BUILDING A GREEN ECONOMY

BUILDING A
GREEN ECONOMY

PERSPECTIVES FROM
ECOLOGICAL ECONOMICS

Edited by Robert B. Richardson

Michigan State University Press

East Lansing

♾ The paper used in this publication meets the minimum requirements of ANSI/NISO Z39.48-1992 (R 1997) (Permanence of Paper).

 Michigan State University Press
East Lansing, Michigan 48823-5245

Printed and bound in the United States of America.

19 18 17 16 15 14 13   1 2 3 4 5 6 7 8 9 10

LIBRARY OF CONGRESS CATALOGING-IN-PUBLICATION DATA

Building a green economy : perspectives from ecological economics / edited by Robert B. Richardson.
    pages cm
Includes bibliographical references.
ISBN 978-1-60917-393-7 (ebook) — ISBN 978-1-61186-102-0 (cloth : alk. paper) 1. Sustainable development—United States. 2. Environmental economics—United States. 3. Environmental policy—Economic aspects—United States. 4. Ecology—Economic aspects—United States. I. Richardson, Robert B.

    HC110.E5B85 2013
    333.70973—dc23
    2012049420

Book design by Scribe Inc. (www.scribenet.com)
Cover design by Erin Kirk New
Cover art © Lorenzo Rossi/Dreamstime.com. All rights reserved.

green press INITIATIVE Michigan State University Press is a member of the Green Press Initiative and is committed to developing and encouraging ecologically responsible publishing practices. For more information about the Green Press Initiative and the use of recycled paper in book publishing, please visit www.greenpress initiative.org.

Visit Michigan State University Press at www.msupress.org

Contents

Preface   vii

PERSPECTIVES ON A GREEN ECONOMY

Building a Green Economy: The Case for an Economic Paint Job
Robert B. Richardson   3

Taking Ecological Economics Seriously: It's the Biosphere, Stupid
David Korten   19

Beyond the Ivory Tower: Why Progress Needs More Ecological Economists to Actively Engage
Kristen A. Sheeran   31

Ruin and Recovery: The Economics of Michigan's Natural Resources
David Dempsey   37

HISTORICAL AND THEORETICAL PERSPECTIVES

Noble Savages or Consummate Consumers: The Behavioral Ecology
of Building a Green Conservation Future
Bobbi S. Low   45

Green Keynesianism: Beyond Standard Growth Paradigms
Jonathan M. Harris   69

The Economics of Information in a Green Economy
Joshua Farley and Skyler Perkins   83

The Evolution of Ego'n'Empathy: Progress in Forming the Centerpiece
for Ecological Economic Theory
William M. Hayes and Gary D. Lynne   101

Civic Empowerment in an Age of Corporate Excess
Ed Lorenz   119

Environmental Justice Challenges for Ecosystem Service Valuation

    Matthew A. Weber   135

APPLICATIONS AND PRACTICE

Assessing the Trade-Offs for an Urban Green Economy

    Myrna Hall, Ning Sun, Stephen Balogh, Catherine Foley, and Ruiqi Li   151

Green Jobs: Who Benefits? Demographic Forecasting of
    Job Creation in U.S. Green Jobs Studies

    Kyle Gracey   171

Great Lakes, Great Debates: Facilitating Public Engagement on Offshore
    Wind Energy Using the Delphi Inquiry Approach

    Erik Nordman, Jon VanderMolen, Betty Gajewski, and Aaron Ferguson   211

Endogenous Environmental Discounting and Climate-Economy Modeling

    Philip Sirianni   223

A Genuine Metric for Assessing Business Sustainability

    Matthew P. H. Taylor, Darrell Brown, David E. Ervin, Jim Thayer, and Brett Cassidy   245

The Case for "Improvement" in Corporate Sustainability Indicators

    Richard Grogan   269

Evolutions in Methods and Technology for Research in Pro-environmental Behavior

    Douglas L. Bessette and Robert B. Richardson   295

Contributors   313

Preface

Few will doubt that humankind has created a planet-sized problem for itself. No one wished it so, but we are the first species to become a geophysical force, altering Earth's climate, a role previously reserved for tectonics, sun flares, and glacial cycles. We are also the greatest destroyer of life since the ten-kilometer-wide meteorite that landed near Yucatan and ended the Age of Reptiles sixty-five million years ago. Through overpopulation we have put ourselves in danger of running out of food and water. So a very Faustian choice is upon us: whether to accept our corrosive and risky behavior as the unavoidable price of population and economic growth, or to take stock of ourselves and search for a new environmental ethic.

—EDWARD O. WILSON, FROM *CONSILIENCE: THE UNITY OF KNOWLEDGE*

THE TWENTY-FIRST CENTURY HAS THUS FAR BEEN MARKED BY SEVERAL IMPORTANT events that have highlighted critical thresholds that limit the capacity of the natural environment to support human activities. Food and energy costs have risen sharply, while many regions reported record-setting temperatures, droughts, and flooding. For nearly three months in 2010, the world watched helplessly while millions of barrels of oil spilled into the Gulf of Mexico, threatening aquatic ecosystems and the livelihoods of coastal communities. World population reached seven billion people in late 2011. World grain prices peaked in 2011 before moderating to levels equivalent only to those at the time of the 2008 food crisis. Damage to crop harvests from exceptionally dry weather in 2012 brought food price indices up again to peak levels, and more than half the U.S. corn crop acreage was listed in poor or very poor condition due to a record-breaking drought. These problems have been compounded by rising inequality, unemployment, and fuel prices that have risen to historic highs. A 2011 report by the Organization for Economic Cooperation and Development noted that the United States has among the highest levels of income inequality and relative poverty among developed countries. Furthermore, on the heels of the 2008 global economic meltdown, a debt crisis in Europe has destabilized its common currency and pushed several countries into a second recession, which has led to an economic ripple across the increasingly integrated global economy.

The challenges presented by this confluence of events are well known to ecological economists, who have long been concerned about these and other impending problems that threaten the sustainability of the human economy and quality of life. Ecological economics acknowledges the importance of the scale of the economic system relative to the ecosystem that sustains it. Perpetual expansion of the human domain will eventually overwhelm the productive capacity of ecological systems and natural cycles. Ecological economists view the destructive events of the last decade as symptoms of an economic system in peril and an environmental system whose limits are being strained.

Ecological economics is known as the science of sustainability, which is grounded in the notion that environmental problems are complex, nonlinear, and require transdisciplinary approaches to solving them. The objective of ecological economics is to enhance theoretical understanding of the human economy and to develop practical solutions to achieve long-term socioeconomic well-being, without undermining the absorptive, regenerative, and resource capacity of the biosphere.

Isolation among academic disciplines and social institutions has led to economic and environmental policies that are mutually damaging in the long term rather than reinforcing. Ecological economics aims to integrate the study and management of "nature's household" (ecology) and "humankind's household" (economics). This integration of economic, social, and ecological systems attracts scholars and practitioners from a variety of natural and social science disciplines who are interested in building a green economy and achieving a just and sustainable future. To that end, ecological economists have developed alternative economic models that recognize and value the functions and services of global ecosystems and that aim to achieve an equitable distribution of resources. In doing so, ecological economists draw upon a range of methods and perspectives in an effort to gain new insights through blurring outdated boundaries that fragment our understanding of the human condition.

Contributions to this edited volume were drawn from research papers and keynote addresses presented at the Sixth Biennial Conference of the United States Society for Ecological Economics, which was held at Michigan State University in East Lansing, Michigan, in June 2011. The theme for the conference was "Building a Green Economy." More than 120 presentations were delivered in plenary and parallel conference sessions, workshops, and panel discussions, with themes that included environmental justice, ecosystem service valuation, biofuel policies, and indicators of sustainability. The seventeen chapters published in this volume represent a selection of a broader range of perspectives that were highlighted in the conference program. These chapters characterize some of the most innovative thinking in ecological economics at a critical time in the reexamination of the human relationship with the natural world.

The volume is organized around three parts and begins with "Perspectives on a Green Economy," which features the views presented by several keynote speakers. Robert Richardson presents the case for an "economic paint job" as a frame for the discussion of building a green economy. David Korten argues that the current economic system should be labeled "suicide economics," and he calls for a new economic model. He suggests that ecological economists are our best hope in meeting the challenge of developing a new paradigm for the human economy that is built on a living relationship with the biosphere. Kristen Sheeran suggests that progressive reform demands new economic thinking, and she calls for ecological economists to step outside the ivory tower to engage with practical, real-world problems. David Dempsey provides a historical perspective on natural resources in Michigan, the site of the conference, and suggests how ecological economics can contribute to discourse on natural resource policy to promote informed choices.

The second part of the volume is entitled "Historical and Theoretical Perspectives" and features six chapters that provide a historical basis and theoretical foundation for building a green economy. Bobbi Low offers an evolutionary perspective on understanding human behavior through an examination of the idea of the "noble savage" and explains the implications for the development of conservation strategies that encourage sustainable human behaviors. Jonathan Harris explores the potential for a "Green Keynesianism" as the basis for solutions to both economic stagnation and global environmental threats. Joshua Farley and Skyler Perkins examine the economics of information in a green economy and call for public investment in open source knowledge. William Hayes and Gary Lynne call for the integration of ego and empathy as a centerpiece for ecological economics in the development of long-term, sustainable solutions to global problems. Ed Lorenz draws upon a historic case of environmental contamination in an assessment of processes that facilitate effective community responses to problems produced by global corporations. Matthew Weber offers an assessment of the pitfalls, strategies, and research needs for the integration of ecosystem service valuation and environmental justice initiatives.

The final part of the book, "Applications and Practice," presents seven chapters that feature applied research related to various aspects of a green economy. Myrna Hall and coauthors offer an assessment of the trade-offs among technologies and infrastructure development in an urban green economy. Kyle Gracey offers an assessment of growth in green jobs by incorporating gender and race equity in an examination of the distribution of benefits of job creation. Erik Nordman and coauthors present the results of an examination of wind energy development in Lake Michigan that used the Delphi Inquiry approach to enhance understanding of the conditions under which offshore wind energy development could be acceptable to nearby residents and communities. Philip Sirianni examines the debate about discounting public investments in environmental sustainability in light of differences in how humans react to imminent and distant threats. He uses climate-economy model simulations to demonstrate that endogenous discount rates lead to more stringent emissions reductions. Matthew Taylor and coauthors propose a comprehensive measure of an individual organization's progress toward sustainability that is based on the concept of a "genuine metric" for sustainability assessment. Richard Grogan calls for improvement in corporate sustainability indicators through the development of a "gross sustainability" measure using corporate sustainability reporting data. Finally, Douglas Bessette and Robert Richardson present an examination of the evolution in research on pro-environmental behavior and explore the potential of the experience sampling method to be deployed using mobile-phone technology in analysis of the determinants of behavior.

Biologist Edward O. Wilson has said that he believes the twenty-first century will come to be known as the Century of the Environment and he calls for the fundamental unity of all knowledge in a search for consilience. This process of convergence of knowledge is transpiring in ecological economics. The breadth of chapters in this volume highlights the critical need for a new economic paradigm and demonstrates the extent of theoretical, methodological, and policy advances that are needed to build a green economy. The perspectives of the authors whose work is represented here contribute to our understanding of the flawed assumptions that undergird the current economic system, demonstrating that a new economy will require advances in holistic thinking, reform of obsolete policies, better metrics and indicators of sustainability, and a broader understanding of the drivers of human behavior. Together, the chapters of this volume represent contemporary thinking in ecological economics and demonstrate how ecological economics may contribute to a unity of knowledge for sustaining quality of life for future generations of humankind.

This book owes a debt of gratitude to the numerous speakers, presenters, session chairs, volunteers, and conference participants whose efforts made the 2011 conference a success.

Particular gratitude is extended to members of the conference committee, which reviewed hundreds of abstracts and organized sessions around conference themes. This committee included Bernardo Aguilar González, Randy Bruins, Jonathan Harris, Valerie Luzadis, Robert Richardson, Laura Schmitt Olabisi, and Paula Sweeden. The conference benefited from the generous support provided by Jim MacInnes, Crystal Mountain Resort and Spa, MSU AgBio Research, the MSU Bioeconomy Network, the Sustainable Michigan Endowed Project, and the Environmental Science and Policy Program at Michigan State University. Of course, the book would not exist without the numerous authors and coauthors whose intellectual offerings are featured in this volume. Their patience and thoughtfulness in developing and revising their papers for the purposes of the book is appreciated. The book was enhanced by useful feedback and suggestions from two reviewers. Finally, appreciation is extended to Julie Loehr and the editorial staff of the Michigan State University Press, whose support of this volume is gratefully acknowledged.

REFERENCE

Wilson, Edward O. 1998. *Consilience: The Unity of Knowledge*. New York: Knopf.

Perspectives on a Green Economy

Building a Green Economy
The Case for an Economic Paint Job

ROBERT B. RICHARDSON

HUMANS IN THE TWENTY-FIRST CENTURY ARE CONFRONTED WITH A NEW GENERATION of environmental and economic problems of an unprecedented scale and scope. The dual demographic forces of population growth and wealth accumulation have led to a global economy that has, by most accounts, exceeded the natural limits of the biosphere in several ways (Global Footprint Network, 2010; Millennium Ecosystem Assessment, 2005). Evidence can be found in studies of the effects of climate change, biodiversity loss, tropical deforestation, and desertification, all of which threaten the long-term viability of economies and livelihoods. Rising levels of greenhouse gas emissions imply an escalating threat of unrestrained climate change, along with potentially calamitous consequences for humans. The damages from climate change are likely to be economically significant and distributed unevenly around the world, based on physical vulnerability and adaptive capacity. Ecosystems are increasingly threatened by both quantitative losses in areal extent (for example, through deforestation) and qualitative degradation of ecosystem structure or functions (for example, from pollution or invasive species). The losses in biodiversity from these ecosystem changes are expected to have dire consequences for human welfare, health, livelihoods, and food security.

Combined with human development stressors such as food insecurity, freshwater scarcity, and malnourishment, the environmental crises are compounding existing social problems related to unemployment, economic inequity, social instability, and poverty. And the widening wealth gap between the rich and poor globally and within the United States highlights grave concerns about the anticipated friction and conflict associated with rising inequality. Increasingly, the global economy can be characterized by its dependence on the ongoing exploitation of Earth's natural resources as well as its people, and it has been described as an extension of a colonial system (Cato, 2009).

The world economy has expanded at unprecedented rates in recent decades; global economic expansion has increased approximately fivefold since 1950, and it has nearly quadrupled in the last quarter-century (UNEP, 2011). This has contributed to an overall rise in average household income, but that growth has been increasingly concentrated in favor of higher-income households. Meanwhile, roughly 60 percent of the world's major ecosystem services that support life and livelihoods have been degraded; world fisheries stocks are declining because of overfishing, and some 40 percent of agricultural land has been degraded in the past fifty years by land use practices that have contributed to erosion, salinization, soil compaction, nutrient depletion, pollution, and urbanization (Millennium Ecosystem Assessment, 2005).

These trends suggest that the current economic paradigm has led to growth that substantially increased material wealth—particularly for higher-income households—but this growth was accomplished through the depletion of natural resource stocks and the degradation of the functions and vital services of ecosystems.

World population reached seven billion people in late 2011, and current estimates of population growth project three billion more people by 2050. Combined with a projected quadrupling of the global economy by 2050, these estimates imply a daunting increase in the demand for food, the consumption of physical goods, the demand for fuels to produce and transport those goods, and the demand for natural resources (especially land and water), leading to escalating impacts on ecosystems and the services they provide (Millennium Ecosystem Assessment, 2005).

For several decades, these issues have been the fragmented concerns of some scientists, economists, and activists, but recently they have begun to converge and attract the attention of policymakers and the media. These accumulated threats are increasingly viewed as an integrated problem, a supersized externality generated by an economic system that is based on competition, profit maximization, and the pursuit of unremitting growth. Furthermore, given the long-term outlook necessary to address these problems, there is growing evidence that our political and economic institutions may be inadequately equipped to deal with these issues because of myopia. Politicians are motivated by short-term election cycles, investors expect quicker payback periods, and financial markets do not reward decisions based on long time horizons. Conventional tools and approaches to these integrated issues will be hopelessly ineffectual at creating the kind of economy that acknowledges the limits of global ecosystems, advances equity and fairness, and facilitates cooperation toward mutually beneficial decisions and policies among and within countries.

Evidence of these mounting problems paints a dark picture of the state of the global economy, and in many ways, the national economy of the United States is emblematic of the greater problem. In chromatic terms, the current global economic system may be characterized as a lifeless brown or gray. Decades of economic growth and unprecedented wealth creation have been based on a reliance on fossil fuels, and the side effects of this gray economy include the depletion of natural resources, the degradation of ecosystems, and the marginalization of millions of people. While the gray economy has delivered rapid global economic expansion, the conspicuous consumption, unrestrained mobility, extreme poverty and hunger, and increasing militarization that have resulted from this growth cannot be sustained (Orr, 2002). The economic and technological complexity of these problems is likely to overwhelm the capacity of traditional institutions to solve them, requiring new thinking about a different economic trajectory.

The economic growth of the past three decades was accompanied by rising property values, low unemployment rates, increasing business profits, expanding financial markets, and unprecedented rates of home ownership. Yet in the first decade of the twenty-first century, the structural problems of the economy started to reveal themselves, and many of the previous gains began to dissipate. Personal property values fell, unemployment rates rose, and economic activity slowed considerably. In spite of recent economic growth in the second decade of the century housing markets remain fragile, unemployment remains at persistently high rates, and wage growth is effectively flat. Public agencies must operate with thinner budgets because of declining tax revenues, even while public infrastructure demands investment for maintenance against depreciation losses.

While recent growth in some green sectors is taking off, economic policy prescriptions seem directed at promoting a return to previous levels of consumption, ignoring the strains of economic growth on global ecosystems. The economy is fundamentally dependent upon non-renewable fossil fuel resources, and growth will require increasing depletion of resource stocks and degradation of ecosystems. In that context, economic policy that is based on increasing levels of consumption is simply unsustainable.

A review of the planetary boundaries of the global economy is presented below, followed by a discussion of the characteristics of a green economy, the case for an economic paint job, and a call for action to green the economy for the benefit of all people and for the ecosystems upon which life on Earth depends.

THE BRINK OF THE GRAY ECONOMY

Two central assumptions about the economy distinguish the visions of a green economy from the current global economic system that has been characterized as gray. First, conventional economics treats the environment as a subset of the economy from which natural resources are extracted for production, and into which waste is emitted. This assumption allows for the pursuit of unrestrained economic expansion, since the only limits to growth are capital and technology. Second, conventional economic models ignore the costs of economic growth—that is, the external costs of pollution and environmental degradation, and the distributional effects that contribute to income inequality are assumed to be negligible and easily resolved through compensation to affected parties by those who benefit from growth.

However, more recent theories and analytical models developed by ecological economists and others have highlighted the fallacy of both of these assumptions. First, the economy is more reasonably characterized as a subset of the ecosystem (Daly and Farley, 2010). As an open system, the economy is wholly dependent upon the energy, land, water, minerals, living organisms, and services provided by ecosystems as inputs for production and for the treatment and absorption of waste. This characterization of the economy implies that the limits to economic growth are ecological, reflecting an appreciation for understanding the scale of any economy relative to the ecosystem upon which it depends. Second, there is growing evidence that the costs of economic growth are substantial and extensive. Models predicting the effects of a continued increase in global emissions of greenhouse gases have estimated detrimental effects to agricultural production, fisheries, biodiversity, water resources, human health, and industry and human settlements (Parry et al., 2007).

Rockström and coauthors (2009) proposed a framework to define preconditions for human development, where crossing certain biological thresholds could have disastrous consequences for humanity. Of the nine interlinked planetary boundaries in their framework, the boundaries in three systems (rate of biodiversity loss, climate change, and interference with the nitrogen cycle) have already been exceeded. They further suggest that humanity is rapidly approaching the boundaries for four other systems—global freshwater use, change in land use, ocean acidification, and interference with the global phosphorous cycle.

The forces of industrialization and globalization and their reliance on the massive expansion of the use of fossil fuels have led some scientists to conclude that human activities are exerting ever-increasing impacts on ecosystems at scales that outcompete natural processes. The Holocene is the term given to the postglacial era of the past ten to twelve thousand years that has been characterized by relatively stable and clement conditions, distinguished by shifts in and out of ice ages. The scale of human activities in the past two centuries—particularly land use changes, deforestation, and the burning of fossil fuels—has persuaded some scientists to conclude that we have entered a new geological epoch known as the Anthropocene, which is characterized by human dominance of biological, chemical, and geological processes on Earth (Crutzen and Stoermer, 2000). Such an alarming shift in geological processes suggests an urgent call to humanity to confront the pressures of population growth, to switch to new sources of energy, to swiftly reduce emissions of greenhouse gases, and to define a new economy that prioritizes socioeconomic well-being over consumerism.

The narrative of the history of economic growth in the United States is typically described as a success story. The U.S. economy has been the largest in the world for over a century, and it has grown at relatively stable rates—roughly 3 percent since World War II—with vigorous periods of sustained growth in the 1960s and the 1990s, in particular. Yet at the same time, U.S. fossil-fuel emissions have doubled since the 1950s, income inequality has risen, and poverty rates have remained stagnant. While the U.S. share of global emissions has declined from 44 percent to 19 percent over the same time period, the decline is related to higher emissions growth rates in other countries, rather than a reduction in U.S. emissions (Boden, Marland, and Andres, 2011). These trends represent the rising environmental and social costs of economic growth.

Although the U.S. economy (measured in terms of the gross domestic product, or GDP) has grown at a greater rate than fossil-fuel emissions, globalization has fueled sharp increases in emissions worldwide, in part through international trade. Of the 337 billion tons of carbon that have been released to the atmosphere from the consumption of fossil fuels and cement production since 1751, half of these emissions have occurred since the mid-1970s. U.S. imports as a percentage of GDP have increased substantially—approximately fourfold since 1960—which suggests that the environmental impacts of rising consumption in the United States have been shifted to other countries. China, for example, has recently attained the status of the nation with the highest emissions rates (up 171 percent since 2000), and it happens to be among the top exporting countries to the United States.

Rising income inequality in the United States is also a by-product of the gray economy. A Congressional Budget Office (CBO) study of trends in the distribution of household income in the United States found that in the period from 1979 to 2007, average household income (adjusted for inflation, government transfers, and federal taxes) grew by 62 percent (Congressional Budget Office, 2011). However, after-tax income for households at the higher end of the income scale increased much more rapidly than income for households in the middle and at the lower end of the income scale. Income for the wealthiest 1 percent of the population rose by 275 percent during this twenty-nine-year period, whereas for the 60 percent of the population in the middle of the income scale, the growth rate of real household income was less than 40 percent. Real after-tax income for the 20 percent of the population with the lowest income grew by only 18 percent during the period. Figure 1 illustrates the growth in real after-tax household income, by income quintile, from 1979 to 2007. (Each quintile contains one-fifth of the population, ranked by adjusted household income.)

These markedly uneven growth rates have led to greater income inequality in the United States now than in 1979. During the study period of the CBO report, the share of income accruing to higher-income households (top 20 percent) increased, whereas the share accruing

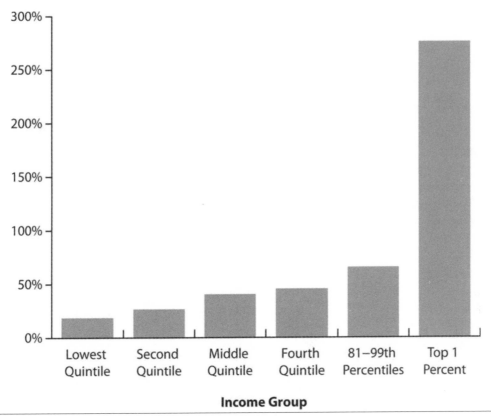

Figure 1. Growth in Real Household (Market) Income from 1979 to 2007
Source: Adapted from Congressional Budget Office, 2011.

to the remaining households (bottom 80 percent) declined. In fact, in just the last three years of the study (2005–2007), the after-tax income of the 20 percent of the population with the highest income exceeded the after-tax income received by the remaining 80 percent. Figure 2 illustrates the shares of market income (before taxes and government transfers), by income quintile in 1979 and 2007.

The CBO study attributes the change in income distribution to two main factors. First, an increase in the concentration of all types of market income heavily favored higher-income households. That is, wealthier households' share of labor income, business income, capital gains, and other income was higher in 2007 than in 1979. Second, shifts in the composition of market income favored wealthier households, further contributing to the concentration of income. The share of income coming from capital gains (from the sale of assets) and business income increased over the study period, while the share coming from labor income and capital income (such as interest and dividends) decreased. Average real household market income for the highest income group nearly tripled over the period, whereas market income increased by about 19 percent for the median household (midpoint of the income distribution scale), leading to a doubling of the share of income received by the top 1 percent. This rapid growth in income at the top may be attributed to technical innovations that have changed the labor market, changes in the governance and structure of executive compensation, increases in firm size and complexity, and the increasing scale of the financial sector.

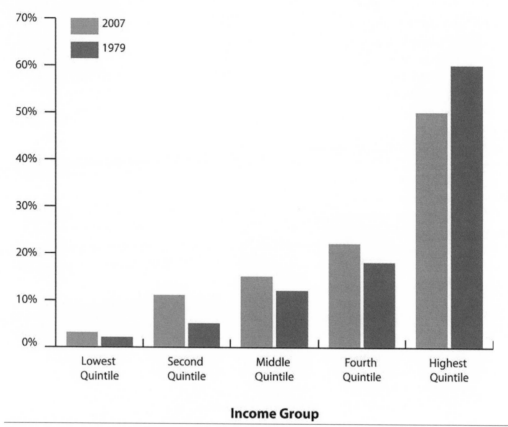

Figure 2. SHARES OF HOUSEHOLD (MARKET) INCOME, 1979 AND 2007
Source: ADAPTED FROM CONGRESSIONAL BUDGET OFFICE, 2011.

CHARACTERISTICS OF A GREEN ECONOMY

The global economy needs a new coat of paint: it is time to paint the economy green. A green economy would be renewable, equitable, and profitable. It would aim to reduce dependence on fossil fuels, minimize impacts to ecosystems, and sustain socioeconomic well-being for all people by ensuring social equity and a fair distribution of wealth. A green economy would be characterized by several principles, including the recognition of the value of ecosystem services, the prioritization of renewable energy and the promotion of energy efficiency, and the enhancement of social equity through the creation of meaningful jobs with fair wages. It is unlikely that a green economy will emerge solely from the agreements of international organizations or by the enactment of national laws; it will not be created through markets that reward short-sighted thinking and short-term growth in corporate profits; and it will not transpire out of the theories of mainstream economics, which treats issues of equity and environmental externalities as peripheral to its growth mission.

A green economy will be developed by the grassroots efforts of individuals, families, neighborhoods, communities, and cities that prioritize the value of environmental sustainability and social justice as fundamental conditions for a productive and meaningful life. To build a green economy, these grassroots efforts will have to increase pressures on governments and the private sector to create new institutional arrangements that are capable of addressing global problems in a dynamic world that is more integrated than ever before.

A green economy will also be developed through innovation and the development of new skills in green sectors such as energy efficiency, clean energy, alternative transportation, green design and construction, recycling, and organic agriculture. The development of a new economy that prioritizes renewable energy, recognizes the value of ecosystem services, and creates meaningful jobs with fair wages will require a fundamental shift in thinking from the outdated objectives, measures, and assumptions that have ushered in decades of gray economic growth. New incentives will be necessary to attract the kind of innovation needed for building a green economy.

A green economy has multiple interpretations, depending upon the definitional context in which it is used. The United Nations Environment Programme (UNEP) defines a green economy as one that results in "improved human well-being and social equity, while significantly reducing environmental risks and ecological scarcities" (UNEP, 2011, p. 16). A green economy has been described in terms of several environmental and social objectives, including

- Sustaining economic, environmental, and social well-being
- Reducing greenhouse gas emissions and other pollution
- Enhancing energy and resource efficiency
- Minimizing biodiversity loss and adverse impacts to ecosystem services
- Increasing social equity and inclusion
- Promoting a fairer distribution of wealth within and among nations

A green economy can be characterized by economic sectors that contribute to the objectives outlined in its definitions. These sectors include

- Green energy—development of renewable sources of energy such as wind, solar, and geothermal energy
- Green transportation—development of renewable fuels, fuel-efficient vehicles, and electric cars; expansion of public and alternative forms of transportation
- Green design and construction—integrated urban environmental planning; advancements in energy and water efficiency; reusable or recyclable products, materials, and infrastructure
- Green agriculture—expansion of organic farming, conservation agriculture, and community-based food systems
- Green water management—water reclamation, reuse, and recycling; rainwater catchment systems; low-water landscaping
- Green waste management—expansion of municipal recycling and composting; recyclable and compostable packaging and products

As the global economy faces mounting challenges from concurrent crises from climate stresses, water shortages, resource scarcity, and spikes in the prices of fuel, energy, and food, the green sectors of the economy are believed to be the engines of future economic growth.

The transition to a clean energy economy is one of the most important long-term challenges facing the United States today, and there has been some recent progress. Investment in new wind power installation is projected to expand from $60.5 billion in 2010 to $122.9 billion in 2020. Investment in installation of solar photovoltaics, modules, and system components is projected to grow from $71.2 billion in 2010 to $113.6 billion by 2020. New installations reached more than 15.6 gigawatts worldwide in 2010, more than double the previous year (Pernick et al., 2011). Global production of biofuels such as ethanol and biodiesel reached $56.4 billion in 2010 and are projected to grow to $112.8 billion by 2020 (Pernick et al., 2011). In 2010, the biofuels market consisted of more than 27.2 billion gallons of ethanol and biodiesel production worldwide, an increase of more than 15 percent over the prior year. Still, the role of biofuels in a green economy is somewhat controversial; some studies have noted that biofuels are associated with lower greenhouse gas emissions relative to petroleum, but others have argued that the aggregate environmental effects of biofuels are considerable. Some biofuels are associated with destruction of native habitats and higher food prices and result in little reduction in overall emissions (Scharlemann and Laurance, 2008).

However, despite growth in alternative energy, investment in green economy sectors in the United States has been slow relative to other nations, and the global market for green technologies is becoming increasingly competitive. China, Japan, and the European Union all invest more in the green economy sectors than does the United States. China alone has spent $200 billion—roughly double the investment by the United States—and this figure is expected to double or triple over the next ten years; China could end up spending $440 billion to $660 billion over the next decade. China has become the global leader in new wind installations and has surpassed the United States in total cumulative installations for wind power, with a capacity of more than 42 gigawatts (Pernick et al., 2011). Private investment in China's clean energy sector increased by 39 percent in 2010 to a world record $54.4 billion. China also is the world's leading producer of wind turbines and solar modules. In 2009, it surpassed the United States as the country with the most installed clean energy capacity.

Still, there is evidence that the United States is on a path toward a green economy, in spite of any clear national policy or participation in global agreements. One-third of the Standard & Poor's index of the top 500 leading companies in the United States are setting and reporting emissions targets through such programs as the Carbon Disclosure Project (King, 2010). Retailers are gathering data about the environmental footprints of suppliers in an effort to track and reduce greenhouse gas emissions associated with their supply chains. Sectors such as green building, information technology, and packaging have been building momentum for more than a decade, and the emergence of solid-state light-emitting diode (LED) technology is likely to dominate lighting production. Furthermore, continued growth is expected in the development of biofuels, wind and solar energy, and the electrification of transportation. Progress toward building a green economy has been driven in part by consumer interest in the environmental and economic benefits of energy efficiency, as well as by corporate sustainability mandates and the assumption of a future price on carbon emissions. But industry leaders believe that a clear national policy is needed to drive broader investment (Pernick et al., 2011; King, 2010).

A recent Brookings Institution report referred to a "clean" economy synonymously as a green economy, which was defined as a low-carbon economy, or as the sector of the economy that produces goods and services with an environmental benefit (Muro, Rothwell, and Saha, 2011). The report acknowledges the difficulty in assessing the scale of the clean economy in part because of its pervasive integration throughout nearly all sectors of the larger economy and because of a lack of standardized definitions of the components of a clean economy. Using county-level data covering the years 2003 to 2010, the report estimates the size of the clean economy in the United States in an assessment of green jobs and their economic impact. Among the findings in the report is the conclusion that the clean economy employs approximately 2.7 million workers across a diverse group of industries, which amounts to greater employment than the fossil fuel-intensive industries such as oil and gas. Although the clean economy grew more slowly than the national economy during the period of study, green jobs were disproportionately more prevalent in manufacturing and export sectors and offered higher wages for skilled workers than the national economy.

A green economy is usually described in terms that include an emphasis on social equity and justice. While not directly related to environmental themes that are typically associated with being "green," increasing income inequality, social marginalization, and injustice are perceived as counter to progress and ultimately unsustainable. If the scale of the human economy has already strained or exceeded the capacity of global ecosystems, high levels of income inequality within a society imply that the rich enjoy lifestyles that draw disproportionately upon the stock of natural capital available to all humans, creating a kind of ecological deficit owed to present and future generations.

In discussing an optimum level of economic growth, Phelps (1966) has referred to the notion of a "golden rule" to concerns about intergenerational welfare. A "golden rule" economy would grow at a rate that could maintain the highest level of consumption per capita indefinitely. Although ecological economics and the science of sustainability did not emerge until twenty years afterward, there is an implicit element of sustainability in the Phelps concept. Building upon that notion, Heal (1998) proposed a "Green Golden Rule" that would aim to provide the highest level of well-being that can be maintained indefinitely, but reflecting the contribution of natural capital and ecosystem services to well-being. In this way, present generations would make decisions about the use of natural resources that consider current benefits as well as the capacity for future generations to benefit as well. This is the path that provides the maximum sustainable utility level, giving equal treatment to the present and future.

If the concept of a green economy sounds familiar, it is perhaps because many of its underlying conditions have been discussed widely in the context of sustainable development, which is concerned with meeting intergenerational needs through achieving a balance across environmental, social, and economic objectives. The concept of sustainable development and its integration with the processes of environmental change has gained worldwide attention through numerous global, regional, and national initiatives and has evolved into the single most prominent paradigm in development discourse. However, despite the traction gained by the propagation of the notion of sustainable development, the challenge of reconciling the development paths of wealthy and poor economies in a global context characterized by energy insecurity, resource scarcity, and the prospects of climate change remains. In light of this fundamental challenge, it is not clear whether sustainable development is even possible.

However, previous efforts to reach sustainability or sustainable development have focused on regulations and policies aimed at fixing environmental and social problems directly, rather than on the economic failures that generated the problems. There is a growing recognition that achieving sustainability depends entirely on "getting the economy right" (UNEP, 2011, p. 16). That is, ensuring environmental sustainability and social equity may not be possible under the terms of the old, gray economy. The recent economic and financial crises present an opportunity to build a green economy by addressing the failed economic structures and institutions that generated decades of economic growth by degrading ecosystem services and widening the income inequality gap. Today's global economic structure may be the single greatest obstacle to achieving environmental sustainability and social justice.

THE CASE FOR AN ECONOMIC PAINT JOB

Ecological economists have been discussing the urgency and necessary conditions for a transition to a green economy for a couple of decades, but recently the concept has gained momentum in mainstream policy discourse. There are several national and global initiatives related to the path toward a green economy, including the Green Economy Initiative of the United Nations and numerous research publications on the topic, including the United Nations Environment Programme's *Toward a Green Economy* (UNEP, 2011), a World Bank research report entitled *Greening Industry* (Wheeler, 2000), and a report by the OECD entitled *Green Development Planning* (Drakenberg et al., 2009).

Ecological economics views environmental resources as a form of capital—natural capital—which is defined as the value of land, water, forests, fisheries, minerals, and other resources. Like conventional notions of capital, natural capital is a stock that yields flows of benefits over time, but it expands upon the means of production created by humans to also include the services and resources provided by nature (Daly and Farley, 2010). Both human-made capital and natural capital contribute to the well-being of humans, a fact that underscores a fundamental understanding that the economy is not separate from the environment; in fact, the economy is dependent upon the environment and upon the ecosystem services that sustain it.

Yet the conventional measures of economic performance—gross domestic product (GDP), inflation rates, or unemployment—completely ignore natural capital, and in some cases, their treatment of natural capital perversely contradicts theories about wealth and socioeconomic well-being (Heal, 2012). In the example of water scarcity, when farmers have to dig more deeply to reach the water table, the increase in expenditures adds to GDP and economic growth, which suggests that a nation is better off. When oil companies are compelled to develop new technologies to reach scarce supplies of petroleum, the additional expenditures they incur also contribute to GDP. Spending associated with water shortages and oil scarcities contribute to economic activity, but treating these expenses as a benefit ignores the looming threat of scarcity to agricultural or energy production that undergirds the global economy. In that sense, measures of economic performance do not provide accurate signals about environmental performance, and in turn, they mask the threats to the sustainability and stability of economic growth itself.

There is a strong case to be made in favor of alternative economic indicators that more accurately depict socioeconomic welfare in a society. One conceptual improvement would be to adjust the GDP for the deprecation of capital, to arrive at net domestic product (NDP) (Heal, 2012). Conceptually, NDP would be reduced by the value of resources extracted for economic production, to reflect the impact of human activity on natural capital. For example, extraction of oil reduces the overall stock of natural capital and can be seen as a kind of depreciation that reduces the value or amount of this capital. Such an adjustment would yield better information about economic output and its effect on natural capital. However, the current system of national accounts only measures human-made capital, so it is the only type of capital depreciation that is reflected in economic measures.

The Genuine Progress Indicator (GPI) is an alternative economic indicator that aims to correct for the fundamental shortcomings of the GDP as a measure of national economic welfare. The GPI is derived from the Index of Sustainable Economic Welfare proposed by Daly and Cobb (1989) as an alternative to the GDP, and it has been updated to account for income inequality, costs of crime, costs of environmental degradation, services of public infrastructure, and the benefits of household and volunteer work. The GPI has been vetted by the scientific community and used regularly by some government and nongovernmental organizations worldwide as a measure of progress. Calculation of the GPI uses the same personal consumption data as GDP, but it makes deductions to account for income inequality and costs of crime, environmental degradation, and loss of leisure, and additions to account for the services from consumer durables and public infrastructure as well as the benefits of volunteering and housework. By differentiating between economic activity that diminishes both natural and social capital and activity that enhances such capital, the GPI and its variants are designed to measure sustainable economic welfare rather than economic activity alone.

However, the GPI is limited in its depiction of socioeconomic well-being, as it merely aims to correct for the shortcomings of consumption as a welfare indicator and does not address notions of life satisfaction. The Happy Planet Index (HPI) is another alternative indicator that estimates the ecological efficiency with which human well-being is delivered in countries around the world by combining measures of environmental impact and human well-being. The HPI is based upon two tenets. First, happy, healthy lives are universally desirable around the world; and second, this desire should not be a privilege of the current generation at the expense of ecosystems and future generations. The HPI combines life expectancy at birth (as an indicator of public health) and happiness (as a subjective measure based on subjective measures of life satisfaction) with ecological footprint (or the environmental demands of lifestyle and consumer choices), based on the notion that the well-being of future generations is dependent upon a respect for ecological limits in the attainment of well-being in the current generation.

Meanwhile, the Living Planet Index (LPI)—one of the longest-running measures of the trends in the state of global biodiversity—shows a consistent overall trend: a global decline of almost 30 percent between 1970 and 2007 (see figure 3). The LPI is based on trends in the abundance of vertebrate populations of species from around the world, and it offers insights into those habitats or ecosystems with species that are declining most rapidly (WWF, 2010). This information can be used to define the impact humans are having on the planet and for guiding actions to address biodiversity loss.

The implications of growing human demands on ecosystems and biodiversity that are depicted by the trend in the LPI are also illustrated by the trend in the Ecological Footprint, which tracks human demands on the regenerative and waste absorptive capacity of the biosphere. The Ecological Footprint is measured by the amount of biologically productive land and water area required to produce all the resources consumed by a population, and to absorb the waste it generates, given prevailing technology and practices. This area can then be compared with biological capacity, or the amount of productive area that is available to generate these resources and to absorb the waste (Ewing et al., 2010). Humanity's footprint was equivalent to about half of the earth's biologically productive capacity in 1961, but grew to a level 50 percent above it in 2007 (see figure 4).

Challenges in data collection limit the ability to produce a single number that reveals the sustainability of economic activity, in part because of the challenges in measuring and valuing some types of natural capital (Heal, 2012). It may be more feasible to supplement existing indicators with measures of some of the most important environmental threats, such as the atmospheric concentration of greenhouse gases, the number of endangered species, and the acidity of the oceans. Methods for measuring the sustainability of economic activities are underdeveloped, and although the data limitations are acknowledged, we can do better than

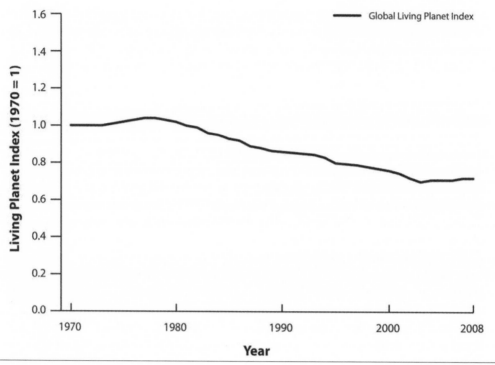

Figure 3. GLOBAL LIVING PLANET INDEX, 1970–2007
Source: WWF, 2010.

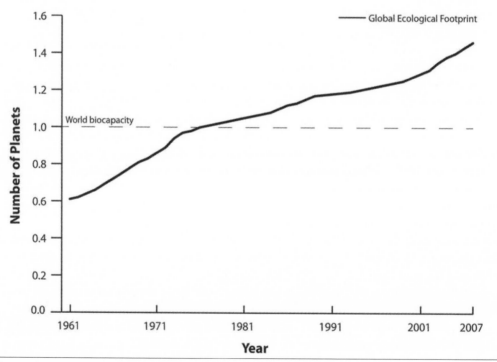

Figure 4. GLOBAL ECOLOGICAL FOOTPRINT, 1961–2007
Source: EWING ET AL., 2010.

the mileposts that marked advancement toward the goals of the gray economy. The question of whether economic activities are sustainable is sufficiently important that the full attention of scientists, economists, and policymakers is warranted in an effort to find the answer.

GREENING THE ECONOMY

There is a widespread disillusionment with the prevailing economic paradigm (UNEP, 2011). There is growing evidence that the unprecedented economic expansion in the last half-century was accomplished through the depletion of natural resource stocks and the degradation of the functions and vital services of ecosystems and has led to rising income inequality, social marginalization, and increasing concentrations of wealth among higher-income households. Yet at the same time, any meaningful change to this economic paradigm is highly unlikely while prevailing economic institutions rely on inaccurate indicators that usher the way toward misguided objectives. The green economy will not be developed by institutional mechanisms that reward myopic thinking in political decisions and short-term growth in markets. It will not be developed by lofty international agreements or by national laws. And it will not be developed through marginal changes to the global economic structures that created the very conditions that made the gray economy possible. A green economy will emerge from both grassroots initiatives and technical innovations that arise out of new ways of understanding the interactions between human and environmental systems. A green economy will emerge from new ways of measuring progress so that economic policies serve the interests of people and respect the limits of the ecosystems upon which the economy depends.

There is a role for governments, industry, and consumers in building a green economy. Governments can level the playing field for greener products by phasing out harmful subsidies, reforming policies and incentives, strengthening market infrastructure, introducing new market-based mechanisms, redirecting public investment, and greening public procurement. Policy reforms that recognize the value of ecosystem services and prioritize the development of renewable energy and greater energy efficiency will create incentives that promote sustainability in market decision-making. Corporations can respond to these policy reforms and incentives by increasing financing and investment, as well as building skills and innovation capacities to take advantage of opportunities arising from a new green economy. Imperfect information and poorly aligned incentives promote inefficient and unwise consumer decisions. Policies that aim to have prices reflect the true social costs of consumption would send more appropriate signals to consumers about the scarcity and spillover effects of particular goods, including the costs of production, transportation, and disposal. Better information and disclosure for consumers would improve feedback mechanisms for greener purchasing choices, energy use, and transportation. Disclosures may activate political safeguards by evoking external pressure from citizens on governments to heed the environmental impacts of particular initiatives.

In conclusion, there is ample evidence that the United States has reached—or exceeded—the brink of the old, gray economy that has delivered the depletion of natural resources, the degradation of the functions and services of ecosystems, and the concentration of material wealth among high-income households and corporations. And this gray economy has, in many ways, chained the American way of life to a dependence on fossil fuels that will be difficult to unleash because of a heavy investment in particular ways of doing things. In the words of the National Research Council (2010), "An inclusive national policy framework is needed to ensure that all levels of government, the private sector, and millions of households and individuals are contributing to shared national goals." The concept of a transition to a green economy provides a framework and a language for the development of shared national goals, as well as a road map to guide the transition. The goals of natural resource conservation, renewable energy development, environmental protection, social equity, and a fair distribution of wealth should be unifying national objectives. The present challenges call for the formulation of a national policy framework and the implementation of an integrated portfolio of tools and approaches to unlock the full potential of a green economy that is renewable, equitable, and profitable. It is time to paint the economy green.

REFERENCES

Boden, T. A., G. Marland, and R. J. Andres. 2011. "Global, Regional, and National Fossil-Fuel CO_2 Emissions." Oak Ridge, TN: Carbon Dioxide Information Analysis Center, Oak Ridge National Laboratory, U.S. Department of Energy.

Cato, Molly Scott. 2009. *Green Economics: An Introduction to Theory, Policy, and Practice.* London: Earthscan.

Congressional Budget Office. 2011. *Trends in the Distribution of Household Income Between 1979 and 2007.* Washington, DC: Congressional Budget Office.

Crutzen, Paul J., and Eugene F. Stoermer. 2000. "The Anthropocene." *Global Change Newsletter* 41(1): 17–18.

Daly, Herman E., and John B. Cobb. 1989. *For the Common Good: Redirecting the Economy toward Community, the Environment, and a Sustainable Future.* Boston: Beacon Press.

Daly, Herman E., and Joshua Farley. 2010. *Ecological Economics: Principles and Applications.* 2nd edition. Washington, DC: Island Press.

Drakenberg, Olof, Sandra Paulsen, Jessica Andersson, Emelie Dahlberg, Kristoffer Darin Mattsson, and Elisabeth Wikstrom. 2009. "Greening Development Planning: A Review of Country Case Studies for Making the Economic Case for Improved Management of Environment and Natural Resources." OECD Environment Working Papers, No. 5, OECD Publishing.

Ewing, B., D. Moore, S. Goldfinger, A. Oursler, A. Reed, and M. Wackernagel. 2010. *The Ecological Footprint Atlas, 2010.* Oakland: Global Footprint Network. http://www.footprintnetwork.org/images/uploads/Ecological_Footprint_Atlas_2010.pdf.

Global Footprint Network. 2010. *The Ecological Wealth of Nations: Earth's Biocapacity as a New Framework for International Cooperation.* Oakland, CA: Global Footprint Network.

Heal, G. M. 1998. *Valuing the Future: Economic Theory and Sustainability.* New York: Columbia University Press.

Heal, G. 2012. "Reflections—Defining and Measuring Sustainability." *Review of Environmental Economics and Policy* 6(1): 147–63.

King, H. 2010. "Green Economy Grows Despite Policy Vacuum." *Daily Climate: A Publication of Environmental and Health Sciences,* March 30, 2010. http://wwwp.dailyclimate.org/tdc-newsroom/2010/03/green-economy-grows-despite-policy-vacuum.

Millennium Ecosystem Assessment. 2005. *Ecosystems and Human Well-Being: Synthesis.* Washington, DC: Island Press.

Muro, M., J. Rothwell, and D. Saha. 2011. *Sizing the Clean Economy: A National and Regional Green Jobs Assessment*. Washington, DC: Brookings Institution.

National Research Council. 2010. "Strong Evidence on Climate Change Underscores Need for Actions to Reduce Emissions and Begin Adapting to Impacts." National Research Council news release, May 19, 2010. http://www.nationalacademies.org/newsroom.

Orr, David. "Four Challenges of Sustainability." *Conservation Biology* 16(6): 1457–60.

Parry, M. L., O. F. Canziani, J. P. Palutikof, P. J. van der Linden, and C. E. Hanson, eds. 2007. *Contribution of Working Group II to the Fourth Assessment Report of the Intergovernmental Panel on Climate Change*. Cambridge: Cambridge University Press.

Pernick, R., C. Wildern, T. Winnie, and S. Sosnovec. 2011. "Clean Energy Trends, 2011." Portland, OR: Clean Edge.

Phelps, E. 1966. *Golden Rules of Economic Growth*. New York: Norton.

Rockström, J., W. Steffen, K. Noone, A. Persson, F. S. Chapin, III, E. F. Lambin, T. M. Lenton, M. Scheffer, C. Folke, H. J. Schellnhuber, B. Nykvist, C. A. de Wit, T. Hughes, S. van der Leeuw, H. Rodhe, S. Sörlin, P. K. Snyder, R. Costanza, U. Svedin, M. Falkenmark, L. Karlberg, R. W. Corell, V. J. Fabry, J. Hansen, B. Walker, D. Liverman, K. Richardson, P. Crutzen, and J. A. Foley. 2009. "A Safe Operating Space for Humanity." *Nature* 461: 472–47.

Scharlemann, Jörn P. W., and William F. Laurance. 2008. "How Green Are Biofuels?" *Science* 319(5859): 43–44.

UNEP (United Nations Environment Programme). 2011. *Towards a Green Economy: Pathways to Sustainable Development and Poverty Eradication*. http://www.unep.org/greeneconomy.

Wheeler, David R. 2000. *Greening Industry: New Roles for Communities, Markets, and Governments*. World Bank Research Report. New York: Oxford University Press.

World Wide Fund for Nature (WWF). 2010. *Living Planet Report, 2010*. Gland, Switzerland: World Wide Fund for Nature.

Taking Ecological Economics Seriously

It's the Biosphere, Stupid

DAVID KORTEN

WE EACH COME TO ECOLOGICAL ECONOMICS FROM OUR OWN DISTINCTIVE EXPERI-ence and perspective. We view the world through different lenses and thereby see different truths. Being interdisciplinary is part of what makes ecological economics interesting and potentially powerful. I come from a business school background with a focus on the design of complex cultural and institutional systems. I am primarily concerned with how the interplay of cultural values and institutional structures shapes individual and collective behavior. I also worked for thirty years in international development. I lived twenty-one of those years in Africa, Latin America, and Asia working to make both public and private institutions effective instruments for ending poverty and avoiding an environmental crash. This gives me a some-what distinctive perspective on the nature and cause of the human crisis.

THE CHALLENGE

My purpose is to share the insights of this perspective and explore the implications for ecologi-cal economics. I am hoping to leave you with a profound new appreciation for the importance of your work as ecological economists and your potential contribution to redirecting the human course. The need to reframe the current economic policy debate grows more urgent by the day. I believe ecological economics is our best hope for producing the tools and advancing the advocacy needed to create an economic system with some prospect of sustaining humans as a viable species. To realize its potential, however, we need to move ecological economics from being an irritant at the margins of the economics discipline to being the defining frame for public policy choices addressing the relationship between humans and the biosphere.

We need a new economics that, as suggested by Herman Daly some forty years ago, truly and unequivocally begins with people and nature—a point that conventional economists to this day fail to recognize and most ecological economists fail to fully engage. We need a truly new economics that reaches as far beyond the understanding of conventional economics as quantum physics reaches beyond the understanding of conventional Newtonian physics.

FATAL FALLACIES OF SUICIDE ECONOMICS

Let us not mince words. The established mainstream of economic thought is driving human societies to collective suicide. It deserves a more evocative label than neoclassical, neoliberal, or even market fundamentalism. Let us call it what it is: a "suicide economics" for a "suicide economy."

Suicide economics gets it wrong on nearly every major issue because it is built on a foundation of fallacies. It ignores natural limits, confuses means and ends, uses the wrong measure of value and the wrong unit of analysis, and relies on a single improperly defined criterion function. And this is only my short list of personal favorites. Let's go through these five fallacies one by one.

The first fallacy, the failure to address natural limits, is a foundational theme of ecological economics. No need to say more about that here.

The second fallacy, the confusion of ends and means, is reflected in the convention of treating people and nature as externalities. The practical implication is that rather than treating the well-being of people and nature as the purpose of economic activity, suicide economics treats people and nature merely as means for making money for people who have money, a grotesque reversal of ends and means. De Graaf and Batker pointedly ask in the title of their documentary film and book, *What's the Economy For Anyway?* (de Graaf and Batker, 2011). The answer should be obvious. Serving people and nature is the only legitimate purpose of an economy.

The third fallacy is the wrong measure of value. Suicide economics uses money rather than life as the basic measure of value. So gold, which we could easily live without, is considered more valuable than air, soil, and water, which we cannot live without. This leads to the destruction of air, soil, and water to extract gold from under the ground so we can refine it—all at enormous cost to people, soil, air, and water—and then lock it away back underground in great vaults. This seems to make perfect sense to suicide economists. There is truth to the cliché that "an economist is a person who knows the price of everything and the value of nothing."

The fourth fallacy, the wrong unit of analysis, is expressed in the choice to build the analytical structure of suicide economics around the firm rather than the household. This leads to measuring economic performance by financial returns to pools of money aggregated as firms, rather than by contribution to increasing the health and happiness of people, households, and communities. Consequently, maximizing corporate profits becomes more important to policymakers than ensuring that people have living-wage jobs.

The fifth fallacy is the improperly defined single criterion function. Have any of you had the experience of piloting an airplane? If you have not, perhaps you can at least imagine trying to pilot an airplane with your windows blacked out, an airspeed indicator as your only instrument, and a decision rule that says do whatever increases your airspeed. You are absolutely guaranteed to fly the plane right into the ground—which is exactly what we are doing with the economy by using gross domestic product (GDP) growth as our primary indicator of success.

Successfully piloting an airplane under conditions of limited visibility requires a whole dashboard of instruments: altimeter, rate of climb and descent, air speed, a directional indicator, engine rpm, fuel gauge, oil pressure, engine temperature, and so on. Making policy adjustments to guide a complex national economy is no less complicated and requires a dashboard of indicators.

Promoting these fallacies as truths, suicide economists have demonstrated their ability to misdirect society to create an economic system that converts the real living-wealth of the many to the phantom financial-wealth of the few and counts it as gain for everyone. The results demonstrate that it is a very bad idea, and people are waking up to the reality that suicide economists have a limited grasp of reality, are knowingly fronting for the Wall Street oligarchy, or some combination of the two.

We all know that the standard measure of GDP counts a lot of bad things as goods. Joshua Farley takes it a step further by pointing out that GDP is best treated not as a measure of benefit, but rather of the aggregate economic cost of producing any given level of human well-being (Farley, 2010). That is the real bottom line.

We are measuring economic performance based not on benefits, but on costs, and no one even seems to notice. That explains why, as Herman Daly once famously observed, we are managing the world as if we were holding a going-out-of-business sale (Daly, 1991).

Let us go a bit deeper on the issue of the firm versus the household as the unit of analysis. Suicide economics focuses on financial returns to the firm rather than the well-being of the household, which accounts for a lot of faulty conclusions.

ORGANIZATION AND MANAGEMENT OF THE HOUSEHOLD

We need to start with basics. As you know, the term *economics* is derived from the Greek *oikos nomos*, which means household management. Ecology is derived from *oikos logos*, which means household organization. Therefore, ecological economics translates into the organization and management of the household. The household writ large is the Biosphere—Earth's extraordinary dynamic, self-organizing evolving band of life—the sum total of all of Earth's ecosystems.

If we are to be true to our name, it is our responsibility and calling to develop ecological economics as the primary discipline concerned with the organization and management of the human relationship to the biosphere. It will be a discipline that bears little resemblance to economics as we currently know it.

A first step is to recognize that we humans are not entities separate from the biosphere. We are integral to it. We have a living relationship to the biosphere that cannot be reduced to mere financial transactions or calculations, as economists are wont to do. Of course, this is not news to ecological economists, but we are prone to lose sight of the full implications.

A STRANGE RULER

Money is the favored metric of conventional economics. It has the advantage of providing an elegant simplicity. On the downside it leads to bad decisions. Money is very useful as a medium of exchange between businesses and their customers, but any household that bases relationships among its members solely on profitable financial exchange rather than mutual caring is in deep trouble.

Life, not money, must be the primary metric of ecological economics. It is much harder to quantify but is more likely to produce the decisions we need to secure the human future.

If you think about it, money is a very strange choice of metric. Indeed, money—useful as it is—is one of the strangest of human inventions. In our modern world, most money is nothing more than a number on a computer hard drive. It is an accounting entry that has no meaning or reality outside the human mind. Nothing in nature can directly detect or experience it. Indeed, there is no equivalent to money in nature. Even we humans depend on computers as our intermediary to observe and manipulate it.

It seems a bit odd that we take these invisible numbers as our measure of wealth, organize our lives and societies around them, and yield control of our lives to those who have the biggest numbers encoded on a computer hard drive we cannot see. It is stranger still that we allow a small oligarchy to rule the whole of the human household by granting them the power to create these numbers from nothing and to allocate them as they choose for their exclusive private benefit with no public accounting or recourse.

I also find it both strange and alarming that our language gives us no tools to easily distinguish between real wealth—land, labor, technology, even peace, and a healthy happy child—and money, a simple accounting chit that can be exchanged for many things of real value but has no real value in itself. A clear distinction between money and real wealth is essential to any valid resource allocation decision.

When economists, or anyone else for that matter, use the terms *wealth, capital, resources,* and *assets,* we have no way to know whether they are referring to something of real value or merely to money. This leads to serious confusion and very bad decisions.

SACRED COMMUNITY

I will return a bit later to the subject of money as a system of power and the implications for how we design the money, banking, and finance system. First, I want to bring the biosphere to the forefront of our conversation.

You likely noted that the phrase "It's the Biosphere, Stupid" is a reference to the story that President Bill Clinton, during the 1992 U.S. presidential campaign, kept a reminder taped to his mirror, "It's the Economy, Stupid." I suggest that all of us who seek to create an economics with the power to heal the world take a hint from the Clinton example and post on our bathroom mirror a reminder that we will see first thing every morning: "It's the Biosphere, Stupid." The biosphere needs to be the foundation of everything we do as ecological economists.

The biosphere is not simply a resource to be priced, as if with enough money we could afford to do without it. It is the foundation of life, and as such it is sacred and beyond price. Maintaining its healthy function is a sacred and nonnegotiable responsibility, not only to future generations, but as well to creation itself. A life-serving living-world economics requires a fundamentally different frame than that of suicidal dead-world economics.

We modern humans are just beginning to confront the reality of our nature as living beings—the reality that living beings, because of the way life manages energy, exist only in active relationships to other living beings. Life can only exist in community. In a fit of adolescent hubris, we humans sought to liberate ourselves from the responsibilities of life in community. In so doing, we confused individual autonomy with personal liberty and created economies that reduce caring human relationships to soulless financial exchange. We have structured our physical space around buildings and auto-dependent transportation systems that wall us off from one another and nature.

Living in isolation from nature, we seek to dominate, overwhelm, control, and expropriate nature's life-serving generative processes to grow a number on a computer hard drive. The resulting destruction of the biosphere, the source of life and all real wealth, is an act of collective insanity.

FROM SEPARATION AND DOMINATION TO INTEGRAL PARTNERSHIP

To work in partnership with Earth's biosphere, we must first understand its structure and dynamics as an exquisitely complex planetary-scale fractal structure 3.5 billion years in the making. It self-organizes everywhere in a dynamic, constantly evolving, locally and globally adaptive process to optimize the sustainable use of nutrients, energy, and water in support of life. All resources are continuously locally repurposed and recycled with zero waste. Redundancy and diversity optimize local adaptation, resilience, and creative potential. It is an incredible system, in which suicide economists take virtually no interest beyond figuring out new ways to extract its wealth for immediate financial gain.

Suicide economics has supported the creation of a global economic system that isolates people and communities from the sources of their food, energy, water, materials, and manufactured goods—and leaves them dependent on corporate-controlled global supply chains that are wasteful, unstable, unaccountable, and environmentally and social destructive. This isolation is psychologically, socially, and environmentally devastating.

The underlying system structure and dynamics of the suicide economy are in most every respect opposed to those of the biosphere. Working in opposition to the biosphere, the global suicide economy is maintained only by unsustainable dependence on a nonrenewable fossil fuels subsidy. That economy is already failing, and its ultimate collapse is only a matter of time. As ecological economists, we are all aware that so long as the current economic system remains in place, there will be no economic recovery for the mass of humanity. The economic stresses experienced by 99 percent of the world's people will only increase. We pay a terrible price for our arrogance.

The human future depends on navigating a transition to the culture and institutions of a New Economy system that works in cooperative integral partnership with the biosphere and self-organizes toward

- *Ecological balance* between aggregate human consumption and the regenerative capacity of Earth's biosphere
- *Equitable distribution* of real wealth to meet the needs of all
- *Living democracy* to secure economic and political accountability to people and community through active citizen participation

This New Economy must be a system that aligns and integrates with the structure and dynamics of the biosphere.

It requires segmenting the borderless global economy into a planetary system of interlinked bio-regional living economies that function as locally self-reliant subsystems of their local ecosystems, each rooted in a community of place and organized to optimize the use of local resources to meet the needs of all who live within the community's borders.

In the manner of the biosphere, these regional economies will meet most needs with local production using local resources in the manner of local ecosystems. They will benefit from trading their surplus with their neighbors in return for that which they cannot reasonably produce for themselves.

A NEW ECONOMICS

Ecological economics has made an important start on defining a new economics. But it has squandered far too much of its intellectual energy on a futile effort to gain the respect of diehard suicide economists. So rather than boldly framing the new economics we need, it has embraced many of the frameworks and conventions that an authentic ecological economics must displace.

Ecological economics must become a true living-systems economics that deals with the organization and management of the human relationship with the biosphere—the household writ large. It properly takes the health and happiness of people and nature as its defining purpose and standard of value. It begins with the household as its defining unit of analysis. It defines appropriate institutional structures. And it replaces GDP with a dashboard of living system indicators.

Instead of tweaking suicide economics at the margin with natural resource pricing studies, it must offer a true alternative and establish a strong public communications outreach presence devoted to redefining the public debate on economic policy choices.

It is a hugely ambitious intellectual and activist undertaking, but someone has to do it, and no group is better positioned to pull it off than ecological economists.

PRACTICAL AGENDA

The New Economy Working Group, which I co-chair with John Cavanagh of the Institute for Policy Studies in Washington, DC, has been working to frame a policy agenda for advancing the transition from the institutions and dynamics of the suicide economy to the institutions and dynamics of a New Economy that self-organizes toward ecological balance, equitable distribution, and living democracy.

We have framed a seven-part agenda, each part focused on a critical system pressure point. It provides a useful framework for thinking through the practical implications of taking ecological economics to the next level. Each of the seven action clusters is defined by a critical systemic source of suicide economy failure, paired with a needed system redesign intervention. The goal of this agenda is to move the locus of economic power from global financial markets to local communities and shift the values focus from making money for the rich to creating community wealth for everyone. This is a crucial step toward bringing the structure and dynamics of our human economies into alignment with those of the biosphere.

I want to briefly review each action cluster so you get a sense of the scope of the issues and needs to be addressed.

- *Problem 1: Financial indicators.* The use of financial indicators like gross domestic product and the Dow Jones Industrial Average to assess the performance of the economy gives priority to making money for rich people over improving the lives of all.

Solution: A dashboard of Living indicators. Optimize sustainable human well-being by evaluating economic performance against an array of indicators of human- and natural-systems health. The Bhutan experiment with a happiness index is an excellent start (Royal Government of Bhutan, 1999).

- *Problem 2: A Wall Street money and banking system.* Wall Street control of the creation and allocation of money gives control of our lives and national priorities to institutions devoted solely to maximizing private financial return through financial games that contribute nothing to the creation of anything of real value.

  Solution: A Main Street money and banking system: Decentralize and democratize the money system so that the power to create and allocate money resides in a system of community banks, mutual savings and loans, and credit unions accountable to local people and devoted to serving local financial needs. I'll elaborate on this in a moment.

- *Problem 3: Wealth concentration.* Wall Street interests use their political power to cut taxes for the rich and advance trade, fiscal, workplace, and social policies that suppress wages, erode worker protections, and cut services and safety nets for those most in need—creating an ever more extreme concentration of wealth and social dysfunction.

  Solution: Equitable distribution. Implement fiscal, workplace, and social policies that distribute income and ownership equitably. Equitable societies are healthier, happier, and more democratic and avoid both extravagance and desperation.

- *Problem 4: Soulless corporations with absentee owners.* An ideology of market fundamentalism has embedded a belief in the public culture that the sole purpose and responsibility of a business enterprise is to maximize financial returns to its owners. This belief legitimates the control of productive resources by soulless corporations possessed of artificial rights bestowed by unelected judges that seek immediate profit for absentee owners and sociopathic managers and deny responsibility for negative social and environmental consequences.

  Solution: Living enterprises with responsible living owners. Advance public policies that favor living enterprises with living, locally rooted responsible owners who seek a living return that includes a healthy community and a healthy natural environment. Cooperative, worker- and community-owned enterprises are positive examples. Tax away the profits of short-term capital gains to discourage the speculative public trading of corporate shares by absentee owners.

- *Problem 5: Market monopolies and big-money politics.* Global corporations operate beyond public accountability to monopolize economic and political power under unified management with no external accountability. They use this power to manipulate markets, extract public subsidies, and externalize social and environmental costs—all in violation of foundational principles of socially efficient, fair-market competition and one-person, one-vote democracy.

  Solution: Properly regulated markets and real democracy. Break up concentrations of corporate power, bar corporations from competing with living human beings for political power, and implement rules and incentives that support cost internalization and fair competition. Corporations are creations of government, and government has a responsibility to ensure that they are democratically accountable and play by proper market rules.

- *Problem 6: Fragmented, colonized local economies.* Fragmented local economies dependent on global corporations for jobs and basic goods and services leave people and nature captive to the financial interests of distant institutions that are interested only in extracting community wealth, not creating it.

  Solution: Self-reliant bio-regional economies. Pursue local economic development programs that build diversified, self-reliant, energy efficient, democratically self-organizing regional economies comprised of locally owned living enterprises accountable to local owners and devoted to serving local needs.

- *Problem 7: Global rules by and for corporations.* Global rules formulated and enforced by corporate dominated institutions like the World Trade Organization facilitate and enforce the concentration of corporate power and shield it from democratic accountability.
  Solution: Global rules by and for people. Restructure global rules and institutions to limit the concentration of corporate power, support balanced trade and national ownership, and secure the economic sovereignty of people by ensuring that any corporation that operates across national borders is democratically accountable to the communities in which it does business.

You will notice the recommended interventions focus on realigning the cultural values and institutional structures that shape the economic system's function.

Beyond dangerously simplistic ideological calls for free trade and deregulation to give free reign to antimarket, antidemocratic global corporate oligopolies, suicide economists pay little attention to issues of system organization that should be a centerpiece of any discipline that presumes to serve as a guide to the organization and management of the human household writ large.

Unfortunately, ecological economics, in its current state, appears to be similarly impaired and similarly neglects essential institutional issues. We must remedy this impairment if we are to live up to the promise of our name.

MONEY AS A FALSE CONSTRAINT

I now want to turn to the money system. Suicide economists are notorious for their lack of understanding of life. The more surprising thing is that they also lack a basic understanding of their favored metric—money. This is revealed most clearly by their failure, which I noted earlier, to distinguish between money and real wealth.

In a modern society in which access to most every essential of a secure and happy life depends on money, the accounting chits we call money take on great significance. Where they flow there are jobs; where they do not flow, there is unemployment. Where they flow there is food, shelter, health care, and education. Where they do not flow there is starvation, homelessness, disease, and illiteracy.

Has it ever struck you how absurd it is that, as a society, we cannot put our millions of unemployed people to work meeting critical unmet needs or shelter the homeless in houses that sit empty—only for lack of money the Federal Reserve can create with a keystroke?

We now know that when Wall Street collapsed in 2008, the Federal Reserve responded by creating $13 trillion out of nothing with a few computer keystrokes and fed it into Wall Street by issuing short-term credit, purchasing securities, and providing guarantees for securities. Wall Street recovered in a flash with record profits, bonuses, numbers of billionaires, a reinflated stock market bubble, and record idle corporate cash reserves. When it comes to employing teachers, nurses, police, and firefighters, however, we do not have the money. To paraphrase Kenneth Boulding, anyone who thinks this makes sense is either a madman or a suicide economist.

There are many real resource constraints to dealing with human needs and the money supply must be kept in balance with resource availability, but for a society, money, which can be created with a simple accounting entry, should never be the defining constraint.

MASTER OR SERVANT?

It is instructive to recall that, prior to European colonization, the indigenous peoples of Africa organized to meet their needs with little need for money. Consequently, the colonizers found it difficult to extract their labor. The solution was to impose a tax payable in money that could be obtained only by providing labor on the estates of the colonizers. Control of money gives Wall Street the power to reduce most of society to the status of colonial serfs.

The proper function of money is to facilitate the sustainable and equitable utilization of resources to fulfill the needs of people, communities, and nature. This calls for a community-based and democratically accountable system of money, banking, and finance that functions to create and allocate money as a well-regulated public utility responsive to community needs and supportive of a natural human alignment and partnership with the biosphere.

We had that sort of a system of community banks, mutual savings and loans, and credit unions not long ago. Indeed, during the years of my growing up, it financed the United States' victory in World War II, produced an unprecedented period of economic stability and prosperity, made America the world's industrial powerhouse, and created the American middle class. That system served us extremely well until Wall Street launched its "financial modernization" experiment to restore the system conditions that plunged the world into the Great Depression.

Wall Street interests mobilized in the 1970s with the support of armies of suicide economists to advance a host of policy initiatives that shifted control of the institutions of money, banking, and finance from Main Street to Wall Street and redirected their purpose from funding real productive investment in response to community needs and opportunities to funding phantom wealth financial speculation. This resulted in the erosion of the middle class, an extreme concentration of wealth, a costly financial collapse, high rates of unemployment, bankruptcy, and housing foreclosure, accelerating environmental systems failure, and the hollowing out of U.S. industrial, technological, and research capacity. Wall Street profited at every step and declared its social engineering experiment a great success—to the applause of its suicide economist cronies.

LIBERATION FROM WALL STREET

I have just completed a report for the New Economy Working Group titled *How to Liberate America from Wall Street Rule*. It outlines an agenda for rolling back Wall Street's disastrous experiment and rebuilding a community-based, publicly accountable money and banking system responsive to the needs and opportunities of the twenty-first century. It presents four major recommendations in addition to those I have just outlined.

- *Item 1: Break up the megabanks and implement tax and regulatory policies that favor community financial institutions* organized as cooperatives or as for-profits owned by nonprofit foundations devoted to community wealth building. These institutions will keep money circulating in the community rather than sucking it up into the Wall Street casino.
- *Item 2: Establish state-owned partnership banks* that serve as depositories for state financial assets. These banks keep state funds circulating in the state by working with and through community

financial institutions to cofinance local enterprises engaged in construction, agriculture, industry, and commerce. The North Dakota State Bank established in 1919 is a model and is a major reason why North Dakota was relatively unscathed by the Wall Street collapse (Public Banking Institute, 2012; Center for State Innovation, 2011). State bank legislation has already been introduced in twelve states.

- *Item 3: Restructure the Federal Reserve* to function as a federal agency subject to strict standards of transparency, public scrutiny, audit by the U.S. Government Accountability Office, and congressional oversight. Its sole responsibility would be to manage the money supply. Responsibility for the regulation of banks and so-called shadow-banking institutions would be assigned to a new regulatory agency established specifically for that purpose.
- *Item 4: Direct all new money created by the Federal Reserve to a Federal Recovery and Reconstruction Bank*, which would use these funds to finance critically needed green public infrastructure projects as designated by Congress.

Newly created Fed money would thus flow directly into the real economy to address real needs rather than serving as a subsidy to Wall Street banks.

A NEW PARADIGM ECONOMICS

So what does all this suggest for the future of ecological economics as an intellectual discipline? These issues of values, institutions, and power that shape our human relationship to the ecosphere must all be at the fore of a fully formed ecological economics.

At the beginning, I made the statement, "We need a truly new economics that reaches as far beyond the understanding of conventional economics as quantum physics reaches beyond the understanding of conventional Newtonian physics." I did not make that statement lightly. The underlying paradigm of science is shifting in the most dramatic ways. Whereas Newtonian physics was based on a premise that only the material is real, the new quantum physics suggests that matter is an illusion and only relationships are real. It is an incredible advance in expanding human understanding of the nature of reality.

From attempting to define and explain the cosmos as a giant machine, we are beginning to recognize that it is better understood as some combination of a great thought and grand living organism. This has vast implications for the life and social sciences, as well as the physical sciences. The old biology sought to understand life by grinding up cells to identify their chemical composition. The new biology studies living cells and organisms to understand life on its own terms—including its extraordinary capacity for self-organization, learning, and resilience. It is an exciting quest with extraordinary implications for a true ecological economics.

To address the human place in the biosphere, ecological economists must align with and build on the most advanced work of the new paradigm life and social sciences. We must draw from their insights to create the tools and frameworks needed to create a new civilization dedicated to working in partnership with the biosphere's generative systems to secure the health and vitality of all of life for all generations to come.

From a futile effort to salvage the discipline of suicide economics from within, we must direct our energy instead to saving the world by creating and popularizing a wholly new economics. The world hungers for new ideas and leadership. The discredited ideas of suicide economists continue to prevail only because there is no organized public voice offering a credible alternative. We can be that voice.

We who work to bring forth a New Economy that works in cooperative alliance with Earth's biosphere engage in an epic undertaking. Now is the hour. We have the power. We are the ones that we have been waiting for.

REFERENCES

Center for State Innovation. 2011. State banks initiative. Madison, WI: Center for State Innovation. http://www.stateinnovation.org/statebanks.aspx.
Daly, Herman E. 1991. *Steady-State Economics.* 2nd edition. Washington, DC: Island Press.
de Graaf, John, and David K. Batker. 2011. *What's the Economy For, Anyway? Why It's Time to Stop Chasing Growth and Start Pursuing Happiness.* New York: Bloomsbury Press.
Farley, Joshua. 2010. Ecological Economics. In *The Post Carbon Reader: Managing the 21st Century's Sustainability Crises,* ed. Richard Heinberg and Daniel Lerch. Healdsburg, CA: Watershed Media.
Public Banking Institute. 2012. "Resurrecting Main Street: An Introduction to Public Banking." Sonoma, CA: Public Banking Institute. http://publicbankinginstitute.org/public-banking.htm.
Royal Government of Bhutan. 1999. *Bhutan 2020: A Vision for Peace, Prosperity and Happiness.* Thimphu: Royal Government of Bhutan, Planning Commission.

Beyond the Ivory Tower
Why Progress Needs More Ecological Economists to Actively Engage

KRISTEN A. SHEERAN

FOR MANY, THE CHOICE OF ECONOMICS AS A CAREER REFLECTS A DESIRE TO UNDER-stand the system of production and consumption, explain the inner logic of economic institutions, and above all to improve economic outcomes. But those who come to economics seeking to improve the world often end up disappointed. They enter a shadowy realm of ever-escalating abstraction from which emerges, again and again, a conservative antireform agenda. Today's challenges demand new economic thinking; conventional economics falls short of envisioning a way through current crises. Useful new economic theory, however, will only arise as economists engage with practical, real-world problems. Ecological economics has been at the forefront of this movement for a new economics paradigm that is fundamentally linked to the natural systems that support economic activity. But even this important body of work can often be divorced from public discourse and real-world policy decisions.

As scholars, we know that there is a large and growing body of published literature that supports active protection of human health and the environment; yet the evidence is rarely translated for decision makers, stakeholders, the media, and the public in language that is compelling and accessible. The most innovative research, persuasive evidence, and best new ideas are reserved for academic journals and academic conferences, largely hidden from the public's eye. Economic arguments, however, heavily influence public support for environmental policy. In the absence of alternative economic voices, the antiregulatory "economics" wielded by interests opposed to reform echo ever more loudly. The debate over national climate policy offers an excellent example of this dynamic: decision makers and the public largely feared that emissions control would destroy jobs and income, despite overwhelming support by economists for immediate and aggressive climate action. In other words, opponents of climate action controlled the public discourse more effectively than scientists and economists.

At the United States Society for Ecological Economics (USSEE) conference in Tacoma Washington, in the summer of 2005, there was a panel discussion led by Frank Acker-man, James Boyce, and Dave Batker about the importance of creating an applied, more relevant economics that is committed to social equity at its very core. The impetus for that conversation was the growing awareness on the part of foundations and environmen-tal organizations that economic arguments were increasingly dominating decision making about the environment and natural resources. It was clear that environmental organizations had the science and legal capacity to inform public policy, but almost all lacked the third leg of the policy stool: the economics. But as economists, they also knew that neoclassical economics was mostly ill suited to offering the tools and perspectives the environmental community was seeking.

The conversations at the USSEE conference led to the creation of Economics for Equity and the Environment Network (E3) at Ecotrust. E3 is a national network of ecological and progressive economists committed to building a new and applied economics that is safe for people and the planet. Its goal is to support research on real-world environmental issues and to create opportunities for productively engaging economists in the public and policy discourse. There are now more than 250 economists in the network across the country. As director of E3 Network for the past four years, I have witnessed firsthand the enormous value of translating economics for the broader policy community and public and the dire need to involve more economists directly in this work.

I would like to reflect on the lessons we have learned since that USSEE meeting in 2005 and issue a challenge to readers to find ways to actively engage beyond the academy in discussions and debates about the enormous challenges and opportunities confronting us in the twenty-first century. Ecological economists are aware that business as usual in theory and in practice locks us into a collision course between human needs and natural constraints. We also know that the solutions to these civilizational challenges—though neither cheap nor easy—are feasible. How can we use our expertise and our credentials to convince others that it is political will, not economic obstacles, that limits us? How can we paint the picture of a more just and sustainable future in strokes broad and bold enough for others to understand? Scientific inquiry, research, and publication are absolutely essential; but I wager that they are not enough and that we can all be doing more.

ECONOMICS AND CLIMATE CHANGE

Climate change offers an excellent example of how conventional economic thinking has failed and where more productive engagement by a broad range of economists could help us move beyond the current impasse on climate and energy reform. As the debate over climate and energy policy intensified over the last ten years, economic analysis played an increasingly central role. Today, the case for inaction on climate change is more likely to be argued from the perspective of economic costs rather than skepticism about the science.

The standard toolkit of conventional economics does not apply well to climate change. Stabilizing the earth's climate system is as much a scientific and moral issue as it is an economic issue. There are limits to applying cost-benefit analysis to climate change when the damages accrue to future generations and involve consequences for human lives and ecosystems that are virtually incalculable. Risk management is a more appropriate frame for evaluating the climate policy objectives for these reasons.

There are widely cited economic models that predict doom and gloom from reducing carbon emissions; others that recommend a "go-slow" approach with only modest emissions reduction in the short term. But there is a large and growing body of scholarship in economics that is consistent with the urgency of the problem as seen from a climate science perspective.

This body of research and its results are far less known to the public, media, and decision makers.

As with most economic research, it is difficult to decipher. How does a reporter or decision maker understand what distinguishes these models—and how do they explain discount rates, fat tails, quadratic damage functions, and welfare weights to their readers or constituents? These are the issues reporters and decision makers need to understand if they are to evaluate the results of climate economic models and understand why some of these models seemingly contradict the more dire predictions of climate scientists. Unable to distinguish between contradictory results, the media's tendency will be to report both sides as if both are equally valid, or bias their reporting toward the side that favors the status quo.

Political scientist Jules Boykoff analyzed coverage of climate change by the major media outlets immediately before and after the UN climate meetings in Cancún in 2010. Of the ninety-eight news stories about climate change that he identified, only three explicitly discussed the negative economic impacts climate change would have on the global economy—all of which appeared in the *New York Times*.[1] In the ninety-eight news stories, only two economists (besides Christina Romer, who wrote an op-ed about the economic risks from climate change) were cited: Robert Stavins of Harvard and David Kruetzer of the Heritage Foundation. Both are highly reputed neoclassical economists; but neither is strongly associated with the large and growing body of research in economics that calls for immediate and aggressive emissions reductions to avoid future damages of climate change.

Scholars will continue to hash out these differences in academic publications, and a new consensus (to the extent economists ever come close to consensus) may someday emerge. But the slowness of publishing in economic journals means that new findings in economics cannot help but lag behind climate science and policy. The vast majority of economic studies of the costs and benefits of climate stabilization, for example, assume a climate stabilization goal of 550 or 450 ppm CO_2 equivalent. Many in the science and climate advocacy communities, however, now call for stabilization targets as low as 350 ppm to minimize the worst risks of climate change. Far less is known about the economic feasibility of achieving 350 ppm. There is a real disconnect between the work on the front lines of the policy and advocacy communities and what is happening in the academy. As a result, many important policy decisions are made on the basis of gray literature rather than scholarly publication.

How can we address real-world policy relevant questions in a time frame that can inform decision making and public opinion? And how can we provide answers that empower decision makers, advocates, and the general public to take action? Framing is key. The relevant question is not whether or not we can afford to stabilize the earth's climate system. The relevant question is whether we can afford not to? Economists can debate how issues such as discount rates, equity weights, and damage functions influence the economic case for climate action, but noneconomists understand more simply that we've abdicated our responsibilities to future generations if we have left them a world in which the capacity to grow food and access fresh water is very limited.

Translating climate science into economic impacts that people can understand and relate to will go a long way toward building broad support for climate action in the United States. So economists need to find more opportunities to engage the public in support of climate protection. The following are some suggestions based on my experience with the E3 Network. It is not an inclusive list. These strategies can be adopted to address other real-world environmental issues as well.

STRATEGIES

Debunking/Rapid Response

In the debate over national climate legislation, there was seemingly no end to industry-sponsored studies predicting massive job loss, lost competitiveness, and economic decline. These studies and their release were typically well orchestrated in advance and reported on widely in the press. Results were often shared directly with key members of Congress and decision makers at the state and local levels. This was true despite the fact that some of these models were proprietary and not subject to public or peer scrutiny. Academic publications often provided better arguments and contrary evidence, but these were largely invisible to the public and decision makers. There is a very strong need for economists to debunk the results of flawed politically driven analyses and provide alternative perspectives and data.

The public is typically skeptical of analyses that make assumptions that contradict their perceived realities and their value systems. Daylighting the assumptions that underlie economic analyses goes a long way toward raising doubts about their credibility. It removes the cloak of "hard science" that a lot of economic analysis hides behind. Ecological economists have done an excellent job calling neoclassical economics to task for many of its basic assumptions about economic growth and the substitutability of natural and economic systems. But it is not enough to debate assumptions in academic journals and conferences; we need to expose those perversities as they manifest regularly in the public discourse. The real battle is not with neoclassical (or any school of economics) per se, but rather with how those paradigms are used to justify the status quo and thwart genuine progressive reform.

Better Communication

The best defense, of course, is a good offense. So we need economists to do a better job of communicating economic arguments for protecting people and nature. Economists are not especially good at communicating with noneconomists. We tend to be too equivocal—we pack every statement with contingencies and assumptions. Our language also tends to be rich in jargon. I've watched communications professionals work with economists and scientists to craft the message of their research and results for a broader audience. It succeeds in generating attention to new ideas. Now more than ever, the lines between fact and fiction are routinely blurred by special interests. We can stay true to what we know but also be very strategic in how we communicate it. I would encourage ecological economists to reach out to communications staff at nonprofits, think tanks, and universities to aid in this process.

Outreach

There is a very strong yearning out there for clarity on economic issues and ideas by noneconomists. At E3 Network, we've discovered that some of the most widely read pieces on our website are two-page policy briefs on issues that are fairly straightforward for most economists; for example, the differences between a carbon cap and tax. We encourage economists in the E3 Network to write a short brief or blog post in plain language to accompany every academic paper they write. It expands readership and allows economists to communicate the practical importance of their research.

Similarly, there are many opportunities in the community to engage with civic groups, schools, churches, and the business community. We need to avail ourselves of those opportunities; they may yield more fruit than talking to each other at academic conferences. We also need to have more and varied economic viewpoints represented on the op-ed pages, quoted in articles, and testifying before key committees. This is not easy to facilitate, but communications professionals at the nonprofits economists partner with can help identify these opportunities.

Research

As we contemplate new research directions, we need to be practical and strategic. We should be prioritizing the questions that concern the public and impede decision making and planning. I have learned that some of the philosophical and theoretical questions that pique my interests and have inspired my scholarship are not necessarily the ones that can mobilize social change. We need to be more deliberative and seek a greater balance between the two. Of our intended research projects we need to ask: how will this research affect change in the world?

OBSTACLES

It is not an accident that progressive economic research remains largely outside of the public discourse and divorced from real-world decision making. There are numerous obstacles that our profession puts in the way. Economics typically does not value research that challenges dominant precepts and existing hierarchies, applied research work, or research that is associated with advocacy. These are strong disincentives for junior scholars pretenure, and tenured faculty who must meet the profession's publishing standards to receive things such as merit pay or course releases.

As much as there is a strong demand for alternative economic perspectives, the scholar who provides them is vulnerable to criticism, often labeled as a radical or a crank. I have observed the media, NGOs, and the philanthropic community fall victim to this trap—a trap that has them returning to the same economists and models time and time again expecting different results.

The more fundamental issue at play here is the line between research and advocacy—between positive and normative inquiry. As scholars we are trained to adopt a very neutral tone in our publications, even when our evidence clearly supports a particular position or worldview. Indeed, that may be the right tone for scholarly publications. But if our expertise and findings clearly support a particular position or action and can inform a public debate, should we shy away from saying so? Why shouldn't we be explicit about the values we bring to our work and the change we are hoping to affect? Not only is it intellectually honest, it may help to attract wider support if others can see themselves in the work. Whenever I address an audience about climate change, I always explain that my work in this area is driven by my understanding of climate science; and my strong belief that we have a moral obligation to protect vulnerable people today and in the future from the impacts of climate change.

CONCLUSION

Ecological economics has been enormously successful in challenging many of the dominant orthodoxies of neoclassical economics and creating safe spaces in which economists of varied heterodox traditions may practice. As the U.S. community of ecological economists contemplates its future and next directions, I encourage greater engagement beyond the academy.

If you believe that a better world is possible; if you believe that the wealth and power of humanity in the twenty-first century is capable of creating a far better world—find new and innovative ways of informing and inspiring others. Economic ideas do not drop from the sky fully formed, nor do they emerge from a politically neutral process of academic research. Rather, they are supported by people with agendas and the resources to back them up. The progrowth, antiregulatory economics that is now so widely accepted and threatens to reverse decades of hard-fought battles to protect human health and the environment is the result of the well-funded, decades-long efforts of ideologically driven institutions. If we want to provide an effective counterweight to those claims and create a more relevant ecological economics for the twenty-first century, we need to more effectively and deliberately step outside of the academy and confront the power structures that support the dominant orthodoxy.

NOTE

1. Jules Boykoff, "US Media Coverage of the Cancún Climate Change Conference," *PS: Political Science and Politics* 45, no. 2 (April 2012): 251–58.

Ruin and Recovery
The Economics of Michigan's Natural Resources

DAVID DEMPSEY

IF EVER THERE WAS A PLACE WHOSE HISTORY ILLUSTRATES THE DANGER OF EXPLOIT-
ing natural resources to the point of economic ruin, that place is Michigan. Located at the
heart of the Great Lakes, the world's largest freshwater ecosystem and the source of nearly
one-fifth of available global surface water, Michigan has risen and fallen with the conservation
and exploitation of that liquid resource, as well as timber, fish, wildlife, and land. The conservation and environmental movements helped dig the state out of previous economic collapses
by fashioning policies with long-term economic benefits from sustainable forest, fish, and
game management, clean air and water, and sensitive natural areas. What remains to be seen is
whether the state's current prolonged recession will produce a similar result—or instead lead
to further stripping of natural resources to realize immediate gains at the expense of the future.
Ecological economics can contribute to the debate and promote informed choices, but it has
not yet developed roots in Michigan public policy.

Well before Michigan became a state in 1837, its natural resources shaped its identity and
accessibility. The state's 32,000 miles of rivers and streams and the nearshore waters of the
Great Lakes were transportation corridors for Native American communities and early European explorers and settlers. On the other hand, extensive wetland enclaves in the southern
region of the Lower Peninsula persuaded early United States surveyors that settling it was nigh
hopeless. In the fall of 1815, the surveyor general of the United States, Edward Tiffin, sent
men into southeastern Michigan. They examined land in Jackson County during a wet season,
and "Tiffin, in turn, reported to President Madison early in 1816 that Michigan apparently
consisted of swamps, lakes and poor, sandy soil not worth the cost of surveying. He declared
that in his opinion not more than one acre in a hundred, or perhaps one in a thousand, could
be cultivated" (Dunbar and May, 1995, p. 157). With the ardent help of later state officials,
the draining of many of these soils would produce rich agricultural lands that today continue
to produce a variety of products from sugar beets to soybeans.[1]

More to the taste of early Michigan explorers and settlers was the abundant, seemingly
inexhaustible supply of fish and game. Michigan's fisheries were the first natural resource
to be ruinously exploited. In 1860 the state's commercial fish catch climbed to 17.5 million pounds. The industry employed 620 workers in the Lower Peninsula and accounted for
$109,838 in value added. But whitefish catch in Lakes Superior, Michigan, and Huron plum-
meted from 8.1 million pounds in 1885 to 5.3 million pounds in 1893, with an even more
marked decline from 315 pounds per net to 127 pounds per net in the same period. Fishing

effort was increasing at the same time catch was declining. In 1885, fifty-eight steamers and 733 smaller boats trolled for whitefish; in 1891, seventy steamers and 1,423 boats crowded the lakes (Michigan Department of Natural Resources, 1974). Although the state created the position of superintendent of fisheries in the early 1870s to run hatcheries to restock fish, commercial fishermen frustrated conservationists' efforts to legislate limits on catch and seasons. In an annual report for 1873–74, the superintendent lamented, "In the times of our fathers these same waters swarmed with the choicest varieties of fin life, contributing a no scanty support to many a pioneer and frontier home. . . . Now, why are not such or similar catches reported in the 'tracts' and papers of today? Ignorance, improvidence, living out the proverb, 'After us a famine'—fishing in season and out of season, but oftener out of season—not knowing the significance of close times nor caring" (Michigan Department of Natural Resources, 1974, p. 59).

Timber was the resource that captured the fancy of both individuals and tycoons in the second half of the nineteenth century. Millions of acres of virgin white pine and hardwood forests spread across the northern two-thirds of the Lower Peninsula and the entire Upper Peninsula. Although largely untouched into the 1850s, the north woods became the fodder for amazing industrial growth in the next decade. The number of lumber firms in the Lower Peninsula rose from 926 to 1,641 between 1860 and 1870. Employment in the industry jumped from 6,394 workers to 20,575. And the value added to the economy by lumber rose from $1,820,971 to $11,390,940.

But even at the time, observers began to warn that Michigan's forests were not inexhaustible. A few voices began to sound an alarm that the massive cut was impossible to sustain. In 1868, the *North American Review* discussed Michigan's future at length. The magazine dismissed claims that the white pine would last forever—or at least 500 years, as some had said: "It is common to speak of the pine lands of Michigan as 'inexhaustible.' We hear of the supply that may be expected for 'ages to come' from this prolific source. Men think of the lumber forests of the Peninsula as they do of the coal-beds of Pennsylvania and Ohio, and laugh at the predictions of the alarmists. Yet these predictions are not hasty, but are based on exact calculations. . . . The most sanguine calculation cannot carry the lumber business beyond the present century" (Brigham, 1868, pp. 95–96).

Absolute timber volume began to fall after a few decades of intense harvest. In 1870, Michigan ranked first among the states in production of lumber, turning out an amazing 2.25 billion board feet. The state maintained its lead in 1880 and in 1890, hitting a peak of 4.25 billion board feet in the latter year. Then production shrank. In 1899, Michigan fell back to second behind Wisconsin, producing 3.01 billion board feet. In the next five years production shrank to just over 2 billion board feet, putting the state fourth. By 1920 Michigan was sixteenth in timber production among states, turning out just less than 750 million board feet (Reynolds and Pierson, 1923).

Left behind were communities with shrunken economies and populations and a cutover landscape that regularly roared into extreme fires, killing hundreds of Michiganders. The owners of the large-scale forest tracts moved onto the Pacific Northwest after depleting most of the timber of northern Michigan, Wisconsin, and Minnesota. Often the land was simply abandoned and reverted to state ownership when taxes were not paid.

The human disasters that came on the heels of the era of timber exploitation, coupled with the gospel of utilitarian conservation championed by President Theodore Roosevelt and others in the first decade of the 1900s, spurred the state's initial forest conservation policies. In 1908, a fire that erupted from cutover land in northeast Michigan killed twenty-five near the village of Metz—part of a record 2.3 million acres of Michigan forest that burned that year. The press expressed outrage. In a *Detroit News* cartoon not long after the murderous fire, a fattened politician, wearing a tag labeling him the "G.O.P. Machine," fiddled "politics" while families raced from forest flames. The caption under the cartoon read: "Our Nero has been fiddling a good many years."

In a subsequent editorial entitled "A Crime Against Humanity," the *News* lamented the "destruction of the state's forests by the ax of the woodsman," adding, "Man and the elements are combining to make this not only a forestless, but a valueless commonwealth. . . . What a commentary is this on state officialdom. What utter neglect it shows of those things for which state officials are elected and appointed." The newspaper called for reforestation. Armed with such support, forestry advocates successfully petitioned the legislature the following year to establish a state Public Domain Commission to improve management of state-owned lands.

Then and throughout the next half-century, conservationists outside of government spurred on the decision makers. The Michigan Forestry Association and the Michigan Association for the Propagation of Fish and Game were leading nongovernmental organizations that pressed for institutional reforms separating lawmakers' immediate political concerns from long-term, sustainable management of state forests and fish and game populations.

Whether the result of institutional reforms or other policies promoted by the advocates, natural resources ravenously consumed up to 1910 began to recover over the next several decades. In May 1901, state lawmakers approved a reserve of approximately 35,000 acres—the genesis of the modern state forest system (State of Michigan, 1901). Michigan's state forests ultimately expanded to approximately 3.9 million acres, the largest such state system east of the Mississippi. Beginning with creation of a State Parks Commission in 1919, the state has now developed a ninety-eight-unit park system attracting more than 20 million visitors annually. Populations of coveted fish and game species like lake trout and deer generate hundreds of millions of dollars for local economies and the state treasury. Founded in 1937, the sportsman's group Michigan United Conservation Clubs continues to act as watchdog over these resources.

At the same time forests, fish, and game were recovering, the state's waterways and air were noticeably deteriorating. In 1936 the chief smoke inspector for Detroit estimated that 350 tons of "soot, fly-ash and dirt" fell each year on every square mile of Detroit, up from 56 tons in 1931. "Smoking factory chimneys, long pointed to as symbols of civic prosperity, actually are signs that money is being wasted and health menaced," he said. Suburbs downriver from Detroit were especially afflicted by uncontrolled emissions to the air during the postwar period. South Wyandotte received 69.6 tons of fly ash one weekend in 1947. Calling the fallout "a veritable hurricane," the *Detroit Free Press* reported that harassed homeowners had called on local governments for relief. As Michigan was rewriting its constitution in 1961, one of the authors observed, "A great many people in the Detroit area are half-sick or below par physically because of the contaminated air they breathe." He added he sometimes used a gas mask on his commute to work in Detroit from suburban Birmingham. Partially as a result, the revised constitution imposed a duty on the state to protect public health, which supported the establishment of strong air pollution control laws in the mid-1960s.

The degradation of water was even more pronounced. A study published by the International Joint Commission in 1918 observed that typhoid death rates per 100,000 population in Michigan's boundary waters communities ranged as high as 163 at Trenton in 1907 and 123 at Wyandotte in 1908, far above normal levels. Until the advent of chlorination, these mortality rates were the price of pollution.

Soon there would be profound clashes between industries and regulators—with communities in the middle—over the perceived choice between clean water and a healthy economy. The Kalamazoo River was a prime example. The site of a more than a dozen papermaking plants at one time, the river regularly suffered from pollution that smothered fish and rendered it unfit for recreation. But the dumping of raw waste also helped the papermaking industry remain profitable. In 1925, ten companies with sixteen paper mills and thirty-four paper-and-board machines employed 5,200 employees and had an annual payroll of $7 million. Related industries provided 2,500 jobs with a payroll of $3.5 million annually. Seeking to protect the jobs, community leaders joined the industry in fighting strict pollution controls for more than forty years.

Worsening conditions and media attention helped galvanize reform. In September 1953, the river attracted national attention when the oxygen demand caused by the paper wastes killed thousands of carp near Allegan. "Their corpses gorged the valley's streams, as in Dumont Creek, where four acres of carp choked the waters in glistening, smelly death," *Life* magazine reported beside a picture of the casualties. It was also *Life* that declared Lake Erie, downstream of Detroit's massive wastewater plant, "dead," spurring state and provincial bans on high-phosphorus laundry detergents and tougher sewage controls. By 1975 the lake had nearly recovered from massive algae blooms that had inspired *Life*. Ultimately, as popular opinion began to turn strongly in favor of clean water rules, Kalamazoo River industries were required to comply with them.

The pollution legacy of the papermaking and other industries would continue in the twenty-first century. Tons of toxic PCBs used in the papermaking process were found downstream in the 1980s, creating a forty-mile Superfund site in the Kalamazoo River and costing over $100 million in private and public cleanup. By 2005, state taxpayers had shelled out over $1.5 billion to clean up some of more than 3,000 contaminated industrial and business sites across Michigan, ranging from automobile manufacturing sites to dry cleaners and gas stations. Many of the sites were abandoned, as the cutover forests had once been.

As had been the case in the early twentieth century with forestry and fish and game, the initial impulse and long-term energy for the environmental cleanup reforms came from citizens and nongovernmental organizations. Founded in 1968, the state's first modern environmental organization, the West Michigan Environmental Action Council, was the source of policy and pressure for Michigan's 1970 Environmental Protection Act (MEPA, 1970). Such groups and individuals harnessed public opinion, often articulated in the media, to influence decision makers.[2] Their arguments typically challenged political leaders to think of the welfare of Michiganders yet unborn.

While the cleanup of air and water was hailed by most of civil society, Michigan's continued sharp economic downturns resulted in public debates over whether environmental safeguards were choking job creation. Beginning in the late 1980s, environmental advocates at both the national and state levels countered the economic impact arguments in favor of less protective regulations with dollar estimates associated with increased disease and mortality, which they argued would result from more polluted air, for example. Largely, however, these costs were regarded by decision makers as nebulous externalities not pivotal in specific regulatory debates.

The relationship of healthy natural resources to job-creating industries, including tourism, outdoor recreation, and agriculture—three of Michigan's top four industries, eclipsed only by manufacturing—did not significantly influence the debate, either. The relationship of a specific proposed polluting facility to tourism, for example, was regarded as unclear if mentioned at all.

These responses by decision makers might also apply to discussions of ecosystem services as well. But it was impossible to know because the topic was rarely raised and good data did not exist on either a macro- or microeconomic scale. Without an approximate dollar value that could be assigned to ecosystem services provided by wetlands, green space, forests, and waterways, the debates often pitted jobs against intrinsic or aesthetic values.

Strengthening the role of ecological economic concerns in Michigan environmental decision making, then, is likely to require the following:

- Robust, peer-reviewed analysis of statewide and local (at least watershed) ecological services
- Incorporation of ecosystem services as a consideration under Michigan environmental laws and rules[3]
- Public communication and education on the meaning and significance of ecosystem services valuation.

While a general concern about the welfare of future generations motivated forestry, fish and game, and environmental advocates in successfully promoting sustainable Michigan natural resource policy from approximately 1900 to 1980, more tangible arguments and stronger ecological economic analysis tools were required after that period to settle the policy argument more often in favor of protection and conservation. Even now, Michigan governments and environmental advocates have not yet deployed such tools.

NOTES

1. According to the U.S. Fish and Wildlife Service, Michigan's original 11 million acres of wetlands dwindled to approximately 5.5 million in 1980, the same year the state's wetland protection act took effect.
2. A striking example of news media attention to the growth of environmental concerns was a one-hour prime-time special on CBS-TV on April 22, 1970, the first Earth Day, entitled *Earth Day: A Question of Survival*. Hosted by Walter Cronkite, the program featured student activists at Michigan's Hillsdale College collecting and compacting discarded aluminum containers. The same spring, WOOD-TV in Grand Rapids broadcast a series, *Our Poisoned World*, detailing serious local air, water, and noise pollution and the problem of garbage disposal.
3. An appropriate place to begin with statutory reform would be the broad-based Michigan Environmental Protection Act (MEPA, 1970), whose genesis is discussed earlier. MEPA establishes a broad state environmental policy calling for the "protection of the air, water, and other natural resources and the public trust in these resources from pollution, impairment, or destruction." MEPA has been codified as 324.1701-1706 of the Michigan Compiled Laws.

REFERENCES

Brigham, C. H. 1868. "The Lumber Region of Michigan." *North American Review* 107:77–103.

Dunbar, Willis F., and George S. May. 1995. *Michigan: A History of the Wolverine State*.3rd edition. Grand Rapids, MI: William B. Eerdmans.

Michigan Department of Natural Resources. 1974. *Michigan Fisheries Centennial Report, 1873–1973*. Lansing: Department of Natural Resources, Fisheries Division.

Michigan Environmental Protection Act (MEPA). 1970. Michigan Compiled Laws Annotated (MCLA) 324.1701-1706, chapter 324, Natural Resources and Environmental Protection Act.

Reynolds, R. V., and Albert H. Pierson. 1923. "Lumber Cut of the United States, 1870–1920." Washington, DC: U.S. Department of Agriculture.

State of Michigan. 1901. Journal of the House of Representatives, May 28, 1901, p. 2378. Lansing: State of Michigan.

Historical and Theoretical
Perspectives

Noble Savages or Consummate Consumers

The Behavioral Ecology of Building a Green Conservation Future

BOBBI S. LOW

SCHOLARS IN MANY FIELDS KNOW THE LITANY OF ECOLOGICAL PROBLEMS WE FACE today: a changing climate, increasingly severe floods and droughts, the extirpation of many species. Today we are more numerous and consume more per capita than ever before. One prominent "explanation" is that we are so isolated from ecological forces that we have no idea of our impacts. If we were to return to our "Noble Savage" state, consuming less, all would be well. This old romantic notion of "noble" indigenous peoples, consuming little (with an implied concern for future resources) dates at least back to John Dryden's *Conquest of Grenada* (1669–70, pt. 1, act 1, scene 1): "I am as free as Nature first made man, / Ere the base laws of servitude began, / When wild in woods the Noble Savage ran."

Those of us who study human behavior in an evolutionary perspective—behavioral ecologists and evolutionary anthropologists and psychologists—know something about the resource consumption patterns of peoples in traditional societies and may have something to offer about what kinds of conservation strategies are more, and what kinds are less, likely to convince ourselves to behave sustainably in particular cases.

HUMAN LIFE HISTORIES: WHY ARE WE SUCH EXPENSIVE ANIMALS?

Behavioral ecology argues that environmental conditions shape the lifetimes and behavior of organisms, and that by crafting testable hypotheses and making the right observations, we can understand the basic rules that drive a species' behavioral ecology, including consumption patterns. Darwin understood this; that is why he began his *Origin of Species* (1859) with the observation that organisms are generally well suited to their environments.

But what about that really smart, social ape, *Homo sapiens*? Because we are changing environmental conditions in ways that have strong impacts on other organisms, we need not only to study others' life histories and behavior, but also to turn the same lens on our own behavior. Recently, behavioral ecologists have turned their attention to humans, applying the same rigor and rules that we use for other species (e.g., Cronk, 1991a, 1991b, 1991c, 1993, 2000, 2004; Irons, 1979; Borgerhoff-Mulder, 1991).

In some ways, our life history is quite mundane for a primate of our size; in other ways, our life history is odd. For example, many features of life history are driven by size, so we make predictions based on mother's size. Newborn human infants are large for their mother's size (compared to other primate infants). Human pregnancies are almost exactly the length one would predict from size (again, relative to other primates), though: how do we make large babies in a relatively short time? Human infants are weaned earlier than the "general" primate pattern; if we weaned our babies at the "standard" rate, our kids would be almost four before we weaned them; instead they are about two or two and a half in traditional and historical societies, and as young as six months in some modern cultures. (Here we know something about the important factors: whereas a mother gorilla or chimpanzee nurses her infant alone, in humans, others besides the mother bring food and care.) Babies' brains are much larger at birth than we would predict—and while the brains of other primate babies grow very slowly after birth, in human infants, The postnatal growth rate continues to be really fast (Low 2013).

Men are the real superconsumers in most societies. Most traditional societies, though not necessarily most individuals alive today, are polygynous (about 85–90 percent depending on the sample; e.g., Murdock, 1967, 1981; Murdock and White, 1969; Human Relations Area Files, 2013). How does a man succeed in marrying more than one wife? Though the particulars vary, the key to a man's lineage success in these societies is *access to reproductively important resources* (e.g., Low and Heinen, 1993; Low and Ridley, 1994; Low, 1996a, 1996b; Low et al., 2002). In many societies, resources are exchanged, and the patterns are interesting. In bride-price societies, in which men "buy" their wives with, cattle, horses, and so on, women typically make large contributions to subsistence and have high economic and reproductive value; most of these societies are polygynous, and wealthier men get to marry "earlier and more often" than poorer men; in return, they reap the value of several women's labor. In dowry systems, in which the bride's father pays, women contribute far less to the agricultural and economic well-being of the household.

RESOURCES AND HUMAN BEHAVIORAL ECOLOGY

All of these factors mean that humans are real consumers of resources. There are excellent general treatises on human behavioral ecology, but I have a specific focus here (cf. Low, 1996a, 1996b, 2004; Ridley and Low, 2003). If natural selection has shaped human behavior and life histories, as well as those of other species, *how has it shaped the ways humans seek and use resources?* Further, how does human resource striving affect the lifetimes and behavior of other species? Behavioral ecology can help us predict not only the vulnerability of other species, but also something about our own behavior and its results.

We humans have evolved to be a really intelligent ape; today we introduce rapid changes resulting in evolutionary novelty, and often create evolutionary "mismatches." Human behavioral ecology is thus crucially important to our conservation and management of other species and ecosystems. Much conservation effort is prescriptive ("Just Save It" or "return to being a Noble Savage"), without taking into account the dilemmas of human behavior—this is why, even when we understand intellectually what will help us be "green," we may have trouble convincing ourselves to do it. Perhaps behavioral ecology can offer us guidance in shaping our conservation efforts. To what conservation pleas will we respond?

THE RESOURCE ECOLOGY OF OUR PAST: TRADITIONAL AND HISTORICAL SOCIETIES

Even ancient *Homo* (and pre-*Homo*) affected other species. We know something of the evolution of primates, including humans, but mostly we rely on physical remains: seeds, skeletal remains, potsherds, arrowheads. These tell us, for example, where and when people lived, how large and fast they grew, how big and complicated their populations became. They tell us how people made a living—did they hunt and gather, did they fish, depend on agriculture? Though we have relatively little information on our ancient interactions with other species, we do know that traditional societies have sometimes overexploited resources (e.g., Clay, 1988; Bodley, 1990). There are documented human-caused extinctions from the Quaternary (Martin and Klein, 1984). In Pleistocene North America, we humans extirpated large mammals, some large birds, and a few small mammals. Less well known extinctions in South America, Australia, and New Zealand in the Late Pleistocene (which ended about 10,000 years ago) followed the same pattern. As Polynesians spread across the islands of the Pacific, they extinguished all of the giant flightless birds, a number of other flightless and flying birds, many marine mammals, frogs, lizards, and flightless insects—not to mention a number of plant species (Anderson, 1984; Cassels, 1984; Trotter and McCullough, 1984; Crosby, 1986). The arrival of Polynesians on the Hawaiian Islands appears to have wiped out more than half (54 percent) of the endemic bird species.

Humans caused harm in several ways: unintended introduction of fellow-travelers like rats and flies, whose competitors and predators were left behind; intentional introduction of agriculture, of animals we husbanded (goats, sheep, cattle, pigs), and of carnivorous pets like cats and dogs; weapons that made hunting efficient; and more. To learn more about earlier people's attitudes and behavior about resource use and about their impact on other species, typically we look at contemporary traditional societies: hunter-gatherers and slash-and-burn agriculturalists, for example. When we do, several facts emerge. First, for these populations, resources, status, and reproductive success are intimately tied together, just as they are for other species (review by Low, 2000). Across societies, resource consumption is essentially always positively related to family (lineage) success, more dramatically for men than women. Usually, this happens because men with more resources can marry more, and often younger, wives, who then produce more children than other women.

"Too many resources" is seldom, if ever, reported by people in a traditional society; but "we need more" is common. Further, although speech itself is a behavior, what people *say* about conservation and helping others is often not what they *do*: despite what we all say about favoring altruism, when you actually watch behavior, people act in ways that enhance family success—including resource extraction (keep in mind that this is a statistical, not a universal, statement).

The basics seem clear: consider people's resource behavior in a few well-studied societies.

The Amazonian Piro

The Piro of Amazonian Peru are hunters and gatherers. Anthropologist Michael Alvard (1993, 1994, 1995, 1998, 2000), who worked among the Piro, is one of the few scholars to ask specifically, and in a testable way, about conservation strategies among people in a traditional society. The idea of the "Noble Savage" is that people in traditional societies are intrinsic conservators. It is used in the sense of a morally superior human, uncorrupted by civilization. This concept was strong in Western thought from the sixteenth through nineteenth centuries. In the popular imagination, indigenous peoples showed far-sighted ecological concern; they were "Noble Savages." Anthropologist Ray Hames (2007) has an excellent review of the flaws in this approach.

Alvard's Piro data allow real testing between these two hypotheses: (1) hunters are conservationists ("Noble Savages") versus (2) they maximize their rate of return from hunting—they are optimal foragers, just as other species. What does it mean "to conserve"? Some species hunted by the Piro are endangered. Suppose a Piro hunter encounters a prime reproductive-age female of an endangered species: do we imagine he will kill her? There is no doubt that hunters in traditional societies know quite well what species are common, what are rare, and what are extremely rare. If a Piro man is an optimal-returns hunter, he will kill her: she is excellent caloric return for his hunting investment. On the other hand, if he is a deliberate conservator, he will pass her by. You probably already suspect that he will kill her, and he does. In fact, the Piro are extremely good at maximizing their caloric returns—young (too small) individuals are passed up, and prime animals are always taken, even if they are an endangered species.

This example suggests an important set of criteria for judging what constitutes actual conservation: low impact is insufficient to infer "conservation." There must be deliberate restraint in conditions in which higher consumption is both possible and profitable. I will return to this topic below.

Why don't the rare species always disappear? When hunters try to maximize their caloric return, it does not necessarily lead to overhunting or real depredation. With their population densities (rather low) and available technology (often inefficient), people in most traditional societies simply are unlikely to devastate local game populations. When hunters in traditional societies do overhunt, they typically affect only some species (ones most visible or frequently encountered). Among the Piro, for example, Alvard has shown that while several large primates are overhunted, collared peccaries (a pig-like species) are not.

The Ache

The Ache hunter-gatherers of Paraguay tell us other things about our past. They live in small bands of fifteen to seventy individuals, moving throughout the forest. Their demography and issues of conservation have been well studied by anthropologists Kim Hill and Magdalena Hurtado (1996). Bands comprise closely related kin and some long-term friends. Daily life centers on hunting and gathering. Women spend about two hours a day gathering; they collect fruits and insect larvae and extract the fiber from palm trees. Women also carry the family's children, pets, and possessions. Their care of children and possessions constrains women's ability to forage. Men may travel with the women's group, but more often they set off in small groups to search for game, spending about seven hours per day hunting white-lipped and collared peccaries, tapir, deer, pacas, agoutis, armadillos, capuchin monkeys, capybara, and coatis. Food not only serves nutritional needs, but can be shared or traded for other reasons: in particular, men can trade meat for sexual access and political alliances (Hurtado et al., 1985; Hawkes, 1993; Hill and Hurtado, 1996; Winterhalder, 1997).

Ache hunters rarely eat from their own kills, and much food is shared; this led early observers to argue that the society was completely egalitarian. But in fact hunting success and mating success—resources and reproduction—are closely related. Men often hunt in ways that look inefficient from standard optimal foraging perspectives, but when you look closely, such men are actually pursuing a high-risk, high-gain "showoff" strategy, just as in many cases of sexual selection in other species (e.g., Hawkes, 1993). Many men who attempt such strategies fail, but the few who succeed produce big, flashy hunting successes—and, with success, more sexual access to women. Men share meat relatively evenly in many circumstances, but share with each other as a sort of political favor-trading, and with women for sexual access. Honey and plants gathered by women are not shared evenly; they tend to remain in the family.

Despite the fact that the Ache have little in the way of heritable wealth, they keep track of likely paternity, and a man's status matters (Kaplan and Hill, 1985; Hill and Hurtado, 1996). The importance of a father in the family is stark: when a man dies, his young dependent children (under ten years of age) are far more likely to die than if he had lived. When a man has died, he can no longer reciprocate in men's political meat-trading, and other men do not share meat with his widow and children (though men may still offer meat for sexual favors). This means that small children whose father dies are also likely to die (Hill and Hurtado, 1996; Hawkes, 1993). Resources and family success are strongly linked.

The Mukogodo

Among the Piro and the Ache, men are the major resource-getters, and male status is important to a man's ability to mate and marry; sons are typically favored. The Mukogodo of central Kenya, foragers and beekeepers until early in this century, show important and informative differences (e.g., Cronk 1991a, 1991b). Today they are at the bottom of the socioeconomic hierarchy of local peoples. As in many pastoral areas, people in this region use livestock for bride-wealth: a bride costs so many cattle, or pigs, or other livestock. The Mukogodo are so poor that men have little chance of raising enough bride-wealth to marry a woman from a high-status neighboring group like the Maasai. But because men pay livestock for brides, when Mukogodo daughters marry men of neighboring groups, cattle, sheep, and goats go home to the women's families.

Thus, for the Mukogodo, daughters are more valuable than sons in reproductively important ways (Cronk, 1991a, 1991b, 1993, 2000). And this gives rise to an oddity: if you ask a Mukogodo, he or she will tell you it is better to have sons than daughters; this is exactly what the high-status Maasai say. But Mukogodo parents actually treat their daughters better than their sons. This is sex-biased investment of the same sort as in certain other species (e.g., Fisher, 1958; Trivers and Willard, 1973; Charnov, 1982; Trivers, 1992). Mukogodo mothers nurse their daughters longer than their sons; Mukogodo caregivers (mothers and others) stay closer to girls than boys and hold them more. Parents take their daughters more frequently than their sons to the dispensary and clinic for treatment, and they enroll their daughters more in the local Catholic mission's traveling baby clinic. Furthermore, probably because of this biased care, girls grow better than boys: better height for age, weight for age, and weight for height. Mukogodo parents appear to favor the (resource/reproductively) profitable sex in their children—even though they *say* (and possibly think) they do otherwise.

These societies suggest three things relative to the behavioral ecology of resource use in humans. First, in some basic ways, many human patterns are just what we would predict for any species (e.g., optimal foraging). Second, again as in other species, resource acquisition is essential for surviving and for marrying and raising children successfully, and sexual selection can be important. Finally, humans present some complications: what they *say* may not be what they *do*; we can learn some things only by observation.

Indigenous Americans

The resource ecology of Native Americans tells us some other important things: the interplay of technological efficiency and profitable markets makes a big difference to a population's impact on any resource. Two resource mainstays for several Native American groups were beaver and buffalo. In North America, Great Lakes Indian societies had efficient technology for trapping beaver (*Castor canidensis*) well before recorded times. Northern Algonquians, for example, used beaver for food and clothing and used the incisors as cutting and sharpening tools. But the local indigenous markets became relatively saturated by the eighteenth century: what can one do with the twenty-fifth beaver hide?

As a result, beaver populations remained relatively stable until the Hudson's Bay Company entered eastern North America in the late eighteenth century. Hudson's Bay introduced a growing market economy, and the value of beaver pelts soared. A male beaver pelt, according to company records in Albany Fort (1773), was worth a brass kettle, or twenty steel fishhooks, or two pounds of Brazilian tobacco. "Mountain men" arrived to trap beaver, and indigenous groups increased their harvests. The number of beaver declined. By the beginning of the nineteenth century, beaver harvests, having first increased, had fallen to one-tenth of their level a century before (e.g., Krech, 1999), and beaver were nearly extirpated.

Indigenous technology was always sufficient to take far more beavers than people did. But there was no point, no advantage, to intense trapping (figure 1). Three factors drive consumption: population density, technological efficiency, and possible profit. It was the market, and thus the *profit*, that changed, driving intensified hunting and beaver decline. Many cases of anthropologists' "postcontact" extinction and ecological degradation relate, as in this example, simply to changes in profit and/or technological efficiency.

To infer "conservation ethic" from low impact is specious: if the human population is small, the technology ineffective, or no good market exists, impact will necessarily be low. *Only* when high consumption is possible and profitable, *yet* remains low, can one infer deliberate conservation.

This is exactly what behavioral ecology would predict: that people will take as many useful resources as they can from the environment (and if extraction technology increases faster than the resource . . . watch out!). Because people in traditional societies seldom were sufficiently numerous or efficient to create problems for themselves in the short term, there was no point to doing otherwise.

Plains societies displayed another common outcome related to technology. Bison (*Bison bison*) were once plentiful on the North American plains; it was hard for people in the

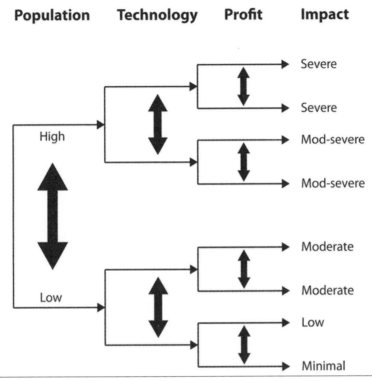

Figure 1. THE INTENSITY OF IMPACT OF HUMAN ACTIVITIES

The intensity of impact of human activities depends on several things: population size and density, efficiency of technology, and profitability. Low impact alone does not imply restraint; it can result simply from too few people, inefficient technology, and/or no economic point to taking resources. There must be clear evidence of restraint with long-term impacts to infer deliberate conservation.

nineteenth century to imagine anything but abundant buffalo. Although no accurate counts were made when buffalo were plentiful, historical sources from the seventeenth and eighteenth centuries provide dramatic testimony to their large populations (e.g., Peter Fidler, cited by Krech, 1999). Bison ranged from the Northwest Territories to Mexico, from Georgia and South Carolina to Washington, Oregon, and Nevada. It was unimaginable that buffalo would ever become rare. Yet by 1884, buffalo were almost extinct.

Why and how did we almost lose the buffalo? Believers in the Noble Savage think that indigenous peoples, in contrast to European settlers, husbanded buffalo populations as they did most or all other resources. The rhetoric goes this way: indigenous peoples were skillful, ecologically sensitive conservationists, but white settlers wasted buffalo, causing their extermination. It's a nice story, but belied by the evidence. Indeed, white hunters, often hunting from trains, did kill buffalo wastefully. But as indigenous peoples' extraction techniques became more efficient—from the use of horses on—their consumption increased. In the early 1800s, Indians took approximately 60 million buffalo; in the mid-1840s, they sold 100,000 buffalo hides to the American Fur Company.

Perhaps the most (inadvertently) wasteful indigenous technique was the "cliff jump." When topography allowed, hunters on horseback could drive the bison up a small rise— which ended in a cliff, not obvious until the running buffalo were too close to turn. Buffalo would charge off the cliff, to be butchered below. Plains Indians who hunted bison using cliff jumps were highly selective in their use of meat, hides, and other by-products of the hunt, seeking particularly fat and fatty meat (and embryos), and leaving heavy, less nutritious parts at the kill. Cliff jumps were *too* efficient in production; they produced far more meat for less effort than competing technologies. However, huge amounts of meat rotted at the base of cliffs, because hunters took only the choicest meat. The extraction technology was highly efficient, but the storage technology lagged behind (e.g., Hames, 1990; Speth, 1990; Krech, 1999; Hames, 2007).

CROSS-CULTURAL GENERALIZATIONS

In the case of the beaver, technology was well up to the job of harvesting far more beaver than were actually taken—the market was missing. In some other cases effective markets existed, but old technologies could not produce sufficient supply. For example, when steel axes were introduced in New Guinea, with a market available for wood exports, serious ecological degradation followed (Salisbury, 1962). On the other hand, among the Ye'kwana, enhanced technology increased hunting efficiency but did not increase exploitation (Hames, 1979). Game could neither be stored nor traded regardless of the presence of a market economy.

Are there general patterns? A cross-cultural study (Low, 1996b) of societies in the Standard Cross-Cultural Sample found that in about a third of societies (39/122) for which data existed, severe environmental degradation existed. Degradation was positively correlated with recent population growth ($p = 0.0001$) and recent technological improvements ($p = 0.0005$), although neither was universally present as a driver of degradation. These crude cross-cultural data are consistent with the more detailed ethnographic data on the societies above, suggesting that resource acquisition is a primary goal for most peoples.

OTHER ANCIENT AND HISTORICAL SOCIETIES

Hunter-gatherer societies tend to be small and to lack complex political hierarchies. What about more "complex" societies? Jared Diamond (2005) reviewed several major societies that thrived and then collapsed: Easter and Pitcairn Islands, the Anasazi, the Mayans, and Norse Greenland. In some cases (Anasazi, Mayans, Greenland) climate change interacted with population growth; hostile neighbors were a factor in the Mayan and Norse Greenland cases, and weakened trading mattered in Pitcairn and Greenland. Two things were present in *every* case: first, population growth combined with human environmental damage, and (perhaps partly as a result) failure to solve large-scale societal problems. As we look at the simpler societies above, it seems likely that individual striving and competition, largely hidden from view in large complex societies, may nonetheless matter as much there as in simpler societies—just as recent financial near collapses of several large nation-states may have been driven by the behavior of a relatively small group of powerful individuals (e.g., Stiglitz, 2010).

WHAT DOES THE PAST TELL US ABOUT THE FUTURE?

Everything we learn from traditional and historical societies is that humans are not exempt from selection: what we do reflects how past natural selection on our resource use influences our decision-making daily, even today. And there is, so far as we can find, no evidence of a highly successful society that deliberately short-changes itself in the short term to husband resources for the distant future. Among traditional societies we see good midterm managers, mostly in rather local, stable-membership, somewhat isolated groups—groups in which social currencies are important, and "take the money and run" is not a viable option.

In our evolutionary past, crucial resources were hard to get. Our main problems were getting enough resources from the environment for our needs, maintaining satisfactory and stable friendships, finding mates, and raising families. Improving technology was always good. Predicting the effect of our actions decades in the future was never a priority, and in fact, inability to predict future environmental conditions made such long-term planning futile. Most of the time, our populations and technology were sufficiently limited that even with our fiercest striving, we did only local damage to our environment.

The result was that *we evolved to strive for resources and seldom—if ever—found ourselves evolutionarily "rewarded" for conscious current restraint for future gains—especially gains for strangers*. We evolved to be efficient short-term environmental managers, not long-term global conservationists.

Now we are so numerous, with such effective technology, that our short-sighted, self-centered tendencies, which have served us well in the past, can cause us difficulties today. Today we have far more technological effectiveness than the Maya or the Anasazi. We can harvest more resources for less human effort. But efficient technology can sometimes mean that we destroy too much "natural capital" (e.g., the biomass of the species we are hunting or fishing); when that happens, recovery is likely to be neither quick nor easy—and sometimes not possible.

Further, well-meaning people, including scholars, have been, at least since the Rio Conference of 1992, talking past each other. Underneath the polite rhetoric, first-world nations complain about population growth in developing nations, and developing nations respond that we could afford such growth if first-world nations were not such superconsumers. In developed nations, we have broken the link between resources and *number* of children, but we invest enormously in our fewer superchildren (e.g., Low et al., 2002). The result is that we consume somewhere between seven and twelve *times* the resources per capita consumed in least developed nations. This is why biologist Joel Cohen (1995) answered the question, "How many people can the earth support?" with a resounding "It depends"—on the degree of equity and the living standard you seek. Figure 2, using 2005 data from the Global Footprint Network, summarizes the problem. Total global hectares per capita consumed (figure 2.a) reminds us that $I = PAT$ (Impact = Population × Affluence × Technology; Ehrlich and Holdren, 1972); and China's population means that the Asia-Pacific region has huge (and growing) consumption. But if we take the poorest nations (the African region), we can compute what the consumption would be of other regions were they equally poor; this highlights the proportion of consumption that is over and above subsistence (figure 2.b). North Americans enjoy consumption levels that are utterly luxurious compared to the rest of the world. And it is worth noting that figure 2 lumps the United States and Canada; the U.S. figures are three times those of Canada.

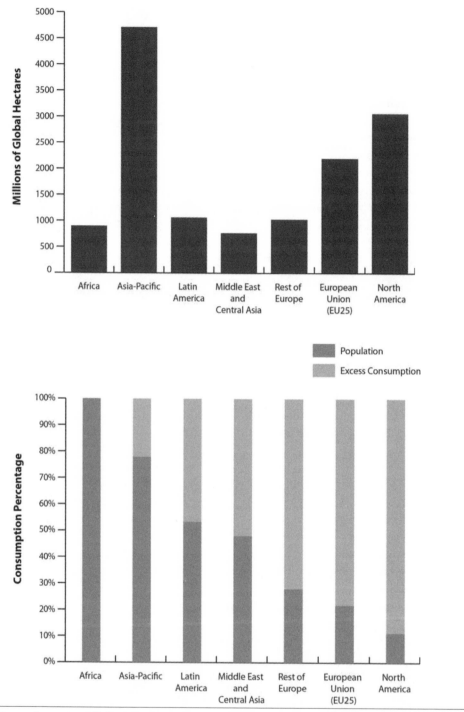

Figure 2. GLOBAL CONSUMPTION BY REGION

Both population and consumption levels matter to environmental impact. A. Largely because of China's existing population numbers, the Asian-Pacific region has high total consumption. B. Using the poorest region (Africa) as a benchmark, we can estimate the proportion of total consumption due to affluence in each region; here North America has the highest per capita consumption above sheer subsistence levels.

Source: GLOBAL FOOTPRINT NETWORK, 2005.

THE LIFE HISTORIES OF EASY- AND DIFFICULT-TO-MANAGE NONHUMAN SPECIES

We know some species are far more vulnerable to human actions than others; we need to understand better the *pattern* behind what makes cockroaches resilient, and condors vulnerable, to our actions (e.g., Boyer, 2009; Collen et al., 2011). Here again, an organism's evolutionary past can help us predict its future: whether it will be easy or difficult to manage, whether it will thrive or disappear with human changes to the environment. To create effective conservation, then, we need not only an understanding of our own behavioral ecology: what drives us, what rewards us. We also need good information on the species' ecology, life history, and behavior, and we will have to find the right matches for good strategies. We further will have to deal, in specific cases, with the fact that there are many "actors" with varying interests and differential power; decisions can be made, or discarded, at many levels.

As in the past, today we affect other species in several major ways. Sometimes (hunting, the bushmeat trade, fishing) we consume them directly. We also have introduced species, both deliberately (cattle, camels, goats) and accidentally (rats, some snakes) that wreaked havoc with native species. We may also manage populations to increase them, perhaps by putting out nest boxes for certain birds, or regulating hunting or fishing. Such actions often reflect a narrow focus on some part of the species' ecology, ignoring other aspects.

Our indirect impacts can create another of the most difficult problems to solve: those in which we have changed one of the environmental aspects that are so important in shaping life history: extremeness, range of variation, spatial patchiness, and temporal predictability. For example, when we change climate (for reasons unrelated to any aspect of species management), we can disrupt a coevolved system in which different species use different cues—except, before disruption, we never knew that a delicate balance existed (e.g., Grossman, 2004).

Our actions have modified all of these factors—extremeness, range of variation, spatial patchiness, and temporal predictability—in various cases, in ways mundane to extraordinary. Cities, for example, are "urban heat islands": cities are warmer (more extreme) and the range of temperature variation is smaller than in the surrounding countryside. The soil in cities is more compacted, and the air is dustier (more extremeness). No wonder horticulturalists and landscape architects selectively breed plants that can tolerate very compact soil, dust on the leaves, and specific temperature ranges.

When the problem is large scale, indirect, and long term (as in the case of global climate change), solutions can be elusive. For some time, we were unaware of many secondary impacts of our use of fossil fuels to power societal expansion, for example. But climate change has multiple impacts, some of which are only now surfacing. Understanding both organism life history and our own predilections is important to solving these problems.

CONSIDER THE COD: FISHING IMPACTS

If we are dealing with a species for which we have very slow feedback, or for which we do not know the actual resource base (the biomass, the population), we face a true management nightmare. It is obviously easiest to manage the populations of other species if we know how many there are, and if we get rapid feedback on our impact—for example, if we overhunt this year, we know our impact by next year. Fishing is particularly difficult to "manage": it is very difficult to estimate populations and biomass accurately, to know whether regulating catches or another strategy is best, and so forth. The organism's life history matters greatly.

Consider cod: the eastern U.S. cod fisheries once seemed vast. Cod mature rapidly and lay many eggs; and because they are "continuous growers," very old females keep getting bigger and bigger—and laying ever more eggs. With a life history like that, much harvesting can be supported. Further, cod seemed as if they were everywhere. In the western Atlantic, fishers have been harvesting cod for more than five centuries, always under the impression that the cod population is huge, stretching all along the coast of North America, and then to Greenland, Iceland, and northern Europe, from the White Sea to the Bay of Biscay. If ever there were an endless resource, it should be cod. And through the nineteenth century, everyone thought this was true (Kurlansky, 1998).

Even as cod populations declined through the twentieth century, catches increased because of improved technology. Cod are harder to find and catch today, and those caught are much smaller than a few decades ago. In the case of cod, there is a hidden ecological story, beyond greed, that will make the recovery of cod fisheries more difficult than we might hope. It involves the interplay between ever-more-efficient harvesting technology and cod population structure. We did not understand the population structure of cod (Wilson et al., 1999); we assumed we were exploiting a single large population, so that as we removed fish, neighboring fish would move in and replace those we caught. In fact Atlantic cod live in structured metapopulations: multiple, small, spatially discrete populations that do not travel freely across subpopulations. This means that when we exhaust a particular local subpopulation, cod do not necessarily move in from nearby areas (Wilson et al., 1991; Wilson et al., 1994). The various local subpopulations are less connected than we imagined. But we don't see that; we only know that we must search farther each year to fish, because places that once were rich with cod are now depauperate.

We have exhausted one after another local population, and the overfished populations are not regrowing or drawing immigrants from nearby. This is a serious form of overfishing and may well require more recovery time than overfishing in a "single" population. It is as if the fish in nearby subpopulations don't recognize that places we have overfished are appropriate places into which they can expand—another ecological trap imposed by human changes. Our ignorance, combined with our evolved striving, has created real problems.

When the extinction rate of local populations exceeds the recolonization rate, as with cod, the metapopulation is eroded. This kind of failure is happening not just for cod, but for many commercial (and predatory) fish species around the world (e.g., Myers and Worm, 2003). Fishers all up and down the coast have, quite naturally, tended to fish where it was most efficient and most convenient. Atlantic cod are bottom-dwellers, and modern fishers use highly efficient trawls. These scrape the ocean floor, removing corals and bottom vegetation, and actually recontouring the ocean floor's surface. Some scholars have compared the effects of trawling to forest clear-cutting: removing species, reducing diversity, creating big bare patches, with resulting changes in species composition as the area is recolonized (Watling and Norse, 1998). (Some recolonizing species are commercially profitable, like scallops.) Now fishers face a scarcer, ever patchier, and more variable resource than in the past; they must explore more to fish, involving more problems in transport and storage, fuel, and danger.

LOBSTER VERSUS COD: LIFE HISTORY AND SUCCESSFUL MANAGEMENT

The case of cod highlights the fact that above and beyond the life history issues of nonhumans as well as humans, sometimes we must work with larger-scale ecological issues: we must recognize, on a case-by-case basis, just how interconnected (or not) particular populations are, if we are to exploit them sustainably. Successful management really requires a lot: understanding a species' life history (and its vulnerabilities), its population dynamics and geographic range, and more. Life history dynamics are perhaps the most central, and certainly the least well understood, of these. Comparing lobster to cod highlights this.

Fishers of cod roam widely for their prey. In contrast, lobstermen are more "local" and territorial, marking out each traditional lobsterpot area with clear buoys that tell whose area this is. It is a common-property regime, in which outsiders are excluded, and members decide the rules. And that makes sustainable lobster fishing easier—but there are still some difficulties. For many years, the lobster harvest, for example in Maine, roughly matched lobster productivity. Lobster was rare and expensive, and the "lobster gangs," groups of senior lobstermen, enforced rules of take—which included measures that enhanced conservation (Acheson, 1988). Almost like related fisheries in traditional societies, the scale, the costs and benefits, were all local and immediate. Compliance with the rules was, for many years, easy.

The combination of lobster site fidelity (which meant that, once settled, lobsters ranged only locally) and local associations of lobstermen was very successful when harvests were low. But as gourmet appreciation of lobster in the United States spread and harvests increased, both biological and political considerations conspired to produce problems. Maine lobstermen agreed that only lobsters near or at the age of maturity would be marketable in Maine. When egg-bearing lobsters (females carry eggs on their tails for about eight to ten months) are caught, they are marked with a "V" notch in the tail and released. Immature lobsters and very large lobsters (maybe ten years old and over) are also V-notched as illegal to sell. Larger lobsters are presumed to provide a reproductive stock—a cushion that protects against one or several years of recruitment failure.

In Maine, no one could legally market marked (V-notched) lobsters. However, because no such restrictions applied in New Hampshire and Massachusetts before the mid-1990s, lobstermen from these states could line up at the state boundaries and happily harvest V-notched lobsters. Unable to enforce the V-notch conservation strategy across states, Maine lobstermen had little incentive to conserve—a classic conservation dilemma. Outsiders can be free riders, whose actions mean a failure of a common-property arrangement and a greater risk of recruitment failure (very low success of young) when ecological perturbations occur. This was a clear mismatch between the harvest rules (outside Maine) and ecological realities: there is biological transfer by lobsters at a certain life stage across systems, but only local harvest rules, and no higher-order control. This is a recipe for management failure (Costanza et al., 2001, p. 236–38).

Maine lobstermen could have decided, as have many others in this situation, that because free riders were reducing their profits, they should remove the V-notch protection for themselves. But they did not: today they still follow the V-notch rule. Why? Maine lobstermen have been successful in lobbying other states, through multistate management plans, to adopt similar rules throughout the Gulf of Maine. In part, this is because colleagues Jim and Carl Wilson and Yong Chen produced accurate but easily understood models of how harvests affect lobster populations and reproduction—connecting the theoretical to the delicious and profitable. In Maine, lobstermen at town hall meetings ran these models to explore population dynamics. At the beginning it took Maine lobstermen appealing to the larger (above state level) East Coast Fisheries Board. Other states, initially under pressure, adopted the V-notch rule, and in fact, more recently, the V-notch restriction has been extended to recreational lobster harvesting across states (it always applied in Maine). Small groups of local lobstermen, who have long familiarity with lobster life history and ecology and with very local costs and benefits, have been highly successful in managing lobsters sustainably, even when quite large-scale issues had to be solved.

SOLVING UNINTENDED MANAGEMENT MISMATCHES

We work at managing populations of many other species: controlling (or trying to eliminate) pests, arranging things so that other species will (we hope) increase in numbers. But sometimes well-intentioned management efforts fail, if we don't know enough about the behavior and life history of the species we want to "help." Consider wood ducks (*Aix sponsa*), in which males are one of the most dramatically colored ducks in existence. Wood ducks nest in tree cavities near open water; they were almost extinguished in the early twentieth century as logging destroyed their nesting habitat. Nest boxes became a popular management tool and remain so to this day.

It probably seemed reasonable that "the more nest boxes the better," but wood ducks, like a number of bird species, practice what is called "dump-nesting" (intraspecific brood parasitism): females, usually relatively young ones, may sneak into others' nests and lay eggs. In places where nest boxes are concentrated, a free-riding female can make many "dumps"; such egg parasitism occurs even when there are suitable, previously successful, unused nest sites. Wildlife biologist Brad Semel and behavioral ecologist Paul Sherman found nest parasitism rates as high as 95 percent in one locality. Occasionally a ("host") female would be trying to incubate as many as thirty-seven eggs, with the outcome that many eggs got broken, and many (often laid by a parasite after incubation had started) never hatched (Semel and Sherman, 1986; Semel et al., 1988).

The concentration of nest boxes in this case, far from enhancing nesting success in wood ducks, created easily found concentrations of nests and increased nest parasitism and failure. This initial failure arose because people focused only on part of the problem and failed to account for the life-history dump-nesting phase. Fortunately, this example had a straightforward solution: space nest boxes farther apart and place them in the woods, where they are less visible than on the shoreline (Semel and Sherman, 1986; Semel et al., 1988; Eadie et al., 1998).

OUR HIDDEN UNINTENDED HARM: CLIMATE CHANGE

A major and widely discussed human-caused environmental change affecting life history and behavior is shifting global climate. Here we see problems that we have caused *indirectly*, and with no conscious intent. What we want is energy to do what we do—but by consuming so much of it, we affect our climate. Variance in temperature is increasing, and in many places, so is extremeness (e.g., as summers get hotter). The earth's climate has warmed 0.3 to 0.6 degrees Celsius over the last one hundred years, most rapidly during the periods 1925–44 and 1978–97. Climate variability, including the frequency and magnitude of extreme events, has also been changing over the past one hundred years. By and large, scientists in relevant fields agree on the facts. A review of all publications with keywords of "global climate change" found 928 articles in scientific journals; not one dissented significantly from the view that our globe is warming and that human activities are a major cause (Oreskes, 2004). The media may have complicated the picture; about half of all articles in the popular press on global warming followed the "he said, she said" format—including (without assessment) some divergent view, typically by a single person.

Rapid, widespread climate change affects more than people's energy bills. Consider the plight of a Magellanic penguin (*Spheniscus magellanicus*) as the climate warms. The geographic distribution of the fish these penguins feed to their chicks is changing with ocean temperature, and now parents must be gone from their nests longer than before. If parents are away more than fifteen days, the chicks are likely to starve—and these longer trips mean that parents are increasingly away beyond that threshold. Starvation is not the only problem. The chicks' down is adapted to keep the chicks dry when it snows; now, however, rather than harmless snow, the chicks experience freezing rain—which is typically lethal (e.g., Boersma, 2008). Penguin numbers are declining. How might we approach this life-history-conservation problem?

Interestingly, the most endangered penguins are not the Antarctic penguins. Penguins in the Galapagos are endangered: warming may play a role both in simple survivorship (these are the world's most northern penguins) and in food availability (again, warming has shifted prey distributions) and direct human disturbance. Erect-crested penguins on the Bounty and Antipodes Islands are endangered: they suffer declining food resources, probably from prey distribution shifts and possible impacts of overfishing. Humans again appear to lie at the root of endangerment: overfishing and oil spills also contribute.

Coral reefs are among the most productive ecosystems in the world; they form the basis of many fisheries on which we depend. But they are quite vulnerable to warming: an increase of as little as one degree Celsius (above the "normal" summer maximum) for as little as two days appears to be enough to kill the algal symbionts of coral. If the heightened temperature lasts less than a month, the coral apparently may recover. But when waters stay hot for too long, the physiological stress may be irreversible, as in the 1988 worldwide coral bleaching event: coral bleaching was reported in sixty countries and island nations around the world (Wilkinson et al., 1999).

WHAT CAN BEHAVIORAL ECOLOGY DO?

The behavioral ecology and life history strategies of nonhuman species are critical in management; fortunately we learn more every day. It is *human* behavioral ecology, of which many have remained largely ignorant, that might make significant future contributions. Early environmental protection in the United States and elsewhere has implicitly or explicitly relied on conventional wisdoms, like the "Noble Savage," that are simply wrong, or a Rousseau-shaped view of human society as inevitably evil (e.g., Oelschlanger, 1991). We can do better now.

There are also issues of who pays. Many centralized approaches to issues such as species and natural area conservation, pollution abatement, and so on, develop into commons dilemmas. If they produce inherent benefits for society at large but also produce local or regional costs, they become one kind of commons: widely dispersed benefits, concentrated costs (spotted owl management; figure 3). Or they can become another major kind of commons (with concentrated benefits and dispersed costs: e.g., cattle leases by the Bureau of Land Management) first highlighted by Garrett Hardin in the 1960s (Hardin, 1968). Not surprisingly, even when such programs have general public support, implementing them can be difficult: there are frequently free-rider problems and stark local dissent. Further, the issues are typically scientifically complex as well as highly emotional; as a result, definitions of, and opinions about, "success" vary greatly.

I do not want to repeat the frequently cited litany of disasters—whole books exist to do just that. I want to begin delineating the fact that *while impacts are worldwide and have many proximate causes, there is a potentially important underlying pattern.* In each of these cases above, we can classify the danger as arising from a change in one of our limited

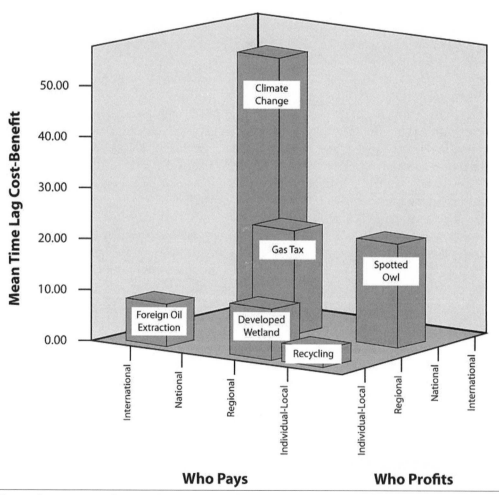

Figure 3. DISTRIBUTION OF COSTS AND BENEFITS OF ENVIRONMENTAL IMPACTS

Costs and benefits may be separated across people (and space), and time. The farther they are separated, the more difficult a problem will be to solve. Thus here, issues of global climate change will be far more difficult to solve than issues of household recycling, in which both costs and benefits are typically local, and results are relatively immediate.

set of attributes: *extremeness, range of variation, patchiness,*and *predictability* (e.g., Low, 1989). None of these is intrinsically "good" or "bad"; rather, we need to be able to tie the *kind* of change we introduce to the evolved life history and behavior traits of the species. We need to recognize, for example, that species with a long evolutionary history of little change in some environmental trait (say temperature) will have a narrow tolerance range that we can easily exceed; once we know this, we can deliberately change environmental characteristics with regard to these aspects in our recovery efforts. We can, and do, reduce isolation (e.g., in building or maintaining corridors, for example) or increase it (as in quarantine, to reduce certain disease spread possibilities). But conscious deliberation is necessary: sometimes we create isolated populations because we fail to consider things like dispersal paths.

Can we design programs that are fair, workable, and effective? I am convinced that the most effective strategies will involve two things: (1) understanding the life history and ecology of affected species, and (2) designing conservation programs that work *with*, not against, our evolved human tendencies as a very smart, long-lived, and highly social mammal.

Conventional wisdoms sometimes assume that we will find it easy to be "global altruists." But is this true? People—you, I—are unlikely to give up short-term individual or familial benefits happily for widely dispersed long-term societal or global gains. This is not a new phenomenon associated with technological innovation. And it shouldn't surprise you that human behavior reflects benefit-cost relationships, just like the behavior of other species. We humans, like other species, evolved to be aware only of proximate rewards and punishments, not of ultimate (reproductive, lineage) costs and benefits. We have evolved to maximize short-term rewards that, in our past, correlated with reproductive success. What makes us proud, what makes us feel good, is also generally what gives us status among our group and makes us attractive to others. In novel evolutionary environments, these strategies may be harmful ecological traps—but of course, that was never something that mattered in our evolutionary past!

We do not often think of ourselves as having evolved in response to pressures on our reproductive success, but increasing evidence supports this idea. *If* we could simply set aside our evolutionary past and use logic, perhaps we could easily act as if the earth were our family, regardless of personal rewards. We could "Just Save It." But as several scholars (e.g., Cross and Guyer, 1980; Costanza, 1987) have noted, we typically have the technological know-how to solve environmental problems. It is the conflicts of interest, the "social traps," that hinder us. And these conflicts are, it should now be obvious, older than humanity.

Even the crucial problems of population numbers and per capita consumption arise in part from us as individuals satisfying our (evolved) proximate desires to have children and invest well in them, to give them a good start in life. We have, I suggest, simply become ever more efficient, better and better at doing *exactly* what we evolved to do, until today we literally could destroy the earth to satisfy our proximate goals. Appeals to people to make relatively small individual sacrifices for the ultimate good of all people everywhere have had limited success; we have not evolved to consider the global population our family.

Predictions

These general patterns lead to specific predictions about human resource use and reproductive patterns. The most difficult resource issues to solve, from a human behavioral ecological perspective, are those in which (1) some actors are able to externalize their costs, and/or (2) do not have well-defined property rights or (if rules are agreed upon) the ability to monitor, detect, and punish cheaters (e.g., Ostrom, 1990, 1998, 2009).

Can we design better strategies by taking our evolutionary past into account? Successful approaches for convincing people to shift their resource use to more "conserving" patterns must often, we suspect, appeal to people's perceived short-term, familial and local, interests (Low 1989, 2004; Low and Heinen 1993; Low and Ridley 1994; Low 1996a, 1996b). If perceived benefits of conservation can be made to outweigh costs for people, then conservation strategies are likely to persist and spread. In most nations today, these are likely to involve economic or other incentives that confer immediate or short-term benefits to individuals and/ or their families and potential reciprocators.

What strategies do we use now, and when are they each likeliest to work? Because we are such a social species, *social incentives* (and disincentives), rather than monetary rewards, may work in small, stable-membership societies without high-profit options—many traditional societies. If we are correct, it may be productive to devise policies that create real, personal incentives to conserve: *the more immediate the benefit, the more successful should be the response.* Indeed, some political scientists, such as Elinor Ostrom in her presidential address to the American Political Science Association, have strikingly convergent ideas about how incentives work (Ostrom, 1998, 2009). But even in large modern societies, perhaps we can make use of social incentives; consider that many household recycling efforts use highly visible signals to advertise cooperation.

Some strategies will be easier than others, and matching the characteristics of proposed solutions to problems will be crucial (figure 3). The more costs and benefits are separated (across individuals, across space, or across time), the more difficult the problem will be to solve. This is why household recycling (in the "front" corner of figure 3) has been relatively easy to tackle in quite varied situations: the costs and the benefits are not widely separated across time, space, or people. In contrast, to ask ourselves for possibly expensive changes in policy and behavior now, to avoid eventual harmful climate change—especially when we may not know for fifty years whether we are successful—meets with intense resistance (figure 3). The "bottom line" is that what comprises rational behavior for an individual is not necessarily (or even usually) a rational policy for society as a whole.

The question then becomes how to change incentives so that individuals are likely to behave in ways that enhance conservation. The most difficult resource-use problems have the following characteristics: *inadequately-known resource base; slow feedback; externalized costs; and used by many, unrelated, noninteracting individuals.* Like the cod example above, we can't fix our negative impacts if we can't yet perceive them. This is also a problem with evolutionarily novel dangers (e.g., chemicals we cannot see or taste); most of us are far more averse to mammal excrement than to something like chemical spills we cannot smell or see.

Temporal and spatial discounting can be problematic. Humans are likely to discount some kinds of environmental problems in particular ways, such as "species" discounting (many more people care about conserving large charismatic mammals than, say, toads or millipedes). The farther away or the more distant in the future, the more we discount the problem and the less we are willing to commit any real resources to its solution. These are "scale" issues; in one form or another they influence what solutions will work (e.g., Low, 1996b, 2004). Because humans evolved in relatively small groups of reciprocating individuals, to varying degrees genetically related to other group members, we are likely to respond most immediately to relatively small-scale, short-term problems that affect us individually and our families and friends directly. Notice that if humans were, in fact "group selected" to do (regardless of cost; see Low 2000 for multiple definitions of group selection) what is best for the whole group, we would have few problems; we would easily convince people to do things that increase their own short-term cost for the long-term good of humanity.

The *scale* of inherent costs and benefits influences potential solutions, as does the fact that there are likely to be multiple currencies. For example, it is relatively straightforward to calculate the economic benefits of maintaining national parks and protected areas. Benefits may include increased foreign exchange and general revenues for a variety of service industries (airlines, hotels, restaurants, etc.); nature tourism is now a major industry worldwide, and the major industry for some developing nations. However, the costs are frequently not national but quite local (as above): restricted or lost access for families to formerly unrestricted resources, job losses, crop damage, livestock depredation, even human death from wildlife.

The most successful strategies for protected areas allow local people greater access to resources and allow them to benefit more directly from the protected area. Any long-term national benefits are secondary, and programs that rely only on them (like many national conservation strategies) are not likely to be stable. Similarly, some endangered species recovery programs are locally costly but nationally beneficial, while others are locally profitable. Recovery programs for large mammalian predators such as wolves in the United States, threatened species like grizzly bears and the northern spotted owl in the Pacific, tend to generate conflict (figure 3). In contrast, the recovery plan for the Kirtland's warbler, an endangered bird that nests in early-successional pine forests, with frequent fires, in north-central Michigan, has never been controversial—because of the warbler's life history. This program includes regular cuttings and sales of pine that generate local short-term profits, unlike many other endangered species recovery plans; this is only possible because the warbler uses young forests for breeding (e.g., Solomon, 1998).

The scale of environmental issues and solutions interacts in another way with our evolutionary past. We had little control over our environment for much of our existence: hurricanes, droughts, all sorts of environmental phenomena were beyond our control (although note that we do not control them perfectly now). It never made sense to worry about the world your grandchildren would see, or the fate of people you would never actually see who lived far away (mostly we didn't even know they were there).

The result is our amazing human ability to *discount* (Hannon, 1990): what is not here, now, and clear matters little. This ability is an evolved response to living with environmental unpredictability. The longer or farther something is away in time or space from our immediate reproductive interests, the less it pays to invest time, resources, or energy in its consideration. Discounting theory, widely applied in economics, is applicable here.

The sum of approaches we use in the face of management and conservation problems is still rather limited, and our most-used strategies are arguably not the most effective (Low, 2000, 2004). *Information* is obviously necessary, but not sufficient. *Teaching* and exhortation (e.g., to do the right thing) may sometimes be effective, but the data tend to be sparse and anecdotal. *Social incentives* may have an influence when your reputation matters more to you than profit, typically in small, stable-membership groups—a situation not really common in today's Western world, at least. *Economic incentives* of various sorts are the most widely used strategies today, from regulations to tradable permits to voluntary agreements. No one type of solution is applicable in all conflicts; clearly we have a large task, an uphill battle!

SUMMARY

Human life histories and behavior, like those of other species, are shaped by natural selection. Some life history traits arise from an unusual combination of high intelligence and extreme sociality. The same intelligence and sociality appear to have meant, over human evolution, that we have become ever smarter and more efficient about extracting resources for ourselves. We are doing what other species do, extracting resources from the environment in order to survive and reproduce—*but* we have become so good at it that we are having an ever-increasing impact on populations of other species. We may well be increasing the extinction rate, even of some keystone species. Their reactions depend in part on their life history, shaped by their evolutionary past: have they repeatedly confronted extremes? Changes? Or, if they have had a long history of relatively little change in important environmental variables, how can they cope? It is clear that understanding life histories, both of other species and of ourselves, is important for our future.

REFERENCES

Acheson, J. M. 1988. *The Lobster Gangs of Maine*. Hanover, NH: University Press of New England.

Alvard, M. S. 1993. "Testing the 'Ecologically Noble Savage' Hypothesis: Interspecific Prey Choice by Piro Hunters of Amazonian Peru." *Human Ecology* 21:355–87.

Alvard, M. S. 1994. "Conservation by Native Peoples: Prey Choice in Depleted Habitats." *Human Nature* 5:127–54.

Alvard, M. S. 1995. "Intraspecific Prey Choice by Amazonian Hunters." *Current Anthropology* 36:789–818.

Alvard, M. S. 1998. "Evolutionary Ecology and Resource Conservation." *Evolutionary Anthropology* 7:62–74.

Alvard, M. S. 2000. "The Impact of Traditional Subsistence Hunting and Trapping on Prey Populations: Data from the Wan of Upland Central Sulawesi, Indonesia." In *Hunting for Sustainability in Tropical Forests*, ed. J. G. Robinson and E. Bennett, 214–30. New York: Columbia University Press.

Anderson, A. 1984. "The Extinction of the Moa in Southern New Zealand." In *Quaternary Extinctions: A Prehistoric Revolution*, ed. P. S. Martin and R. G. Klein, 728–40. Tucson: University of Arizona Press.

Bodley, J. H. 1990. *Victims of Progress*. 3rd edition. Mountain View, CA: Mayfield.

Boersma, R. D. 2008. "Penguins as Marine Sentinels." *Bioscience* 58(7): 597–607.

Borgerhoff-Mulder, M. 1991. "Human Behavioral Ecology." In *Behavioural Ecology*, ed. J. R Krebs and N. B. Davies, 69–98. London: Blackwell.

Boyer, A. 2009. "Consistent Ecological Selectivity through Time in Pacific Island Avian Extinctions." *Conservation Biology* 24:511–19.

Cassels, R. 1984. "Faunal Extinctions and Prehistoric Man in New Zealand and the Pacific Islands." In *Quaternary Extinctions: A Prehistoric Revolution*, ed. P. S. Martin and R. G. Klein, 553–73. Tucson: University of Arizona Press.

Charnov, E. L. 1982. *The Theory of Sex Allocation*. Princeton, NJ: Princeton University Press.

Clay, J. W. 1988. *Indigenous Peoples and Tropical Forests*. Cambridge, MA: Cultural Survival.

Cohen, J. E. 1995. *How Many People Can the Earth Support?* New York: Norton.

Collen, B., L. McRae, S. Deinet, A. De Palma, T. Carranza, N. Cooper, and J. Loh. 2011. "Predicting How Populations Decline to Extinction." *Philosophical Transactions (Royal Society) B* 366:2577–86.

Costanza, R. 1987. "Social Traps and Environmental Policy." *Bioscience* 37:407–12.

Costanza, R., B. S. Low, E. Ostrom, and J. Wilson, eds. 2001. *Institutions, Ecosystems, and Sustainability*. Washington, DC: Lewis Publishers.

Cronk, L. 1991a. "Preferential Parental Investment in Daughters over Sons." *Human Nature* 2:387–417.

Cronk, L. 1991b. "Wealth, Status, and Reproductive Success among the Mukogodo." *American Anthropologist* 93:345–60.

Cronk, L. 1991c. "Human Behavioral Ecology." *Annual Review of Anthropology* 20:25–53.

Cronk, L. 1993. "Parental Favoritism toward Daughters." *American Scientist* 81:272–79.

Cronk, L. 2000. "Female-Biased Parental Investment and Growth Performance among Mukogodo Children." In *Adaptation and Human Behavior: An Anthropological Perspective*, ed. L. Cronk, N. A. Chagnon, and W. G. Irons, 203–21. Hawthorne, NY: Aldine de Gruyter.

Cronk, L. 2004. *FromMukogodo to Maasai: Ethnicity and Cultural Change in Kenya*. Boulder, CO: Westview Press.

Crosby, A. 1986. *Ecological Imperialism: The Biological Expansion of Europe*. Cambridge: Cambridge University Press.

Cross, J., and M. Guyer. 1980. *Social Traps*. Ann Arbor: University of Michigan Press.

Darwin, C. 1859. *On the Origin of Species by Means of Natural Selection, or the Preservation of Favored Races in the Struggle for Life*. London: John Murray.

Diamond, J. 2005. *Collapse: How Societies Choose to Fail or Succeed*. New York: Viking.

Eadie, J., P. W. Sherman, and B. Semel. 1998. "Conspecific Brood Parasitism, Population Dynamics, and the Conservation of Cavity-Nesting Birds." In *Behavioral Ecology and Conservation Biology*, ed. T. Caro, 306–40. Oxford: Oxford University Press.

Ehrlich, P., and J. P. Holdren. 1972. "Impact of Population Growth." *Science* 171:1212–17.

Fisher, R. 1958. *The Genetical Theory of Natural Selection: A Complete Variorum Edition*. New York: Dover Books.

Global Footprint Network. 2005. http://www.footprintnetwork.org/en/index.php/GFN/.

Grossman, D. 2004. "Spring Forward." *Scientific American*, January 2004, 85–91.

Hames, R. 1979. "A Comparison of the Shotgun and the Bow in Neotropical Forest Hunting." *Human Ecology* 7:219–52.

Hames, R. 1990. "Game Conservation or Efficient Hunting?" In *The Question of the Commons: The Culture and Ecology of Communal Resources*, ed. B. J. McCay and J. M. Acheson, 192–207. Tucson: University of Arizona Press.

Hames, R. 2007. "The Ecologically Noble Savage Debate." *Annual Review of Anthropology* 36:177–90.

Hannon, B. 1990. "Early References to Discounting in Biology." *Mathematical Biosciences* 100:115–40.

Hardin, G. 1968. "The Tragedy of the Commons." *Science* 168:1243–48.

Hawkes, K. 1993. "Why Hunter-Gatherers Work: An Ancient Version of the Problem of Public Goods." *Current Anthropology* 34:341–61.

Heinen, J. T., and B. S. Low. 1992. "Human Behavioural Ecology and Environmental Conservation." *Environmental Conservation* 19:105–116.

Hill, K., and A. M. Hurtado. 1996. *Ache Life History: The Ecology and Demography of a Foraging People*. New York: Aldine de Gruyter.

Human Relations Area Files. 2013. eHRAF World Cultures online. Cultures Covered. www.yale.edu/hraf/collections.htm.

Hurtado, M., K. Hawkes, and K. Hill. 1985. "Female Subsistence Strategies among Ache Hunter-Gatherers of Eastern Paraguay." *Human Ecology* 13:1–28.

Irons, W. 1979. "Natural Selection, Adaptation, and Human Social Behavior." In *Evolutionary Biology and Human Social Behavior: An Anthropological Perspective*, ed. N. Chagnon and W. Irons, 4–39. North Scituate, MA: Duxbury Press.

Kaplan, H., and K. Hill. 1985. "Hunting Ability and Reproductive Success among Male Ache Foragers." *Current Anthropology* 26:131–33.

Krech, S. 1999. *The Ecological Indian: Myth and History*. New York: Norton.

Kurlansky, M. 1998. *Cod: A Biography of the Fish That Changed the World*. New York: Penguin.

Low, B. S. 1989. "Human Responses to Environmental Extremeness and Uncertainty: A Cross-Cultural Perspective." In *Risk and Uncertainty in Tribal and Peasant Economies*, ed. E. Cashdan, 229–55. Boulder, CO: Westview Press.

Low, B. S. 1996a. "Men, Women, and Sustainability." *Population and Environment* 18:111–41.

Low, B. S. 1996b. "Behavioral Ecology of Conservation in Traditional Societies." *Human Nature* 7:353–79.

Low, B. S. 2000. *Why Sex Matters: A Darwinian Look at Human Behavior*. Princeton, NJ: Princeton University Press.

Low, B. S. 2004. "Human Behavioral Ecology and Conservation." *Endangered Species Update* 21:14–22.

Low, B. S. 2013. "Fertility: Life History and Ecological Aspects." In *Evolution's Empress: Darwinian Perspectives on the Nature of Women*, ed. Maryanne L. Fisher, Justin R. Garcia, and Rosemarie Sokol Chang, 222–42. New York: Oxford University Press.

Low, B. S., and J. Heinen. 1993. "Population, Resources, and Environment: Implications of Human Behavioral Ecology for Conservation." *Population and Environment* 15:11–38.

Low, B. S., and M. Ridley. 1994. "Why We're Not Environmental Altruists—and What We Can Do about It." *Human Ecology* Review 1:107–36.

Low, B. S., C. P. Simon, and K. Anderson. 2002. "An Evolutionary Perspective on Demographic Transitions: Modeling Multiple Currencies." *American Journal of Human Biology* 14(1): 149–67.

Martin, P. S., and R. G. Klein, eds. 1984. *Quaternary Extinctions: A Prehistoric Revolution*. Tucson: University of Arizona Press.

Murdock, G. P. 1967. *Ethnographic Atlas*. Pittsburgh: University of Pittsburgh Press.

Murdock, G. P. 1981. *Atlas of World Cultures*. Pittsburgh: University of Pittsburgh Press.

Murdock, G. P., and D. White. 1969. "Standard Cross-Cultural Sample." *Ethnology* 8:329–69.

Myers, R., and B. Worm. 2003. "Rapid Worldwide Depletion of Predatory Fish Communities." *Nature* 423:280–83.

Oelschlanger, M. 1991. *The Idea of Wilderness: From Prehistory to the Age of Ecology*. New Haven: Yale University Press.

Oreskes, N. 2004. "The Scientific Consensus on Climate Change." *Science* 306(5702): 1686.

Ostrom, E. 1990. *Governing the Commons: The Evolution of Institutions for Collective Action*. Cambridge: Cambridge University Press.

Ostrom, E. 1998. "A Behavioral Approach to the Rational Choice Theory of Collective Action." Presidential Address, American Political Science Association, 1997. *American Political Science Review* 92:1–22.

Ostrom, E. 2009. "A General Framework for Analyzing Sustainability of Social-Ecological Systems." *Science* 325:419–22.

Ridley, M., and B. S. Low. 1993. "Can Selfishness Save the Environment?" *Atlantic Monthly* 272:76–86.

Salisbury, R. F. 1962. *From Stone to Steel: Economic Consequences of a Technological Change*. Melbourne, AU: Melbourne University Press.

Semel, B., and P. Sherman. 1986. "Dynamics of Nest Parasitism in Wood Ducks." *The Auk* 103:813–16.

Semel, B., P. Sherman, and S. Byers. 1988. "Effects of Brood Parasitism and Nest-Box Placement on Wood Duck Breeding Ecology." *The Condor* 90:920–30.

Solomon, B. D. 1998. "Impending Recovery of Kirtland's Warbler: Case Study in the Effectiveness of the Endangered Species Act." *Environmental Management* 22:9–17.

Speth, J. D. 1990. "Seasonality, Resource Stress, and Food Sharing in So-Called 'Egalitarian' Foraging Societies." *Journal of Anthropological Archaeology* 9:148–88.

Stiglitz, J. E. 2010. *Freefall: America, Free Markets, and the Sinking of the World Economy*. New York: Norton.

Trivers, R. L. 1992. "Parental Investment and Sexual Selection." In *Sexual Selection and the Descent of Man*, ed. B. Campbell, 136–79. Chicago: Aldine de Gruyter.

Trivers, R. L., and D. E. Willard. 1973. "Natural Selection of Parental Ability to Vary the Sex Ratio of Offspring." *Science* 179:90–92.

Trotter, M., and B. McCullough. 1984. "Moas, Men, and Middens." In *Quaternary Extinctions: A Prehistoric Revolution*, ed. P. S. Martin and R. G. Klein, 708–27. Tucson: University of Arizona Press.

Watling, L., and E. A. Norse. 1998. "Disturbance of the Seabed by Mobile Fishing Gear: A Comparison to Forest Clearcutting." *Conservation Biology* 12:1180–97.

Wilkinson, C., O. Linden, H. Cesar, G. Hodgson, J. Rubens, and A. Strong. 1999. "Ecological and Socioeconomic Impacts of 1988 Coral Mortality in the Indian Ocean. An ENSO Impact and a Warning of Future Change?" *Ambio* 28:188–96.

Wilson, J. A., J. M. Acheson, M. Metcalfe, and P. Kleban. 1994. "Chaos, Complexity and Community Management of Fisheries." *Marine Policy* 18(4): 291–305.

Wilson, J. A., J. French, P. Kleban, S. R. McKay, and R. Townsend. 1991. "Chaotic Dynamics in a Multiple Species Fishery: A Model of Community Predation." *Ecological Modeling* 58:303–22.

Wilson, J., B. S. Low, R. Costanza, and E. Ostrom. 1999. "Scale Misperceptions and the Spatial Dynamics of a Social-Ecological System." *Ecological Economics* 31:243–57.

Winterhalder, B. 1997. "Delayed Reciprocity and Tolerated Theft." *Current Anthropology* 38:74–75.

Green Keynesianism
Beyond Standard Growth Paradigms

JONATHAN M. HARRIS

We have involved ourselves in a colossal muddle, having blundered in the control of a delicate machine, the working of which we do not understand. The result is that our possibilities of wealth may run to waste for a time—perhaps for a long time.

—JOHN MAYNARD KEYNES, *THE GREAT SLUMP OF 1930*

IN THE WAKE OF THE GLOBAL FINANCIAL CRISIS, KEYNESIANISM HAS HAD SOMETHING of a revival. In practice, governments have turned to Keynesian policy measures to avert economic collapse. In the theoretical area, mainstream economists have started to give grudging attention to Keynesian perspectives previously dismissed in favor of New Classical theories. This theoretical and practical shift is taking place at the same time that environmental issues, in particular global climate change, are compelling attention to alternative development paths. Significant potential now exists for "green Keynesianism," combining Keynesian fiscal policies with environmental goals.

But there are also tensions between the two perspectives of Keynesianism and ecological economics. Traditional Keynesianism is growth-oriented, while ecological economics stresses limits to growth. Expansionary policies needed to deal with recession may be in conflict with goals of reducing resource and energy use and carbon emissions. In addition, long-term deficit and debt problems pose a threat to implementation of expansionary fiscal policies. This chapter explores the possibilities for green Keynesianism in theory and practice and suggests that these apparent contradictions can be resolved and that green Keynesian policies offer a solution to both economic stagnation and global environmental threats.

A REINTERPRETATION OF THE KEYNESIAN VISION

Keynes's "colossal muddle" seems to apply well to the confusion and dismay characterizing both economists and policymakers in the face of the events of 2007–9 and continues to ring true as we grapple with slow and inadequate recovery and the possibility of a "double-dip" recession, especially in Europe. Ecological economists might also recognize the concept of a blundering approach to a delicately balanced machine in a different sense, considering the widespread damage wrought on ecosystems that we only partially understand, as a result of unrestrained economic growth. But can the remedies suggested by Keynes—government intervention through fiscal and monetary policy to rebuild aggregate demand and economic confidence—also be reinterpreted in a more ecological sense?

In a recent paper, Paul Krugman suggests that "Keynesian economics remains the best framework we have for making sense of recessions and depressions" (Krugman, 2009). With reference to current economic controversies, Krugman has pointed out that "not only do these disputes involve many of the same issues Keynes grappled with 75 years ago, we are—frustratingly—retracing much of the same ground covered in the 1930s" (Krugman, 2011). The issues include the need for government stimulus to respond to recession, and the counterproductive nature of "austerity" programs, which do indeed echo the 1930s. But a major difference from the crisis of the 1930s is the current importance of global environmental crises. Environmental issues were not absent in the 1930s (one important aspect of the New Deal was the Civilian Conservation Corps), but they have much greater scope today.

The financial and economic crisis had the temporary effect of eclipsing major environmental issues in public debate. But these issues have, if anything, gained in urgency. The scientific evidence supporting human-induced climate change has grown stronger, the possibilities of catastrophic outcomes more significant, and the recommendations of scientists for carbon reductions more drastic, within the last few years. Water shortages, species loss, ocean pollution and fisheries decline, and a host of other issues have grown more pressing as human population crosses the 7 billion mark. How do these issues relate to the shifting perceptions of macroeconomic realities as we enter the second decade of the twenty-first century?

On the recent economic crisis, I have suggested that there was a possibility of a synthesis between Keynesian macroeconomics and the kind of environmental macroeconomics originally called for by Herman Daly (Daly, 1991a, 1991b, 1996):

> Keynes did not focus on issues of ecological sustainability, but from our current standpoint in the first decade of the twenty-first century, it certainly seems reasonable to include environmental degradation as one of the "outstanding faults" of the economic system. The implementation of ambitious programs for social investment and redirection of the macro economy towards sustainability will be essential for preserving economic systems in the twenty-first century. It will, however, require a turn away from conventional macroeconomics. (Harris, 2009, p. 183)

To explore whether such a synthesis might be possible, it is important to reconsider the essential vision of Keynes concerning the *causes* of economic disruptions such as recession and depression, before looking at policy solutions. Keynes, of course, rejected the classical notion of an automatic tendency toward full employment based on price and wage adjustment. But the key element in his vision is not, as is frequently assumed, market imperfections or "sticky" prices. These may play a role. But the central point that Keynes emphasized, although it was lost on many of his later followers and exponents, was the essential instability of investment due to the uncertain connection between present and future.

Theories of efficient markets depend on the idea of perfect information about market conditions—probably not possible even in the present. But perfect information about the future is clearly impossible. This is what gives rise to bubbles, boom and bust, and periods of irrational optimism or pessimism. Current investments are based on current prices and expectations about the future. But expectations vary and may be wildly wrong. The resulting variations in investment can generate self-reinforcing cycles in aggregate demand, leading to long periods of expansion or depression. Hence the clear need for government to stabilize the economy with countercyclical fiscal and monetary policy.

Here again there is an interesting parallel to a central issue in ecological economics. One of the key points about resource management is the inadequacy of market incentives for long-term resource conservation. Similarly, market mechanisms deal poorly with cumulative pollutants whose impacts build up over time. These resource and environmental issues have moved from being specific concerns about individual resources to macro-level issues of global climate change, forest loss, fisheries collapse, groundwater depletion, and other ecosystem-wide impacts. So it is evident that however well markets may deal with efficient allocation of resources in the short term, they clearly fail to balance short-term (static) efficiency considerations with long-term (dynamic) efficiency. A clear government policy role is indicated to prevent resource overdraft and to sustain long-term resource and environmental balance.

If the current macroeconomic crisis forces a reassessment of the market-based, minimal government intervention approach that has characterized most mainstream economic theory, it seems necessary to take into account both the traditional Keynesian and the environmental critiques. A revised approach might be something like the following:

> Both inherent economic instability and the incompatibility between many market outcomes and environmental sustainability mean that national economies, and the world economy, are vulnerable to major economic fluctuations and to degradation of the essential resource and environmental base for economic activity. This necessitates government intervention to stabilize economic systems and to preserve essential ecological functions.

In considering appropriate government policy initiatives, monetary intervention is not enough. While central bank policy can to some extent mitigate economic fluctuations, it has crucial limitations. One limitation is the Keynesian "liquidity trap"—the inability of central banks to push interest rates below zero, or to ensure that additional monetary reserves will be deployed to create expanded aggregate demand. (A current demonstration of this phenomenon is evident in a 2011 *New York Times article*, "In Cautious Times, Banks Flooded with Cash.")[1] Another is the inability of monetary policy to create jobs directly, or to target interventions toward environmental investment. For these reasons, fiscal policy is essential and needs to be focused specifically on the goals of full employment, social equity, and environmental sustainability. Monetary policy should be used both to enable these targeted fiscal interventions and to promote traditional monetary goals of adequate liquidity and price stability.

As a description of the main principles of macroeconomic theory and policy, this clearly stands as rank heresy in terms of what up until recently has been the mainstream consensus.[2] But, as noted, this consensus is now in serious question, and perhaps defunct. This creates a major opportunity for a new kind of macroeconomics to emerge—one that is "old" in that it returns to some traditional Keynesian principles, but "new" in that it incorporates the ecological realities of the twenty-first century. It provides an opportunity to address some of the major problems of the contemporary economy, including growing income and wealth inequality, inadequate infrastructure investment, fossil fuel dependence, and the adverse impacts of economic growth on the environment.

This revised approach does not provide a definitive answer to the question of whether or when a limit to macroeconomic growth—Daly's concept of "optimal macroeconomic scale"—may be required. It does, however, provide a framework to address this question as a central issue in macroeconomics. Daly first called for a move to a steady-state economy over a quarter of a century ago (Daly, 1973), but his perspective has never been taken seriously within mainstream macroeconomics. A revised macroeconomics will incorporate the possibility of a steady state, but there are many questions to be resolved about what this really means, and what a transition from current growth-oriented macro might look like.[3]

A REVISED APPROACH TO KEYNESIAN THEORY

In previous articles, I have suggested that a new breakdown of the major sectors of aggregate demand is useful in thinking about alternatives to current economic growth patterns (Harris, 2007, 2009). Specifically, the three major sectors of consumption, investment, and government spending can be divided into subsectors representing material goods, services, resource-intensive and resource-conserving investment, and investment in human and natural capital.

The idea is that we can then distinguish between those macroeconomic aggregates that should be strictly limited—resource-intensive consumption and investment, and energy-intensive infrastructure—and those that can expand over time without negative environmental consequences. The latter would include large areas of health, education, cultural activity, and resource- and energy-conserving investment. The conclusion is that there is plenty of scope for growth in economic activity, concentrated in these categories, without growth in resource throughput,[4] and with a significant decline in the most damaging throughput, that of carbon-intensive fuels.

A revised breakdown of macroeconomic categories would look something like this:[5]

C_g = consumption of nondurable goods and energy-intensive services
C_s = consumption of human-capital intensive services[6]
C_m = household investment in consumer durables
I_{me} = investment in energy-intensive manufactured capital
I_{mc} = investment in energy-conserving manufactured capital
I_n = investment in natural capital[7]
I_h = investment in human capital
G_g = government consumption of nondurable goods and energy-intensive services
G_s = government consumption of human capital-intensive services
G_{me} = government investment in energy-intensive manufactured capital
G_{mc} = government investment in energy-conserving manufactured capital
G_n = government investment in natural capital
G_h = government investment in human capital

These categories are conceptual and do not correspond to current categories of national income accounting. The do, however, resonate with the extensive literature on "greening" the national income accounts, which makes similar distinctions between socially or environmentally beneficial and harmful GDP categories.

Thus the basic equation of macroeconomic balance can be restated:

$$Y = C + I + G + (X - M) \tag{1}$$

$$Y = [C_g + C_s + C_m] + [I_{me} + I_{mc} + I_n + I_h]$$
$$+ [G_g + G_s + G_{me} + G_{mc} + G_n + G_h] + (X - M) \tag{2}$$

While ecological principles imply limits on C_g, I_{me}, G_g, and G_{me}, the other terms in the equation can grow over time without significant negative environmental impact, and indeed with a positive effect in the case of natural capital or energy-conserving investment.[8] The equation can be rearranged to distinguish between macroeconomic aggregates that we wish to limit, and those that we wish to encourage:

$$Y = [C_g + I_{me} + G_g + G_{me}]$$
$$+ [C_s + C_m + I_{mc} + I_n + I_h + G_s + G_n + G_{mc} + G_h]$$
$$+ (X - M) \tag{3}$$

To satisfy sustainability criteria, the terms in the first set of brackets should be stabilized or reduced over time, but the terms in the second set of brackets can be expanded. These categories are sensitive to various kinds of government policy, so different options are available to achieve the desired results. Regarding the government-spending terms, these are clearly in the domain of fiscal policy (more on this below). The investment categories are responsive to a variety of tax and other incentives, as well as possibly preferential provision of credit to certain sectors. The consumption categories may also be affected by tax policy, in particular a carbon tax or equivalent that raises the price of fossil fuels and all fossil-fuel-intensive goods and services, as well as by subsidies and tax credits for favored activities.

Regarding the foreign sector term, which has here been left in the traditional form, it would certainly be possible to break the import and export categories down in a similar fashion. Trade policy to affect these is a trickier question. If, for example, "greener" production in one country is offset by imports of more energy- and carbon-intensive goods from abroad, either border tariffs or some kind of globally coordinated policy will be required to prevent "leakage." Without going into the many ramifications of this issue, it can simply be noted that trade policies will need to complement domestic "green Keynesian" policies. It is likely that this would require significant revision of some World Trade Organization (WTO) guidelines that largely prevent environmental considerations from being a part of trade policy.

GREEN KEYNESIANISM AND THE CURRENT CRISIS

One interpretation of the crisis that began in 2007–8 is that the global economy has in some sense reached the limits of growth. This perspective has been presented by analysts such as Richard Heinberg (2011). Heinberg summarizes the case thus:

> Economic growth as we have known it is over and done with. The growth we are talking about is the expansion of the overall size of the economy . . . and of the quantities of energy and material goods flowing through it. The economic crisis that began in 2007–2008 was both foreseeable and inevitable, and it marks a permanent fundamental break from past decades—a period during which most economists adopted the unrealistic view that perpetual economic growth is necessary and also possible to achieve. There are now fundamental barriers to ongoing economic expansion, and the world is colliding with those barriers. (2011, pp. 1–2)

The problem with this argument is that it conflates two quite different possible causes for a cessation of growth. One is based on ecological limits. This argument is very familiar to those who have followed the discussion in ecological economics since Daly introduced the idea of fundamental macroeconomic limits. Its most pressing manifestation today, as I have emphasized, has to do with the impacts of global climate change:

> The cognitive disconnect between scientists' warnings of potential catastrophe if carbon emissions continue unchecked on the one hand, and the political and economic realities of steadily increasing emissions on the other, defines the outstanding economic problem of the twenty-first century. Can economic growth continue while carbon emissions are drastically reduced? (Harris, 2009, p. 169)

The other possible cause for limits to growth is financial. According to Heinberg, the factors that stand in the way of further economic growth would include the following:

> Financial disruptions due to the inability of our existing monetary, banking, and investment systems to adjust to both resource scarcity and soaring environmental costs—and their inability (in the context of a shrinking economy) to service the enormous piles of government and private debt that have been generated over the past couple of decades. (Heinberg, 2011, pp. 2–3)

But the financial crisis of 2008 and the European debt crisis of 2010–11 had little to do with resource scarcity or environmental limits. It is certainly true that the management of private and government debt was a central feature of these crises, but it does not appear that the housing bubble and subsequent recession that caused and accentuated debt and default issues in the United States and Europe had any significant environmental dimension. Nor is the failure to resume growth centered on environmental factors. It is true that there have been some significant increases in oil and commodities prices since 2006, but price trends have been variable since 2008 and have generally fallen somewhat as a result of recession.

The real causes of continued sluggish growth or "double-dip" recession lie in the financial sphere. The U.S. banking system has not recovered from the 2007–8 crisis, so credit remains tight despite efforts by the U.S. Federal Reserve Bank to expand it. So long as the

Fed's policies are not accompanied by expansionary fiscal policy, they will be limited in their effectiveness (as noted above, this is the Keynesian "liquidity trap"). In Europe, the problem has had more to do with willful policy errors, in particular a reliance on austerity policies and the unwillingness of the European Central Bank to provide sufficient credit to allow debt-strapped countries to recover, thereby promoting a vicious cycle of economic decline and worsening debt problems.

These problems, and their remedies, are well described by long-established Keynesian analysis. In order to restart an economy mired in recession, the Keynesian formula is a combination of expansionary fiscal and monetary policy. In the United States, this approach was followed during the period 2009–10, but fiscal expansionism came to a screeching halt with the Republican electoral victories in 2010. This has placed the burden of fighting recession entirely on monetary policy. In Europe, a misplaced emphasis on excessively contractionary fiscal and monetary policies threatened to plunge the continent back into recession. During 2012, European monetary policies eased, with very positive results, but fiscal policy remained dangerously restrictive, prolonging the crisis and endangering recovery. Thus the reasons for a failure of economic growth to resume lie in mistaken policy approaches as well as the continuing financial damage from the collapse of excessively leveraged and inadequately regulated investment in housing and other areas.

This is not to suggest that resource and environmental problems are not significant. But their current impact is primarily to degrade the quality of the ecosphere rather than to limit economic growth. There is a good argument that economic growth, or at least growth in resource and energy throughput, *should* be limited to prevent further ecological damage, especially climate change (Victor, 2008; Jackson, 2009; Harris, 2009 and 2010). There is also a likelihood that resource demands from China, India, and other growing economies will eventually raise oil and other commodity prices to the point where there will be significant impacts on growth. But given a general lack of policies to internalize environmental costs into prices through carbon taxes or similar mechanisms, the economic system is currently insensitive to ecological damage, and environmental constraints do not serve as a limit on growth in most areas.

From the point of view of a "green" Keynesian analysis, this distinction between financial and environmental limits to growth is crucial. If indeed Keynesian policies can offer a route out of economic stagnation and high unemployment, then it is vital to implement such policies. As numerous analysts have pointed out, the social and political costs of continued high unemployment are staggering, not just in terms of current deprivation but also in loss of human capital and the possibility of political breakdown and the rise of antidemocratic demagogues. The experience of the 1930s indicates that the alternative to democratic Keynesian policies to create employment, such as Roosevelt's New Deal, is a collapse of democracy and the rise of authoritarian alternatives.

But if environmental problems are not the immediate cause of the crisis, there is nonetheless a danger that a solution to the problems of recession and unemployment will worsen pressures on the environment. A resumption of standard-style economic growth, even if possible, will increase demand for fossil fuels, minerals, water, and greater carbon emissions, implying greater ecological damage and worsening the drivers of climate change. So either a different type of growth, or an adaptation to a lower- or no-growth economy, is needed. How can this be compatible with solving the unemployment problem?

GREEN KEYNESIANISM IN PRACTICE

Fiscal policy is the central element of an environmentally oriented Keynesianism. As noted above, expansionary monetary policy is essential for recovering from recession, but it lacks any differentiation between environmentally beneficial and harmful GDP categories. Fiscal policy can be specifically targeted. There are recent examples of this in the Obama administration's 2009–10 stimulus package. In part this was directed toward traditional types of spending such as highway maintenance, but a significant portion (about $71 billion) was specifically oriented toward "green" investments, together with another $20 billion in "green" tax incentives.[9]

The double benefit of such policies is that they promote employment and also advance a transition to a more environmentally sustainable economy. In terms of the GDP categories outline above, they expand the beneficial categories, with a focus on public and private investment. It is easily possible to envision much larger programs of this nature. For example, the stimulus program included $5 billion for weatherization programs. A major nationwide program for building energy efficiency retrofit could easily be ten times as large. The stimulus program temporarily quadrupled U.S. spending on energy research and development; a permanent increase of this magnitude would have enormous long-term benefits in promoting a transition to efficiency and renewables.

And energy is by no means the only option for beneficial spending. Investment in education and the development of human capital is one of the most productive forms of investment. The stimulus program helped avert teacher layoffs and other educational cutbacks; unfortunately, after 2010 these fiscal policies were largely eliminated and widespread teacher layoffs at the state level have resulted. What sense does this make in an era of 8–9 percent unemployment? Surely a program to *expand* teacher hiring and raise incentives for young people to enter teaching professions would make much more sense.

A European example of green Keynesian policy is provided by Portugal, which has achieved an impressive government-led transition from fossil fuels toward renewable power, with the percentage of renewable supply in Portugal's grid up from 17 percent in 2005 to 45 percent in 2010.[10] This involved a $22 billion investment in modernizing its electrical grid and developing wind and hydropower facilities. Portugal will recoup some of its investment through European Union carbon credits and will save about $2.3 billion a year on avoided natural gas imports. Unfortunately, the current one-sided emphasis on austerity policies in Europe makes such ecologically friendly, employment-generating projects much less likely, despite their clear long-term benefits. It also raises the more general question of whether green Keynesianism is sustainable from a fiscal point of view. What are the limits to "green" expansionary policies?

POTENTIAL LIMITS TO GREEN KEYNESIANISM

Deficits and Debt

The main counterweight to Keynesian expansionary polices as a solution for recession comes from arguments related to deficits and debt. The most extreme form of this is the New Classical assertion that government deficit spending is completely ineffective in stimulating the economy—it merely replaces private spending. This seems to have been refuted in practice by the experience with the 2009–10 stimulus package, which clearly helped to fill a widening gap in aggregate demand following the 2008 collapse. According to a recent analysis by Alan Blinder and Mark Zandi, aggressive federal policy action (including the "green" investments discussed above) "probably averted what could have been called Great Depression 2.0 . . . without the government's response, GDP in 2010 would be about 11.5% lower, payroll employment would be less by some 8½ million jobs, and the nation would now be experiencing deflation" (Blinder and Zandi, 2010, p. 1).

A more realistic concern is that mounting deficits and debt will eventually lead to inflation, or to European-style sovereign debt crises. Certainly economies cannot continue indefinitely with ever-rising debt loads. But in recessionary times, successful expansionary policy may actually lower long-term debt through generating employment and higher tax revenues. As Paul Krugman points out: "Suppose that government uses borrowed money to buy useful things like infrastructure. The true social cost will be very low, because the spending will put resources that would otherwise be unemployed to work [and allow private debtors to pay down their debt] . . . the argument that debt can't cure debt is just wrong" (Krugman, 2011).

To a significant degree, the European sovereign debt crisis arose from unwillingness to use the European Central Bank to finance debt, allowing indebted players to recover. Instead, "austerity" policies make debt harder to manage and threaten major defaults and financial catastrophe.[11] In a situation of crisis and looming economic collapse, arguments about moral hazard and rewarding improvident behavior have to take a back seat to the urgent need to restore economic health and full employment—which can only be achieved through expansionary fiscal and monetary policy. The dangers of such an approach—essentially some degree of inflation—pale beside the prospect of massive and spreading economic decline, perhaps on the scale of the Great Depression, that could result from failure to act.[12]

Similarly in the United States, a focus on debt reduction undermines the ability to support a still-weak economy with further stimulus spending. Just as in 1937, a withdrawal of federal spending to accommodate calls for fiscal prudence could very well plunge the economy into a "double-dip" recession. While managing expenditures, increasing revenues, and bringing the budget closer to balance are all worthy long-term goals, what Keynes called "the Treasury view" urging balancing the budget during recession is likely to be disastrous—and actually worsen long-term debt problems. Instead, the government needs to borrow excess savings and put them to work in ways that can generate long-term growth in revenues. Distinguishing between short-term and long-term goals on debt management is vital—and the longer term need to keep debt at a manageable level is also consistent with green Keynesianism, as we will discuss.

Environmental Limits to Growth

The short-term case for deficit spending is that we need economic growth to generate both employment and revenues. But ecological economists point out that we can't grow forever, and therefore can't rely on growth to pay down debt. Undoubtedly there are long-term limits to growth. But this is true primarily of "throughput" growth (growth in energy and resources and resulting waste streams). There is plenty of scope for growth in services, human capital, environmental infrastructure, renewable energy, and other beneficial areas. In many cases these forms of growth are labor intensive, promoting greater employment. (For example, organic agriculture is typically more labor intensive, so shifting from highly mechanized and chemical-dependent agriculture is likely to increase employment).

In the longer term, there is a strong ecological case that we will have to adapt to a steady-state economy (Daly 1991b, 1996). But we don't need a steady state with 8–9 percent unemployment! It is essential to promote employment growth, and, as Peter Victor has pointed out, labor market institutions encouraging a shorter workweek can allow higher employment with less resource and energy throughput (Victor, 2008).

Should the economy reach a point at which debt reduction becomes a major issue, there are many options that are consistent with green Keynesianism. The Keynesian policy toolkit includes contractionary as well as expansionary measures, and these too can be adapted for environmental ends, especially by placing taxes on environmental "bads" or higher-income segments of the population. Such policies could include health care reform to limit growth of unnecessary health spending and high administrative costs; a carbon tax with partial per capita rebate to generate revenues while inducing a shift away from fossil fuels and preserving or improving income equity; and higher taxes on upper-income earners and capital gains (Ruffing and Horney, 2011).

The most pressing environmental limit is the need for drastic reductions in carbon emissions (Harris, 2009). In theory, there is no barrier to reducing carbon by imposing steadily increasing carbon taxes or their equivalent (Ackerman and Stanton, 2011). The revenues from carbon taxes or auctioned carbon permits can be used for a variety of purposes consistent with social and environmental objectives, including a per capita rebate to promote income equity and eliminate the regressive nature of an energy tax (see e.g. Boyce and Riddle, 2009); subsidies for research and development, renewable energy, and energy efficiency (which also indirectly benefit lower-income consumers by reducing energy costs); or simply deficit reduction if this is considered a priority. Higher energy costs resulting from a carbon tax or equivalent would constrain traditional energy-intensive growth but would not significantly impact human services or investment in human capital and would promote investment in energy efficiency and energy alternatives.

Political Barriers

The main barrier to implementation of green Keynesian policies is not economic or environmental limits, nor deficits and debt. Rather, it is a broadly held but erroneous perception that government action is the problem rather than the solution. In the United States, this takes the form of a belief that the Obama economic stimulus "failed" and that taxpayers paid dearly for a Wall Street bailout. This belief (strongly supported by more conservative members of the economics profession)[13] was largely responsible for the rightward turn in U.S. politics in 2010 and the subsequent focus on deficit reduction and cutting back government spending. But it correlates poorly with the facts.

As noted above, the economic stimulus saved or created about 8.5 million jobs (Blinder and Zandi, 2010). At a total cost of $787 billion in Federal spending and tax cuts, this works out to about $92,000 per job. But even this figure is too high, as the stimulus also paid for substantial real infrastructure investment that conveys long-term economic benefits (a substantial part of it, as noted above, being specifically "green" investment). Considering the alternative—a cascade of negative multiplier effects forcing the United States and world economies into depression conditions—this seems like a bargain. The fact that the stimulus was not large enough to overcome the massive effects of the 2008 collapse argues for more stimulus, not less, but the fact that unemployment remained high led many to the seemingly commonsense, but erroneous, conclusion that the stimulus failed.

Even the much-maligned bank and industrial bailouts have proved to be good investments. So far, taxpayers have not paid a penny for either stimulus or bailout. In fact, taxes have gone down significantly, and are now at levels not seen since the 1950s. Most of the bailout money was repaid; the government made a profit on much of it.[14] The auto industry bailout saved Michigan and most of U.S. industry from depression, and its eventual net cost was almost zero ($74 out of $86 billion had been repaid as of mid-2010).[15]

So good political slogans are not necessarily good economics. It is of course true that government fiscal policy may well involve some inefficiency and waste. But the perception that government action is necessarily bad undercuts our ability to respond both to economic and environmental crises. In addition, the allergic reaction in the American political system to anything involving the word "tax" (unless followed by "cuts") greatly constrains sensible fiscal policy. Overcoming these political barriers may be difficult. But economists should not endorse the pessimistic view that we are impotent in the face of economic crisis, recession, and debt. A sensible combination of fiscal and monetary policy options holds great potential for responding both to unemployment and to environmental priorities including carbon reduction. We need to expand, not contract, the Keynesian toolbox to respond to this combination of twenty-first-century economic and environmental issues.

POLICIES FOR FULL EMPLOYMENT, CLIMATE STABILIZATION, AND ECOLOGICAL BALANCE

What would a green Keynesian policy mix aimed at a combination of economic and environmental goals look like? There are many options, but here are some possibilities:

- Increased hiring in the public sector: teachers, police, transit and park workers, and youth employment programs
- Large-scale building retrofit publicly financed but carried out by private contractors
- Increased public R&D expenditures with accompanying higher education investment (like the "Sputnik" push for stronger science education in the 1950s)
- Major energy efficiency and renewables investment, partly public and partly incentivized private investment
- Investment in public transit and infrastructure
- Carbon tax or equivalent (cap and trade with auction)
- Recycling of carbon tax revenues for energy efficiency, renewables, progressive rebates
- Infrastructure investment—high-speed rail, public transit, green buildings
- Efficiency standards for cars, machinery, buildings
- Preferential credit or subsidy for energy efficiency investments

- Financial reform and reregulation including the equivalent of Glass-Steagall "firewall" between basic banking and risky investments (another Keynesian precedent)

And at the international level:

- A Global Investment Fund for efficiency and renewable energy investment (like the World Bank but with a noncarbon energy focus)
- Integrated cap-and-trade schemes for industrialized economies with carbon credits for developing countries, including agriculture and forestry
- Efficiency and renewables technology transfer, with waiver of intellectual property and WTO subsidy rules for least developed economies
- Microcredit schemes for local solar, wind, ecological preservation, water and sanitation, and community development

This list of policies is by no means comprehensive, but it is meant to suggest the outlines for a new and more optimistic approach to economic policy. Just as the impact of Keynesian analysis helped to break through the seemingly intractable problems of the Great Depression, a revised and "greened" Keynesian vision can help us escape the daunting problems of economic stagnation, debt crisis, and global environmental threats that confront us today.

The needed theoretical and policy reorientation requires a turn away from the narrowed vision that has until recently characterized modern economics. The tools are available, drawing both on the historical tradition of Keynesianism and the modern vision of ecological economics, to guide a new social response that can mobilize the strengths of both human capital and technology to respond to economic, social, and environmental problems. The main difficulty lies not in the practical challenges, large though they are, but in overcoming the restrictive habits of thought that limit the scope of economic theory and policy.

NOTES

1. According to the article, "Bankers have an odd-sounding problem these days: they are awash in cash. Ordinarily, in a more robust environment, an influx of deposits would be used to finance new businesses, expansion plans, and home purchases. But in today's fragile economy, the bulk of the new money is doing little to spur growth" (*New York Times*, October 25, 2011).
2. For a macroeconomics text that advances this nonmainstream view, see Goodwin, Nelson, and Harris, 2009.
3. For more extensive discussion of this issue, see Harris, 2010.
4. Throughput, a term introduced by Herman Daly, refers to the combined processes of input of resources and output of wastes.
5. The categories and equations that follow are adapted from Harris, 2009.
6. In GDP accounting, the term "services" refers to a wide range of activities including health care, education, and information services, as well as transportation and utility services. Here we divide services into more energy-intensive types such as transportation and more human-capital-intensive types such as education.

7. The concept of "natural capital" has been promoted by ecological economists to emphasize the importance of healthy ecosystems and natural resources to economic production and human well-being. Investment in natural capital preserves or improves these resource functions—for example, conserving forests and wetlands or rebuilding soils.

8. Not all services are environmentally benign, but many services such as education and health care typically have less environmental impact than goods production. This formulation also assumes that investment in natural capital is wisely managed; for example, replacement of natural forest with plantation forest would not count as investment in natural capital.

9. Specific provisions included spending on energy efficiency in federal buildings and Department of Defense facilities ($8.7 billion); smart-grid infrastructure investment ($11 billion); energy and conservation grants to state and local governments ($6.3 billion); weatherization assistance ($5 billion); energy efficiency and renewable energy research ($2.5 billion); grants for advanced battery manufacturing ($2 billion); loan guarantees for wind and solar projects ($6 billion); public transit and high-speed rail ($17.7 billion); environmental cleanup ($14.6 billion); and environmental research ($6.6 billion). See "U.S. Economic Stimulus Package Includes Billions for Energy and Environment," http://environment.about.com/od/environmentallawpolicy/a/econ_stimulus.htm.

10. "Portugal Gives Itself a Clean-Energy Makeover," *New York Times*, August 10, 2010.

11. "German Fears about Inflation Stall Bold Steps in Debt Crisis," *New York Times*, December 2, 2011.

12. "New Reports Warn of Escalating Dangers from Europe's Debt Crisis," *New York Times*, November 28, 2011.

13. See, for example, Metzler 2010. Metzler argues that "government spending has failed to bring about an economic recovery . . . more than a trillion dollars of spending by the Bush and Obama administrations has left the economy in a slump and unemployment hovering above 9%" and recommends a program of government spending cuts.

14. "As Banks Repay Bailout Money, U.S. Sees a Profit," New York Times, August 30, 2009.

15. "Government Could Recoup Most of Auto Bailout Funds," *Detroit Free Press*, July 25, 2010.

REFERENCES

Ackerman, F., and E. A. Stanton. 2011. "Climate Risks and Carbon Prices: Revising the Social Cost of Carbon." Report for the Economics for Equity and the Environment Network. http://www.sei-us.org/publications/id/399.

Boyce, James K., and Matthew Riddle. 2009. "Cap and Dividend: How to Curb Global Warming While Promoting Income Equity." Chapter 9 in *Twenty-First Century Macroeconomics: Responding to the Climate Challenge*, ed. Jonathan M. Harris and Neva R. Goodwin. Northampton, MA: Edward Elgar.

Blinder, Alan S., and Mark Zandi. 2010. "How the Great Recession Was Brought to an End." http://www.economy.com/mark-zandi/documents/End-of-Great-Recession.pdf.

Daly, Herman E., ed. 1973. *Toward a Steady-State Economy*. San Francisco: W.H. Freeman.

Daly, Herman E. 1991a. "Elements of Environmental Macroeconomics." Chapter 3 in *Ecological Economics: The Science and Management of Sustainability*, ed. Robert Costanza. New York: Columbia University Press.

Daly, Herman E. 1991b. *Steady-State Economics*. Washington, DC: Island Press.

Daly, Herman E. 1996. *Beyond Growth: The Economic of Sustainable Development*. Boston: Beacon Press.

Goodwin, Neva, Julie A. Nelson, and Jonathan M. Harris. 2009. *Macroeconomics in Context*. Armonk, NY: M.E. Sharpe.

Harris, Jonathan M. 2007. "Reorienting Macroeconomic Theory towards Environmental Sustainability." Chapter 2 in *Frontiers in Ecological Economic Theory and Application*, ed. John M. Gowdy and Jon D. Erickson. Northampton, MA: Edward Elgar.

Harris, Jonathan M. 2009. "Ecological Macroeconomics: Consumption, Investment, and Climate Change." Chapter 8 in *Twenty-First Century Macroeconomics: Responding to the Climate Challenge*, ed. Jonathan M., Harris and Neva R. Goodwin. Northampton, MA: Edward Elgar. Also available as Tufts University Global Development and Environment Institute Working Paper 08-02, http://www.ase.tufts.edu/gdae/publications/working_papers/index.html.

Harris, Jonathan M. 2010. "The Macroeconomics of Development without Throughput Growth." Tufts University Global Development and Environment Institute Working Paper 10-05. http://www.ase.tufts.edu/gdae/publications/working_papers/index.html.

Heinberg, Richard. 2011. *The End of Growth*. Gabriola Island, British Columbia: New Society Publishers.

Jackson, Tim. 2009. *Prosperity without Growth: Economics for a Finite Planet*. London: Earthscan.

Keynes, John M. 1964. *The General Theory of Employment, Interest, and Money*. New York: Harcourt, Brace. Original publication London: Macmillan, 1936.

Keynes, John M. 1930. "The Great Slump of 1930." *Nation & Athenæum*, December 20 and December 27, 1930.

Krugman, Paul. 2009. "How Did Economists Get it So Wrong?" *New York Times*, September 2, 2009.

Krugman, Paul. 2011. "Mr. Keynes and the Moderns." Paper presented at conference commemorating the seventy-fifth anniversary of the publication of *The General Theory of Employment, Interest, and Money*, Cambridge.

Metzler, Allan H. 2010. "Four Reasons Keynesians Keep Getting It Wrong." *Wall Street Journal*, October 28. http://online.wsj.com/article/SB10001424052970204777904576651532721267002.html.

Ruffing, Kathy, and James R. Horney. 2011. "Economic Downturn and Bush Policies Continue to Drive Large Projected Deficits." Center on Budget and Policy Priorities, May 10. http://www.cbpp.org/cms/?fa=view&id=3490.

Victor, Peter A. 2008. *Managing without Growth: Slower by Design, Not Disaster*. Northampton, MA: Edward Elgar.

The Economics of Information in a Green Economy

JOSHUA FARLEY AND SKYLER PERKINS

BUILDING A GREEN ECONOMY CONFRONTS TWO CRITICAL AND CONFLICTING SCALE issues. To avoid environmental catastrophes, we must dramatically reduce throughput—carbon emissions alone must fall by over 80 percent. However, modern economies are so dependent on fossil fuels and other forms of throughput that far more modest reductions could result in economic catastrophe. New technologies can help bridge the gap between these two conflicting thresholds, but must be developed and disseminated as rapidly as possible. Current efforts to speed up technological innovation rely on strengthening intellectual property rights. However, scientists competing for property rights are unlikely to share information, slowing the advance of knowledge. Environmental catastrophes threaten public goods and are likely to have the worst impacts on the poor, providing little incentive for market investments in technologies that protect them. Patents on new technologies raise their prices for twenty years, slowing dissemination and preventing other scientists from freely improving the technology. Knowledge is expensive to produce, but its value is maximized at a price of zero and as a result is best produced through cooperation, not competition. Building a green economy requires public investment in open source knowledge, ideally funded by fees on throughput.

INTRODUCTION

There is a growing acceptance that we must "green" our economy but little consensus about what that entails. The Organisation for Economic Co-operation and Development (OECD) calls for green growth (OECD, 2011), while others believe that a steady-state economy or even degrowth is a prerequisite for sustainability (Daly, 1973; Flipo and Schneider, 2008; Victor, 2008; Jackson, 2009; Rijnhout and Schauer, 2009; Martinez Alier, 2011; Daly, 1977). The basic criteria for a green economy, however, are quite clear. A green economy cannot use renewable resources any faster than they can regenerate. In fact, we must reduce the rate of use of renewable resources to below their regeneration rate in order to rebuild our seriously depleted stocks. We cannot emit waste products into ecosystems faster than they can be absorbed, and we must be particularly careful when we extract and concentrate toxic elements from the earth's crust and release novel chemicals into the environment, because ecosystems have not evolved the capacity to absorb them. In fact, we must reduce emissions rates well below current absorption rates in order to reduce the harmful accumulated stocks of greenhouse gases (GHGs) and other dangerous pollutants. We must also ensure that neither resource extraction nor waste emissions threaten the supply of life-sustaining ecosystem services, again requiring a reduction in both. Finally, we cannot use nonrenewable resources upon which we depend faster than we develop renewable substitutes. Failure to develop a green economy must ultimately have catastrophic results.

Unfortunately, the path toward a green economy is rocky indeed. Take the relatively straightforward case of achieving climate stability. We know from the report of the Intergovernmental Panel on Climate Change (IPCC) that failure to reduce greenhouse gas emissions by greater than 80 percent will lead to continuing accumulation of GHGs in our atmosphere, likely resulting in runaway climate change (IPCC, 2007). From an economic perspective, the marginal costs of GHG emissions are immeasurably high. However, our economy currently depends on fossil fuels for everything from food supply to communication. Conventional modern food systems, for example, consume over seven calories of fossil hydrocarbons for every calorie of food that winds up on a plate (Heller and Keoleian, 2000; Pimentel and Pimentel, 2008). Reducing fossil fuel consumption by as little as 50 percent would leave us unable to feed 7 billion people with current technologies and likely lead to global economic collapse. The marginal benefits of GHG emissions are also immeasurably high with current technologies.

The loss of ecosystem services in general presents a similar dilemma. Failure to restore global ecosystems and biodiversity threatens a catastrophic loss in ecosystem services, including many essential to agricultural production. There is often a significant time lag between human activities and ecological degradation, and again between degradation and biodiversity loss (Brooks et al., 1999; Metzger et al., 2009). This time lag offers a window of opportunity to restore ecosystem resilience. However, the greatest threats to ecosystem function include nitrogen, phosphorous, greenhouse gas emissions, land conversion, biodiversity loss, freshwater use, and chemical pollution (Rockström et al., 2009). Agriculture is a leading cause of all of these threats (Millennium Ecosystem Assessment, 2005). Measured in terms of ecosystem services lost, the marginal costs of agriculture are immeasurably high. However, for the billion people who are currently malnourished, the marginal benefits of agriculture production are immeasurably high as well.

With current technologies, we face an apparently unsolvable dilemma: failure to build a green economy will lead to a global ecosystem collapse that drags the economy down in its wake, while switching to a green economy with current technologies will likely lead to global economic collapse in the short run. The choice is between disaster now and disaster later. Figure 1 depicts this dynamic.

New technologies alone will be unable to solve this problem, but they are almost certainly an essential part of any viable solution. Technology is nothing more than applied scientific knowledge, applied information. For the specific problem of global climate change, we must develop clean alternative energy sources, more energy efficient technologies, better methods for capturing and storing carbon, and so on. Such technologies will reduce the marginal costs of reducing greenhouse gas emissions, shifting the demand curve for fossil fuel emissions to the left, as shown in figure 2. The quicker we can begin the shift, the less radical it needs to be.

For the specific dilemma of ensuring adequate provision of both food and ecosystem services, we need to develop agricultural systems that replace artificial or nonrenewable off-farm inputs (e.g., nitrogen, phosphorus, pesticides, and fossil fuels) and the mining of soil and water with their renewable but dwindling ecosystem service counterparts (e.g., nutrient cycling, erosion control, biological pest controls, water regulation, and renewable energy)

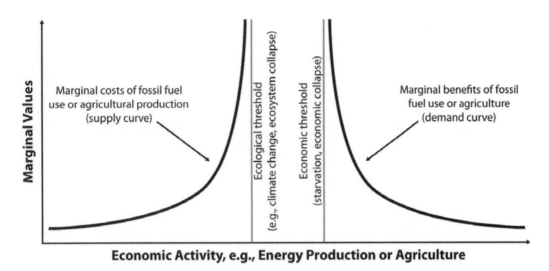

Figure 1. APPARENTLY UNSOLVABLE DILEMMAS

Under current technologies, both the marginal costs and marginal benefits of essential economic activities can become immeasurably high, with the possibility of no 'optimal' solution.

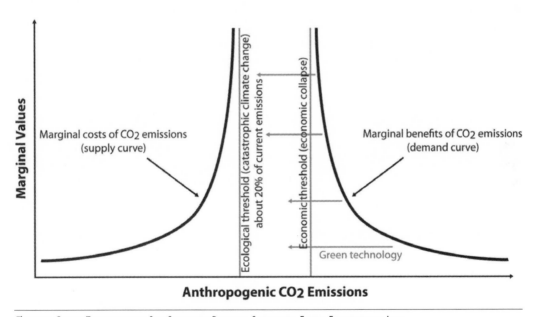

Figure 2. GREEN TECHNOLOGIES CAN SHIFT THE DEMAND CURVE FOR FOSSIL FUELS TO THE LEFT

while simultaneously increasing output (Farley et al., 2011). Agriculture practices must help mitigate climate change and adapt to its impacts. Agriculture must not only maintain the natural resource base, but also actively restore critical ecosystem services. To ensure food actually flows to those who need it most, agricultural systems should pay particular attention to the needs and aspirations of poor farmers in marginal environments. The design of green agricultural systems must be based on ecological principles while simultaneously accounting for social and economic capabilities. Such a system would reduce the marginal costs of agriculture, shifting the supply curve to the right: more land could be dedicated to such systems without threatening vital ecosystem services. Increasing food production per unit of agricultural land and restoring degraded lands with agroforestry systems that also produce food would paradoxically reduce the marginal benefits of agricultural land by reducing the threat of starvation posed by restoring farmland to more native-like ecosystems. The transdisciplinary field of agroecology, defined as the "application of ecological science to the study, design and management of sustainable agroecosystems" is built precisely on these principles to achieve these goals (Gliessman, 2007, p. 18). Figure 3 depicts this dynamic.

We do not believe that technological advance is sufficient to solve these critical dilemmas, but we do believe it is necessary. Information of course is the basic building block of all technology.

The goal of this chapter is to describe the challenges of producing and disseminating the technologies necessary to create a green economy. As an OECD report states, "If we want to make sure that the progress in living standards we have seen these past fifty years does not grind to a halt, we have to find new ways of producing and consuming things" (OECD, 2011, p. 3). We argue that this change is especially important with the production and "consumption" of information. Specific challenges include the promotion of the right type of research and development (R&D), the production of the desired technologies at the lowest possible cost, and maximization of their value once they exist, which for green technologies will require rapid and extensive dissemination. As we lay out these challenges, we will explain why markets are ill suited to overcome them. We then describe a variety of economic institutions that can overcome them and assess their viability. We conclude with suggestions for steps forward.

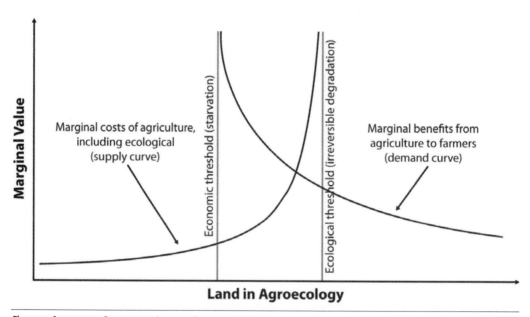

Figure 3. SUPPLY AND DEMAND OF LAND IN AGROECOLOGY

By increasing ecosystem services from farmland, agroecology can shift the marginal costs of farming to the right, and by increasing food output on farmlands and native-like ecosystems, it can shift the starvation threshold to the left.

PROMOTING THE RIGHT TYPE OF RESEARCH AND DEVELOPMENT

Our first challenge is to design economic institutions that promote the right type of technologies for a green economy. This task can be subdivided into a number of subchallenges.

To begin, appropriate technologies must protect and provide critical ecosystem services upon which we depend for survival. However, many of these ecosystem services, such as climate regulation, disturbance regulation, protection from ultraviolet radiations, and regulation of atmospheric gasses, are inherently nonexcludable resources, which means that it is impossible to prevent someone from using the resource if it exists. There is no direct market incentive to provide such technologies because the benefits they generate cannot be bought or sold. Other resources such as oceanic fisheries or waste absorption capacity of unregulated pollutants could be made excludable if we chose to, but until we choose to do so, there are greater incentives to develop technologies that overuse these resources than ones that protect them (Daly and Farley, 2010).

A related problem is that it is difficult and expensive to make information itself excludable. A profit-seeking firm is unlikely to shoulder the costs of developing a new technology if other firms can readily copy it at minimal cost. The traditional solution to this problem is to protect intellectual property rights via patents, but in today's information age, increasing accessibility to information makes this ever more difficult to achieve. Furthermore, the proliferation of intellectual property rights can actually deter the advance of knowledge by making it more difficult to build on the knowledge of others. This is particularly true for scientists seeking to develop technologies that provide public goods or target the poor, as these do not generate revenue to pay royalties on existing patents (Kubiszewski, Farley, and Costanza, 2010). From the perspective of building a green economy, resources spent protecting private property rights to information are simply wasted.

Recent surveys suggest that patents do indeed have a heavy influence on the direction of research. A survey by the American Association for the Advancement of Science (AAAS) found that 35 percent of academics in the biosciences reported difficulties in acquiring patented information necessary for their research; of those scientists, 50 percent had to change the focus of their research, and 28 percent had to abandon it all together (Hanson et al., 2005). Another survey found that the majority of scientists interviewed believed that intellectual property rights to research tools had a negative impact on research in their area (Lei, Juneja, and Wright, 2009). As universities seek ever more patents, they push professors to focus on the production of patentable, market goods. Given a finite supply of scientists, this pressure comes at the expense of producing technologies that provide the public good benefits needed to solve our problems.

Even apart from the costs of enforcing intellectual property rights, appropriate technologies can be very expensive to develop. Costs are often beyond the capacity of a single industry. Information in fact is an ideal example of a natural monopoly, with very high fixed costs of production and negligible marginal costs. For example, developing a safe, clean alternative to fossil fuels may cost hundreds of billions of dollars, while the cost of transmitting that information over the Internet to other potential users is essentially zero. The total cost of providing the information is independent of the number of people using the technology. The more people who use the technology, the lower the average total cost. In other words, the more people who use the knowledge, the lower the total cost per person, as seen in figure 4. Figure 4 also shows the market demand curve for some hypothetical green

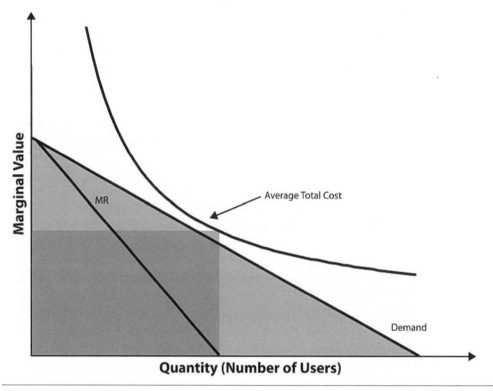

Figure 4. INFORMATION AS A NATURAL MONOPOLY

As depicted here, the costs of developing a natural monopoly always exceed the total revenue it can generate, even when economic surplus is positive.

technology along with the marginal revenue curve. More people will use the technology as the price declines, but marginal revenue falls to zero when the impact of a falling price overwhelms the impact of a growing number of consumers. Lowering prices to increase the number of users at this point also lowers total revenue, hence profits. Since the marginal cost is zero, the economic surplus is given by the area under the demand curve minus the cost of producing the technology, indicated by the shaded rectangle, which is unaffected by the number of consumers. Green technologies of course produce positive externalities or reduce negative externalities. The marginal social benefits of the technology are therefore much higher than the marginal private benefits depicted by the demand curve, but the goal of a private sector firm of course is to maximize profits, so it ignores social benefits. As drawn, there is no price at which the total revenue from the technology will exceed the total cost of producing it, even when the private economic surplus is positive. Competitive markets simply will not produce such technologies.

These problems no doubt contribute to a serious lack of research and development in technologies required for a green economy. For example, the energy sector is one of the most important for a green economy but is also one of the least innovative on the planet. Private sector investment in energy technology fell steadily from the 1980s before rebounding slightly in recent years and accounts for only .03 percent of sales in the United States (Coy, 2010). It invests only 6 percent as much in R&D as does the manufacturing sector (Avato and Coony, 2008).

Finally, technologies must also meet the needs of the poor. The one billion people currently suffering malnutrition are destitute by definition. The worst impacts of global climate change are likely to strike the poorest countries, which ironically are those who made the least contribution to the problem. Market demand is determined by preferences weighted by purchasing power. The purchasing power of the destitute is negligible, so they have no market demand, and market forces will not invest in technologies that target their needs. This is particularly true when scientists must pay royalties on technologies required by their research. For example, when scientists biogenetically modified rice to produce vitamin A, they found that they had infringed upon dozens of patents. While many of the companies holding the patents have agreed to allow poor farmers to eventually obtain the rice, the legal obstacles involved have increased total costs and slowed dissemination of the technology (Potrykus, 2010; Kowalski, 2002).

PRODUCING TECHNOLOGIES AT THE LOWEST POSSIBLE COST

The second challenge is to produce the required technologies at the lowest possible cost. The most important input into new technologies, into new information, is existing information. Information has the unique characteristic that it improves through use. As many people in the open source movement have pointed out, information is like grass that grows longer the more it is grazed. In economic terms, information is nonrival, meaning that use by one person does not leave less for others to use, or even antirival, meaning that use by one person leaves more for others by adding improvements. We need institutions that promote the sharing of information during the research process.

There is a widespread though often faith-based belief that markets are effective at minimizing costs of production, but for information this is unlikely to be the case. Markets require property rights, which in the case of information means patents and royalties, and these increase the cost of doing research in several different ways. First, as pointed out above, they force scientists to pay for access to existing information. For example, studies have found that each new medical technology infringes on an average of fifty existing patents (Heller and Eisenberg, 1998). Paying royalties on these patents can dramatically increase the cost of doing research and of using new technologies. It can also slow the development of knowledge (Paul, 2005; Runge and Defrancesco, 2006). Second, a huge amount of effort goes into creating patents. The U.S. Patent and Trademark Office alone receives 500,000 patent applications per year, which may run to hundreds of pages with hundreds of claims each. There is an existing backlog of 700,000 claims (Wyatt, 2011). Third, the legal costs of enforcing patents can also be quite high for both the patent owner and the court system. Over 1 percent of patents end up in litigation (Lanjouw and Lerner, 1998), with cost per case typically running to $2 million dollars or more (Tyler, 2004; Margiano, 2009). Fourth, patent trolling is the creation or purchase of patents by firms simply to challenge patents held by other firms. Challenged firms frequently settle out of court simply to avoid litigation costs (Magliocca, 2006). Fifth, many firms patent technologies they do not plan to use simply to keep others from using them, further slowing innovation (Turner, 1998).

Finally, the nature of information as a natural monopoly also increases the costs of producing technologies under a competitive market system. In a market economy, firms will compete to be the first to develop a new technology. Each will hire a separate team of scientists with separate laboratories. These teams are unlikely to share information with each other, even though information improves through use, and sharing would likely speed the rate of progress. The result is a duplication of high fixed costs. When one firm wins the race and earns a monopoly, the redundant research of the other firms becomes worthless.

MAXIMIZING THE VALUE OF EXISTING INFORMATION

Building a green economy requires the widest possible dissemination of green technologies. This is intuitively obvious but is also a clear result from economic theory, which tells us that economic surplus is maximized when marginal costs equal marginal benefits. Since the marginal cost of the additional use of information is zero, it should be used until the marginal benefit is also zero, which will only happen at a price of zero. If one views the protection of ecosystem services as a positive externality of green technologies, it might prove optimal to subsidize the use of such technologies, rather than restricting access through patents (Foxon, 2003).

As previously explained, patents create private property rights in information, allowing it to be bought and sold. The problem with this is that prices ration access—only those willing to pay the price are allowed to use the information.

The inefficiency of using prices to ration access to information is perhaps best illustrated through example. The Convention on Biological Diversity awards countries property rights to endemic biodiversity and the genetic information it contains. Historically, countries that find new strains of contagious diseases make them available to the World Health Organization, which allows anyone to develop vaccines or cures for that disease. Typically this means that the genetic information would be passed on to private sector corporations, which would compete to develop a vaccine. As discussed above, such competition is likely to increase the costs of developing the vaccine. Indonesia recently discovered a new strain of avian flu. In terms of allocating a successful vaccine, Indonesia realized that a private corporation would likely price the vaccine at a cost too high for most of the world's poor, including Indonesia's citizens. Indonesia therefore threatened to sell the virus to a single corporation, presumably with the requirement that any resulting vaccine be made available to Indonesia's citizens (McNeil, 2007). Rationing access to the virus would reduce the likelihood of discovering a vaccine, while rationing access to the vaccine would increase the likelihood of a pandemic (Farley and Costanza, 2010). Charging for information fails to maximize its value.

Returning to figure 4, imagine that technological breakthroughs have lowered the cost of developing an environmentally friendly technology, shifting average fixed costs down below the market demand curve, as shown in figure 5. The firm can now make a profit by creating, patenting, and selling the technology. The patent allows the firm to capture monopoly profits, so it will produce where marginal revenue is zero. Total revenue is depicted by the two rectangles. Total costs, which are constant for any level of use, are depicted by the darker rectangle, and profits by the lighter rectangle above it. The net market benefits to society are given by the private profits plus the triangle between the profits and the demand curve.

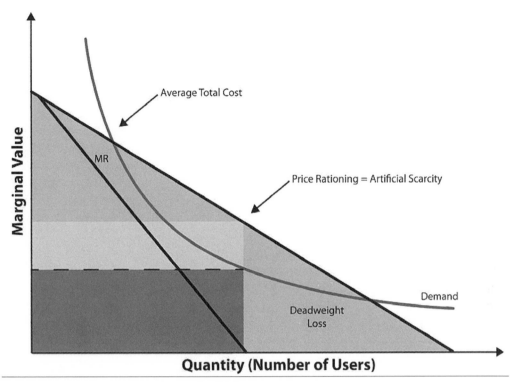

Figure 5. INFORMATION AS A PROFITABLE NATURAL MONOPOLY

Firms will produce less of the new technology than is socially desirable, especially if the technology generates positive externalities.

However, the green triangle labeled "deadweight loss" depicts the additional *net* market benefits to society if the technology were to be given away free of charge. This is the cost to society caused by patent pricing. Any positive price would cause some deadweight loss, but the lower the price, the less the loss. Of course, if the green technology generates positive externalities, then the value of these externalities is also reduced due to price rationing.

If the economic profit made from this technology are large enough, they might attract other firms to create a nearly identical product, sufficiently different that it doesn't infringe on the patent—frequently called a "me too" product (Bennani, 2011). However, this would require new investments in R&D simply to replicate an existing product, thus increasing fixed costs. The more firms that replicate the fixed costs, the greater the total cost to society. Competition under such circumstances can actually drive up the costs. Potentially, another firm will develop a better product, but the likelihood of this happening is far higher if new firms can improve on the existing product instead of producing a new one from scratch.

To maximize the value of existing information, it instead should be freely available to all firms, reflecting its marginal cost of zero. The firms would then compete to produce the new technology as cheaply as possible. Of course, someone must cover the real costs of producing new innovations, and innovators must be rewarded.

THE EFFICIENT PROVISION OF GREEN INFORMATION

The market provision of information confronts an irresolvable paradox. The efficient price of information is zero, but at that price, information will provide an inadequate supply of innovative technologies. Patents create an incentive for the market provision of information, but lead to price rationing and inefficiently low levels of consumption. Markets also fail to provide technologies that protect or restore public goods, and fail to meet the needs of the poor. We require alternative economic institutions based on cooperation, not competition. We quickly review two potential solutions: public sector provision and commons-based peer production.

PUBLIC SECTOR PROVISION

Given the public good characteristics of information, public sector provision seems an obvious solution. This is especially true for the information required for a green economy, for technologies that protect and restore public goods. Public provision is hardly a radical suggestion, as there is a long tradition of government-financed research and development in public goods. The U.S. land grant universities are just one example of organized public support for R&D in agriculture, with results freely disseminated as public goods, that dates back over 150 years (Tansey, 2002). Public sector investment in agricultural R&D averages rates of return on the order of 65 percent (Alston et al., 2000; World Bank, 2007). Investments in agroecology are potentially much higher, especially if one accounts for the environmental benefits generated (Pretty et al., 2005; De Schutter, 2010). In spite of the growing need for R&D that protects public goods, however, the share of public funding for research has declined dramatically in recent decades. In the United States, federal funding for R&D has fallen from well over 60 percent for most of the 1960s to well under 30 percent in recent years, with the private sector making up most of the difference. Federal funding continues to account for the bulk of basic research, however, and the bulk of funding for universities (National Science Foundation, 2010). However, since the Bayh-Dole Act facilitated the creation of patents on publicly funded research, the number of patents held by universities has skyrocketed (Sampat, 2006).

Given globally interconnected ecosystems, green technologies inevitably provide global public goods. Ideally, all countries should therefore jointly invest in the green R&D. Shared investments may be difficult to achieve initially, and one could easily envisage politicians in one country refusing to invest in open source green technologies because other countries would free-ride on their investments. However, the more widely used a green technology, the better off everyone becomes. As other countries use the technologies, they are likely to evolve and improve, benefiting the country that initially invested in their production. Free-riding is virtually impossible.

Unfortunately, it is not clear that governments are effectively allocating R&D resources toward solving society's most pressing problems. As in the private sector, government support of alternative energy R&D has fallen substantially since the 1980s. In the United States, the President's Council of Advisors on Science and Technology has recommended an increase in energy R&D funding from $6 billion to $16 billion, though an actual increase of that magnitude seems unlikely given the pressures to reduce the federal deficit (Johnson, 2010). Global climate chaos could have dramatic impacts on quality of life and life expectancy, while advances in health care can at best add a few years to our lives. Nonetheless, well over half of U.S. nondefense R&D is spent on health, while investments in energy and the environment are negligible (Knezo, 2005). Furthermore, the Bayh-Dole Act of 1980 allows private sector businesses to patent publicly funded research, with the potential for seriously restricting its dissemination.

COMMONS-BASED PEER PRODUCTION

Even prior to public sectors and patents, knowledge thrived. The most important advances in human knowledge such as language, culture, and mathematics, were large-scale "projects" created by the successful collaboration of groups of individuals "following a diverse cluster of motivational drives and social signals" (Benkler, 2002, p. 2). This is known as commons-based peer production. By its very nature, such research is freely available to all. Commons-based peer production tends to be most successful when research equipment is quite cheap (e.g., computers), problems can be broken down into small modules of different sizes, and integration of the modules is relatively easy. The modular nature allows contributors to determine their own level of contribution, and self-select for the tasks at which they excel (Benkler, 2002).

Despite economists' assumptions that humans are perfectly self-interested, we know empirically that individuals freely contribute enormous amounts of time to collaboratively solving problems and generating new technologies. Benkler (2004) argues that "instead of direct payment, commons-based production relies on indirect rewards: both extrinsic, enhancing reputation and developing human capital and social networks; and intrinsic, satisfying psychological needs, pleasure, and a sense of social belonging. Instead of exclusive property and contract, peer production uses legal devices like the General Public License (GPL), social norms, and technological constraints on 'antisocial' behavior" (p. 1110). Within this peer production community, monetary returns may actually have negative connotations and can potentially decrease cooperation (Benkler, 2002). Although some computer programmers report being paid for their contributions (Todd, 2007), there is actually evidence from behavioral economics and psychology that monetary incentives can make people more selfish (Vohs, Mead, and Goode, 2006; Vohs, Mead, and Goode, 2008), and "crowd out' the intrinsic motivations to cooperate that drive much of this research (Frey, 1997; Frey and Jegen, 2001). It thus appears that most contributors participate in order to be part of a gift economy, for the status conferred, or to make the world a better place. However, it does not really matter what the particular motivation is for an individual to participate—different individuals can participate for different reasons (Boyle, 2003).

Throughout history, technological advances in stone knapping, agriculture, architecture, government, and others involved a similar approach, as did language, culture, and music. The advantage of this approach is that it does not require any changes in intellectual property rights. The problem is that some of the most important societal problems we currently face, such as alternative energy technologies, may require substantial and expensive investments in basic science, additional investments to apply the research, and a significant learning curve to achieve economies of scale. Public sector investments may be more suitable in this case.

EFFICIENT DISSEMINATION: OPEN ACCESS AND OPEN SOURCE

Once information has been produced, there are different ways to make it accessible to all. The two dominant approaches are known as open source and open access.

Open access refers to information that is freely available for all, but which cannot be modified. In the scientific realm, most open access publications and the research behind them are generated by academics and paid for with salaries or grants, which may also cover the costs of publication. Publications typically contribute to promotions and higher salaries, but nonmonetary compensation such as status and prestige provide considerable incentive. There is also a strong element of reciprocation, or "gift economies," as scientists know that they will also benefit from the contributions of others. Such payments allow researchers to devote full time to a specific problem. However, many academics jealously guard the data underlying their research at least until publication, which reduces the value of the data to society. Also, at the same time that open access publications are becoming more common, so too are patents on research results.

Open source refers to information that is freely available to all and can be modified by anyone. Open source information is generally produced via commons-based peer production. It can be used as is or modified, as long as it is properly cited. More importantly, it is typically protected by a GPL or copyleft. Though anyone can use and alter the work, all subsequent work is protected by the same license and can never by patented or placed under conventional copyright (Mustonen, 2003).

One promising alternative for production and dissemination is a hybrid of the open source and open access approaches. One example is the Alzheimer's Disease Neuroimaging Initiative (ADNI), in which a large consortium of researchers looking for biomarkers for Alzheimer's shares all their data and makes findings public immediately. No one owns the data and no one submits patent applications. Scientists on the project are paid for their research with salaries and grants, primarily from universities or the public sector, and also gain status and other nonmonetary benefits. Participants have referred to the results as "unbelievable" and "overwhelming" (Kolata, 2010). There are other open source initiatives in the health sciences focused on diseases of the poor, which provide little opportunity for profit in any case (Maurer et al., 2004; Hale, Woo, and Lipton, 2005). The advantage of this hybrid approach is that it allows scientists to work full time on problems that serve the public good.

THE NEED FOR GLOBAL COOPERATION

In ecosystems, everything is connected to everything else (Commoner, 1971). This means that no single nation can develop a green economy; it must be a collaborative global effort. However, the central goal of a green economy is sustainability; we need to make sure that future generations are able to meet their basic needs. But people unable to meet their basic needs today will certainly not sacrifice for future generations. They will deplete as many resources and spew as much waste as required to fill their own bellies. A green economy is virtually impossible in the presence of misery and poverty.

The International Monetary Fund classifies 150 countries as "emerging and developing" (IMF, 2011). Figure 6 depicts the world's countries in proportion to their net forest loss between 1990 and 2000, which shows that many of the "developing" nations are depleting their renewable resource base faster than it can regenerate. Developing nations are frequent exploiters of raw materials in general, and also of commodities produced by the most heavily polluting industries (Gernot, 2010). By the standards of a green economy, these countries are becoming poorer.

To promote poverty reduction, the OECD recommends we focus on "introducing efficient technologies that can reduce costs and increase productivity, while easing environmental pressure" and "alleviating poor health associated with environmental degradation" (2011, p. 1). We heartily concur. However, figure 7 depicts the world's countries in proportion to the royalties and license fees they receive. It is almost the inverse of the map in figure 6. Rather than providing these countries with the necessary technologies, the OECD countries are enriching themselves by rationing access to technology via the price mechanism.

Non-ozone-depleting compounds offer a clear example of the perversity of this approach. Few people realize that the Montreal Protocol allows less-developed nations to use hydrochlorofluorocarbons (HCFCs) as a substitute for chlorofluorocarbons (CFCs). Though HCFCs have less impact on the ozone than CFCs, emissions have been doubling every few years, worsening ozone depletion (Bradsher, 2007). The Antarctic ozone hole broke records in 2006, and an ozone hole appeared in the arctic in 2011 (Barringer, 2011). Non-ozone-depleting substitutes exist, but they are patented, increasing their costs and decreasing their use. Failure to take a cooperative approach to creating and distributing green technologies could prove suicidal.

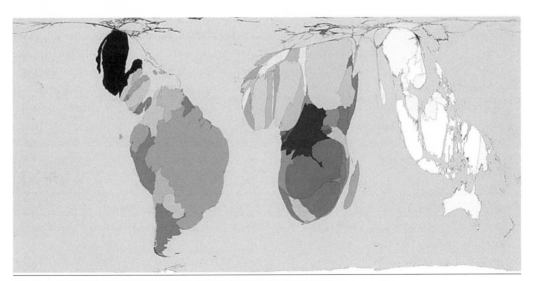

Figure 6. Countries in Proportion to Their Net Forest Loss, 1990–2000
Source: Worldmapper: The World as You've Never Seen It Before. http://www.worldmapper.org/. © Copyright SASI Group (University of Sheffield)

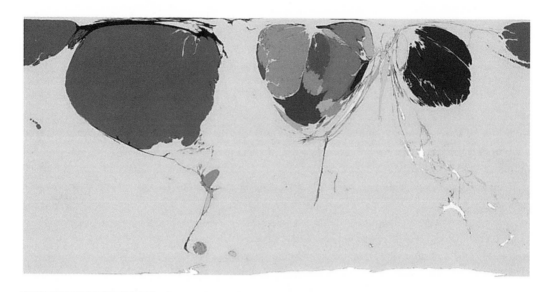

Figure 7. Countries in Proportion to Royalties and License Fees Received
Source: Worldmapper: The World as You've Never Seen It Before. HTTP://WWW.WORLDMAPPER.ORG/. © Copyright SASI Group (University of Sheffield)

FUNDING GREEN TECHNOLOGY

An important question so far left unanswered is the source of financing for investments in green technology. The obvious answer is to capture revenue from antigreen activities, such as waste emissions and resource extraction. Green taxes or cap-and-auction schemes can be used to charge for resource extraction and waste emissions, sending a price signal that reduces resource depletion and pollution while creating a revenue stream for investment in green technologies. As the OECD states, "creating a global architecture that is conducive to green growth will require enhanced international co-operation. Strengthening arrangements for managing global public goods, especially biodiversity and climate, hold the key to addressing co-ordination and incentive problems" (OECD, 2011, p. 13). We will ultimately require a broad suite of policy changes to complement green technologies. The wealthy countries have done the most to cause the problems we face and have a moral obligation to start the ball rolling.

REFERENCES

Alston, J. M., M. C. Marra, P. G. Pardey, and T. J. Wyatt. 2000. "Research Returns Redux: A Meta-analysis of the Returns to Agricultural R&D." *Australian Journal of Agricultural and Resource Economics* 44(2): 185–215.

Avato, P., and J. Coony. 2008. *Accelerating Clean Energy Technology Research, Development, and Deployment.* Washington, DC: World Bank.

Barringer, F. 2011. "A Significant Ozone Hole Is Reported over the Arctic." *New York Times*, October 3, 2011.

Benkler, Y. 2002. "Coase's Penguin, or, Linux and the Nature of the Firm." *Yale Law Journal* 4(3): 369–446.

Benkler, Y. 2004. "Commons-Based Strategies and the Problems of Patents." *Science* 305(5687): 1110–11.

Bennani, Y. 2011. "Drug Discovery in the Next Decade: Innovation Needed ASAP." *Drug Discovery Today* 16(17–18): 779–92.

Boyle, J. 2003. "The Second Enclosure Movement and the Construction of the Public Domain." *Law and Contemporary Problems* 66: 33–74.

Bradsher, K. 2007. "The Price of Keeping Cool in Asia; Use of Air-Conditioning Refrigerant Is Widening the Hole in the Ozone Layer." *New York Times*, February 23, 2007.

Brooks, T. M., S. L. Pimm et al. 1999. "Time Lag between Deforestation and Bird Extinction in Tropical Forest Fragments." *Conservation Biology* 13(5): 1140–50.

Commoner, B. 1971. *The Closing Circle: Nature, Man, and Technology*. New York: Knopf.

Coy, P. 2010. "The Other U.S. Energy Crisis: Lack of R&D: R&D Neglect Is Holding Back Innovative Energy Technologies." *Bloomberg Business Week*, June 17, 2010.

Daly, H., ed. 1973. *Toward a Steady-State Economy*. San Francisco: W. H. Freeman.

Daly, H. 1977. *Steady-State Economics: The Political Economy of Bio-physical Equilibrium and Moral Growth*. San Francisco: W. H. Freeman.

Daly, H., and J. Farley. 2010. *Ecological Economics: Principles and Applications*. 2nd edition. Washington, DC: Island Press.

De Schutter, O. 2010. Report submitted by the Special Rapporteur on the right to food. New York: United Nations Human Right Council.

Farley, J., and R. Costanza. 2010. "Payments for Ecosystem Services: From Local to Global." *Ecological Economics* 69(11): 2060–68.

Farley, J., A. Schmitt Filho, J. Alvez, and N. R. de Freitas Jr. 2011. "How Valuing Nature Can Transform Agriculture." *Solutions* 2(6): 64–73.

Flipo, F., and F. Schneider, eds. 2008. *Proceedings of the First International Conference on Economic Degrowth for Ecological Sustainability and Social Equity*, Paris, April 18–19. http://events.it-sudparis.eu/degrowthconference/en/.

Foxon, T. J. 2003. *Inducing Innovation for a Low-Carbon Future: Drivers, Barriers and Policies*. London: Carbon Trust.

Frey, B. S. 1997. "On the Relationship between Intrinsic and Extrinsic Work Motivation." *International Journal of Industrial Organization* 15(4): 427–39.

Frey, B. S., and R. Jegen. 2001. "Motivation Crowding Theory." *Journal of Economic Surveys* 15(5): 589–611.

Gernot, W. 2010. "Energy Content of World Trade." *Energy Policy* 38(12): 7710–21.

Gliessman, S. R. 2007. *Agroecology: The Ecology of Sustainable Food Systems*. Boca Raton, FL: CRC Press.

Hale, V. G., K. Woo, and H. L. Lipton. 2005. "Oxymoron No More: The Potential Of Nonprofit Drug Companies to Deliver on the Promise of Medicines for the Developing World." *Health Affairs* 24(4): 1057–63.

Hanson, S., A. Brewster et al. 2005. *Intellectual Property in the AAAS Scientific Community: A Descriptive Analysis of the Results of a Pilot Survey on the Effects of Patenting on Science*. Washington, DC.: Directorate for Science and Policy Programs, AAAS.

Heller, M. C., and G. A. Keoleian. 2000. *Life Cycle-Based Sustainability Indicators for Assessment of the U.S. Food System*. Ann Arbor, MI: Center for Sustainable Systems.

Heller, M. and R. Eisenberg. 1998. "Can Patents Deter Innovation? The Anticommons in Biomedical Research." *Science* 280: 698–701.

IMF (International Monetary Fund). 2011. *World Economic Outlook (WEO): Slowing Growth, Rising Risks*. Washington, DC: International Monetary Fund.

IPCC (Intergovernmental Panel on Climate Change). 2007. *Climate Change 2007: Synthesis Report. Summary for Policymakers*. Cambridge: Cambridge University Press.

Jackson, T. 2009. *Prosperity without Growth? The Transition to a Sustainable Economy*. Sterling, VA: Earthscan.

Johnson, J. W. 2010. "Panel Urges Jump In Energy R&D." *Government and Policy Concentrates* 88(48): 32.

Knezo, G. J. 2005. *Federal Research and Development: Budgeting and Priority-Setting Issues, 109th Congress*. Congressional Research Service. Washington, DC: Library of Congress.

Kolata, G. 2010. "Sharing of Data Leads to Progress on Alzheimer's." *New York Times*, August 12, 2010.

Kowalski, S. P. 2002. "Golden Rice: A Case Study in Intellectual Property Management and International Capacity Building." Pierce Law Faculty Scholarship Series, Paper 7. http://lsr.nellco.org/piercelaw_facseries/7.

Kubiszewski, I., J. Farley, and R. Costanza. 2010. "The Production and Allocation of Information as a Good That Is Enhanced with Increased Use." *Ecological Economics* 69(6): 1344–54.

Lanjouw, J., and J. Lerner. 1998. "The Enforcement of Intellectual Property Rights: A Survey of the Empirical Literature." *Annales d'Economie et de Statistique* 49(50): 223–46.

Lei, Z., R. Juneja, and B. D. Wright. 2009. "Patents versus Patenting: Implications of Intellectual Property Protection for Biological Research." *Nature Biotechnology* 27(1): 36–40.

Magliocca, G. N. 2006. "Blackberries and Barnyards: Patent Trolls and the Perils of Innovation." *Notre Dame Law Review* 82:1809–35.

Margiano, R. 2009. "Cost and Duration of Patent Litigation." Managing Intellectual Property, February 1, 2009. http://www.managingip.com/.

Martinez Alier, J. 2011. "Socially Sustainable Economic Degrowth," Chapter 11 in *Herman Daly Festschrift* (e-book), Encyclopedia of Earth, ed. Cutler J. Cleveland. http://www.eoearth.org/article/Herman_Daly_Festschrift_%28e-book%29.

Maurer, S. M., A. Rai et al. 2004. "Finding Cures for Tropical Diseases: Is Open Source an Answer?" *PLoS Med* 1(3): e56.

McNeil, D. G., Jr. 2007. "Indonesia May Sell, Not Give, Bird Flu Virus to Scientists." *New York Times*, February 7, 2007.

Metzger, J. P., A. C. Martensen, M. Dixoa, L. C. Bernaccib, M. C. Ribeiroa, A. M. G. Teixeiraa, and R. Pardinic. 2009. "Time-Lag in Biological Responses to Landscape Changes in a Highly Dynamic Atlantic Forest Region." *Biological Conservation* 142(6): 1166–77.

Millennium Ecosystem Assessment. 2005. *Ecosystems and Human Well-Being: Synthesis*. Washington, DC: Island Press.

Ministério do Meio Ambiente. 2011. *Relatório de Inspeçã:o Área atingida pela tragédia das chuvas: Região Serrana do Rio de Janeiro: Áreas de Preservação Permanente e Unidades de Conservação & Áreas de Risco: O que uma coisa tem a ver com a outra? S. d. B. e. Florestas*. Brasília, DF: Ministério do Meio Ambiente.

Mustonen, M. 2003. "Copyleft: The Economics of Linux and Other Open Source Software." *Information Economics and Policy* 15(1): 99–121.

National Science Foundation. 2010. "National Patterns of R&D Resources: 2008 Data Update Detailed Statistical Tables." NSF 10-314, March.

OECD (Organisation for Economic Co-operation and Development). 2011. *Towards Green Growth.* Paris: OECD.

Paul, A. D. 2005. "Can 'Open Science' Be Protected from the Evolving Regime of IPR Protections?" *Journal of Institutional and Theoretical Economics* 160(1): 9–34.

Pimentel, D., and M. Pimentel. 2008. *Food, Energy, and Society.* Boca Raton, FL: CRC Press.

Potrykus, I. 2010. "The Private Sector's Role in Public Sector Genetically Engineered Crop Projects." *New Biotechnology* 27(5): 578–81.

Pretty, J. N., A. D. Noble, D. Bossio, J. Dixon, R. E. Hine, F. W. T. Penning de Vries, and J. I. L. Morison. 2005. "Resource-Conserving Agriculture Increases Yields in Developing Countries." *Environmental Science & Technology* 40(4): 1114–19.

Rijnhout, L., and T. Schauer, eds. 2009. *Socially Sustainable Economic Degrowth.* Proceedings of a workshop in the European Parliament on April 16, 2009, upon invitation by Bart Staes MEP and The Greens / European Free Alliance. http://www.clubofrome.at/2009/degrowth/proceedings.html.

Rockström, J., W. Steffen et al. 2009. "A Safe Operating Space for Humanity." *Nature* 461(7263): 472–75.

Runge, C. F., and E. Defrancesco. 2006. "Exclusion, Inclusion, and Enclosure: Historical Commons and Modern Intellectual Property." *World Development* 34(10): 1713–27.

Sampat, B. N. 2006. "Patenting and U.S. Academic Research in the 20th Century: The World before and after Bayh-Dole." *Research Policy* 35(6): 772–89.

Tansey, G. 2002. "Patenting Our Food Future: Intellectual Property Rights and the Global Food System." *Social Policy & Administration* 36(6): 575–92.

Todd, M. H. 2007. "Open Access and Open Source in Chemistry." *Chemistry Central Journal* 1(3): 1–4.

Turner, J. S. 1998. "The Nonmanufacturing Patent Owner: Toward a Theory of Efficient Infringement." *California Law Review* 86(1): 179–210.

Tyler, C. 2004. "Patent Pirates Search for Texas Treasure." *Texas Lawyer*, September 20.

Victor, P. 2008. *Managing without Growth: Slower by Design, Not Disaster.* Cheltenham: Edward Elgar.

Vohs, K. D., N. L. Mead, and M. R. Goode. 2006. "The Psychological Consequences of Money." *Science* 314(5802): 1154–56.

Vohs, K. D., N. L. Mead, and M. R. Goode. 2008. "Merely Activating the Concept of Money Changes Personal and Interpersonal Behavior." *Current Directions in Psychological Science* 17(3): 208–12.

World Bank. 2007. *World Development Report 2008: Agriculture for Development.* Washington DC: World Bank.

Wyatt, E. 2011. "Fighting Backlog in Patents, Senate Approves Overhaul." *New York Times*, September 9, B4.

The Evolution of Ego'n'Empathy

Progress in Forming the Centerpiece
for Ecological Economic Theory

WILLIAM M. HAYES AND GARY D. LYNNE

THIS CHAPTER EXPLORES THE EVOLUTION OF HAYES AND LYNNE'S (2004) Ego'n'Empathy(EnE) hypothesis working to move beyond neoclassical economics (NCE) and nudge toward a centerpiece for ecological economics (EE). Results are encouraging, transdisciplinary support is good, new directions are considered, and there is new and common ground for EE and NCE. Empathy is in that ground, a key force in the adoption of conservation technologies, choices in recycling, and overall better potential for achieving a sustainable way of life that recognizes the thermodynamic realities that undergird EE. It is the key force in tempering-shifting the pivotal principle in mainstream economics, self-interest (ego) to include other interests (empathy). Our (2004, p. 299) claim about NCE still stands and evolves stronger: "If empirical testing results in failure to reject the null hypothesis of 'no empathic, other-interest at work' and 'no lack of substitution possibilities,' we are back to the standard neoclassical economic model." There is no evidence to go back, and substantive evidence to support going forward, together on new and shared grounds. A grand case in point is the recent 2008 financial crisis and near economic collapse: Only through bringing empathy to the fore can we hope to move to better policy development and practice globally. Further, we bring empirical tests and scientific content to Rifkin's (2009) contention that global consciousness about empathy is the hope for a long-term, sustainable solution to global problems, especially as related to food, fiber, energy, and climate change.

INTRODUCTION

The Ego'n'Empathy (EnE)hypothesis (Hayes and Lynne, 2004), as a theoretical framework, includes both the philosophical and scientific meanings of "hypothesis."[1] The science formulates a proposition made on the basis of limited evidence as a starting point for undertaking further scientific investigation. The philosophy formulates the hypothesis as a supposition made as a basis for reasoning, without any assumption that it is positively truth. Together, Hayes and Lynne formed the hypothesis and a theoretical framework was put forward in "Towards a Centerpiece for Ecological Economics" (2004). We see ourselves as providing a paradigm shift back to the economics implied in Adam Smith's *Inquiry* (1776)as a "real" spectator and investigative undertaker of the scientist; but, with his *Theory* (1759) as an "ideal" spectator and overseer of the philosopher.

That the hypothesis and theory evolve stronger with science and philosophy is developed further, especially relative to new and shared grounds with EE and NCE. We envision a shared ground for a new mainstream economics in the future. Thus, our claim about neoclassical economics (NCE) still stands: "If empirical testing results in failure to reject the null hypothesis of 'no empathic, other-interest at work' and 'no lack of substitution possibilities,' we are back to the standard neoclassical economic model (Hayes and Lynne, 2004, p. 299)." There's no evidence to go back, and substantive evidence to support going forward, together on new and shared grounds.

When it was published in 2004, the main hypothesis was claimed as a movement toward, rather than asserted as the, centerpiece for EE. This implied we preferred not to be seen as overbearing and wanted to be more deferential. We also felt a dialog was needed, between the different disciplines involved in EE, about what is or should be the centerpiece or pivotal principle(s) of EE. In nudging the EnE hypothesis and theory toward the center, we hope the time is now even more right for a healthy discussion, especially when economic theory, in the mainstream, is appearing increasingly irrelevant.

We have been disappointed that the paper has not stirred more conversation in the literature regarding a pivotal principle to develop a centerpiece for ecological economics, with its fundamental focus on achieving sustainability. This pivotal principle points to empathy as the key to achieving sustainability. Yet our proposal has had some notable attention, including Konchak and Pascual (2006, p. 11), who see the hypothesis as a "potentially ground-breaking solution . . . a new basis for social theory . . . a workable theoretical framework . . . a new paradigm for environmental policymaking." Sneddon, Howarth, and Norgaard (2006) note how their paper works to "complement and extend discussions within ecological economics" as stirred in the 2004 and related papers of that era. Still others have not only used but empirically tested the dual-interest framework, including Chouinard and coauthors (2008) and Bishop, Shumway, and Wandschneider (2010). Both highlight how shared interests work to temper self-interest, with self-sacrifice quite common, although they see the substantive heterogeneity in individual paths. Larson (2010) notes how the framework recognizes conflict in divergent attitudes, which arise between the egoistic and empathetic interests. Importantly, these works implicitly if not explicitly support our contention that empathy will likely play a perhaps superordinate role and needs to be made explicit in a new economic theory built in the interstice of NCE and EE theory.

Rifkin (2009) has made it a point to highlight, in most recent developments relating to empathy, the substantive, indeed essential, role to be played by empathy especially in solving energy and related climate change problems. It is only through expressions of empathy that will we be able to resolve the entropy (ego)-empathy dialectic (Rifkin, 2009, esp. p. 26), moving to an "empathic civilization" on the eco-path of sustainability. De Waal (2009, p. ix) in *The Age of Empathy* sets the stage for his behavioral science-based story of empathy tempering behavior by proclaiming, "Greed is out, empathy is in."

We first explore the current state of our empathy theory. Second, we bring this frame to life in brief applications, moving away from greed as the main driver. We distinguish between the philosophy underlying the hypothesis of EnE as a reasonable ideal to work toward and the science supporting the hypothesis as a rationalized reality with empirical testing. We briefly address the role of greed and lack of empathy leading to the 2008 financial crisis and near economic meltdown, and the most basic of the economic processes essential to achieving sustainability, that of a sustainable food and fiber system.

THE MAINFRAME: IDEAL TYPE FRAMEWORK AND DUAL-INTEREST FRAMEWORK

We have oftentimes been in awe of the power of simple diagrams in economics, like the familiar circular flow diagram in macroeconomics and the Marshallian demand and supply curves in microeconomics. They are simple structures that fit with a discernment to give an Aha! Relative to the hypothesis and theory we remain hopeful our diagrams will also stir a substantive Aha! Personally, we've been amazed at how the philosophy and (especially behavioral) science have evolved since the 2004 paper. While the philosophy has generally rested with the hypothesis, the science has gone on to develop it with hard, robust empirical tests that shore up the philosophical propositions.

Type Framing for Ego'n'Empathy: Suppositions and Headway in Ideality and Reality

Two frames are used for the EnE hypothesis and theory relative to a centerpiece for ecological and green economies. In figure 1, we illustrate the philosophical framework that is part of the overall mainframe in partnership with the scientific dual-interest framework. In figure 2, we illustrate the frame that was used for integrated resource management moving toward sustainable development in the Lakelse Watershed (Hayes, 1992a, 73). Learning with the ideal frame and the metaeconomic approach has led the science to work on parts and prove a real path toward the ideal: We realize that the ideal can only be approached, not fully realized. The vision began with intuitive insight, though we now have reason to believe that EnE science is rationally possible and provable. We offer a useful guide for a worldwide perception, for seeing more than the sum of the parts—parts cannot be fully understood without reference to the whole.

In contrast to the ideal frame, learning a particular part with a real frame leads the participant to work on parts along a path toward a positive reality that has the potential to be fully realized. Take, as an ecological example, the Social element of Nature defined by the boundaries of a whole watershed, classified as Fabricated, Natural, or a Domesticated ecosystems. With this classification, the important dimensions in each of the three ecosystems with energy, throughput, material cycles, biodiversity, and more are measurable with ecosystem science (as in Odum, 1989).

Further, notice in figure 2 how the categories correspond as complementary opposites between Nature and Culture: Natural ecosystem to Aboriginal culture; Fabricated ecosystem to Urban culture; Domesticated ecosystem to Agrarian culture. This outlines a unique social anthropology or ways of life, with people culturally embedded and part of each ecosystem. As such it's a way of classifying and guiding those involved, like the metaeconomic approach that also sees the embeddedness within green economies.

The social element frame was also used in action research in a multicultural setting "evenly balanced between aboriginal, rural and urban cultures" as an educational program where each

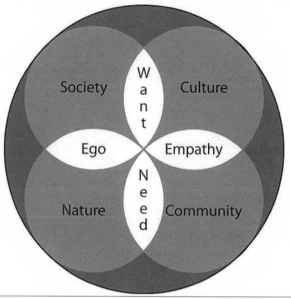

Figure 1. VISION OF THE SOCIAL SPHERES

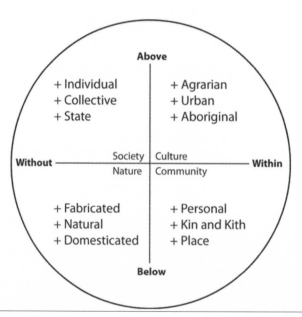

Figure 2. SOCIAL ELEMENTS AND VALUE PARAMETERS

of the cultures gained a real appreciation of each other's culture (Hayes, 1996). Also there was increased understanding in the ways of living in providing good, services and understanding natural capital in natural and domesticated ecosystems. This action research was extended to England and furthered in education and developed in psychology (Beattie, 2005).

The vision of the social spheres is a framework for heuristic holism, proven good for science to develop a real path; it is also a philosophical hypothesis whose theoretical development as a normative social philosophy constitutes a comprehensive worldview that has proven suitable to encompass various learning themes, values, emotions, and ethics with a common vision to work toward. The epistemology can be summed up in a German word: *Weltanschauung* or, in more words, a wide-world perception with reference to a framework of ideas and beliefs practically covering a lot of ground in education, psychology, ecology, and economics—which helps in making some headway as wide-world perception for ever more people.

There is also another feature about the philosophy needed for understanding the mainframe and difference between the science and the philosophy. This is especially so in that Lynne's science is closely connected but not the same as Hayes's philosophy.

Hayes's philosophy worked originally with "as if" heuristic fictions using the root metaphor method (Pepper, 1942) about EnE in a fable (see http://agecon-cpanel.unl.edu/lynne/socialcapital/fableegonempathy.pdf) that, to this day, remains rough and a work in progress. It was used as an Internet reference for peer reviewers of Hayes and Lynne (2004). The fable was supposed simply to get the reviewers in the ballpark to see the problem and solution as we saw it in fiction. Curiously the fable has since been around the Internet a bit; and, relevant to a main topic here, was accepted as the best answer to questions on Answerbag: "Is there a middle ground between selfish and selfless? If there is, would that be a worthy goal for all of us to reach? The quote from the Fable of Ego'n'Empathy was given as the answer:

> When he brought Ego and Empathy together it was love at first sight. The two horses happily lived and worked well in tandem alternatively taking lead roles. Ego was up front when working objectively in the outer world for the bilateral symmetric shaping of reality. Empathy led subjectively "within": what one seer suggested was the radial symmetric shaping of actuality. And, side-by-side, they discovered that an emergent principle came into play: a symbiotic level of activity like two people working together on common purpose indeed do far more than two people working apart.[2]

Now, let us unpack this relative to Ego'n'Empathy moving three ways: two down-to-earth and one up in the air. The personification is changed from divine horses in a fictional place to humans in an economic household, which exemplify the two down-to-earth movements. This is relevant to the field of economics, as it provides some light into the black boxes of households and firms in microeconomics and macroeconomics (like the famous circular flow chart in Econ 101 that depicts perpetual motion, which cannot be sustained) to give economists and other social scientists an insight as to how humans (and divine horses) work optimally and normatively with healthy egos and good empathies on sustainable paths.

Objectively, Ego leads and Empathy supports, as sometimes a man leads in constructing a house in nature and society (a firm is societal), while his mate supports him. The second movement . . . more subjective, less objective . . . has Empathy leading and Ego following as a woman or man or friend leads in creating a home in community and culture while the mate is supportive. Lynne's empirical science and proof has been about the objective side of the hypothesis: Lynne has been measuring the ego drive by a man or woman constructing a house and the mate oriented more to empathy, tempering that construction. Next is for the science to be about the more subjective side, where empathy leads and ego follows.

On leaving down-to-earth matters, let us fly up in the air to mind and gain understanding of the third movement of Ego'n'Empathy that the philosophy hypothesizes. We do this by going back to the personification of Ego and Empathy as the two heavenly horses, as stated in the conclusion to the Fable of Ego'n'Empathy: "But the greatest satisfaction was when the pair of Pegasus, side by side, had free rein gaining the freedom and capacity to fly to the higher plane where everyone could impartially observe Pangaia below."

What the philosophy is metaphorically saying is about a higher mind having two consciousnesses that are interconnected. There are two ways of awareness, with a superego consciousness and a superempathy consciousness that ride together on a "higher plane." The discussion between Hayes and Lynne continues and evolves about this "higher plane." Can the science get with rationality where the philosophy is in ideality? Perhaps: Lynne now models "the higher plane" in what is called "meta-interest," as explained below. Lynne can now rationalize the more objective side (like constructing a house) with the metaeconomic approach and moves onto rationally proving the more subjective side (like creating a home) with the final aim to find a rational basis for the "higher plane" of Hayes's philosophy about mind.

Dual-Interest Framing for the Metaeconomics Approach

The Marshallian diagrams of demand and supply curves are parsimonious and very powerful. The foundation that was built under those propositions is represented in utility theory that undergirds the demand construct and in production/cost theory that undergirds the supply construct. Utility theory came to be based in the indifference curve of the household, while production theory was based in the isoquant of the firm. Econ 101 starts with these constructs, such as depicted in the array of iso-curves around path 0G in figure 3. The self-interest is reflected along a path 0G, the egoistic-hedonistic path to maximum profit (max P) in isoquant space, which produces the maximum income used in moving on an egoistic-hedonistic, utility-seeking path 0G through indifference space to maximum utility (max U). These autonomous, independent, separable entities seek their single interest, their self-interest, on this path 0G. Metaecon 101, in contrast, starts with the recognition that households and firms are inextricably intertwined with others, not only within households and firms, but also these households are embedded within communities and firms within industries, within society influenced by culture; and, in turn both within physical and natural ecosystems of this spaceship Earth. Econ 101 extracts community from economy and serves to undermine it (see Marglin, 2008); Metaecon 101 puts community back, better serving to sustain it along with a green economy. Metaeconomics was inspired by the work of the first economist to be awarded the Nobel Prize, Ragnar Frisch, who saw this interdependency. Frisch (1965) posits that interdependency and the resultant joint, multiple production is best characterized, in a simple diagram, by drawing two sets of isoquants in the same space: We agree, as argued in Lynne (1988), that a far superior way to represent the real production embedded in the ecosystem of spaceship Earth would be to recognize the always attendant joint products and joint costs. Stimulated by Frisch's overlapping isoquants, we introduced the same construct into the utility structure, first offered in Lynne (1995), and elaborated in Lynne (1999).

Bottom line: Econ 101 posits a single self-interest as the own-interest. In contrast, Metaecon 101 posits a joint self-interest and other-interest, which together form the internalized own-interest. Further, this leads to the notion of a meta-interest that could easily be called the "Hayes higher plane" depicted in the I_S curves of figure 4. This higher plane works to resolve the self- and other-interest in the best overall own-interest on path 0G.

Special and distinguishing features of dual-interest theory and the metaeconomics ("meta" meaning "transcending" and "going beyond") approach include

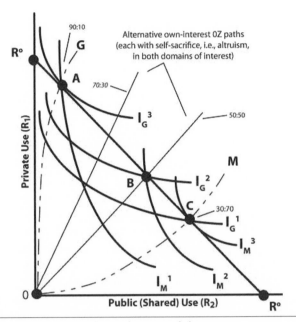

Figure 3. Joint Self-Interest (I_G) and Other (Shared)-Interest (I_M) Indifference Curves for the Allocation of a Resource R between Self (R_1) and Sharing Jointly with Others (R_2)

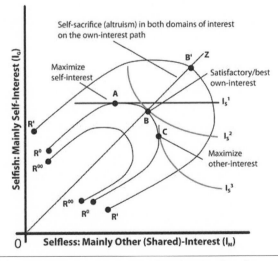

Figure 4. Synthesis, Synergy, and Self-Sacrifice on the Best Own-Interest Path Determined by the Meta-interest I_S^2

- Absolute jointness, nonseparability of the interests: Every choice, every decision results in two distinct outcomes at the intersection of a self-interest (I_G) and an other-interest (I_M) isocurve. So one cannot pursue one interest exclusively of the other, except on the vertical (greed) and horizontal (selfless) axes.
- The jointness depicted in figure 3 gives a unique mapping of an interests possibilities frontier in the meta-interests space of figure 4. The simple analytics of metaeconomics points to moving along a constraint R^oR^o in figure 3 to plot a possibilities frontier R^oR^o in figure 4. Notice how the interests are complementary in the regions R^oA and CR^o while also complementary in the technical sense (see Lynne, 2006a, 2006b) as the interest-possibility frontiers expand ever more rapidly apart for equal increments in resources. Even Scrooge gains something in the way of self-interest by being just a bit more empathetic-sympathetic at point A rather than completely selfish at the intersection of R^oR^o at the vertical axis, the "greed axis." Mother Teresa, too, gains by moving away from the "selfless axis" at the intersection of R^oR^o and the horizontal axis, moving to point C. Both would do even better on path 0Z, as the interest frontiers get ever further apart.
- Economic choice is about a bit of self-sacrifice in both domains of self-interest and other-interest; notice the best outcome at point B in figure 3 shows $I_G^2 < I_G^3$ and $I_M^2 < I_M^3$. So we can seek the best outcome in the meta-interest on a higher plane as represented in the I_s curves of figure 4 only with some self-sacrifice (altruism) in both domains of interest represented in figure 3.
- Both paths 0G and 0M tend to be in the subconscious of the individual, with path 0M likely, even more so out of conscious (more dots in the 0M than in the 0G path) access most of the time. This is also to say that empathy-sympathy gets quite subtle expression in the underlying institutions (norms and traditions; working rules of organizations; property rights and duties) that temper and condition egoistic-hedonistic expression of self-interest.
- Perhaps most importantly, commensurability becomes an empirical question, rather than an utilitarian presumption of only self-interest in meta-interest I_s^1 (figure 4). To the individual represented in this figure, there is only one kind of utility easily commensurable in money terms, so both max P and max U are pursued at point A. We have to surmise this individual can put a price on the head of his firstborn, at least implicitly (a shadow price if not in an actual market transaction). That is, NCE proclaims everything has a price, an implicit shadow price in revealed preferences if not a price revealed explicitly in markets. In contrast, an individual with a meta-interest represented in I_s^3 would likely be appalled by the question, "Just what would you be willing to sell your firstborn for (or, be willing to accept to destroy a rain forest)." It is often quipped that "Economists (read NCEs) know the price of everything and the value of nothing." Yes, because NCE presumes commensurability in "utils" that are easily converted to dollars/money units in any currency—so, everything has a price, including (let's stay consistent here) one's firstborn. In complete contrast, someone with a meta-interest I_s^3 would likely see the inherent conflict that often arises within the self- and other-interest domains, often finding themselves with a great deal fewer of the material comforts afforded the more selfish among us for the sake of "doing the right thing" in a moral community and ethical society sense. A holder of the meta-interest function I_s^3 at best would likely see commensurability in a world of material comfort with limits and more likely see complete incommensurability in a world of endless hedonistic pursuits.

Intriguingly, it is when I_s^3 is squared against I_s^1 that the most important EnE case arises, applicable to most of the people most of the time: This potentially leads to the temperate self, one who acts to integrate across all the virtues, with the meta-interest emerging and evolving as I_s^2. This is more about finding an integrated, best balance than maximizing either self-interest or other-interest. We act neither with selfish, prudence-only-based max P and max U on path 0G, nor with selflessness-only-based max O (other-interest) on path 0M. Instead, we would find the prudence-only virtue being integrated and balanced with the other six virtues, temperance, justice, courage, faith, hope, love, on path 0Z. McCloskey (2009) has made this point cogently, in arguing the role that the other bourgeois virtues have played over the centuries in conditioning the tendency to the prudence-only virtue exemplified in max U. That is, truly successful (and they have peace of mind on a sustainable path) businesspeople, the bourgeois, condition the max U tendency.

Another possibility that also needs consideration sees justice as being the prevalent virtue integrated with prudence, the other five less so. Traditionally, classical (and medieval theological) philosophy argued that the virtue of justice lay in moderation between selfishness and selflessness. To Aristotle individual justice is social justice. To seek more than a fair share is greediness (*pleonexia*). The just person renders to each and all what is due to that person. Dual-interest theory and metaeconomics can also handle this possibility and in some ways favor highlighting just the most important other-interest, in this case economic justice. Sen (2009) would also likely favor focusing on justice, seeing it needing to play a substantive role with prudence (and the other virtues to a lesser degree), but this justice is really about the capability "to be and to do," and not about the amount of income and wealth that is shared. On this latter point, he's at odds with Aristotle and the meta-interest of the philosopher.

Figure 3 also points to the empirical evidence from the behavioral and neuroeconomics literature (for overviews, see the comprehensive handbooks by Altman, 2006, and Glimcher et al., 2009) as found in laboratory experiments of various kinds. Ultimatum, dictator games, and variations on them invariably point to individuals choosing to absolutely avoid the private-public balancing in sharing of resources (i.e., capital, means) at any ratio higher than 90:10 (see figure 3), and more generally stay in the range of 50:50 to 70:30. The latter break point is especially revealing, in that often countries choose marginal tax rates upward of around 30 percent; perhaps this tells us something profound about the nature of human nature. Being reasonably satisfied with a 70:30 share implies empathy at work, as only ego puts one at least on the 90:10 path (i.e., presuming religious leaders could indeed induce a "tithe" of 10 percent), and perhaps even the vertical axis when "extreme greed is deemed extremely good," which has been the "American way" for the past three decades (and which has been exported globally, promoted as the "American dream," which has become the world's nightmare). By the same token, few venture toward the 30:70 range, albeit there are some notable exceptions, as in the relatively recent decisions by Bill Gates and Warren Buffett to essentially give away the bulk of their amassed fortunes, well below the 30:70 line of figure 3. It is also intriguing where they are putting that money, largely being into the domain of "incommensurables," working on such issues as general health of the population in underdeveloped regions of this spaceship Earth, working more on the capabilities to be and to do than to redistribute wealth.

The classic paper by Fromm (1939) made it quite clear that selfishness integrated and balanced with self-love (the latter making possible a degree of selflessness, conditioning selfishness) was essential. Path 0Z in figure 3 could be relabeled the "Fromm path," as he gave us a key idea. If so, what do we do, as individuals? Do we "maximize" the outcome, the payoff we individuals experience from this integration at points like B (see esp. figure 4)—or do we instead think of this as "satisficing" with a meta-interest at work—good enough, never perfect, doing the best we can under the circumstances, with self-sacrifice in both of the other domains of interest?

It is intriguing that when one turns this into mathematics (Lynne, 2006a, 2006b), it seems one can think of "maximizing" on path 0Z, which is the "best" path through "Fromm space"—the space between and including the two paths 0G and 0M. We can actually maximize while sacrificing, something the NCE frame cannot do. NCE claims the soldier jumping on the hand grenade to save fellow soldiers is maximizing while sacrificing self-interest utility, which lacks common sense and makes no behavioral science sense. However, dual-interest theory can reasonably posit that the soldier sacrifices self-interest utility, moving toward more other-interest utility, hoping to be on path 0Z. Yet humans sometimes make mistakes and pay the ultimate price in sacrificing the entirety of their self-interest payoffs, going too far by hitting the horizontal axis. They lose all self-interest utility in this life, and who knows about the hereafter?

Again, this suggests we would now represent "greed" on the vertical axis and "selfless" on the horizontal axis. Selfish and self-love are in the space between the axes. We would also now see the irrational selfishness and self-love in areas above and below the paths 0G and 0M, respectively, in contrast to the rationality in the "Fromm space" between and including paths 0G and 0M.

APPLICATIONS

Greed and the Financial Ecosystem

The role of greed without empathy starts with the introduction of derivatives trading, which ultimately played a major role in the 2008 financial crisis and near economic meltdown. This all started rather innocently. The very first derivative trade, a credit default swap (CDS), as they came to be called, was arranged by J.P. Morgan, involving Exxon, as related to the problem with the Valdez oil tanker spill. After being threatened with a $5 billion fine, Exxon asked for a $4.8 billion credit line. J.P. Morgan wanted to provide it (Tett, 2009, p. 47), even though there was little money to be made from so doing, due to loyalty to an old customer, Exxon. With this example we see the ongoing self-sacrifice I_G on path 0Z driven by the commitment represented in I_M. It was realized that a CDS could not only keep J.P. Morgan on 0Z (keep their loyalty, commitment) but could also free up funds. It was found that the European Bank for Reconstruction and Development (EBRD) might be willing, for a fee, to carry the risk of default by Exxon. EBRD needed to increase their income flow; J.P. Morgan wanted to free up capital to lend to other entities. This is to say, providing this credit line to Exxon raised their reserve capital requirements as well as pushed on credit limits imposed on this part of J.P. Morgan (Tett, 2009, p. 46). A deal was struck, with J.P. Morgan paying EBRD to cover the risk of default, which EBRD was happy to accept, due to the risk of Exxon defaulting being exceedingly small. J.P. Morgan had found a way through trading in CDS instruments to maintain loyalty with less self-sacrifice, that is, due to now being able to make interest income on at least part of the $4.8 billion credit line more than sufficient to cover the fee payment, moving 0Z upward toward path 0G. As Tett (2009, p. 48) tells it, such trading in CDSs fed the dream to free up reserve cash:

" credit derivatives would allow J.P. Morgan—and in due course all other banks, too—to exquisitely fine-tune risk burdens, releasing banks from age-old constraints and freeing up vast amounts of capital, turbocharging not only banking but the economy as a whole." The problem became that not all banks and their traders had as well-defined loyalty and "doing the right-thing" paths 0M as did J.P. Morgan, which as Tett (2009) shows, resulted in failure to temper the greed, which now is even more easily expressed by using nonregulated derivatives that famously impressed on the 2008 financial crisis.

The CDS derivatives became one of just many types of derivatives. By the time of the crash in 2008 derivatives were represented in currency, interest, and, the one that broke the bank, the CDO (collateralized debt obligation) of ABSs (asset-backed securities), especially the CDO squared (CDOs of CDOs) and CDO cubed (and CDOs of CDOs of CDOs) versions, the ultimate in facilitating speculation and greed. The CDOs associated with subprime mortgages became especially problematic due to the higher interest rates to which these mortgages were supposed to move (and, thus, produce ever higher payoffs to the investors), and the substantive default rates that emerged as those interest rates increased: These were viewed like "gold dust" (Tett, 2009, p. 95) to greed-driven, returns-hungry investors. The problem was really very simple: the derivatives, especially the CDOs that had been extended way beyond any reality in the underlying, actual asset markets. The underlying asset markets themselves, too, were moving way beyond reality, fed by cheap credit and plentiful money made possible by reduced reserve requirements from selling the risk. The result was runaway bank lending and massive accumulation of private debt. The system did not self-regulate on any kind of shared ethic other than "greed is good and extreme greed is extremely good."

The "good, ethical lot" (Tett, 2009, p. 110, quoting Jamie Dimon, who was brought into the new J.P. Morgan Chase by the merger with Bank One) from the old J.P. Morgan were also disturbed by what happened. Blythe Masters, one of the original swap team members at the old J.P. Morgan "was livid . . . at how bankers had perverted her derivatives dream" (Tett, 2009, p. 249). Masters also noted (quoted in Tett, 2009, p. 251) that the economic (read NCE)models being used to drive the derivative trading "were right in a sense, but the problem is that they did not give enough emphasis to all the human issues, the regulatory structures, and things like that. . . . The idea was that those issues were just noise in the models but that is just dead-arsed wrong. We don't live in that kind of world of perfect economic models." Greenspan, too, admitted he had made a mistake in applying free-market notions, as Tett (2009, p. 251) quotes him, admitting he was in a "state of shocked disbelief"; he admitted that he made a "mistake" in believing that banks would protect shareholders and institutions: No path 0M at work in most banks.

The saga continues. Wall Street continues taking undue amounts of capital out of the system for private use (buying yachts) at point A in figures 3 and 2—capital then not available to the rest (except yacht builders) for productive use. An article in the *Omaha World Herald* (May 16, 2011) tells the story, with the headline declaring: "Oil Speculators on Wall Street Siphon from Drivers' Wallets," referring to the surge in gasoline prices with no substantive reason for it, other than to line wallets, playing on the emotions of the market. Wall Street needs to embrace empathy, which will contribute in substantive ways in providing the capital needed in building a green economy on sustainable path 0Z. It is only through empathy-sympathy, too, that we can work through government to develop economic policy that works for the entire economy, including the Wall Street self(ish)-interests, but tempered by the other(shared)-interest in economic justice.

Greed and the Food/Fiber Production Ecosystem

It is clear that focusing on "max Profit" and the utility it can buy in "max Utility" choices is not working to move spaceship Earth onto a sustainable path. If truth be told, in food, fish, and fiber, a productive ecosystem that combines "max Yields" and "max Monoculture" with "max Profit" and "max Utility" has proven to be the most profitable over the shortest time. However, it is short-term gain and long-term pain.

Two cases are presented: A case of fish and forest production ecosystems in British Columbia and a case of food production ecosystems, both considered relative to the movement toward sustainable technology and practice.

Case of a Fish and Fiber Productive Ecosystem

The British Columbia (BC) case goes back to the release of the UN Bruntland Commission Report (World Commission on Environment and Development, 1987), which was relative to a pilot project about sustainability with integrated resource management in the Lakelse Watershed of northwestern British Columbia from 1988 to 1992 (Reese-Hansen et al., 1992). The federal, provincial, and regional governments, in their wisdom, sought to resolve the "war in the woods" between environmentalists and corporations (the war over what is to be shared in path 0M) and sought to have more efficient government (on path 0G) with integrated resource management (on path 0Z). The new concept of sustainable development was an opportunity for a win-win-win scenario, and so it turned out to be, with a notable exception.

The idea was to get all the stakeholders involved, which included government agencies, landowners, forest leaseholders, and environmental groups. The formed group was given a planning project to address the fishery, wildlife, forestry, biodiversity, and recreational values, resulting in the Thunderbird Integrated Management Plan accepted by the BC Ministry of Forests in 1992 as "operational guidelines to be developed by government agencies" (Downie, 1992).

Hayes represented the BC Farmers' Institute on the Committee and was in a unique position as a commissioner for regional planning who had identified problems of overlapping and contradicting jurisdictions in government (Kirby, 1984) and had introduced whole-watershed management planning. This experience, essentially about applied sustainable development, speaks to the origins of the EnE hypothesis developed in Hayes and Lynne a decade later (2002–4). The question of whether clear-cutting was sustainable was taken off the table, as was the stakeholder model, though the "stakeholders" remained. That model basically represented a competition over the sizes of the slices of the resource pie. In its place was a roundtable model based on a consensus process (Birdsell, 1992, p. 71).

Consensus building around values virtually eliminated the economic system premised on greed in the fishery and forestry economics of "max Utility" and "max Profit." It also tempered max yields and max monoculture in consideration of other values such as biodiversity within forest core areas (Hayes, 1992a, p. 73). While the authors did not talk in terms of empathy, no doubt it was there in the committee's interaction and focus on a common, viable, and sustainable future.

In hindsight, taking the clear-cut off the table was a mistake. While BC forestry experts at the time admitted that they couldn't prove the clear-cut was sustainable, they were hopeful.

On the other hand, a noted researcher had declared the clear-cut not sustainable and was only suited for pioneer species, but even they "rarely generate on clear-cuts in sufficient density to secure the production of high quality timber. This excludes clear cutting as a practical method" (Plochmann, 1968, p. 29). In agreeing to participate with the clear-cut off the table, there was the promise that alternate methods were to be included with clear-cuts; a forested area was to be set aside for research and education (Hayes, 1992b, p. 72). Neither came to fruition—and now the clear-cut is accepted and assumed as part of sustainable development, which may have some validity in the even-aged stands of the boreal forests. The proof remains lacking that the great temperate rain forests on the west coast and great tropical rainforests can be sustained with the clear-cut.

Still, while the clear-cut remains by far the dominant form of forest management and is promoted as sustainable, it still appears an unsustainable path 0G choice to us. The other values, practices, and plan developed were huge steps toward sustainable development, with integrated resource management in a plan reflecting path 0Z considerations that the government was prepared to implement (Reese-Hansen et al., 1992). As noted, this process was crucial background experience for the hypothesis, and also points to how to better expedite building a future green economy.

Case of Conservation Tillage on U.S. Farms

We first wish to connect sustainability with the notion of using soil and water conservation technologies on U.S. farms, with a special focus on soil conservation, and thus on tillage technologies, because this is after all what we think of in the notion of a "farmer" and "farming," being about plowing, tilling, and otherwise stirring in the soil. Sustainability, then, is about finding ways to till less and thus move away from the mining of soil capacity while shifting toward sustaining that capacity.

The specific story about no-till starts in the late 1980s, at which time we had come to realize that the soil and water conservation adoption literature was quite ad hoc, with no integrating theory and framework for making sense of why some farmers adopt conservation technologies, while others do not. Lockeretz (1990) had come to the same conclusion. After all, if farmers are all profit maximizers on path 0G (or all networked in conservation-minded communities on path 0M, as mainstream sociology presumes), they should all be doing the same thing, as technology options are quite homogenous. Other than some variation in land and growing conditions, the adoption of such technologies (or not) should be universal. Indeed, in the specific case of no-till, technical NCE-based analysis always shows it more profitable on 0G, mainly because no-till saves huge amounts of fuel, so why would any profit maximizer not adopt no-till? Is it only because they are "uneducated" to the possibilities, which is the common presumption?

We set out to find out, with the first studies by Lynne, Shonkwiler, and Rola (1988), Lynne and Rola (1988). While not yet explicitly using the dual-interest framework, as it was yet to be developed, the other-interest dimension as represented in shared conservation norms, which arise in the domain of empathy, was shown prominent in decisions to adopt no-till, tempering the economic based drives. These findings led to a kind of "creative period" in the evolution toward dual-interest theory, involving a sabbatical leave with immersion into institutional economics, anthropology, psychology, sociology, and social psychology (e.g., see the testing of the "theory of planned behavior" [Ajzen, 1991] model, as modified to including economic variables in a "theory of planned demand" model in Lynne et al., 1995), leading to the notion of overlapping "I & We" (later the Self & Other) interest framework in Lynne (1995), and further refinements in Lynne and Casey (1998), and the eventual proposal of the metaeconomics approach in Lynne (1999). This idea was first applied in Lynne (2002), examining the underlying framing in the agricultural industrialization question as reflected in the "strict father" (mainly egoistic-hedonistic based) versus "nurturant parent" (mainly empathetic-sympathetic) framing of food system issues and organization. The mathematics of what would become dual-interest theory (at that time still using the "dual motives" vernacular) was introduced in Lynne (2006a, 2006b), which was also empirically tested in a nonagricultural setting about consumer recycling at about this same time (see Kalinowski, Lynne, and Johnson, 2006). Also, at this time, the framework still referred to the egoistic-hedonistic based self-interest tendency and the empathy-*altruistic* (as was also the use in Hayes and Lynne, 2004) based "others"-interest tendency. The latter was eventually refined and replaced with the empathy-*sympathy*-based notion of an other (shared, yet internalized within the individual) interest in Sheeder and Lynne (2011). Also, by this time, as represented in Ovchinnikova and coauthors (2009) using a laboratory based experiment, and another survey-based study in Sautter and coauthors (2011), the dual-interest frame is focusing on how other-interest works to condition through tempering of the self-interest. Bishop, Shumway, and Wandschneider (2010) and Chouinard and coauthors (2008) also use the metaeconomics approach, with testing finding further support for the role of an other-interest. And, most importantly, all of these studies show either directly or indirectly, with the most explicit and robust finding about this phenomenon emerging in the most recent study by Sheeder and Lynne (2011), that *Empathy has been the key, missing factor in understanding what drives and motivates the adoption of conservation technology by U.S. farmers, and finding the way to a green food economy.* While profit, habit, control, and capital all play roles, the missing variable is empathy: The extent to which U.S. farmers empathize (and join into sympathy with shared cause) with "downstream" users is key in explaining the huge variability in choices about conservation technology, the key in solving the tragedy of the commons. Conservation is at the core of long-term sustainability of this spaceship Earth's food system, as embedded in the larger ecosystem, so moving to the eco-path of sustainability depends upon empathy.

The role of empathy is also implicitly recognized in Sollner (1997), who insightfully pushes the understanding that bringing thermodynamic reality into economic framing requires addressing "the normative problem" in that it "turns out to be decisive" regarding the "integration of thermodynamic concepts" into economic framing. We can now so integrate these thermodynamic concepts, within dual-interest theory, through the construct of the empathy-sympathy-based other-interest, the other now referring to empathizing, walking-in-the-shoes-of-unborn-generations, and asking, "How would I wish to be treated?" with respect to the pace to maximum entropy, which works to resolve the normative problem. Instead of looking to the future in terms of the present through discounting the future, we instead empathize while looking to the present in terms of the future (for a discussion of this substantive difference, see Bromley, 2006). Also, note how the substitution possibilities are likely quite limited in and around the path 0Z, with the two interests better framed as complementary, a common argument in EE, going back to Georgescu-Roegen (1971). The interests in both utility and production space are better described as being more in fixed proportions around path 0Z than infinitely substitutable, the latter a common presumption in NCE. Also, we see the benefits of complementarity in figure 4 space, as the interest frontiers become increasingly further apart for equal increments in RR, on this sum-greater-than-sum-of-the-parts path for a green economy.

GREED AND ENERGY/ENTROPY INDUCED CLIMATE CHANGE

We finish out our examples with a brief note on energy and climate change. As argued, a financial system aimed at exponential growth is an insane greed game that creates superficial and shallow people; we are, as economist Tim Jackson said,: "being persuaded to spend money we don't have, on things we don't need, to create impressions that don't last, on people we don't care about" (Jackson, 2010). This scenario and model for stakeholders also appears central to the failed process as part of the continuing conversation started prior to the offering of the Kyoto protocol in 1997, each nation seeing it not in its self-interest to sacrifice anything, while a consensus of almost two hundred countries was needed.

This matter could be resolved with empathy, as Rifkin makes clear. Rifkin (2009, p. 26) makes the substantive point that "The underlying dialectic of human history is the continuous feedback loop between expanding empathy and increasing entropy." The reconciliation of these opposites, the synthesis, occurs on path 0Z at point B-type choices, on the path to a green economy and sustainability.

CENTERING FOR THE FUTURE: *HOMO ECONOMICUS* EVOLVING AS *HOMO EGO:EMPATHICUS*

That the new theory is relevant with a workable framework there is no doubt. Ever more others are starting to find the theory useful and relevant. As more get involved, its increasing reliability proves that it is generally valid, with the development of dual-interest theory, tests, and the metaeconomic approach. The new theory has huge implications for, and can move us away from and go beyond, misplaced policy, that is, policy evolved without sufficient expressions of empathy (and sympathy) in so many realms.

There is also past experience and local examples of moving toward sustainability and the development of sustainable practices in finance (i.e., we have fixed this more than once before, e.g., after the 1930s, with empathy the driver) as well as the food- and fiber-productive ecosystems. Empathy works to bring about sense in finance and conservation in food/fiber on the way to sustainability. Basic economic processes essential to achieving sustainability of a financial and physical economy, the latter ensuring the most fundamental and essential, sustainable food production system as related to energy and climate change, will be stirred as well as conditioned by empathy. We see dual-interest theory as resting on the foundation of thermodynamic principles, as well as the most fundamental of human principles represented in empathy-sympathy. We invite your participation in building a new EE theory, starting with this new Metaecon 101 proposition. The empirical evidence justifies a new theory; an empathic civilization needs it; and the result will be a centering theory with solid foundations in both EnE philosophy and science, providing the frame for deciding just how to build a truly green economy.

NOTES

1. The philosophical part of the hypothesis is the work of Hayes. The scientific part of the hypothesis is the work of Lynne.
2. http://www.answerbag.com/q_view/1963207#ixzz1NdcOlkqD.

REFERENCES

Ajzen, I. 1991. "The Theory of Planned Behavior." *Organizational Behavior and Human Decision Processes* 50:179–211.

Altman, M., ed. 2006. *Handbook of Contemporary Behavioral Economics: Foundations and Developments.* Armonk, NY: M.E. Sharpe.

Beattie, L. C. 2005. *The Elemental Wheel: From Metaphor to Meaning. 2005 Adlerian Year Book.* Lennoxtown, Scotland: Adlerian Society (UK) and the Institute for Individual Psychology.

Birdsell, F. 1992. "Consensus Decision Making." In L. Reese-Hansen, S. Sandhals, W. Hayes, D. Webb, M. Graham, A. W. MacDonald, G. Payne, R. Seaton, K. Kline, G. Bloomer, R. Mikaloff, D. Keating, T. Goyert, and A. Lubke. Thunderbird Integrated Resource Management Plan. Kalum Forest District, Terrace, BC.

Bishop, C. P., C. R. Shumway, and P. R. Wandschneider. 2010. "Agent Heterogeneity in Adoption of Anaerobic Digestion Technology: Integrating Economic, Diffusion, and Behavioral Innovation Theories." *Land Economics* 86:585–608.

Bromley, D. W. 2006. *Sufficient Reason: Volitional Pragmatism and the Meaning of Economic Institutions.* Princeton, NJ: Princeton University Press.

Chouinard, H. H., T. Paterson, P. R. Wandschneider, and A. M. Ohler. 2008. "Will Farmers Trade Profits for Stewardship? Heterogeneous Motivations for Farm Practice Selection." *Land Economics* 84:66–82.

de Waal, F. 2009. *The Age of Empathy: Nature's Lessons for a Kinder Society.* New York: Harmony Books.

Downie, B. D. 1992. Letter to "Thunderbird Resources Advisory Committee Members." In Reese-Hansen, L., S. Sandhals, W. Hayes, D. Webb, M. Graham, A. W. MacDonald, G. Payne, R. Seaton, K. Kline, G. Bloomer, R. Mikaloff, D. Keating, T. Goyert, and A. Lubke. Thunderbird Integrated Resource Management Plan. Kalum Forest District, Terrace, BC.

Frisch, R. 1965. *Theory of Production.* Chicago: Rand McNally.

Fromm, E. 1939. "Selfishness and Self-Love." *Psychiatry: Journal for the Study of Interpersonal Process* 2:507–23.

Georgescu-Roegen, N. 1971. *The Entropy Law and the Economic Process.* Cambridge: Harvard University Press.

Glimcher, P. W., C. F. Camerer, E. Fehr, and R. A. Poldrack. 2009. *Neuroeconomics: Decision Making and the Brain.* New York: Elsevier.

Hayes, W. M. 1992a. "Forest Fragmentation & Core Areas." In L. Reese-Hansen, S. Sandhals, W. Hayes, D. Webb, M. Graham, A. W. MacDonald, G. Payne, R. Seaton, K. Kline, G. Bloomer, R. Mikaloff, D. Keating, T. Goyert, and A. Lubke. Thunderbird Integrated Resource Management Plan, p. 73. Kalum Forest District, Terrace, BC.

Hayes, W. M. 1992b. "Research and Education Forest." In L. Reese-Hansen, S. Sandhals, W. Hayes, D. Webb, M. Graham, A. W. MacDonald, G. Payne, R. Seaton, K. Kline, G. Bloomer, R. Mikaloff,

D. Keating, T. Goyert, and A. Lubke. Thunderbird Integrated Resource Management Plan, p. 72. Kalum Forest District, Terrace, BC.

Hayes, W. M., 1996. Equilibriums of Rational and Emotional Education. The Roy C. Hill Awards Program. BC Teachers' Federation, Vancouver, BC.

Hayes, W. M., and G. D. Lynne. 2004. "Towards a Centerpiece for Ecological Economics." *Ecological Economics* 49:287–301.

Jackson, T. 2010. "Tim Jackson's Economic Reality Check." TED Talks. http://www.ted.com/talks/tim_jackson_s_economic_reality_check.html.

Kalinowski, C. M., G. D. Lynne, and B. Johnson. 2006. "Recycling as a Reflection of Balanced Self-Interest: A Test of the Metaeconomics Approach." *Environment and Behavior* 38:333–55.

Kirby, N. 1984. Greater Terrace Official Settlement Plan. Prepared for the Regional District of Kitimat-Stikine, BC.

Konchak, W., and U. Pascual. 2006. "Converging Economic Paradigms for a Constructive Environmental Policy Discourse." *Environmental Science and Policy* 9:10–21.

Larson, K. L. 2010. "An Integrated Theoretical Approach to Understanding the Sociocultural Basis of Multidimensional Environmental Attitudes." *Society and Natural Resources* 23:898–907.

Lockeretz, W. 1990. "What Have We Learned about Who Conserves Soil?" *Journal of Soil and Water Conservation* 45:517–23.

Lynne, G. D. 1988. "Allocatable Fixed Inputs and Jointness in Agricultural Production: Implications for Economic Modeling: Comment." *American Journal of Agricultural Economics* 70:948–49.

Lynne, G. D. 1995. "Modifying the Neo-classical Approach to Technology Adoption with Behavioral Science Models." *Journal of Agricultural and Applied Economics* 27:67–80.

Lynne, G. D. 1999. "Divided Self Models of the Socioeconomic Person: The Metaeconomics Approach." *Journal of Socio-economics* 28:267–88.

Lynne, G. D. 2002. "Agricultural Industrialization: A Metaeconomics Look at the Metaphors by Which We Live." *Review of Agricultural Economics* 24:410–27.

Lynne, G. D. 2006a. "On the Economics of Subselves: Toward a Metaeconomics." In *Handbook of Contemporary Behavioral Economics: Foundations and Developments*, ed. M. Altman, pp. 99–122. Armonk, NY: M.E. Sharpe.

Lynne, G. D. 2006b. "Toward a Dual Motive Metaeconomic Theory." *Journal of Socio-economics* 35:634–51.

Lynne, G. D., and C. F. Casey. 1998. "Regulatory Control of Technology Adoption by Individuals Pursuing Multiple Utility." *Journal of Socio-economics* 27:701–19.

Lynne, G. D., C. F. Casey, A. Hodges, and M. Rahmani. 1995. "Conservation Technology Adoption Decisions and the Theory of Planned Behavior." *Journal of Economic Psychology* 16:581–98.

Lynne, G. D., and L. R. Rola. 1988. "Improving Attitude-Behavior Prediction Models with Economic Variables." *Journal of Social Psychology* 128:19–28.

Lynne, G. D., J. S. Shonkwiler, and L. R. Rola. 1988. "Attitudes and Farmer Conservation Behavior." *American Journal of Agricultural Economics* 70:12–19.

Marglin, S. A. 2008. *The Dismal Science: How Thinking Like an Economist Undermines Community*. Cambridge: Harvard University Press.

McCloskey, D. 2009. *The Bourgeois Virtues: Ethics for an Age of Commerce*. Chicago: University of Chicago Press.

Odum, E. P. 1989. *Ecology and Our Endangered Life-Support Systems*. Sunderland, MA: Sinauer Associates.

Ovchinnikova, N., H. Czap, G. D. Lynne, and C. Larimer. 2009. "'I Don't Want to Be Selling My Soul': Two Experiments in Environmental Economics." *Journal of Socio-economics* 38:221–29.

Pepper, S. C. 1942. *World Hypotheses: A Study in Evidence.* Berkeley: University of California Press.

Plochmann, R. 1968. *Forestry in the Federal Republic of Germany.* Corvallis: Oregon State University.

Reese-Hansen, L., S. Sandhals, W. Hayes, D. Webb, M. Graham, A. W. MacDonald, G. Payne, R. Seaton, K. Kline, G. Bloomer, R. Mikaloff, D. Keating, T. Goyert, and A. Lubke. 1992. Thunderbird Integrated Resource Management Plan. Kalum Forest District, Terrace, BC.

Rifkin, J. 2009. *The Empathic Civilization: The Race to Global Consciousness in a World in Crisis.* New York: James P. Tarcher/Penguin.

Sautter, J., N. Czap, C. Kruse, and G. Lynne. 2011. "Farmers' Decisions Regarding Carbon Sequestration: A Metaeconomic View." *Society and Natural Resources* 24(2): 133–47.

Sheeder, R. J., and G. D. Lynne. 2011. "Empathy Conditioned Conservation: 'Walking-in-the-Shoes-of-Others' as a Conservation Farmer." *Land Economics* 87:433–52.

Sen, A. 2009. *The Idea of Justice.* Cambridge: Harvard University Press.

Smith, A. 1776. *An Inquiry into the Nature and the Causes of the Wealth of Nations.* Ed. E. Cannan. New York: Modern Library, 1937.

Smith, A. 1982. *The Theory of Moral Sentiments.* Ed. D. D. Raphael and A. L. Macife. Indianapolis: Liberty Classics.

Sneddon, C., R. B. Howarth, and R. B. Norgaard, R. B. 2006. "Sustainable Development in a Post-Bruntland World." *Ecological Economics* 57:253–68.

Sollner, F. 1997. "A Reexamination of the Role of Thermodynamics for Environmental Economics." *Ecological Economics* 22:175–201.

Tett, G. 2009. *Fool's Gold: How the Bold Dream of a Small Tribe at J.P. Morgan Was Corrupted by Wall Street Greed and Unleashed a Catastrophe.* New York: Free Press.

World Commission on Environment and Development. 1987. *Our Common Future.* New York: Oxford University Press.

Civic Empowerment in an Age of Corporate Excess

ED LORENZ

They were careless people . . . they smashed up things and creatures and then retreated back into their money or their vast carelessness, or whatever it was that kept them together and let other people clean up the mess they had made.

—F. SCOTT FITZGERALD, *THE GREAT GATSBY*

WHILE INNUMERABLE HISTORIC EXAMPLES EXIST OF ABUSE OF INDIVIDUAL POWER and excessive self-interest, recent financial crises illustrate that today such abuses can impact large numbers of people and communities around the globe. Individual excess transitioned into fundamental societal problem when its pathologies are magnified in corporations no longer properly controlled by either civic processes or cultural norms. As the early twenty-first-century financial crises unfolded, a common error of analysis focused on relatively recent changes in law or policy that encouraged imprudent behavior, such as the repeal of bank regulations or public finance modifications (Grumet, 2009). The problems that became evident in the fall of 2008 had been brewing in American business and civil society for decades and were grounded not merely in contemporary leadership mistakes, however grievous, but primarily in much longer-term civic, economic, and environmental ideologies and practices.

There is no better way to see this than through a case study of a group of firms that at one time or another were linked to Fruit of the Loom. Politically and economically they often modeled exploitation if not contempt for local communities, their workers, and their investors. Environmentally, the former chemical subsidiary Velsicol left a multistate legacy of carelessly dumped chemical and radioactive wastes. Rather than be distracted by recent flagrant financial misjudgments, we should understand what this case study reveals about the need for widespread and systematic reforms, ranging from U.S. institutional leadership practices to renewed citizen empowerment, if the real sources of the current problems are to be addressed. The case of Fruit of the Loom exposes two primary sources of the economic and cultural maladies of the new millennium as well as effective ways of curing them.

First, the firm's history illustrates how poor corporate and civic leadership can negatively affect workers and residents of host communities, the natural world, and ultimately the economic viability of companies themselves. Advocates of sustainable capitalism have called these three dimensions of corporate impact the triple bottom line (Gray and Bebbington, 2001;

Hawken, 1993; Hawken, Lovins, and Lovins, 1999). Velsicol's behaviors, which first appeared confined to egregious environmental practices, demonstrated that disregard for any of the three dimensions likely will undermine continued success in the other two. The business media, as well as the scientific and technical professionals who worked for and with the firm, blindly dismissed early concerns with Velsicol's environmental impact or later the movement of Fruit's jobs out of historic host communities as inevitable adjustments to allow the firms to remain competitive. Fruit's bankruptcy in late 1999 proved the error of such compartmentalized economics.

Reviewing the history of this company is especially helpful because of its links to some of the most flawed leaders in finance and government. As the national economy unraveled in 2008 and 2009, even casual observers of U.S. leadership recognized Fruit's collaborators as failures. Whether junk bond promoters such as Michael Milken, insurance schemers at AIG, or officials of the Federal Reserve, all had helped Fruit flounder yet had survived its collapse. The core danger of the 2008–9 collapse, as the earlier problems in with savings and loans, was not the loss of jobs and wealth, but that the response would be the use of short-term public subsidies to allow failed leaders and practices to continue. The public therefore urgently needs to review the longer-term history of the behaviors that underlay contemporary crises rather than focus only on mistakes tied to mortgages, auto production, or public finance. The study of Fruit of the Loom and the companies that became part of its complex structure shows, for example, that the insurance giant AIG did not merely speculate carelessly in the "subprime" mortgage market, but speculated more generally in other high-risk insurance schemes (Dobaro, 2009). Examining the history of Fruit of the Loom also shows the long-term consequences of deregulation of the financial sector and promotion of excessive debt financing (Barth, Brunbaugh, and Wilson, 2000). While detrimental to the firm's workers, host communities, natural environment, and outside investors, these schemes transferred massive amounts of wealth, especially savings accumulated over many years of productive business activity, to the private accounts of speculators, much as the 2008–9 bank bailout transferred public subsidies to the private accounts of bank owners.

Second, beyond the details of corporate skullduggery and administrative incompetence revealed by the Fruit of the Loom case, the firm's history, especially that of the Velsicol subsidiary, chronicles the evolution of an ideology and methodology for exploiting the environment and people. Firms like Velsicol relied heavily on the power arising from professional expertise and effectively used it to control citizen objections to their egregious behavior. As with so many mid-twentieth-century U.S. manufacturers, the respect for the leaders of Fruit of the Loom arose from a long history of innovation and entrepreneurship within components of the Fruit "empire." The firm's experts pioneered the production of ubiquitous products such as underwear and the window envelope and made technological advances in aluminum casting and fluorescent lighting. A Nobel laureate praised one of its chief scientists. Community leaders celebrated the philanthropy of its owners. Yet several of the firm's great philanthropists equally symbolized the pursuit of naked self-interest.

Environmentally, the history of the firm exemplified what Thomas Berry (1999, p. 59) called "the central human issue and the central Earth issue of the twenty-first century. . . . [T]hat after . . . centuries of industrial efforts to create a wonderworld we are in fact creating wasteworld, a nonviable situation." Socially, the history of Fruit demonstrated how separation of corporate ownership and leadership from the communities in which the firm operated encouraged the transfer of wealth from the producers. It also imposed excess risk on the workers and their workplace, exorbitantly enriching managers and their institutional collaborators (Hacker, 2006). Finally,the firm's behavior illustrated the timeless need for civic institutions to adopt and enforce regulations to protect communities and the natural world from pillage and abuse. With the rise of what political scientists labeled "interest group liberalism" in the middle of the century, Fruit exemplified how firms undermined, even corrupted, civic capacity. They retrained citizens to pursue individual interests in jobs and cheap consumer goods rather than seek the more amorphous but much more important long-term public interest (Barber, 2007).

The leadership at Fruit of the Loom and its affiliates created numerous problems that parallel fundamental troubles in the U.S. policymaking process. While some link these difficulties to the Reagan administration's advocacy of "deregulation" and neoliberalism, this study shows those problems had earlier manifestations more deeply rooted in the dominant American theory of "political-economy" (Diggins, 2008). The company's controversial abuses of the environment and workers began in periods often marked by progressive regulatory regimes. This investigation suggests that the widely shared free-market ideology that dominated both political parties in the second half of the twentieth century facilitated these abuses. The transition to an era of "deregulation" did not correspond to intensification of these wrongs; in fact, some progress in addressing the firm's problems occurred after the appearance of Reaganomics. The Fruit case is important because it clarifies that neither the liberal nor the neoliberal ideology behind the dominant U.S. policy process effectively protects the public interest, and it also suggests a procedural approach and supporting ideology that do identify and defend that common good (Stone, 1990).

ALTERNATIVES

Since the early republic some of the great works of social analysis and literature have noted the tension between the excesses of individual freedom and the need to define and protect community. For example, after touring the United States during the 1830s, Alexis de Tocqueville produced a classic assessment of these tensions in a large federal democracy. He understood all societies walked a fine line between the twin scourges of anarchy and oligarchy. On both sides, a few powerful or violent leaders emerged, bringing oppression, exploitation, and, at its worse, pillage and rape to the many. After observing the young U.S. democracy, Tocqueville concluded his visit hopeful that the U.S. political culture controlled the worst tendencies inherent in individual freedom through its "habits of the heart." These habits included a distinctive mix of commitment to republican principles and personal self-restraint, reinforced especially by the country's vigorous and competing churches. Although people in the United States sought individual success without hesitation or shame, they qualified that pursuit by "explaining almost all the actions of their lives by the principle of self-interest rightly understood." Tocqueville added:

> The principle of self-interest rightly understood produces no great acts of self-sacrifice, but it suggests daily small acts of self-denial. By itself it cannot suffice to make a man virtuous; but it disciplines a number of persons in habits of regularity, temperance, moderation, foresight, self-command; and if it does not lead men straight to virtue by the will, it gradually draws them in that direction by their habits. (Tocqueville, 1956, 2:123)

In 1985, *Habits of the Heart* shifted from Tocqueville's concept to become a title of a best-selling study of the decline of community and the rise of individualism in America (Bellah et al., 1985). *Habits of the Heart* was neither the first nor only investigation of growing concern with personal interest. What came to be called communitarianism produced numerous studies during the last third of the twentieth century that critiqued the abandonment of "rightly understood" as a modifier for self-interest and its replacement with "naked" or "radical" (Slater, 1970; Etzioni, 1993; Elshtain, 1995; Ehrenhalt, 1995). Of course, even before the communitarians, the general culture had described the extreme pursuit of wealth at all costs as "greed" and listed it as a deadly sin. A number of leading business scholars had expressed concern with the negative consequences of entrepreneurship as much as they celebrated the innovation. William Kapp (1950, p. vii) once summarized his research as presenting "a detailed study of the manner in which private enterprise under conditions of unregulated competition tends to give rise to social costs which are not accounted for in entrepreneurial outlays but instead are shifted to and borne by third parties and the community as a whole." When the management guru Peter Drucker (1985) examined the topic in the 1980s, he likewise emphasized the need for observing warning signs of entrepreneurship gone wrong rather than focusing on "success stories." The prevailing justification for entrepreneurial creative destruction was progress. Communities like St. Louis, Michigan, in the late twentieth century experienced a contrary fate. They witnessed job loss and environmental pollution arising from earlier enterprise with no replacement innovation, only abandonment.

REACTION

What makes this study important is that in St. Louis, Michigan, the only town with three of the firm's highly contaminated sites, citizens awakened and found their "habits of the heart." At the turn of the new millennium, they organized to challenge irresponsible corporate leadership and the media and experts who defended the leadership. The uniqueness of their action is visible through a review of the problems, both environmental and economic, in all the communities that hosted company facilities. Citizens in a number of these also tried to confront the closures and contamination left by the company, only to fail. St. Louis took advantage of all possible structures and processes to sustain corrective efforts. The community's story can be emulated, and that makes the story worth telling.

In St. Louis, citizens took advantage of provisions in the Superfund regulations to create a community advisory group (CAG) to advise EPA—the Pine River Superfund Citizen Task Force (U.S. Environmental Protection Agency, 1995). When the task force started in 1998, it saw its role as raising technical questions about government decisions. Slowly, it pioneered ways to directly challenge elite expertise in and out of government and in the press. By the end of the next year it sought large funding for a sophisticated health study and in 2000 filed a $100 million claim when Fruit of the Loom filed for bankruptcy protection. Partnering with a local college for free technical expertise, the Task Force did not stop with aggressive legal tactics. In 2002, CAG leaders forced the Department of Justice to hold three hearings in the community on environmental settlements with Fruit (U.S. Department of Justice, 2000, 2002). At the second of these, the local community expanded its focus beyond its region, inviting people from Memphis, Tennessee, who faced Velsicol contamination there, to come to the St. Louis hearing. This step inaugurated the community's awareness that local groups needed to join together to confront problems created by irresponsible global leadership. The question was how small communities could link with others outside the United States where firms such as Fruit of the Loom found few requirements to report their impacts on the triple bottom line. Relying on weak international regulatory mechanisms, the leadership of modern multinational firms can exploit workers, abuse the environment, and ignore investor protections far more easily than when they clearly were tied to one nation.

Long advised by policy experts to "think globally and act locally," local environmental activists usually focus on reviewing general environmental issues and then apply those lessons to their specific circumstances. By implication, the local groups lack the expertise or resources to shape the national or global policy process. In 2006–7, the Pine River Task Force learned it was being outmaneuvered in complex policy negotiations by the "perceived wisdom" developed by global experts and the mechanisms they controlled for justifying policy—conferences, peer-reviewed technical publications, and global forums. The catalyst for the task force's new strategy materialized when global petrochemical lobbyists began to undermine the global consensus on the restricted use of dichlorodiphenyltrichloroethane (DDT) (Marco, Hollingworth, and Durham, 1987).

VELSICOL'S LONG LOBBYING CAMPAIGN

The post-2000 lobbying in favor of DDT had its origins in the battles to regulate the pesticide in the 1960s. Those conflicts, tied to the publication of *Silent Spring* (Carson, 1962) made the pesticide the symbol of all later environmental regulation. In fact the battles began even before Carson's book appeared. For example, in 1960, when George Wallace, a widely respected ornithologist at Michigan State University, quite cautiously reported that songbirds dying in Michigan had high levels of DDT in their tissue, state agricultural interests called for his firing (Hayes, 1960). A midcareer, tenured professor, Wallace kept his job only because a sympathetic member of Congress intervened on his behalf (Lowe, 1989; Nichols, 1993).

Two years later, when Houghton Mifflin prepared to publish *Silent Spring*, Velsicol and its allies in higher education and the professions struck back, as had Wallace's critics. Prominent faculty, such as Frederick Stare at Harvard School of Public Health and William Darby of Vanderbilt, wrote caustic reviews of Carson's book (Brooks, 1972). However, the strongest institutional effort to oppose Carson came from the University of California at Berkeley. In the summer 1962, John Martinson, who coordinated the program in "Science and the Citizen" in the extension program at Berkeley, had informed readers of the *Science Guide*, published by his program, that the *New Yorker* was serializing Carson's work. The *Guide* merely referred readers to the series. Martinson did not endorse it. As he reported in a confidential letter to *TheNew Yorker*:

> The day following the appearance of this issue someone within the University made a confidential call to the University Public Information Officer in charge of science news releases. The substance of the call as relayed to us by P.I.O. (without telling us who the caller was) was to the effect that Rachel Carson is not a chemist, the University has a number of chemists working on insecticides, and this is a controversial question which it would be better not to discuss in a bulletin distributed by the University. (New Yorker, 1962)

Martinson was not confused about the nature and reasons for the communication from the anonymous caller. It was "censorship." He also guessed what he faced was "a very minor kind of annoyance compared to the economic pressures that must be exerted by chemical interests when you do a series like 'Silent Spring.'" He concluded, "In a way I'm glad this incident occurred because it provides me with an excellent argument in favor of establishing an independent journal of science criticism" (New Yorker, 1962).

A few weeks later, Velsicollaunched an unprecedented attack on the book and its publisher. In a letter dated August 2 from the company's general counsel, Louis McLean, Velsicol asserted that it wished to warn Houghton Mifflin of "legal and ethical" problems with the book. Then it made its threat:

> From a legal standpoint, we call to your attention the fact that several of the chemicals named, including, for example, aldrin, chlordane, dieldrin, endrin, and heptachlor, are patented chemicals. Chlordane and heptachlor are manufactured solely by this company. You no doubt are familiar with the fact that disparagement of products manufactured solely by one company creates actionable rights in the sole manufacturer. (McLean, 1962)

The ethical problems with the book, according to McLean, were that the publishers "are willing to publish anything to make a dollar." By contrast, the pesticide industry tests its products to ensure they are safe. He added quotations from the *Journal of the American Medical Association* (1961), which stated, "There is no reason to believe that the present use of chemicals in foods is endangering the health of people." Furthermore, he insisted that "pesticides and other agricultural chemicals are essential if we are to continue to enjoy the most abundant and purest foods ever enjoyed by any country of this world."

Velsicol and McLean followed their initial attacks on Carson with an aggressive defense of pesticides and corporate behavior. Much like the later attacks on DDT regulation, the rhetoric seemed out of touch with reality. McLean and Velsicol's lobbyist, Samuel Bledsoe, repeatedly took the lead in attacking critics of pesticides, especially those calling for government regulations. Beginning in 1964, Bledsoe, working with lobbyists from Shell Oil and Geigy Chemical, developed a plan to publish a defense of pesticides. They recruited Rep. Jamie Whitten, the longterm congressman from Mississippi and a staunch defender of big agriculture, as the author. They assembling a text from material submitted to hearings before his committee and added information supplied by the staff at the Library of Congress. Velsicol and its corporate allies first approached M. B. Schnapper of the Public Affairs Press in Washington to publish the book. Schnapper recalled he found the book "substantively weak and . . . poorly written." However, what worried him more was that the three firms assured him there would be sales of the book, since they planned to buy thousands for distribution. the *Washington Post* quoted Schnapper saying, "I really felt squeamish about what was going on in terms of industrial sponsorship of the book" (March 14, 1971, p. A4). Unfortunately, few were as cautious as Schnapper.

Eventually, Velsicol got D. Van Nostrand, the scientific publishing firm in Princeton, to produce the book, with the provocative title *That We May Live* (Whitten, 1966).

RENEWED BATTLES WITH GLOBAL LOBBYISTS

In 2005, a St. Louis, Michigan, CAG member noticed an editorial in the *Wall Street Journal* (November 8, p. A16) entitled "DDT Saves Lives." As with Velsicol's approach in 1962, powerful interests could not resist tying their defense of DDT to attacks on the ghost of

Rachel Carson, the *Journal* asserted: "The perception—going back to Rachel Carson—that DDT spraying is dangerous has long since been debunked." Later in the month, the *Journal* published three letters to the editor praising the newspaper for its courage in printing the editorial, under a heading "DDT Hysteria Has Killed Millions of People." The letter writers were Harold M. Koenig, Jason Urbach, and Richard Tren.

Koenig, former surgeon general of the air force, would be one of two retired Defense Department health experts who would be prominent in the pro-DDT campaigns of the era. Koenig in 2005 was a partner in Martin, Blanck and Associates, a Washington health-lobbying firm. However, in his letter to the *Journal*, he did not reference his role in lobbying but instead identified himself as the director of the Annapolis Center for Science Based Public Policy. Funded by ExxonMobile and the National Association of Manufacturers, the Annapolis Center described itself as a "national, non-profit educational organization that supports and promotes responsible energy, environmental, health and safety policy-making through the use of sound science. . . . The Center is committed to ensuring that public policy decisions are based on scientific facts and reasoning" (Annapolis Center, 2005). As would be typical of the pro-DDT advocates, the Annapolis Center took on a number of other deregulation issues, such as attacking renewable energy programs.

Jason Urbach and Richard Tren, like many associated with the pro-DDT campaign, had free-market economics backgrounds. Urbach had worked for the South Africa Free Market Foundation and Enterprise Africa. Tren, who led Africa Fighting Malaria, previously had written pro-tobacco and climate skeptic essays linked to the Competitive Enterprise Institute (Mamadu, 2008). According to lobbying monitoring websites, Africa Fighting Malaria's (AFM) supporters included mining giant BHP Billiton, the Earhart Foundation of Ann Arbor, DeBeers diamonds, its Anglo-American Chairman's Fund, and the fortune of Hans Rausing, one of the richest Englishman. AFM obtained public relations help from free-market organizations such as the White House Writer's Group.

Among Tren's works was an attack on Doctors Without Borders in *Capitalism Magazine* entitled "Doctors Without Principles" (June 30, 2002). On multiple occassions, Tren criticized health professionals opposed to persistent organic pollutants (POPs), including staff of the World Health Organization (WHO). For example, in 2003, Tren wrote to the editor of the *Daily Telegraph*:

> In developing countries, DDT is still being used very effectively in malaria control and saves thousands of lives every day. Any restriction on its use will cost lives and hamper development. It is absurd . . . to call for the same environmental standards around the world when the risks faced from communicable diseases, pests and poor sanitation are vastly different. . . . Eco-imperialism will only lead to increased death and misery in Africa and should be stopped in its tracks. (May 2, p. 29)

The attacks on DDT regulation shared several characteristics with the pro-tobacco, climate skeptic, and related free market campaigns. First, they attacked the policy process as antiscience and controlled by powerful "funders." Henry Miller, who worked on the pro-DDT campaigns through a series of what should be called "junk science" think tanks, attacked both the Gates Foundation and the UN for resisting DDT spraying, quoted in the Thai periodical, *The Nation* in May 11, 2010, "[F]or someone as smart as Gates . . . some of the foundation's strategies are baffling. . . . [P]olicies based on science and data have a short half-life at the UN." In a pro-DDT book published by AFM in 2010, Tren and his coauthor wrote, "As an ideological movement, environmentalism has been astonishingly powerful, controls vast resources, and is not answerable to any government. . . . In the United States, the EPA, National Institute of Environmental Health Science and Agency for Toxic Substances and Disease Registry are functional components of this empire" (Roberts and Tren, 2010, p. 332). Second, they directly questioned the integrity of academic scientists and the public institutions that base policy on peer-reviewed science. In the same book, Tren, praised J. G. Edwards for a critique of the journal *Science*. "The record supports Edwards' claim that *Science* refused to publish articles favorable to DDT" (Roberts and Tren, 2010, p. 224) Another ally, S. Fred Singer, also a tobacco advocate and climate skeptic, regularly attacked peer-reviewed science. What appeared to a general reader as both cautious and specialized became for modern laissez-faire proponents fodder for a strategy to undermine public respect for scientific consensus (Starobin, 2006).

The final characteristic common to DDT advocates both in the late 1960s and in the early twenty-first century was a fixation on Rachel Carson. Koenig, in his 2005 letter to the *Wall Street Journal* captured this approach. "Many of the world's leading scientists predicted 30 years ago that Carson's crusade against DDT would allow some of the world's deadliest diseases to return with dreadful consequences. The truth of that prediction is now upon us . . . right on schedule" (November 19, 2005). The attacks on Carson could take a strange turn, for what billed itself as "sound science." In the 2010 AFM book, the authors attacked Carson for "not writing about personal experience . . . at no point did she claim to have personally witnessed the killing of birds from use of DDT" (Roberts and Tren, 2010, p. 106).

As so much antiscience propaganda of the era, at the core of the pro-DDT strategy was conversion of empirical testing of hypotheses into a source for debates about the results of testing (Oreskes and Conway, 2010). Chris Mooney said of the American Petroleum Institute's campaign against global warming, "Victory will be achieved [when] recognition of uncertainties becomes part of the 'conventional wisdom'" (Starobin, 2006, p. 24). Henry Pollack (2003) explained how these efforts build upon public misunderstanding of "scientific theory" and scientific "uncertainty." Pollack stressed the need for media intelligence in handling lobbying efforts to turn the meaning of theory on its head. Yet AFM realized the media's search for controversy worked to its advantage. Soon policy change seemed to prove the wisdom of their strategy.

LOCALS AND GLOBAL LOBBYISTS

Whether in 1962 or 2005, one of the repeated claims of the pro-DDT forces was that they were on the side of "locals against outside do-gooders" (Dunlap, 1981, p. 235). That distortion as well as news in 2006 that World Health Organization (WHO) was reversing its DDT policy, made the Pine River locals decide they had to confront—as "locals"—those advocating bad policy. Already concerned with the *Wall Street Journal's* position, National Public Radio's (NPR) treatment of the issue appalled the CAG. NPR not only praised WHO's leadership for its policy change, but did so by attacking Rachel Carson:

> The World Health Organization today announced a major policy change. It's actively backing the controversial pesticide DDT as a way to control malaria. . . . While DDT repels or kills mosquitoes that carry the malaria parasite, it doesn't get much good press. In 1962, environmentalist Rachel

Carson wrote a book, *Silent Spring*, about how it persists in the environment and affects not just insects but the whole food chain.

In the early 1960s, several developing countries had nearly wiped out malaria. After they stopped using DDT, malaria came raging back, and other control methods have had only modest success.

Which is why Arata Kochi, head of the WHO's antimalaria campaign, has made the move to bring back DDT. His major effort at a news conference Friday in Washington, DC, was not so much to announce the change, as to deflect potential opposition from environmental groups (Silberner, 2006).

The account briefly noted the resignation of a number of WHO staff in protest over Kochi's policy change, but the pro-DDT propaganda campaign worked so well that NPR quickly returned to the theme of saving little African children.

Rather than lament the power and influence of AFM, the CAG chose to confront it. The CAG would show AFM's true colors, not as defender of third-world locals but as a classic Washington special interest lobby. In the fall of 2007, the CAG contacted a large number of global malaria and DDT experts to determine if they would participate in an international conference on DDT. When the CAG received a number of encouraging responses from widely respected scholars, it decided to commit some of the resources from an earlier environmental settlement to the event. Alma College's Center for Responsible Leadership, under the direction of John Leipzig, agreed to cosponsor the conference with the College's Public Affairs Institute. The CAG named the conference for the late Eugene Kenaga, one of the founders of the Society for Environmental Toxicology and Chemistry (SETAC) and of the CAG. Eventually the CAG won the official sponsorship of SETAC and the International Society for Environmental Toxicology. It recruited medical, public health, and environmental experts from as far as South Africa and from some of the leading universities in the United States. While the CAG paid travel expenses, the scholars donated their time.

As if CAG sponsorship were not enough to reflect a new local community role in shaping policy, the group designed a format for the conference that implemented their evolving theory of lay involvement. Half the attendees would be people from the region, who would both hear and interact with the global experts. As the CAG finalized arrangements for the conference, a controversy erupted related to an Agency for Toxic Substances and Disease Registry (ATSDR) study of "areas of concern" in the Great Lakes basin. Giving the lie to the AFM claim that agencies such as the ATSDR were under the control of well-funded anti-insecticide lobbyists, the CAG learned that ATSDR had blocked release of the study that identified the Pine River as one area of concern. The agency also had reassigned the scientist responsible for the report, Christopher DeRosa, to a vacant office with no duties. For several months, the CAG had tried to get ATSDR to send a representative to the Kenaga International DDT Conference, only to be rebuffed. Now David Carpenter at Albany University urged the CAG to invite DeRosa privately. By this point, DeRosa's name was in the national media; he had told the ATSDR director, Howard Frumkin, that the delay in release of the study had "the appearance of censorship of science and the distribution of factual information regarding the health status of vulnerable communities" (Kaplan, 2008). Two Michigan members of Congress, Bart Stupak and John Dingell, demanded that CDC release both the report and information on its treatment of DeRosa. They warned, "ATSDR's apparent withholding of this report raises grave questions about the integrity of scientific research at CDC and ATSDR, as well as treatment of its scientist" (Stupak and Dingell, 2008).

Without support from ATSDR, DeRosa became the keynote speaker, traveling on vacation time and with the college and CAG paying for his ticket. On the evening before the conference, with DeRosa on his way to Michigan, ATSDR released the embargoed Great Lakes report. Doris Cellarius of the Sierra Club captured the mood of all saying, "This is totally wonderful. Dr. DeRosa is a scientist with the greatest integrity and has been standing up for the best science possible" (Cellarius, 2008).

DeRosa's keynote directly challenged the contempt of groups such as AFM for both the "precautionary principle" and Rachel Carson (Goklany, 2001; Wiener, 2002). He summarized his thoughts:

> I began to focus in my graduate career on DDT alternatives, DDT substitutes. A very elegant article by Ian Nisbet turned me on to that idea and I did early research on the effects of carbon made pesticides on reproduction in wildlife populations. Then I started to think about the confluence of some of the remarks that have been shared with us by the different speakers [at the DDT conference], and the fact that one of the themes we have to recognize is that there are limits of our knowledge base that is circumscribed by the questions we choose to ask and they change over time. That is why Bernardino Ramazzini in the 16th [*sic*, seventeenth] century, the father of occupational medicine, invoked the precautionary principle said it is better to prevent than to cure. So we banned DDT after the epiphany of *Silent Spring* and we thought perhaps that was the end of the problem, but that was the end of the beginning of the problem as we have heard today. (DeRosa, 2008)

At the conclusion of the Kenaga Conference, the participants requested that the experts draft a consensus document, summarizing all that had been learned. Drafted initially by Brenda Eskenazi as she returned to the University of California, it was edited and signed by fifteen experts, including the three South African medical and environmental scholars who had participated: Maria Bornman and Christiaan de Jager from the University of Pretoria and Henk Bouwman from North-West University. Other signatories came from Cornell, Creighton, Indiana, Rockefeller, and Wisconsin, as well as the hosts from Alma College. The statement's conclusion exemplified the unofficial slogan of the conference, "Think Locally, Act Globally." After reviewing hundreds of studies, it concluded:

> Current evidence on DDT exposure to human populations and on its potential health effects support the Stockholm Convention on Persistent Organic Pollutants which emphasizes that DDT should be used with caution, only when needed, and when no other effective, safe and affordable alternatives are locally available. . . . Given the paucity of data in populations who are currently potentially exposed to high levels of DDT, we urge the global community to monitor exposure to DDT and to evaluate its potential health impacts both in malaria endemic regions of the world and in locations where DDT use has been historically high such as the Pine River Superfund site. (Eskenazi et al., 2009, p. 1369)

The official announcement of publication in the NIEHS's journal, *Environmental Health Perspectives,* received national coverage. *Scientific American* summarized the findings: "The scientists from the United States and South Africa said the insecticide, banned decades ago in most of the world, should only be used as a last resort in combating malaria" (Cone and Environmental Health News, 2009). Institutions that sent experts to the conference such as the Sprecher Institute for Cancer Research at Cornell and the School of

Public Health at the University of California at Berkeley celebrated the publication that resulted. Its title, the "Pine River Statement," epitomized its link to the CAG, its community, and the world.

In the fall 2008. the CAG learned the draft Pine River Statement had been discussed at the "Stakeholder Meeting of the UN Environmental Program on the Stockholm Convention" attended by two of the Kenaga Conference experts, Hank Bouwman and Riana Bornman. This discussion took place in front of Richard Tren, who attended as a representative of a nongovernmental organization. He would attack the "Pine River Statement" in his pro-DDT book, *The Excellent Powder*, which was published by a vanity press (Roberts and Tren, 2010). Following up on the commitment started with the Kenaga Conference, the CAG sent its public health chair to the Washington press conference for Tren's book.

LESSONS

Whatever the long-term impact of the Pine River Statement, its publication represented a model for other isolated communities facing well-funded global threats to their sustainability. St. Louis residents and the CAG experimented with many strategies and tactics in order to be heard and taken seriously by government agencies and polluters. Their experiences provided other communities with several lessons in civic empowerment:

- Defend the rights of the community to control its structure and processes as the community defines its expectations. Do not allow outside special interests to set the agenda or decide with whom negotiations will take place.
- Expect and be prepared to use the law to achieve justice. Confront legal challenges, even from the highest levels of government, if they are compromised by special interest influence. Understand that while the legal system may be biased against poorly funded communities, the door is never completely closed to presenting a community case.
- Do your research and be prepared to challenge experts, even the most well trained and respected, as in the community's battle with NIEHS. Realize, however, that the community must find some professional help to have an opportunity to influence experts.
- Neither ignore nor fear global special interests that may seem so far away as to be irrelevant or beyond local influence. Dismiss slogans such as "Think globally, act locally." Certainly know and think about the global forces and movements that may threaten the community, but do not retreat into only local actions. With modern globalization, such a retreat opens the door to being hopelessly outmaneuvered by forces seemingly beyond one's control.

A CIVIC GOAL

This study ends with advocacy of building sustainable communities by promoting alternative forms of policymaking and responsible leadership. The evidence from this case study attests to the urgency of the task. While the word is used too frequently, sustainability means, at a minimum, that "the present generation has the obligation to pass on to future generations an average capital stock,—of goods, services, knowledge, raw materials—that is equivalent to today's" (Mazmanian and Kraft, 2001, p. 17) A stronger version assumes that "some natural resources and ecological processes are critical; they cannot be depleted below a certain level without dramatic ramifications" (Mazmanian and Kraft, 2001, p. 19). While people, economic institutions, and technological tools and practices change, building a sustainable community embraces permanence and not short-term exploitation. Good stewards of such a community struggle to reject the short term and destructive, while laboring to promote the general welfare by preserving resources, maintaining public law, and encouraging vigorous civic life.

The consequences of poor leadership at Velsicol, its last parent, Fruit of Loom, and other firms linked to them proves the need for renewal of civic life as a defense against those who were formerly called robber barons. Despite the complacent neoliberal demands for less regulation, this case makes clear that ideology is fatally flawed. The pattern for this new civic vitality complies with Tocqueville's "habits of the heart." The community advisory group (CAG) process of the U.S. Environmental Protection Agency modeled this approach. Without glorifying a rather minor governmental procedural change, the CAG was one example of empowered citizens, a rare species at the start of the new millennium in America. The CAG at the Velsicol site in Michigan regularly objected to legal interpretations and decisions that failed to acknowledge the equity implicit in protecting the environment for future generations. In the mid-twentieth century, political scientists Grant McConnell (1966) and Theodore Lowi (1969) warned that U.S. civil society was in peril because "justice" had come to be considered the product of a deal between powerful interests. This study concludes with an appeal to minimize the power of special interests and to enhance involvement of the general public in enactment and enforcement of law through enhanced CAG-style procedures.

As a corrective to the emotions and fears that are emboldened by modern environmental regulation, one school of modern legal scholars calls for injecting natural and social science expertise into the law. Chicago's Cass Sunstein (2002) has modeled this solution, advocating precise, scientific calculations of risks and benefits. He assumes that with enough data the experts can determine accurately the perils of alternative government decisions (Sunstein, 2003). While tempting to an academic, no amount of research can detect precisely all risks, since the long-term ones may be assessed incorrectly or remain obscure to contemporary scientists (Czarnezki and Zahner, 2005). There are innumerable precedents of more general failures of what James Scott (1998) terms "high-modernist" planning. Thus, this study maintains the experts must serve as consultants to an active citizenry.

In 1978, as the Velsicol problems in St. Louis led to the closure of the town's factory, an environmental aide to Governor William Milliken, an expert employed by a thoughtful public figure of the era, voiced concern with local citizens' input into the environmental policy process (Dempsey, 2006). In a letter to a county commissioner, he said, "I have reservations about the kind of citizen committee that [the state senator] was proposing. We have learned from past experience that it's awfully easy to frighten the public to a degree which may be unwarranted about toxic chemical problems" (Rustem, 1978). The expert-dominated process that followed yielded a solution that not only failed to contain the pollution but exposed inhabitants to additional toxins for at least another quarter century. The citizens could not have done worse.

This study teaches that the most basic principle of democracy is right: the collective citizenry must control the leaders, even their highly trained experts. The average citizen is not always correct, and there clearly is the need for professionals employed in the civil service to monitor policy implementation. However, experts and self-interested individualists also can be wrong and can be more dangerous if mistaken than a single, ordinary citizen. Whatever the merits for specific environmental policy, reinvigorated public engagement is essential for the good of civil society. The United States needs a corrective to excessive individualism. The St. Louis case, especially when contrasted to the other communities harmed by Fruit of the Loom, demonstrates processes and structures to control neoliberal excess and the professionals in the media and the natural and social sciences who endorse it. This case therefore highlights the endless need to control "robber barons" and also to regain control of the policy process and mark it with restraint and integrity.

This study does not end as a pessimistic account of the triumph of neoliberal cynicism, but with descriptions of a community empowerment process that has had at least modest success. Such empowerment resembles other historical examples. As this investigation concludes, the St. Louis, Michigan, example is linked, hopefully not presumptuously, to the battle for humanistic civic life throughout the modern world. That linkage illustrates the value of pondering the struggles of the past that pitted special interests against the public good and, more importantly, restores confidence that communities can achieve a good society (Kristeller, 1961). As citizens seek to restore expectations and methodologies that support their vision of the long-term public interest, they can perceive that this is an old fight that must be renewed periodically to restore control over elite economic leaders and their accomplices. It is about civic empowerment to direct innovation and enterprise toward the creation of a good society.

This study celebrates the historic strengths of the American system, such as the multilayered federal policy structure with a preference for public decisions, which most impact daily lives, legislated at the local level. Another attribute has been the distrust of the corruption and hunger for power of faraway experts, beginning with the minions of George III. This examination does not reject the civic tradition; rather, it challenges the twentieth-century policy innovation that empowered professionals, linked to special interests, at the expense of those with a vision of the long-term public interest. As Frank Fischer (2000, p. 1) phrased the current debate, "Already talk of democracy all too often serves as little more than a thinly veiled guise for elite government. The question is: Can the democratic process be rescued from the increasingly technocratic, elitist policy-making processes that more and more define our present age?" Max Weber (1946), one of the great defenders of the virtues of the modern bureaucratic state but also a perceptive critic of its vices, warned citizens to find mechanisms to assert their values.

While celebrating vigorous local participation in technocratic policymaking, this study is not guided by simplistic adulation of local wisdom or by a bias against either business or national political leadership. Local people often can be foolish, primitive, superstitious, and bigoted. They seldom possess the expert knowledge of modern professionals, whether physicians, accountants, or economists. Nor do they understand global and national political imperatives as do better-trained leaders. Yet this study maintains that local weaknesses must be balanced by concern with the potential immorality of the specialist or the corruption of the Washington official. The only checks on experts and insiders is either a benevolent dictator or a vigorous public policy process that allows outspoken or outraged citizens to say "No!" The locals can do a lot of irrational things, but those may be not nearly as evil in intent or consequence as the health problems spawned by the irresponsible chemists at Velsicol or the theft of worker and investor wealth by the devious accountants in the pocket of Fruit of the Loom's officials. An unqualified local manager may cost a handful of his neighbors work when his incompetence causes his business to fail. Such behavior pales by comparison to the impact of the leadership at Fruit of the Loom, whose actions caused

65,000 workers to lose their jobs and more to surrender their pensions, health insurance, and investments.

Welcoming business creativity has given the United States its great wealth, permitting most residents to live more affluent lives than almost anyone else in the world. This study is not oblivious to that achievement. In fact, many communities adversely affected by the behavior of Fruit of the Loom wish they had an innovative entrepreneur to bring good jobs to their hometowns. Nothing written in this study seeks to inhibit innovation, some of which inevitably results in failures and errors. The cases examined here are not examples of random business failures, inevitable in a free economy. They are not random accidents, such as the unavoidable odds that for every mile driven by millions of drivers, some misjudgments will lead to injury and death. These cases are more analogous to the accidents of the chronically drunk. The public response is no-fault insurance for the random driver errors and criminal prosecution for the severely impaired. However, there have been no criminal prosecutions of leaders involved in the events chronicled here, with the exception of one set of charges against Velsicol's officials, punished by token fines after the firm hired one of the best-connected law firms in the country, Williams, Connolly and Califano, to guide it to victory (Velsicol, 1977). Their success in enriching themselves at the expense of their workers is reason to cease protecting the recklessness of the civically and socially impaired. That our media consults them as economic experts rather than exposes their disingenuousness suggests the extent of collusion in their actions and ideology. This story intends to encourage corrective actions and embrace of an ideology that envisages reform of our failing civic processes.

REFERENCES

Annapolis Center for Science Based Public Policy. 2005. http://www.Annapoliscenter.org.

Barber, Benjamin. 2007. *Consumed: How Markets Corrupt Children, Infantilize Adults and Swallow Citizens Whole.* New York: Norton.

Barth, James R., R. Dan Brunbaugh Jr., and James A. Wilson. 2000. "Policy Watch: The Repeal of Glass-Steagall and the Advent of Broad Banking." *Journal of Economic Perspectives* 14 (Winter): 191–204.

Bellah, Robert N., Richard Madsen, William M. Sullivan, Ann Swidler, and Steven M. Tipton. 1985. *Habits of the Heart: Individualism and Commitment in America Life.* New York: Harper and Row.

Berry, Thomas. 1999. *The Great Work: Our Way into the Future.* New York: Bell Tower.

Brooks, Paul. 1972. *The House of Life: Rachel Carson at Work.* Boston: Houghton Mifflin.

Carson, Rachel. 1962. *Silent Spring.* New York: Houghton Mifflin.

Cellarius, Doris. 2008. Email to Ed Lorenz, March 5. In DDT Presenter—DeRosa, Chris File. Pine River Files, Alma College Archives.

Cone, Marla, and Environmental Health News. 2009. "Should DDT Be Used to Combat Malaria?" *Scientific American* (May 4). http://www.scientificamerican.com/article.cfm?id=ddt-use-to-combat -malaria.

Czarnezki, Jason J., and Adrianne K. Zahner. 2005. "The Utility of Non-Use Values in Natural Resource Damage Assessments." *Boston College Environmental Affairs Law Review* 32:509–26.

Dempsey, Dave. 2006. *William G. Milliken: Michigan's Passionate Moderate.* Ann Arbor: University of Michigan Press.

DeRosa, Chris. 2008. DDT Conference Presenter File. Pine River Files, Alma College Archives.

Diggins, John P. 2008. *Ronald Reagan: Fate, Freedom, and the Making of History*. New York: Norton.

Dobaro, Gene. 2009. Acting Controller General of the U.S. *A Framework for Crafting and Assessing Proposals to Modernize the Outdated U.S. Financial Regulatory System*. U.S. General Accountability Office Report 09–216, January 8.

Drucker, Peter F. 1985. *Innovation and Entrepreneurship: Practice and Principles*. New York: Harper and Row.

Dunlap, Thomas R. 1981. *DDT: Scientists, Citizens, and Public Policy*. Princeton: Princeton University Press.

Ehrenhalt, Alan. 1995. *The Lost City: The Forgotten Virtues of Community in America*. New York: Basic Books.

Elshtain, Jean B. 1995. *Democracy on Trial*. New York: Basic Books.

Eskenazi, Brenda, et al. 2009. "The Pine River Statement: Human Health Consequences of DDT Use." *Environmental Health Perspectives* 117 (September): 1359–67.

Etzioni, Amitai. 1993. *The Spirit of Community: Rights, Responsibilities, and the Communitarian Agenda*. New York: Crown Publishers.

Fischer, Frank. 2000. *Citizens, Experts, and the Environment: The Politics of Local Knowledge*. Durham: Duke University Press.

Goklany, Indur M. 2001. *The Precautionary Principle: A Critical Appraisal of Environmental Risk Assessment*. Washington, DC: Cato Institute.

Gray, Rob, and Jan Bebbington. 2001. *Accounting for the Environment*. 2nd ed. London: Sage Publications.

Grumet, Lou. 2009. "Commentary: A Financial Frankenstein; Deconstructing the Argument for the Return of Glass-Steagall." *Accounting Today*, January 5.

Hacker, Jacob. 2006. *The Great Risk Shift: The Assault on American Jobs, Families, Health Care and Retirement*. New York: Oxford University Press.

Hawken, Paul. 1993. *The Ecology of Commerce*. New York: HarperCollins.

Hawken, Paul, Amory Lovins, and L. Hunter Lovins. 1999. *Natural Capitalism: Creating the Next Industrial Revolution*. Boston: Little Brown.

Hayes, Wayland, Jr. 1960. Testimony of Chief, Toxicology Section, U.S. Public Health Service, September 20, before the Michigan Senate Hearings on Pesticides. Michigan Archives, Lansing, Michigan, Michigan Department of Agriculture Records, Record Group 69-17, Box 47-51.

Kaplan, Sheila. 2008. "Great Lakes Danger Zones." The Center for Public Integrity. http://www.publicintegirty.org/GreatLakes/index.htm.

Kapp, K. William. 1950. *The Social Costs of Private Enterprise*. Cambridge: Harvard University Press.

Kristeller, Paul Oskar. 1961. *Renaissance Thought: The Classic, Scholastic, and Humanist Strains*. New York: Harper and Row.

Lowe, Kenneth S. 1989. "George Wallace and the Fight against DDT." *Michigan Out-of-Doors*, June, 56–58.

Lowi, Theodore. 1969. *The End of Liberalism*. New York: Norton.

Mamudu, Hadii, Ross Hammond, and Stanton Glantz. 2008. "Tobacco Industry Attempts to Counter the World Bank Report Curbing the Epidemic and Obstruct the WHO Framework Convention on Tobacco Control." *Social Science and Medicine* 67 (December): 1690–99.

Marco, Gino J., Robert M. Hollingworth, and William Durham. 1987. *Silent Spring Revisited*. Washington, DC: American Chemical Society.

Mazmanian, Daniel A., and Michael E. Kraft. 2001. "The Three Epochs of the Environmental Movement." In *Toward Sustainable Communities: Transition and Transformations in Environmental Policy*, ed. Daniel A. Mazmanian and Michael E. Kraft. Cambridge: MIT Press.

McConnell, Grant. 1966. *Private Power and American Democracy.* New York: Vintage Books.

McLean, Louis. 1962. Letter to William Spaulding, August 2. Carson Papers, Yale Collection in American Literature, Beinecke Rare Book and Manuscript Library, Box 89, Folder 1575.

New Yorker. 1962. Memo to Rachel Carson. "Confidential excerpt for Miss Carson's information only. Taken from letter received by staff member." Carson Papers, Yale Collection in American Literature, Beinecke Rare Book and Manuscript Library, Box 85, Folder 17 July: 1496.

Nichols, Sue. 1993. "Wallace's Stand on DDT Bears Remembering." *MSU News Bulletin*, August 5, p. 6.

Oreskes, Naomi, and Erik Conway. 2010. *Merchants of Doubt: How a Handful of Scientists Obscured the Truth on Issues from Tobacco Smoke to Global Warming.* New York: Bloomsbury Press.

Pollack, Henry N. 2003. *Uncertain Science . . . Uncertain World.* New York: Cambrudge University Press.

Roberts, Donald, and Richard Tren. 2010. *The Excellent Powder: DDR' Political and Scientific History.* Indianapolis: Dog Ear Publishing.

Rustem, William. 1978. Letter from Special Assistant to the Governor of Michigan to Arnold Bransdorfer, County Commissioner, March 27. Michigan, State of, 1978 File, Pine River Files, Alma College Archives.

Scott, James C. 1998. *Seeing Like a State: How Certain Schemes to Improve the Human Condition Have Failed.* New Haven: Yale University Press.

Silberner, Joanne. 2006. "WHO Backs Use of DDT against Malaria." National Public Radio. *All Things Considered*, September 15.

Slater, Phillip. 1970. *The Pursuit of Loneliness.* Boston: Beacon Press.

Starobin, Paul. 2006. Who Turned Out the Enlightenment?" *National Journal*, July 29, 20–26.

Stone, Walter J. 1990. *Republic at Risk: Self-Interest in American Politics.* Pacific Grove, CA: Brooks Cole.

Stupak, Bart, and John Dingell. 2008. Letter to Julie Gerberding, Director CDC, Fenruary 28. DDT Presenter—DeRosa, Chris File. Pine River Files, Alma College Archives.

Sunstein, Cass R. 2002. *Risk and Reason: Safety, Law, and the Environment.* New York: Cambridge University Press.

Sunstein, Cass R. 2003. "Beyond the Precautionary Principle." *University of Pennsylvania Law Review* 151 (January): 1003–10.

Tocqueville, Alexis de. 1956. *Democracy in America.* Ed. Phillips Bradley. Vol. 2. New York: Alfred A. Knopf.

United Nations Environmental Program. 2008. Stakeholder Meeting to Review the Draft Business Plan to Promote a Global Partnership for Developing Alternatives to DDT. UNEP/POPPS/DTBP.1/11, Geneva, November 3–5.

U.S. Department of Justice. 2002. Public Meeting concerning the St. Louis Facility (Velsicol Chemical Superfund Site), Gratiot Senior Center, St. Louis, Michigan, June 19.

U.S. Environmental Protection Agency. 1995. Office of Solid Waste and Emergency Response (OSWER) Directive 9230.0-28, December.

Velsicol Chemical Corporation v. Honorable James B. Parsons. 1977. United States Court of Appeals for the Seventh Circuit, 561 F.2d; July 29.

Weber, Max. 1946. "Science as a Vocation." In *From Max Weber: Essays in Sociology*,ed. and trans. H. H. Gerth and C. Wright Mills. New York: Oxford University Press.

Whitten, Jamie L. 1966. *That We May Live.* Princeton, NJ: D. Van Nostrand.

Wiener, Jonathan B. 2002. "Precaution in a Multi-risk World." In *Human and Ecological Risk Assessment: Theory and Practice.* Ed. Dennis D. Paustenbach. New York: J. Wiley.

Environmental Justice Challenges for Ecosystem Service Valuation

IN PURSUING IMPROVED ECOSYSTEM SERVICES MANAGEMENT, THERE IS ALSO AN opportunity to work toward environmental justice. The practice of environmental valuation can assist with both goals, but as typically employed obscures distributional analysis. Furthermore, valuation techniques may provide misleading or flawed information for weighing outcomes across groups. Pitfalls, solutions, and research needs are summarized at the nexus of valuation and environmental justice.

INTRODUCTION

Improving environmental management for the benefit of humanity requires a better understanding of the value of nature. The discipline of ecosystem services seeks this understanding and has become a popular research paradigm. Daily (1997) provides one of the earliest ecosystem services references, and the Millennium Ecosystem Assessment (2005) provides the first global view. There are now thousands of publications on ecosystem services (Cox and Searle, 2009).[1]

A traditional focus of the literature is to use information on nature's value to consider ways of increasing the aggregate net benefits of ecosystem services and thus utilize those resources more efficiently. Given the attraction of efficiency and the difficulties in its achievement, it can be easy to forget further social goals. Yet while revising ecosystem services management, there is also an important opportunity to work toward environmental justice. This raises new research issues since distributional impacts must be assessed.[2] A process must also be undergone to decide what does and does not constitute a just outcome. A specific procedure for environmental justice analysis is not outlined here—instead this chapter takes the related goal of examining how well the tools of ecosystem service valuation support such an analysis in general. If ecosystem service benefits are misrepresented, both efficiency and distributional analyses will be flawed. While many of the issues discussed here are not new, the tools of valuation are specialized, and their limitations may not be well known. Furthermore, some problems are particularly troublesome when cast in the light of the intentions of environmental justice.

For our purposes, the term "valuation" refers to a subset of ecosystem service research that attempts to estimate ecosystem service benefits in dollar terms, so results are compatible with a formal benefit-cost analysis (hereafter BCA). Valuation is a challenge since ecosystem service benefits are often unpriced in markets and require specialized research to monetize their value. A variety of nonmarket valuation techniques have been developed for this purpose (for background see Freeman, 2003). Governmental responsibilities lend motivation, for example, all new U.S. federal regulations with an expected impact of $100 million per year on the national economy require use of BCA by Executive Order 12866.[3] Without valuation there is no direct way to account for nonmarket environmental benefits in the balance, and we risk assigning them an effectual value of zero.

The promise of improved accounting has spurred the spread of ecosystem service thinking into government, marking a new level of maturity for the field. Notable examples in the United States include the 2008 Farm Bill naming of a new Office of Ecosystem Services and Markets housed within the U.S. Forest Service (U.S. Forest Service, 2010); the U.S. Environmental Protection Agency (EPA) ecology research program being reorganized as the Ecosystem Services Research Program (U.S. EPA, 2010a), including a multiyear plan (U.S. EPA, 2008a); and the National Ecosystem Services Partnership, encompassing federal and nonfederal members (Duke University, 2009). Governmental involvement is significant since agencies manage a significant share of natural resources. In the United States, roughly 30 percent of the land is federally managed; 50 percent in the West (Natural Resources Council of Maine, 2000).[4] In addition, the U.S. EPA regulates navigable water resources through the Clean Water Act and air through the Clean Air Act.

Governmental involvement also underscores the further challenge to environmental management of incorporating environmental justice. Environmental justice is a broadly recognized social goal (e.g., background in Cole and Foster, 2001) and is a mandated consideration for U.S. federal agencies by Executive Order 12898. However there is a complication in that there is no single approach to addressing environmental justice. The U.S. EPA offers a general definition (U.S. EPA, 2010b):

> Environmental Justice is the fair treatment and meaningful involvement of all people regardless of race, color, national origin, or income with respect to the development, implementation, and enforcement of environmental laws, regulations, and policies. EPA has this goal for all communities and persons across this Nation. It will be achieved when everyone enjoys the same degree of protection from environmental and health hazards and equal access to the decision-making process to have a healthy environment in which to live, learn, and work.

While the above passage refers only to hazards, recent interim rulemaking guidance for EPA notes the agency has expanded the role of environmental justice "to include not only the consideration of how burdens are distributed across all populations, but also how benefits are distributed" (U.S. EPA, 2010c). An additional passage from Executive Order 12898, Section 1-101, describes a test for fairness as being the absence of "disproportionate impacts" and identifies low-income and minority populations as groups to focus on:

> Each Federal agency shall make achieving environmental justice part of its mission by identifying and addressing, as appropriate, disproportionately high and adverse human health or environmental effects of its programs, policies, and activities on minority populations and low-income populations.

These passages demonstrate that federal language exists but should not be taken as the exclusive interpretation of environmental justice. For our purposes, it is not necessary to have a specific definition of environmental justice, but only to appreciate that there is a regulatory backdrop for distributional analysis, as a goal distinct from the more familiar goal of efficiency. The crucial point is that aggregate analysis is insufficient—we also need to know which groups win, and which groups lose.

The next section further describes an example of textbook efficiency analysis, highlighting how distributional issues can be obscured in the typical conceptual model. Succeeding sections describe potential sources of error in estimating benefits, which can underrepresent certain groups. Note any associated disadvantage does not need to be borne by a recognized environmental justice group, such as low-income or minority groups. Any tendency toward exclusion or non-neutral treatment of any group is included. The intent of the chapter is not to dismiss valuation, but rather to summarize potential pitfalls, describe strategies for their remediation, and outline areas needing research. In so doing it is hoped that a contribution is made toward conjunctive environmental justice and ecosystem service management.

BACKGROUND: EFFICIENCY VERSUS DISTRIBUTIONAL IMPACTS

Economics and valuation typically focus on overall efficiency. There have been relatively few contributions on distributional impacts (as noted by Loomis, 2011), the central concern of environmental justice. Recent guidelines on preparing economic analyses from EPA remain incomplete on distributional impacts, with additional information on the subject to be posted "as it becomes available" (U.S. EPA, 2010d, Ch. 10, p. 1). In pursuing overall efficiency, the typical test is a "potential Pareto improvement," in which total net benefits are increased. Theoretically winners could compensate any losers to ensure no one is made worse off, resulting in an actual Pareto improvement. However redistributing gains requires overcoming transactions costs. Valuation rarely moves beyond identifying potential Pareto improvements (Gowdy, 2004).[5] Discussions on redistributing wealth are controversial, and texts refer to ethics problems as "normative" rather than "positive" economics (Heath, 1994). Aversion to normative associations may explain why relatively few valuation researchers investigate problems of distribution, even though economic information to assist equity judgments can be furnished in a purely positive sense.

To illustrate, the framework for a typical environmental economics study is shown in figure 1. Taking the example of clean water, there are costs with pollution reduction that may be idealized as the marginal costs curve shown. Cleanup is cheap at first but becomes more expensive as easier methods are exhausted. Benefits of pollution control can be idealized as the marginal benefits curve shown. Societal benefits are high per unit improvement at first but then become smaller as water quality continues to improve, through the normal assumption of diminishing returns. Because costs of cleanup can exceed benefits, zero pollution is usually not justified. The efficient goal in the aggregate is to be at the point where the marginal cost of cleanup equals the marginal benefit, the intersection of the curves. Only if benefits exceed abatement costs at every pollution level (yielding no intersection) would optimal pollution be set equal to zero.

Environmental economists develop cost and benefit curves such as these so optimal solutions can be assessed. While this alone is exceedingly difficult, distributional impacts are not described in aggregate analysis and the information is thus incomplete for management purposes. Imagine if pollution reduction on tribal lands happened to be especially costly. It is

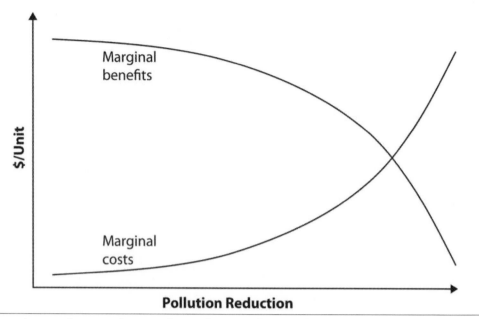

Figure 1. Idealized Aggregate Ecosystem Services Efficiency–Pollution Example

Cleanup becomes more expensive as easier methods are exhausted. Marginal benefits are smaller as water quality continues to improve. The idealized, "efficient" goal in the aggregate is to be at the point where the marginal cost equals the marginal benefit, the intersection of the curves.

clearly an environmental justice concern for a water pollution policy to pursue cleaner water everywhere else, but that would be the solution aggregate logic would offer. It would be elementary if it were more routinely observed in practice; BCA needs to consider distributional analysis to be informative for the goal of environmental justice.

CHALLENGES FOR VALUATION

Systematic Low-Income Disadvantage

Nearly all valuation surveys are presented in willingness-to-pay (WTP) format. That is, they ask respondents for their WTP to avoid an environmental damage, or their WTP for an environmental improvement.[6] This format was recommended as the "conservative choice" by the influential expert panel assembled by the National Oceanic and Atmospheric Administration in the wake of natural resources damages lawsuits associated with the 1989 Exxon *Valdez* oil spill in Prince William Sound, Alaska (Arrow et al., 1993). With WTP, respondents' bids are limited by their income, and a characteristic of high-quality standard surveys is to remind the respondent of their budgetary constraint. As might be expected, those with a higher income tend to have higher WTP for better environmental conditions. Indeed, income is a common regressor in valuation models, often positively correlated and statistically significant.[7] Thus, even if the income percentage high and low-income groups are willing to commit is identical, preferences of the rich would "count" more than the preferences of the poor. One could further imagine situations in which high and low preferences are at odds. With equal numbers in each group, preferences of the high-income group as measured by WTP would sum to a larger number. This contrasts with income-neutral manners of gauging preferences, such as voting.

The positive influence of income on benefits has been codified into valuation's benefit-transfer tools. The field of benefit-transfer offers techniques to adjust values from one or more contexts with data, to a context without data. The most sophisticated techniques are meta-analyses, which draw from multiple existing studies (for an overview, see Bergstrom and Taylor, 2006). One class of meta-analysis regresses on meta-data from multiple similar valuation studies, using a flexible functional specification. Income is a common regressor to explain variation in WTP (see Van Houtven et al., 2007, and Johnston et al., 2005).[8] The influence of income is even stronger in a second form of meta-analysis called structural transfer. Here WTP is derived from an indirect utility functional form defined at the outset, of which income is a traditional component. Thus, income is one of the key variables ultimately used to calibrate the utility function and predict WTP (see Smith, Van Houtven, and Pattanayak, 2002, and Van Houtven, Pattanayak, and Depro, 2011).

The income effect can lead to problems for environmental justice that will be referred to here as blind implementation. When localized projects occur in environmental management, such as selection of a river reach to restore, the reach closest to higher-income groups could be promoted if directed by original or benefit-transfer valuation results. Aggregate benefits would simply tend to be higher. By the same token, using valuation results to prioritize a list of environmental improvements for an entire region also favors high-income groups if their priorities differ from other groups. Since environmental management is inherently regional in implementation and enforcement, a systematic low-income disadvantage results if valuation alone directs that management.

Property Rights and the Income Effect Revisited

As noted in the prior section, WTP is the standard format in valuation. Sometimes this is theoretically appropriate and sometimes it is not, depending on property rights. There are four possible valuation elicitation formats. For environmental damages, the choices are the collective maximum WTP to avoid the loss, or the collective minimum willingness-to-accept (WTA) compensation for the loss. For environmental improvements, the choices are collective maximum WTP for the improvement, or collective WTA to forgo the improvement. Note that in cases of both degradation and improvement, when public environmental rights are stronger, the preferred welfare elicitation question is type WTA. A WTP format implies the lack of a public property right to the better environmental condition. When the public does hold that property right, a WTA format is theoretically preferred. The WTA format removes the income effect and places bids from all income groups on more equal footing. When WTP is used, the income effect again places low-income groups at a disadvantage, and environmental justice would be compromised under conditions of blind implementation.

In some cases the degree to which people have rights to environmental resources is unsettled. However, in many circumstances the public property right is clear. In the United States, the Clean Air Act, the Clean Water Act, and the Endangered Species Act all give citizens environmental rights.[9] High-profile ecosystem services and valuation publications continue to note WTA and/or the importance of observing correct property rights in valuation (Millennium Ecosystem Assessment, 2003, p. 134; U.S. National Research Council of the National

Academy of Sciences, 2004, pp. 47–50; U.S. Office of Management and Budget, 2003, Benefit-Transfer Methods section).

Improper use of WTP can lead to poor efficiency outcomes. Bids with WTA have been shown to be four to twenty-eight times higher than their WTP counterparts (Horowitz and McConnell, 2002). It should be noted that the income effect is only one of several explanations for the discrepancy (Brown and Gregory, 1999; Knetsch, 2007). The solution may not be as simple as switching to WTA, since there are concerns of non-incentive compatibility (inviting strategic behavior), and bid scenarios that sound unrealistic to respondents. In the famous valuation study following the *Valdez* disaster, the authors acknowledge their usage of WTP as theoretically incorrect (Carson et al., 1992, pp. 1-7 to 1-8). For both environmental justice and efficiency reasons valuation needs to overcome issues with estimating WTA, rather than simply defaulting to WTP.

Intergenerational Impacts

Economists apply discount rates evident in society to assess returns on an investment over time. Usually environmental protection has benefits that continue for successive generations. Likewise, failure to protect the environment has costs for successive generations. Discounting the benefits of action, and the costs of inaction, is standard practice and reduces the worth of investing in the environment today. Normally with environmental justice, we think about guarding against disproportionate impacts for the present generation. However, since environmental choices today affect future generations as a group, intergenerational impacts can be seen as an environmental justice issue. This would admittedly be a broad interpretation of environmental justice.

Part of the argument for a positive discount rate is that the next generation is likely to be richer, as has been the historical trend (Arrow et al., 1995, p. 191). Thus, a degree of extractive resource use is justified as a means of borrowing against future wealth. Another argument is that people through their own behavior exhibit positive, and sometimes large, discount rates for environmental goods (Stevens, DeCoteau, and Willis, 1997). Yet another argument is that environment expenditures should be treated like any other investment in a portfolio, and a standard discount rate attached so it can be fairly compared with other investments and their typical returns. Discount rates in keeping with the latter argument are common, with applied rates between 3 percent and 7 percent, following U.S. Office of Management and Budget (2003) recommendations.

A positive discount rate means the future matters less than the present. Over a long time horizon, the effect is substantial. For environmental issues such as climate change with delayed impacts, discount rates make it hard to justify mitigation and adaptation strategies. This is at odds with an interpretation of environmental justice whereby everyone would enjoy the same degree of environmental protection.

Based on an uncertainty argument regarding what future investment returns will actually be, some research has proposed a smaller discount rate for the far future than the near future (Weitzman, 1998, 2001). This is related to an argument for low discount rates for risk-free investments, such as investments in environmental quality (Howarth, 2009). An approach known as the "precautionary principle" also implies low discount rates on environmental assets due to potential irreversibilities in ecological processes. However, note that the theoretic goal of strict intergenerational environmental justice seems unrealistic. Equilibrating all environmental conditions over time would deprive all generations of consuming any nonrenewable resources (among other results). For a sustainability-based review of such issues and a conceptual solution by which present generations could compensate future generations for irreparable environmental losses, see Howarth (2003). Further conceptual and practical explorations of how to maintain the most valuable aspects of environmental quality, and/or value compensation due across generations for differences in environmental quality, are needed.

Limited Geographic Scale

Valuation studies might be done at too small a geographic scale to measure potential benefits to all relevant populations. Preferences of those outside the sample frame are either included imperfectly by proxy or not included at all, excluding potential stakeholders from the analysis a priori. Such "extent of market" issues are persistent in valuation, control how values are aggregated, and have enormous influence over final values (Bateman et al., 2006; Smith, 1993). There are a few studies that have been conducted at a U.S. national scale, including (but not limited to) Carson et al. (1992), Carson and Mitchell (1993), Chestnut and Rowe (1990), Loomis (1996), and Viscusi, Huber, and Bell (2008). The overwhelming majority of studies have localized sample frames. As a standing issue in valuation, researchers continue to explore "distance-decay" functions (Hanley, Schläpfer, and Spurgeon, 2003) that could help extrapolate values to unsampled populations. The emphasis of such functions is improving aggregate value estimates, rather than examining distributional considerations of geographically limited preference information.

Limited geographic scale may or may not disadvantage any particular group—but the analyst should be aware of the possibility. The concern is again intertwined with a potentially poor outcome for efficiency if only a subset of the relevant geography is considered. Valuation needs to develop guidelines on defining the geographic extent of sample frames, including both distributional impact analysis and efficiency analysis criteria.

Survey Methods

Many surveys begin with a qualitative research phase to test ideas and language, sometimes referred to as "pretesting" (Dillman, 2007). Qualitative research has several critical components, one of which is human subjects recruiting (Morgan and Krueger, 1998). Recruits from low-income and minority populations may be underrepresented with simplified recruiting strategies, such as using preexisting contacts, or advertisements distributed in a single language. Input from a narrow sociodemographic profile can result in biased feedback. Paying incentives for participation can broaden the sociodemographic pool, that is, allow those otherwise unable to miss work or pay for child care to attend (Krueger and Casey, 2009), but such incentives are not always budgeted. Governmental agencies typically convene "open door" public meetings to gather feedback, which contrasts with targeted recruiting. The danger is that input beyond the "usual suspects" will be missed. Survey development guided by an incomplete qualitative phase may completely miss topics of concern to some groups.

Qualitative research traditions are largely separate from economics, although some implications for valuation have been described by Hoehn, Lupi, and Kaplowitz (2003), Johnston et al.

(1995), and Kaplowitz and Hoehn (2001). A research opportunity remains to ascertain how to best design qualitative methods to represent environmental priorities of different groups.

After the survey is developed (hopefully as informed by sufficient qualitative research), it is deployed to a sample of the population, and responses are collected from some fraction of that sample. There are several possible sources of survey bias in results, and the preferences of all distinct groups in the population may not be adequately represented, even if the qualitative phase has ensured the questions are relevant for them. Nonresponse bias can occur when certain groups have a lower response rate, systematically lessening their input. Those of lower socioeconomic status and education are prone to nonresponse (Goyder, 1988; Green, 1996). Minority respondents may not even be literate in the language the survey uses. While researchers can take corrective measures and weight the responses in proportion to demographics of the overall target population, precisely the groups environmental justice typically seeks to protect seem most likely to be underrepresented with raw data. Furthermore, when analyzing responses collected from a survey, outlier bids and protest bids are routinely thrown out (Halstead, Luloff, and Stevens, 1992; Jorgensen et al., 1999). This distances our appreciation of environmental values represented by certain segments of society.

Opportunities in Hedonics

Environmental justice studies are found throughout the literature. A common theme is analyzing differential proximity to environmental pollutants, such as air emission sources (e.g., Chakraborty, 2009; Green et al., 2004), or to environmental commodities, such as open space (e.g., Boone et al., 2009). At the same time, valuation studies concerning the same issues are found in many journals. A popular valuation technique called hedonics can be applied to isolate housing price premiums for similar environmental variables as above, that is, WTP to avoid proximity to air pollution sources (e.g., meta-analysis by Smith and Huang, 1995), or WTP for proximity to open space (e.g., Anderson and West, 2006; Riddel, 2001). While the environmental justice studies find statistical evidence of differential impacts detrimental, hedonic environmental economics studies begin with the hypothesis of differential impacts, and only by quantifying this are they able to infer societal value.

The body of hedonic literature is extremely important and informative but is potentially at cross-purposes with environmental justice. Significant valuation outcomes may at the same time be evidence of environmental injustice. The hedonic analyst focusing only on valuation misses an opportunity to investigate how the environmental amenity or disamenity is distributed. In a sense, the researcher could address two concerns of society with one data set. Take a typical study investigating housing prices and statistically isolating the price disparity associated with an environmental amenity or disamenity. For an environmental justice analysis two additional points would be relevant: whether the price disparity is correlated with a certain group (i.e., higher-priced properties belonging to the higher-income group); and whether the environmental feature is something public entities manage (for policy pertinence).

Considering environmental justice can also aid interpretation of a hedonic study. For example, if no effect of park proximity on home value is found, it does not necessarily mean parks have no value. It could mean the community is proactive about providing green space for housing across income levels. As environmental justice actions increase, one could see how the effectiveness of hedonics in estimating values could decrease. In principle, a time-series approach to hedonics would be useful to disentangle a sequence of events, such as whether environmental disamenities are sited in poor neighborhoods, or if those neighborhoods became poor after disamenities were sited within them. For an example of such time-series thinking see Banzhaf and McCormick (2006). Tracking hedonic responses over time could be important information to help judge whether amenity or disamenity siting decisions were discriminatory.

CONCLUSIONS

In large part, the challenge of ecosystem services is in understanding their value such that improved natural resource management may follow for the greater public good. While extraordinarily important, typical aggregate analysis is insufficient for society's goals since it does not consider distributional impacts and the related concept of environmental justice. Only through considering winners and losers of potential environmental decisions can new injustices be ascertained, or opportunities to repair standing injustices be realized. This chapter does not attempt to describe how to make final judgments about whether environmental outcomes are just or unjust. How to make such equity judgments to guide environmental management presents complementary research needs beyond our focus: improving the care with which valuation is conducted and implemented for the purposes of informing subsequent environmental justice analysis. It should be clearly stated that any impacts relevant for environmental justice from flaws in valuation require that valuation is actually used to guide a decision, and that a decision is implemented such that variable effects across different groups in the population are possible.

In many cases valuation practice and implementation can be adapted to better serve distributional analysis. An obvious method is simply to move beyond aggregate analysis and tabulate results for different subgroups of the population (Loomis, 2011). However valuation techniques can also be adapted or implemented more carefully. Potential flaws in valuation for environmental justice boil down to the following:

- The values of certain groups may not be adequately represented.
- The groups themselves may not be adequately represented.
- The technique is potentially at cross-purposes with environmental justice research.

Addressing these problems is difficult, but important for leveling the playing field and capturing fuller returns from valuation research. In some cases, addressing issues will also lead to improved research regarding aggregate net benefits. Some suggestions are the following:

- Additional research on the magnitude of the income effect, and income-neutral modes of valuation when the income effect is significant
- Careful rather than blind implementation of valuation in decisions to reduce outcomes favoring high-income groups due to the income effect
- Observation of environmental property rights

- Consideration of the extent to which groups may be left out of or diminished in valuation analysis either in time (i.e., future generations) or space (i.e., outside of the sampling envelope)
- Development of qualitative research guidelines adapted for valuation
- Consideration of whether protest and outlier bids in surveys correspond to certain sociodemographic groups in society
- While engaged in hedonic research, consideration of simultaneously investigating environmental justice

Topics in this chapter are highlighted not to dismiss valuation, but to advertise environmental justice concerns for those unfamiliar with subtleties of applying valuation techniques or results, to provide suggestions for practice, and to pose challenges for future research. Ecosystem service trade-offs are arguably more and more pressing, while at the same time expectations are on the rise for addressing distributive impacts.

NOTES

Author support is provided by a postdoctoral fellowship with the U.S. Environmental Protection Agency, Office of Research and Development. Randy Bruins, Gerardo Gambirazzio, Laura Norman, Hale Thurston, and anonymous reviewers provided feedback that improved earlier drafts. Errors and views lie solely with the author. This research does not represent official government policy.

1. Concepts mirror dilemmas of public goods discussed in classical economics, expanding the relevant reference list still further.
2. While environmental justice analysis is not the same as distributional impact analysis, the former does require at least some of the latter.
3. It is less clear that federal decisions hinge on monetized economic analysis (Hahn and Dudley, 2007; Weber, 2010) and it is an ongoing debate, beyond the scope of this chapter, as to whether they should.
4. The official government publication "federal real property profile" excludes important areas, such as national parks, national forests, and wildlife refuges (U.S. Federal Real Property Council, 2009). Thus, a nongovernmental source was used that had compiled this data.
5. Gowdy (2004) also questions the theoretical basis for focusing on potential Pareto improvements.
6. There are two main valuation survey methods, contingent valuation, and choice experiments.
7. It should be noted that in a meta-analysis on income effects reported in contingent valuation studies, Schläpfer (2006) finds income effects to be surprisingly low. He speculates this may be due to a methodological problem, not because income effects do not exist.
8. Some meta-regressions have discarded income due to lack of influence (see Johnston et al., 2003, and Rosenberger and Loomis, 2001), although this may be partly due to aggregation bias since income in metadata was sometimes obtained from a secondary source such as the U.S. Census.
9. The Clean Water Act requires fishable and swimmable status for all "Waters of the U.S.," with rare exceptions. Waters of the United States generally include all interstate waters; intrastate waters used in interstate and/or foreign commerce; tributaries of the above; territorial seas at the cyclical high tide mark; and wetlands adjacent to all the above (U.S. EPA, 2008b). The Clean Air Act requires programs to improve visibility, ensure healthy standards for ambient air quality, protect

against toxic emissions from point sources, and reduce chemicals that destroy stratospheric ozone (U.S. EPA, 2010f). Specific standards for ambient air quality to which the public has a right are posted by U.S. EPA (2010e). The Endangered Species Act prohibits a "taking" of listed species and requires development and implementation of recovery plans, including designating critical habitat (U.S. Fish and Wildlife Service, 2010).

REFERENCES

Anderson, S. T., and S. E. West. 2006. "Open Space, Residential Property Values, and Spatial Context." *Regional Science and Urban Economics* 36:773–89.

Arrow, K. J., W. R. Kline, K.-G. Mäler, M. Munasinghe, R. Squitieri, and J. E. Stiglitz. 1995. "Intertemporal Equity, Discounting, and Economic Efficiency." In *Climate Change 1995: Economic and Social Dimensions of Climate Change*, ed. J. P. Bruce, J. Lee, and K. F. Haites for the Intergovernmental Panel on Climate Change. Cambridge: Cambridge University Press.

Arrow, K. J., R. Solow, E. Leamer, P. Portney, R. Rander, and H. Schuman. 1993. "Report of the NOAA Panel on Contingent Valuation." *Federal Register* 58(10): 4602–14.

Banzhaf, H. S., and E. McCormick. 2006. "Moving Beyond Cleanup: Identifying the Crucibles of Environmental Gentrification." Andrew Young School of Policy Studies Research Paper Series No. 07-29, December.

Bateman, I. J., B. H. Day, S. Georgiou, and I. Lake. 2006. "The Aggregation of Environmental Benefit Values: Welfare Measures, Distance Decay, and Total WTP." *Ecological Economics* 60:450–60.

Bergstrom, J. C., and L. O. Taylor. 2006. "Using Meta-analysis for Benefits Transfer: Theory and Practice." *Ecological Economics* 60:351–60.

Boone, C. G., G. L. Buckley, J. M. Grove, and C. Sister. 2009. "Parks and People: An Environmental Justice Inquiry in Baltimore, Maryland." *Annals of the Association of American Geographers* 99(4): 767–87.

Brown, T. C., and R. Gregory. 1999. "Why the WTA-WTP Disparity Matters." *Ecological Economics* 28:323–35.

Carson, R. T., R. C. Mitchell, W. M. Hanemann, R. J. Kopp, S. Presser, and P. A. Ruud. 1992. *A Contingent Valuation Study of Lost Passive Use Values Resulting from the Exxon Valdez Oil Spill: A Report to the Attorney General of Alaska*. November 10. Retrieved January 6, 2011, from http://mpra .ub.uni-muenchen.de/6984/.

Carson, R. T., and R. C. Mitchell. 1993. "The Value of Clean Water: The Public's Willingness to Pay for Boatable, Fishable, and Swimmable Quality Water." *Water Resources Research* 29(7): 2445–54.

Chakraborty, J. 2009. "Automobiles, Air Toxics, and Adverse Health Risks: Environmental Inequities in Tampa Bay, Florida." *Annals of the Association of American Geographers* 99(4): 674–97.

Chestnut, L. G., and R. D. Rowe. 1990. "Preservation Values for Visibility Protection at the National Parks." Draft Final Report. Prepared for: Economic Analysis Branch, Office of Air Quality Planning and Standards, U.S. Environmental Protection Agency, Research Triangle Park, North Carolina, and Air Quality Management Division, National Park Service, Denver, Colorado.

Cole, L. W., and S. R. Foster. 2001. *From the Ground Up: Environmental Racism and the Rise of the Environmental Justice Movement*. New York: New York University Press.

Cox, S., and B. Searle. 2009. "The State of Ecosystem Services." The Bridgespan Group. December. http://www.bridgespan.org/state-of-ecosystem-services.aspx.

Daily, G. C., ed. 1997. *Nature's Services: Societal Dependence on Natural Ecosystems*. Washington, DC: Island Press.

Dillman, D. A. 2007. *Mail and Internet Surveys*. Hoboken, NJ: John Wiley & Sons.

Duke University. 2009. National Ecosystem Services Partnership. http://nicholasinstitute.duke.edu/sites/default/files/october_kickoff_meeting_summary.pdf

Freeman, A. M., III. 2003. *The Measurement of Environmental and Resource Values*. 2nd edition. Washington, DC: Resources For the Future.

Gowdy, J. M. 2004. "The Revolution in Welfare Economics and Its Implications for Environmental Valuation and Policy." *Land Economics* 80(2): 239–57.

Goyder, J. 1988. *The Silent Minority: Nonrespondents on Sample Surveys*. Boulder, CO: Westview Press.

Green, K. E. 1996. "Sociodemographic Factors and Mail Survey Response." *Psychology and Marketing* 13(2): 171–84.

Green, R. S., S. Smorodinsky, J. J. Kim, R. McLaughlin, and B. Ostro. 2004. "Proximity of California Public Schools to Busy Roads." *Environmental Health Perspectives* 112(1): 61–66.

Hahn, W. R., and P. M. Dudley. 2007. "How Well Does the U.S. Government Do Benefit-Cost Analysis?" *Review of Environmental Economics and Policy* 1(2): 192–211.

Halstead, J. M., A. E. Luloff, and T. H. Stevens. 1992. "Protest Bidders in Contingent Valuation." *Northeastern Journal of Agricultural and Resource Economics* 21:160–69.

Hanley, N., F. Schläpfer, and J. Spurgeon. 2003. "Aggregating the Benefits of Environmental Improvements: Distance-Decay Functions for Use and Non-use Values." *Journal of Environmental Management* 68:297–304.

Heath, W. C. 1994. "Value Judgments and the Principles of Economics Textbook." *Southern Economic Journal* 60:1060–64.

Hoehn, J. P., F. Lupi, and M. D. Kaplowitz. 2003. "Untying a Lancastrian Bundle: Valuing Ecosystems and Ecosystem Services for Wetland Mitigation." *Journal of Environmental Management* 68(3): 263–72.

Horowitz, J. K., and K. E. McConnell. 2002. "A Review of WTA/WTP Studies." *Journal of Environmental Economics and Management* 44(3): 426–47.

Howarth, R. B. 2003. "Discounting and Sustainability: Towards Reconciliation." *International Journal of Sustainable Development* 6(1): 87–97.

Howarth, R. B. 2009. "Discounting, Uncertainty, and Revealed Time Preference." *Land Economics* 85(1): 24–40.

Johnston, R. J., E. Y. Besedin, R. Iovanna, C. J. Miller, R. F. Wardwell, and M. H. Ranson. 2005. "Systematic Variation in Willingness to Pay for Aquatic Resource Improvements and Implications for Benefit Transfer: A Meta-Analysis." *Canadian Journal of Agricultural Economics* 53:221–48.

Johnston, R. J., E. Y. Besedin, and R. F. Wardwell. 2003. "Modeling Relationships between Use and Nonuse Values for Surface Water Quality: A Meta-analysis." *Water Resources Research* 39(12): 1–9.

Johnston, R. J., T. F. Weaver, L. A. Smith, and S. K. Swallow. 1995. "Contingent Valuation Focus Groups: Insights from Ethnographic Interview Techniques." *Agricultural and Resource Economics Review* 24(1): 56–69.

Jorgensen, S. B., G. J. Syme, B. J. Bishop, and B. E. Nancarrow. 1999. "Protest Responses in Contingent Valuation." *Environmental and Resource Economics* 14:131–50.

Kaplowitz, M. D., and J. P. Hoehn. 2001. "Do Focus Groups and Individual Interviews Reveal the Same Information for Natural Resource Valuation?" *Ecological Economics* 36(2): 237–47.

Knetsch, J. L. 2007. "Biased Valuations, Damage Assessments, and Policy Choices: The Choice of Measure Matters." *Ecological Economics* 63(4): 684–89.

Krueger, R. A., and M. A. Casey. 2009. *Focus Groups: A Practical Guide for Applied Research*. 4th edition. Thousand Oaks, CA: Sage Publications.

Loomis, J. 1996. "Measuring the Economic Benefits of Removing Dams and Restoring the Elwha River: Results of a Contingent Valuation Survey." *Water Resources Research* 32:441–47.

Loomis, J. 2011. "Incorporating Distributional Issues into Benefit Cost Analysis: Why, How, and Two Empirical Examples Using Non-market Valuation." *Journal of Benefit-Cost Analysis* 2(1): 1–22.

Millennium Ecosystem Assessment. 2003. *Ecosystems and Human Well-Being: A Framework for Assessment*. Washington, DC: Island Press. http://www.maweb.org/en/index.aspx.

Millennium Ecosystem Assessment. 2005. *Ecosystems and Human Well-Being: Synthesis*. Washington, DC: Island Press. http://www.maweb.org/en/index.aspx.

Morgan, D. L., and R. A. Krueger. 1998. *The Focus Group Kit*. 6 vol. Thousand Oaks, CA: Sage Publications.

Natural Resources Council of Maine. 2000. "Public Land Ownership by State." http://www.nrcm.org/documents/publiclandownership.pdf.

Riddel, M. 2001. "A Dynamic Approach to Estimating Hedonic Prices for Environmental Goods: An Application to Open Space Purchase." *Land Economics* 77(4): 494–512.

Rosenberger, R. S., and J. B. Loomis. 2001. "Benefit Transfer of Outdoor Recreation Use Values: A Technical Document Supporting the Forest Service Strategic Plan (2000 Revision)." General Technical Report RMRS-GTR-72. U.S. Department of Agriculture, Forest Service, Rocky Mountain Research Station.

Schläpfer, F. 2006. "Survey Protocol and Income Effects in the Contingent Valuation of Public Goods: A Meta-analysis." *Ecological Economics* 57:415–29.

Smith, V. K. 1993. "Nonmarket Valuation of Environmental Resources: An Interpretive Appraisal." *Land Economics* 69(1): 1–26.

Smith, V. K., G. Van Houtven, and S. K. Pattanayak. 2002. "Benefit Transfer via Preference Calibration: 'Prudential Algebra' for Policy." *Land Economics* 78(1): 132–52.

Smith, V. K., and J. Huang. 1995. "Can Markets Value Air Quality? A Meta-analysis of Hedonic Property Value Models." *Journal of Political Economy* 103(1): 209–27.

Stevens, T. H., N. E. DeCoteau, and C. E. Willis. 1997. "Sensitivity of Contingent Valuation to Alternative Payment Schedules." *Land Economics* 73(1): 140–48.

U.S. EPA. 2008a. "Ecological Research Program Multi-year Plan 2008–2014." Review Draft, February. http://www.epa.gov/ord/htm/multi-yearplans.htm#eco.

U.S. EPA. 2008b. "Introduction to the Clean Water Act." http://www.epa.gov/owow/watershed/wacademy/acad2000/cwa/.

U.S. EPA. 2010a. "Ecosystem Services Research Program." http://www.epa.gov/ecology/.

U.S. EPA. 2010b. "Environmental Justice." http://www.epa.gov/environmentaljustice/.

U.S. EPA. 2010c. "EPA's Action Development Process: Interim Guidance on Considering Environmental Justice during the Development of an Action." July. http://www.epa.gov/compliance/ej/resources/policy/considering-ej-in-rulemaking-guide-07-2010.pdf.

U.S. EPA. 2010d. "Guidelines for Preparing Economic Analyses." December. http://yosemite.epa.gov/ee/epa/eed.nsf/pages/guidelines.html.

U.S. EPA. 2010e. "National Ambient Air Quality Standards." http://www.epa.gov/air/criteria.html.

U.S. EPA. 2010f. "The Plain English Guide to the Clean Air Act." http://www.epa.gov/air/caa/peg/.

U.S. Federal Real Property Council. 2009. "The Federal Real Property Council's FY 2008 Federal Real Property Report: An Overview of the U.S. Federal Government's Real Property Assets." August. http://www.gsa.gov/portal/content/102880.

U.S. Fish and Wildlife Service. 2010. "Endangered Species Program." http://www.fws.gov/endangered/.

U.S. Forest Service. 2010. "Ecosystem Services." http://www.fs.fed.us/ecosystemservices/.

U.S. National Research Council of the National Academy of Sciences. 2004. *Valuing Ecosystem Services: Toward Better Environmental Decision-Making*. Committee on Assessing and Valuing the Services of Aquatic and Related Terrestrial Ecosystems. Washington, DC: National Academies Press.

U.S. Office of Management and Budget. 2003. "Circular A-4. Regulatory Analysis." September 17. http://www.whitehouse.gov/omb/circulars_a004_a-4/.

Van Houtven, G. L., S. K. Pattanayak, and B. M. Depro,.2011. "Benefits Transfer of a Third Kind: An Examination of Structural Benefits Transfer." In *Preference Data for Environmental Valuation*, ed. J. Whitehead, J. C. Huang, and T. Haab. Explorations in Environmental Economics Series. New York: Routledge.

Van Houtven, G., J. Powers, and S. K. Pattanayak. 2007. "Valuing Water Quality Improvements in the United States Using Meta-analysis: Is the Glass Half-Full or Half-Empty for National Policy Analysis?" *Resource and Energy Economics* 29:206–28.

Viscusi, W. K., J. Huber, and J. Bell. 2008. "The Economic Value of Water Quality." *Environmental and Resource Economics* 41:169–87.

Weber, M. 2010. "EPA Use of Ecological Nonmarket Valuation." *Association of Environmental and Resource Economists Newsletter* 30(1): 26–35.

Weitzman, M. L. 1998. "Why the Far-Distant Future Should Be Discounted at Its Lowest Possible Rate." *Journal of Environmental Economics and Management* 36(3): 201–8.

Weitzman, M. L. 2001. "Gamma Discounting." *American Economic Review* 91(1): 260–71.

Applications and Practice

Assessing the Trade-Offs for an Urban Green Economy

MYRNA HALL, NING SUN, STEPHEN BALOGH, CATHERINE FOLEY, AND RUIQI LI

Advocates of green fuels, green infrastructure, and green jobs propose implementation of various nature-based technologies to revitalize the economies of cities. Some, such as tree planting, provide ecosystem services such as reduction of urban air pollutants, temperatures, and storm water runoff. Others, such as solar energy capture technologies, are intended to reduce dependence on fossil fuel and home energy costs. Yet others, such as community gardens and urban agricultural production, are a means to enhance nutrition and reduce food costs in urban neighborhoods where access to fresh food is often limited. Some technologies (e.g., green roofs, naturally draining bio-retention basins, or porous paving) are very energy intensive to build and all require considerable maintenance. Furthermore, all compete for the limited space and funds available in the urban environment, and installation of one may preclude the benefits of others. Enthusiasm for these technologies is leading to their implementation in cities around the world without much, if any, evaluation of the trade-offs of installing one over another, for example in terms of their economic efficiency, energy costs, energy return on investment, the number of jobs they would contribute to the "green economy," or citizen receptivity, which is key to their long-term success. Such an analysis is critical as world energy supplies dwindle and global unemployment is on the rise. We propose a methodology for the assessment of trade-offs based on net energy gains and apply it to a neighborhood in Syracuse, New York. We find, for example, that the net energy gain of food production and solar thermal installations combined approximately equals that derived from planting trees.

INTRODUCTION

Around the world advocates of green fuels, green infrastructure (GI), and green jobs have proposed various nature-based technologies as means to revitalize the economies of cities (UNECE, 2011). In the United States the Sustainable Communities Partnership consisting of the Environmental Protection Agency (EPA), the Department of Housing and Urban Development (HUD), and the Department of Transportation has recently announced its second round of funding for its Greening America's Capitals program with this goal in mind.

151

Along with "smart growth" and transportation planning the partnership is promoting green building and green infrastructure, including such elements as tree planting, vegetated storm water controls, and solar energy capture. The Partnership suggests that these innovations in design and structure of our communities will not only provide jobs but also save taxpayers energy and money (EPA, 2010).

Science has shown that green infrastructure can positively impact the urban environment. The urban forest reduces the urban heat island effect (Heisler et al., 2007; Murphy et al., 2011) and can influence household summertime cooling demand or provide winter wind protection (Heisler, 1986, 1991). Recent work by Alfredo, Montalto, and Goldstein (2010) has shown the storm flow runoff reduction potential from green roofs, however many storm water management solutions (e.g., green roofs, rain gardens, naturally draining bioswales, or porous paving), are very energy intensive to build. Unfortunately such energy costs are generally not included in the focus of scientific papers that assess their effectiveness. All GI, including trees and gardens, requires considerable maintenance. Furthermore, all technologies compete for the limited space in the urban environment and may preclude other green technologies such as photovoltaic (PV) installations or solar thermal (hot water) systems that can reduce heating or cooling costs. They may also occupy precious space for urban food production, also recognized by many as an essential way to improve inner-city quality of life and health and contribute to overall urban sustainability. Finally, whether or not these technologies can be implemented in neighborhoods either in public or private spaces depends on citizen knowledge, attitudes toward nature in the city, and willingness to participate. Hence the constraints to successfully moving toward a "greener" city physically, ecologically, economically, and socially are many.

Although science has quantified many of the ecological benefits of the urban forest, many of which are included in the US Forest Service collaborative I-Tree software (USDA, 2011), it is difficult to find studies that have quantified the effectiveness of other GI options, let alone analyzed (1) the ecological or economic benefits versus the dollar or energy costs of individual GI technologies, or (2) the trade-offs to be considered when deciding to invest in one over another. Most surprising, given the world energy crisis, is the lack of attention devoted to the energy implications of each "greening" option, particularly when one considers that these options are advanced as desirable for long-term urban sustainability. Before making public and private investment, an analysis of the trade-offs and actual benefits of the many possible options is necessary.

To compare these various green solutions requires a common currency for evaluation of the trade-offs among and between them. In the study of natural ecosystems, quantification of energy flows is key to understanding system metabolism, trophic level efficiencies, and system pulses over time. This should be no less so in human-dominated ecosystems. Furthermore, the uncertainty of future oil supplies (Hall, Powers, and Schoenberg, 2008; Hall, Balogh, and Murphy, 2009; Hall and Day, 2009; Hall and Klitgaard, 2011), competition for the global energy available, and subsequent rising energy costs are already causing economic strain at the household, city, national, and international levels (Hamilton, 2009). Urban green revitalization must be selected to optimize energy use now and into the future and should be customized to each urban situation. We propose, therefore, a methodology of assessment of trade-offs based on neighborhood energy profiles, the net energy surplus, and the energy return on investment of proposed technologies.

Hall (2011) quantified existing urban energy use and green infrastructure in three urban neighborhoods of varying socioeconomic and biophysical structure in a typical rust belt city, Syracuse, New York. This city, like many others across the northeastern United States, has experienced huge economic losses from the drain of industry to the South and overseas, and as a consequence, large population losses and decline of inner-city neighborhood vigor. The analysis showed widely differing energy use and source fuels, depending on average neighborhood household income, housing size, and age. The affluent neighborhood used almost twice as much fossil energy per residence and per person as did the downtown, poorer, and more densely settled neighborhoods. Yet Armory Square, one of the two low-income neighborhoods evaluated, where 50 percent of the population was below the poverty level in 2000 (U.S. Census, 2012), is using a disproportionately large amount of electricity per hectare, per person, and per household when compared to the natural gas use pattern across the neighborhoods (figure 1). This cannot be explained by higher density alone. According to the 2000 census, 64 percent of these homes are heated with electricity. The other low-income neighborhood, the Near Westside (NWS), has the same number of people per household as the more affluent Strathmore neighborhood, but the average square feet of living area is only 37 percent the size of the latter (U.S. Census, 2012). The average household use of natural gas, however, is 78 percent and electricity use 60 percent of the Strathmore homes. According to the 2000 census 25 percent of NWS homes are heated with electricity, versus 5 percent in Strathmore.

Tree cover also varied across these neighborhoods with primary production as low as 5 gigajoules (GJ) per hectare in Armory Square, and as high as 13 GJ per hectare in the NWS and 19 GJ per hectare in Strathmore. The ratio of photosynthetic energy fixed to industrial energy used was approximately 1:700 in the poor neighborhoods, versus 1:400 in the affluent neighborhood. We interpreted this to mean that lower-income people are using more expensive fuel (electricity) for heating and are getting few of the benefits of urban trees listed earlier. The affluent neighborhood is getting an energy boost from the natural ecosystem that affects overall neighborhood socio-ecological metabolism and may contribute to lower household energy use per square foot.

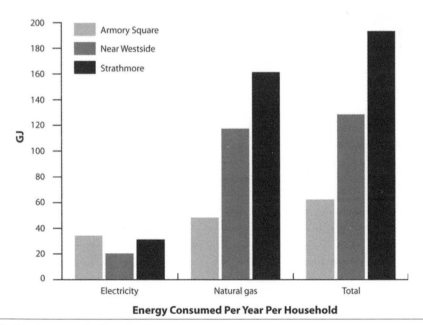

Figure 1. ENERGY CONSUMED PER YEAR PER HOUSEHOLD

Comparison of Neighborhood Household Electricity and Natural Gas Consumption Per Household in Three Neighborhoods of Syracuse, New York, with Varying Tree Cover, Housing Stock, and Household Economic Profiles

In general, both P (production of trees) and R (respiration mostly from fossil fuel consumption) were small relative to incoming solar radiation. Because fossil energy consumption was only 5 to 6 percent of incoming solar radiation, it may be possible to capture a portion of this energy through solar collectors at 5 percent efficiency, which could help alleviate future home energy requirements and provide green jobs. Factors that might work against such a plan include large upfront energy investment costs and the potential loss of large shade trees that can block incoming radiation. Clearly there are trade-offs that need to be evaluated and tailored to individual neighborhoods in order to find the optimal strategy for long-term sustainability.

The objective of this study, therefore, was to create a framework in which alternative strategies for urban greening can be assessed and test that framework within one neighborhood for three proposed green technologies—tree planting, solar thermal (hot water heating) systems, and urban food production. The proposed cost-benefit matrix compiles the estimated energy costs and energy gains for proposed urban greening strategies (table 1). Since our metric for comparison of green installations is energy, we assess the energy investment (cost) to install them and the energy gains to be realized by them through reduced home energy use, reductions in energy required to treat combined sewer/storm water, and caloric contributions to the neighborhood diet. We also calculated the energy return on energy invested, which is the benefit-to-cost ratio. We expect that as we populate this matrix the trade-offs between and among different strategies will emerge.

BACKGROUND

The questions "Who accrues the costs?" and "Who accrues the benefits?" suggest the need for such a matrix for both homeowners and local government. Since some GI technologies are paid for directly by the homeowner and others by homeowners via taxes, the willingness of residents to "buy in" to different technologies will vary according to their perception of immediate costs and eventual benefits. We analyzed the trade-offs at the neighborhood/city scale, rather than at the household scale. Although this implies that policies often encouraged via tax structuring, or low-interest loans, would be in the hands of local governing bodies, we recognize that the householders' attitudes and ability to pay will determine whether or not many, or most, of those policies are actually implemented. In fact we use citizen receptivity, measured via a GI survey (Sun and Hall, 2013; Foley, 2012) to inform the storm water runoff scenarios we employ to evaluate the first of three greening options.

We applied this analysis to one of the three neighborhoods for which baseline energy production-consumption statistics were calculated by Hall (2011). The neighborhood, known as the Near Westside, is located in the city of Syracuse, New York. This area of the city at the time of the 2000 census had one of the highest vacant home rates in the United States, and over 50 percent of the population fell below the poverty level. Due to its proximity to downtown, and particularly to the revitalized Armory Square mixed commercial/residential area, the neighborhood has received a great deal of attention from Onondaga County, the City of Syracuse, the Syracuse Center of Excellence Finance Center, Habitat for Humanity, Home Headquarters, and Syracuse University. This "attention" includes installation of low-impact development (LID) and GI demonstration projects, marketing of homes for "green" rehabilitation, new Leadership in Energy and Environmental Design (LEED) certified construction, an

Table 1. PROPOSED ENERGY COST AND BENEFIT MATRIX FOR MULTIPLE GREEN INFRASTRUCTURE TECHNOLOGIES

Technology	Application	Embodied energy	Energy to install/ maintain	EROI	$ savings	Negative consider-ations
Trees	Storm water management, UHI mitiga-tion, human health					
Solar PV panels	Household energy savings					
Solar hot water heating	Household energy savings					
Pervious paving	Storm water management					
Urban agriculture	Nutrition, health					
Rain gardens	Water con-servation / storm water management					
Rain barrels	Water con-servation / storm water management					

innovative "house for a dollar" program to encourage restoration of decaying properties, fostering reuse of abandoned commercial buildings for artists and cultural events, and introduction of new businesses. The neighborhood's six sewer sheds, which drain into nearby Onondaga Creek, were stipulated for routing to a planned regional sewage treatment facility under a court decision requiring Onondaga County to ensure "that effluent discharges from METRO [Onondaga County Metropolitan Waste Water Treatment Plant] and the combined sewer overflows (CSOs) are in compliance with the limitations set in its State Pollutant Discharge Elimination System ("SPDES") permit and state water quality standards for the receiving waters," that is, Onondaga Lake.[1] An amendment to the original court decision, agreed upon by all the stakeholders in 2006, stopped the building of the plant in favor of using GI and underground storage to avoid CSOs. In response the county executive has announced plans to plant 8,500 trees by 2018 throughout the city. Toward that end the county has received an urban forestry grant of $75,000 from the New York State Department of Environmental Conservation that will provide trees explicitly for the greening of the Near Westside. Greening strategies so far in this neighborhood have, therefore, been focused primarily on storm water reduction. For our analysis we selected one sewer shed (CSO 031) within the neighborhood (figure 2) to evaluate how much trees can reduce storm water runoff, whether it is enough to eliminate CSO events, and if these reductions can contribute significantly to reduced energy expenditures at the Onondaga County Metropolitan Waste Water Treatment Plant (WWTP).

To do this we have developed a submodel to the widely used Environmental Protection Agency Storm Water Management Model (SWMM), hereafter SWMM_GI (Sun, Hong, and Hall, 2013). It allows us to assess the degree to which flow in the combined sewer lines can be reduced by on-site or proposed GI implementations, for example, green roofs, tree cover, rain gardens, rain barrels, pervious paving, or curb extensions, particularly during the peak of a rainfall event, the critical time when overflows dump sewage directly into the city's creeks and nearby lake. Knowing the magnitude of this flow reduction also allows us to estimate how many fewer gallons would need to be treated as the nonoverflow effluent reaches the sewage treatment plant. The land surface cover within the sewer shed evaluated here (CSO 031) is defined at very high resolution so that location-specific alterations can be tested (figure 2). The coefficients of Manning's roughness and depression storage are fundamental to determining the overland flow from the individual types of land cover. The porous paving parameters were collected from field measurements, the tree parameter values were obtained from our previous model calibration procedure (Sun, Hong, and Hall, in revision), and the remaining parameter values were from an extensive recent literature review. Not only the land cover but also the path of runoff flowing over the landscape surface affects the final quantity of flow estimated to reach the combined sewer/sanitary trunk line. Runoff reductions could enhance urban stream water quality and opportunities for recreation. They could also reduce sewage treatment costs by reducing the amount of electricity required to pump the water through the treatment facility, and the cost for various chemicals used to remove phosphorous, or maintenance of bacteria employed in nitrogen removal.

METHODS

To test the net energy return for each of these proposed green technologies we estimated the energy costs and benefits of each and populated the trade-off matrix (table 1). Our

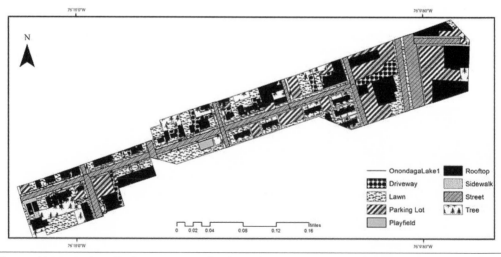

Figure 2. MICROSCALE LAND USE DELINEATION FOR ONE SEWER SHED IN THE NEAR WESTSIDE NEIGHBORHOOD OF SYRACUSE, NEW YORK

analysis began with a citizen survey that allows us to arrive at a realistic estimate of how many households are likely to adopt a green technology. Their receptivity toward tree planting, assessed here, informs the storm water runoff model SWMM_GI. From the predicted runoff we can estimate the reduction in sewage treatment and its energy savings. The number of trees added for each scenario also allows us to calculate household energy gains (if trees are optimally planted), and tree installation and maintenance costs. We also evaluate two alternatives to green the neighborhood. These include solar thermal and urban food production.

Preliminary Citizen Survey Results

From the initial fifty-three surveys analyzed we found that overall 80 percent of respondents are likely or very likely to implement tree planting if the trees are provided for free or if respondents were to save money on their water bill. However 74 percent of respondents also indicated that the cost to purchase and plant trees has "some" to "great" influence on their decision to plant trees, indicating that the true number of persons likely to participate if they were to bear the costs themselves is lower than 80 percent. Other factors influencing tree implementation, according to respondents, is the size of trees. Fifty-four percent indicated that the size of trees would have "some" to "great" influence on their decision to implement trees. Although respondents indicated that the size of trees would factor into their decision they were not given the opportunity to indicate *how* size might influence their decision, that is, if a large tree size is a positive or negative. From this we assumed an acceptability level for citizen tree planting that amounts to an approximate doubling of the current number of yard trees. This information is important to our runoff simulations described next.

Energy Cost and Benefit Calculations for Neighborhood Greening with Trees

Using information from the survey we tested the impacts of three different land cover scenarios on storm water runoff (table 2). The model was calibrated using actual sewer line hydrographs for four storm events in 2009 when combined sewer overflows occurred. According to the record there were eight such events that year. The first simulation is based on the City of Syracuse's plan for the Near Westside neighborhood that would reduce areas of 100 percent impervious cover in public areas to 80 percent impervious with 20 percent tree canopy cover and provide enough trees at maturity to cover all sidewalks. This area amounts to a total of 17.68 percent of the sewer shed or 0.833 ha, an increase of 9.25 percent of the total sewer shed area (table 2). The second scenario is based on the citizen survey and reflects the land cover change on private property as a function of the number of participants, as a percentage of the population, indicating willingness to plant trees. Lawn area is reduced from 22.62 percent of the sewer shed to 13.42 percent, impervious surface area is maintained as is, and future tree canopy area is also increased from 8.43 percent to 17.63 percent. The third scenario combines both the city plan and citizen response and results in a total canopy cover of 26.88 percent or 1.75 hectares (table 2). This is an 18 percent increase in existing canopy cover.

Table 2. THREE SCENARIOS OF LAND COVER INPUTS TO SWMM_GI ACCORDING TO CITIZEN RECEPTIVITY AND GOVERNMENT PLANS

	Surface type	Current	Tree-planting scenario		
			City plan	Neighborhood plan	Combined
Percentage of and cover	Impervious surface	68.95%	59.70%	68.95%	59.70%
	Tree	8.43%	17.68%	17.63%	26.88%
	Lawn	22.62%	22.62%	13.42%	13.42%

Total neighborhood area: 9.47 hectares
Average slope of neighborhood: 0.53%

Hall (2011) reports trees per mile of street in the core Near Westside neighborhood, with an average crown diameter of 6.36 meters. The majority of trees are very young. In another neighborhood of the city, where very mature trees shade the entire sidewalk, the average crown diameter is 11.76 m. We used the latter to calculate the number of new trees to be planted under the combined third scenario as follows:

$$\text{New Trees}_{\text{(City Plan + Citizen Plan)}} = \text{percent proposed area increase * sewershed area} \div \text{average crown area of mature trees}$$

$$= 0.18 * 9.47 \text{ ha}$$

$$= 1.74 \text{ ha} * 10,000 \text{ m}^2 \text{ per hectare}$$

$$= 17,472 \text{ m}^2 \div 109 \text{ m}^2 \text{ per tree}$$

$$= 160 \text{ trees of large crown size or more if smaller species.} \quad (1)$$

Within this sewer shed we counted trees on aerial photos and found approximately twenty existing private yard trees, some of which are the largest in the neighborhood, and another twenty-eight street and park trees for a total of forty-eight trees. The increased canopy under scenario 3 would triple the existing number of trees.

To calculate the energetic cost of increasing tree cover we used McHale, McPherson, and Burke's (2007) estimates of the average cost to plant and maintain a tree. Depending on location, size of tree planted, and labor source (paid or volunteer) this monetary cost can range between $100 and $570 per tree. We chose the median value of $335 per tree. The average energy intensity (energy consumed per dollar of GDP) for the U.S. economy in 2005 was approximately 7.65 megajoules (MJ) per dollar GDP. We use this value to estimate the energy cost per dollar spent on tree planting. This estimate does not include site preparation, which, depending on substrate, can increase this cost. The combined scenario energetic cost is calculated as follows:

$$\text{Cost}_{(trees)} = \text{number of new trees} * \$335 \text{ per tree} * 7.65 \text{ MJ per dollar} \quad (2)$$

The cost calculated should be divided by an expected forty years of tree lifespan since presumably the trees are planted only once, but the mortality rate of trees, and need for replacement, can run between 3 and 20 percent for newly planted trees, according to a summary of urban tree mortality studies done by Bond (2005). The cumulative thirty-year survival rate is between 40 and 75 percent. To make our estimates more realistic, therefore, we assume a 50 percent survival rate by thirty years and so calculate cost of the trees * 150 percent of the number of new trees estimated, and then divide by thirty years to get the annual cost.[2]

To calculate the energy gain derived from using trees for storm water management we have used data from the Onondaga County Metropolitan Waste Water Treatment Plant (WWTP), which treats an average of 84 million gallons a day of waste water. All incoming flows must be raised from their gravity flow arrival point to the secondary treatment level. Five centrifugal pumps of 600 horsepower each can lift up to sixty million gallons a day (MGD) for a total capacity of 240 MGD (OCDWEP, 2011). When flows exceed 124 MGD, the sewage bypasses secondary and tertiary treatment and is routed directly to Onondaga Lake. During lesser storms or during the rising or falling limb of a large precipitation event, when WWTP capacity is not exceeded, reductions in energy and material costs (chemicals, bacteria, and ultraviolet lightbulbs) required to bring the treated sewage to its final "polished" stage might also be realized. For this study we use the energetic cost of only the initial pumping. The conversion of horsepower (HP) per pump, to megajoules per day energy consumed is as follows:

$$\text{MJ per day per centrifugal pump} = ((600 \text{ HP} * 0.746\text{kW per HP} \\ * 24 \text{ hours per day}) * 3.6 \text{ MJ per kilowatt hour})$$

$$= 38,673 \text{ MJ.} \quad (3)$$

We calculate the energy gain in per gallons runoff avoided over the eight largest annual storm events, calculated as the average of four simulated events from our model times eight. The equation used is

$$\text{Gain}_{(trees)} = (\text{number of gallons avoided in 8 intense storm days} \div 60 \text{ million gallons} \\ \text{per day per centrifugal pump}) * \text{MJ per day per centrifugal pump.} \quad (4)$$

In addition to this benefit, we consider the potential savings on home energy use from the shading effect of trees. Studies to date estimate that this can be between 2 and 50 percent depending on latitude and altitude of the cities studied, number of trees, tree size, growth rate, azimuthal location, distance from house, and whether the impact affects heating or cooling (McPherson, 1993 [2–9 percent]; McPherson and Rowntree, 1993 [8–12 percent]; Simpson,

2002 [9 percent]). These estimates, however, require optimal siting of trees, preferably on the west side of homes (Heisler, 1986). In a dense urban environment such as this, where there are twenty-one residences per hectare versus eleven per hectare in more affluent neighborhoods of this city (Hall, 2011), the space required to achieve this level of energy savings may not be possible. Furthermore, homes may be shaded by neighboring homes with little space between for optimal planting. Therefore, we applied the lower 5 percent savings. Finally, the monthly energy use in this neighborhood (figure 3) is highest during January. Since houses are quite close together, already it is not clear that trees will provide much in the way of additional wind break, which is normally the winter benefit. If planted on the south side of houses, given the east-west orientation of the majority of the streets, they could in fact reduce winter solar gain on south-facing walls. We, therefore, estimate that the savings would come primarily in summer and, therefore, adjust the energy savings estimate to 5 percent of the June through August electricity use, assumed to rise at that time due to air conditioning. Hall (2011) reported average Near Westside household electricity consumption of 20 GJ (figure 1). Of this the summer average per household, based on National Grid data for residences in the Near Westside neighborhood, is 1,746 kilowatt hours (kWh) (6.28 GJ) (figure 3), so the second energy benefit of trees due to household energy consumption savings in sixty-seven residences in CSO 031 is

$$\text{Gain}_{(trees2)} = 67 \text{ households} * (\text{average summer electricity use per household} * 0.05). \quad (5)$$

Energy Cost and Benefit Calculations for Neighborhood Greening with Solar Thermal Installations

We generated a second, independent greening scenario for the neighborhood to permit collection of solar energy that might offset the current disproportionate use of expensive

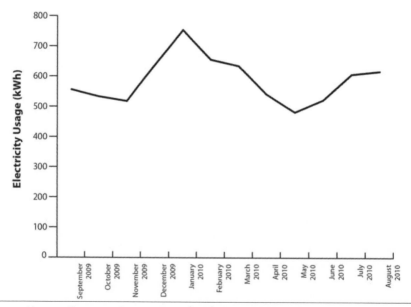

Figure 3. Average Monthly Household Electricity Use (kWh) in the Near Westside Neighborhood of Syracuse, New York, September 2009 to August 2010

electricity in this economically stressed neighborhood (Hall, 2011; Li, 2012). For this analysis we modeled solar thermal rather than photo-voltaic installations given the shorter payback time and efficiency of the former in this climate (Mike Kelleher, formerly of the National Grid Company, personal communication). For this scenario, all rooftops are considered to be without shading, and public housing is currently excluded. Tree canopy could, depending on size and orientation of homes, deprive houses of the potential to capture solar energy via photovoltaic (PV) or solar hot water (SHW) technologies (Heisler, 1986; Simpson and McPherson, 1998); therefore, our scenario makes the assumption that there are no trees on residential properties. To identify residential properties versus commercial and public housing, we used ArcGIS software (ESRI) to select the tax parcels that intersect the sewer shed boundary and are less than 7,000 m². Five of these parcels that drained to the neighboring sewer line were removed. The annual average household use in the Near Westside is 7,059 KWh (Hall, 2011). The Solar Rating and Certification Corporation (SRCC), the only national certification organization for solar thermal products, estimates incoming sunlight to a solar thermal collector mounted at 23° in Syracuse on a cloudy day is 3.2 kWh per square meter per day (SRCC, 2011). Based on SRCC comparison of a variety of solar thermal collector technologies (flat plate, evac tubes, etc.), the Florida Energy Center has computed the expected daily energy production under different climates (FSEC, 2011). For example a stainless steel tubular system is expected to produce a 2.2 kWh per square meter per day equivalent to heat water to 50°C in a cool climate with average insolation of 3.1 kWh per square meter per day. National Renewable Energy Laboratory (NREL) estimates Syracuse average insolation closer to 4.2 kWh per square meter per day (NREL, 2011). Using SRCC average energy production values for different collectors at this rate of insolation, we estimated output per unit installed for the Near Westside of 4.2 kWh per square meter per day. The average cost of installation is $5,000 per collector (table 3). The solar thermal energy gain and cost for the sixty-seven residential parcels located within the sewer shed are calculated as

$$\text{Gain}_{(\text{solar thermal})} = 4.2 \text{kWh per day} * 365 \text{ days} * 67 \text{ houses} * 3.6 \text{ MJ per kWh} \qquad (6)$$

$$\text{Cost}_{(\text{solar thermal})} = \$5,000 \text{ per installation} * 67 \text{ installations} * 7.65 \text{ MJ per dollar.} \qquad (7)$$

Energy Cost and Benefit Calculations for Urban Greening with Food Production

Finally, to estimate neighborhood energy gains from growing food within the neighborhood we allocated urban gardens to all open space. There are approximately 3.0 ha available on both private and public property within the study area, if one takes into account 2.14 ha of current lawns and 0.80 ha that is currently planted with trees. We avoid the issues of lead and other soil contaminants by estimating the cost of materials for building four-foot by eight-foot raised beds ($32 per bed), and trucking in topsoil ($24 per bed) (Alabama Cooperative Extension, 2011) and determine the energy cost by converting from U.S. dollars to energy by the energy intensity of the economy (7.65 MJ per dollar). We assume the need for two–foot-wide pathways between beds and buffer areas along buildings and fences, leaving 53 percent of open spaces to grow food (see figure 4). Thus each raised bed provides 2.97 m² of arable

Table 3. Costs and Payback Periods for Residential Solar Thermal Systems with Savings of 200 kWh Per Month (using 2010 data)

System cost ($)	Subsidy (%)	Effective cost ($)	Electricity cost per kWh ($)	Electricity savings per month ($)	Payback period (yrs)
5,000	30	3,500	0.1158	23.16	12.6

Sources: SRP, 2011 (cols. 1 and 3); EPA, n.d. (col. 2); USEIA, 2010, "Average Retail Price of Electricity to Ultimate Customers by End-Use Sector, by State, Year-to-Date through February 2011 and 2010 (cents per kWh)" (cols. 4–6).

Table 4. Megajoules (MJ) of Embodied Energy per Delivered Kilogram of Nutrient in 10-10-10 Fertilizer

	Nitrogen (ammonium nitrate)	Phosphorus (diammonium phosphate)	Potassium (muriate of potash)	Total
MJ/kg-nutrient	15.1	67	5	87.1 MJ/kg-NPK
kg-nutrient in 1 kg of 10-10-10 fertilizer	0.1	0.1	0.1	8.71 MJ/kg-nutrient of 10-10-10 fertilizer

Source: FCES, 1991; MSU Extension, 2010.

land, with an estimated embodied energy cost of 428 MJ. We then annualize the cost over an assumed fifteen-year lifetime. Average urban production using conventional gardening can yield 4,800 kilocalories (kcal) per square meter (derived from Grewal and Grewal, 2012). We do not account for the calories burned to work the beds, nor those to prepare and maintain (weed, water, or harvest) the garden plots, though certainly this would reduce the net calories available to the residents. Also, under this scenario we do not consider the effects of shading by trees or buildings. Light constraints could reduce productivity and decrease the benefit we estimate. That said, to be conservative in our production estimates, we chose the lowest published productivity values for urban gardens. Intensively managed and maintained gardens are able to produce from 21,600 to 27,000 kcal per square meter (Grewal and Grewal, 2012).

To determine what part of the required local diet could be produced on the available open space we derived a census block area-weighted (necessary because sewer sheds and 2000 census blocks are not spatially congruent) population for CSO 031 of 308 people and we assumed a diet of 3,000 kcal per day per person. This is less than the United Nations' estimate for the United States in 2007 of 3,748 kilocalories per day (FAO, 2011). Energy gain from growing food in the neighborhood is as follows:

$$Gain_{(food)} = Area \ (m^2) \ of \ arable \ open \ space *4,800 \ kcal \ per \ m^2 * 0.004187 \ MJ \ per \ kcal. \quad (8)$$

Each hectare of agricultural production will require approximately 1,200 kg of 10-10-10 NPK fertilizer (as recommended, e.g., by MSU Extension, 2010) with an energy value of 8.7 GJ/ton (derived from FCES, 1991 and MSU Extension, 2010; see table 4). Hence the energetic cost of growing food is

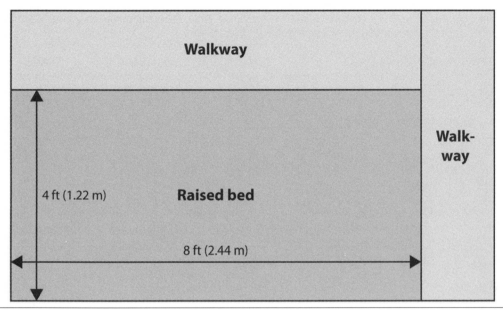

Figure 4. ASSUMED RAISED BED CONFIGURATION, REPEATED OVER THE AVAILABLE OPEN SPACES IN THE NEAR WESTSIDE NEIGHBORHOOD

$$\text{Cost}_{(food)} = (\text{Area (ha)} * 1.2 \text{ ton fertilizer per hectare} * 8.7 \text{ GJ per ton}) + (\text{Area (ha)} * 0.337 \text{ raised beds per m}^2 * 28 \text{ MJ per raised bed}). \tag{9}$$

All calculated values were converted to gigajoules (1,000 MJ per GJ) for comparison.

RESULTS

The largest neighborhood energy profit for this sewer shed from the green options we examined would be derived from solar thermal installation (table 5). It would deliver 267 times the energy benefit derived from planting trees. Growing food in all available urban space produces a net neighborhood energy profit for this sewer shed 150 times that realized from planting trees. Since rooftop installations and ground level gardens do not compete for the same space, together they could provide the maximum net energy return and a preferred greening scenario for a rust belt neighborhood such as the Near Westside in Syracuse, New York, if direct energy provision is the major goal. Given their installation costs, however, the energy return on investment of solar thermal is about 4:1, food production 2:1, and trees almost 1:1. Individual results follow.

Energy Cost and Benefit Calculations for Neighborhood Greening with Trees

Of the three scenarios tested across four storm events of varying intensity and duration, the plan that would rely solely on public participation on private property delivers between 45 and 64 percent of the runoff volume simulated using the city's plan for public spaces (figure 5, table 6).

Table 5. Annual Energy (GJ) Cost and Benefit Derived for Three Proposed Urban Greening Solutions for the Near Westside Neighborhood of Syracuse, New York

Greening strategy	Cost	Benefit	Net energy	EROI
Tree planting	20.5	21.83	1.33	1.06:1
Solar thermal	103	370	267	3.6:1
Food production	170	320	150	1.9:1

Table 6. Modeled Reductions in Storm Water Runoff Volume under Three GI Surface Treatment Scenarios

Event in 2009	Intensity (mm/hr)	Reduced flow (gallons)		
		City plan	Neighborhood plan	Combined plan
August 29	22.78	176,503	79,988	213,922
October 6	5.23	56,912	33,804	71,959
October 7	9.53	58,837	38,121	70,243
October 28	8.32	204,169	99,719	290,304

Clearly the optimal plan for storm water reduction combines both government and citizen planting strategies. Extrapolating the estimated 646,428 gallons from these four events under the combined plan to the entire year yields a runoff reduction of 1,292,856 gallons. If the latter were realized, the cost for tree planting and maintenance would be 20.5 GJ per year. The benefits derived from storm water treatment reduction, however, amount to only 0.833 GJ per year, that is, 16 percent of the annualized cost of the trees. Gains from summertime cooling of residences result in 21 GJ of annual reduced neighborhood household energy use (table 5) for a total 21.833 GJ benefits from trees.

Energy Cost and Benefit Calculations for Neighborhood Greening with Solar Thermal

If "average" solar thermal systems were installed on the roofs of the sixty-seven private homes, the annual energy production could amount to 370 GJ. The cost to install for all homes is $335,000, with an energy cost of 2,563 GJ. Divided by the expected twenty-five-year lifetime of the systems, the annualized cost is 103 GJ (perhaps more due to repairs). This yields a net neighborhood annual energy gain of 267 GJ. Based on the actual Near Westside average annual home energy electrical use from Hall (2011), of 19 GJ per household and total energy use (128 GJ), the sixty-seven homes located in CSO 031 would use about 1,273 GJ and 8,592 GJ respectively. Solar thermal could provide the heat equivalent of up to 21 percent of the current household electricity use (if replacing electric hot water heaters) or 3 percent of the total household energy use.

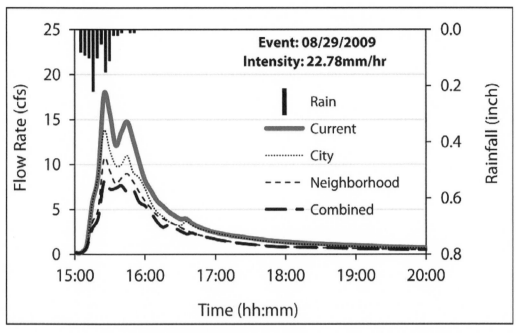

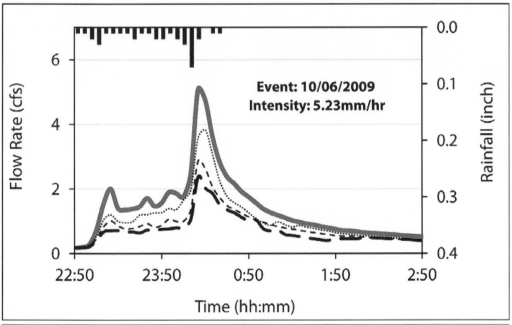

Figure 5a. Actual CSo 031 Sewer Pipe Discharge andSimulated under Three Scenarios for Four Representative Storm Events in 2009

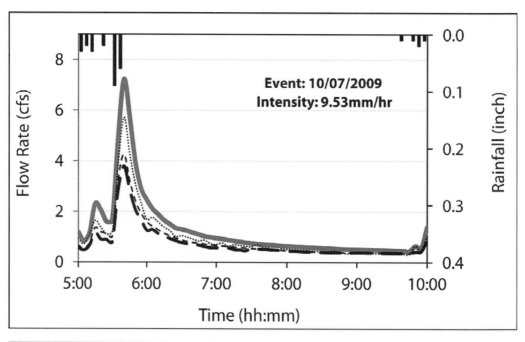

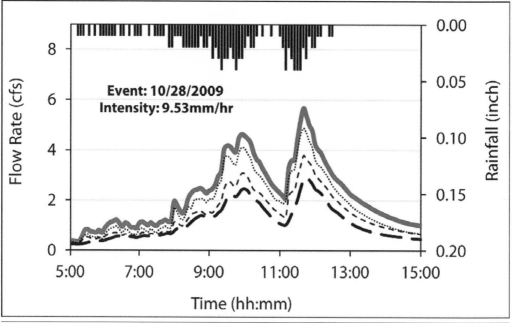

Figure 5b. ACTUAL CSO 031 SEWER PIPE DISCHARGE ANDSIMULATED UNDER THREE SCENARIOS FOR FOUR REPRESENTATIVE STORM EVENTS IN 2009

Energy Cost and Benefit Calculations for Neighborhood Greening with Food Cultivation

We estimate that agricultural yield could total 320 GJ per year (76.3 million kcal per year), enough to feed approximately 70 of the 308 residents (23 percent) of the Near West Side neighborhood 3,000 kcal per day each year. However, 16.9 GJ of fertilizer would be required to maintain productivity each year, and a total of 2,291 GJ of embodied energy in the supplies to build the raised beds and truck in the soil. Spreading the cost of building the raised beds and adding soil over fifteen-year lifespan amounts to 153 GJ per year, and with fertilizer, a sum total of 170 GJ of inputs per year. This reduces the annual net energy gain to 150 GJ per year.

DISCUSSION

One should not necessarily conclude from these results that tree planting is not an effective strategy for maximizing urban greening efforts. There may indeed be other energetic benefits that have not been included in our calculations due to the difficulty of quantifying them, things such as reduced health care expenses due to better air quality, better neighborhood relations, reduced crime, or higher home resale values (McPherson, Nowak, and Rowntree, 1994). In addition it should be noted that we did not account for the time it would take to receive the full benefit of the trees, a calculation that would presumably favor other green technologies even more. The dollar payback of solar thermal installations is 12.6 years (table 3), whereas trees may take thirty years to reach maturity and provide full energy benefits. Annualized benefits based on tree growth over time have not been calculated in the literature. McPherson and coauthors (2005) employed the Street Tree Resource Analysis Tool for Urban Forestry Managers (STRATUM) to model the net benefit of trees as a function of their annual growth in five U.S. cities over one year of growth. They found a benefit-to-cost ratio between 1.37:1 and 3.09:1. Our calculated energy return on energy investment (EROI) of 1.06:1 is slightly less than the minimum they calculated for the five cities investigated. Given the uncertainty of their estimates (pointed out by McPherson et al.) and perhaps our underestimate of benefits or overestimate of costs, they are not that different.

Nonetheless the protocol we have demonstrated here does identify green technologies that will probably have the most long-term *energetic* benefit, with higher EROI than trees, in this climate for this community, given its current energy profile, citizen attitudes, economic, and bio-physical realities. Furthermore, both urban food plots and solar thermal installations can provide some of the same benefits derived from planting trees, such as jobs, neighborhood investment, beautification, and strengthened social ties. In addition, agricultural plots can also provide storm water storage that will help ameliorate storm water runoff. It is easy to imagine other situations where other greening strategies might provide a larger net energy return. However, without an analysis such as this, the greening program selected may not be the one that will provide the largest net energy gain over time.

CONCLUSIONS

Trade-offs of costs and benefits for individual greening technologies, and trade-offs between multiple green options must be quantified. The most meaningful way to do this is to look at energy costs and gains, particularly as we enter a new era where abundant cheap fuel is likely to be less available. This study has demonstrated how to do that for one neighborhood. Among three commonly promoted green economy options, residents would benefit more from investing in agricultural production and rooftop solar hot water systems than from 160 new trees. Continuing work will seek to refine these numbers by evaluating citizen response to more green options, assessing the effect of existing household and tree shading on potential agricultural production, and household solar collector potential. So far we are encouraged that there are significant ecological and economic benefits to be derived from greening our cities, but we caution that careful assessment of the trade-offs must be done prior to investment.

NOTES

We gratefully acknowledge the National Science Foundation Award BSC-0948952 for an Urban Long Term Research Area Exploratory project (ULTRA-EX) that supported and inspired this research. We also wish to thank Dr. Charles Hall for EROI inspiration and help with the energy conversion numbers!

1. Amended Consent Judgment between Atlantic States Legal Foundation, State of New York, and John P. Cahill, as Commissioner of the New York State Department of Environmental Conservation, Plaintiffs, vs. The Onondaga County Department of Drainage and Sanitation and Onondaga County, New York, Defendants, 88-CV-0066, Judge McAvoy, January 20, 1999, p. 2.
2. Nowak, Kuroda, and Crane (2004) found an average annual mortality rate for established trees in Syracuse between 1.4 and 6.4 percent.

REFERENCES

Alabama Cooperative Extension. 2011. Raised Bed Gardening. ANR-1345. http://www.aces.edu/pubs/docs/A/ANR-1345/ANR-1345.pdf.

Alfredo, K., F. A. Montalto, and A. Goldstein. 2010. "Observed and Modeled Performance of Prototype Green Roof Test Plots Subjected to Simulated Low and High Intensity Precipitation in a Laboratory Experiment." *Journal of Hydrologic Engineering* 15(6): 444–57.

Bond, J. 2005. "The Significance of Young Urban Tree Mortality on State Implementation Plan (SIP) Planning." Davey Resource Group, for the National Tree Trust and its partners in the project "Urban Tree Canopy Cover Inclusion in State Implementation Plans," partially funded by USDA Forest Service, Urban and Community Forestry.

Environmental Protection Agency (EPA). 2010. "Partnership for Sustainable Communities: A Year of Progress for American Communities." Office of Sustainable Communities (1807T), EPA 231-K -10-002, October. http://www.epa.gov/smartgrowth/pdf/partnership_year1.pdf.

Environmental Protection Agency (EPA). N.d. http://www.energystar.gov/index.cfm?c=tax_credits
.tx_index.

Florida Cooperative Extension Service (FCES). 1991. Energy Information Handbook—Appendix C.
Document 1028. http://www.p2pays.org/ref/08/07349.pdf.

Florida Solar Energy Center (FSEC). 2011. Estimates of solar thermal energy production. http://www
.fsec.ucf.edu/en/index.php.

Foley, C. 2012. "How Socio-Demographic Factors and the Physical Environment Shape Resident Atti-
tudes Towards Green Infrastructure in Syracuse, NY." Master's thesis, State University of New York
College of Environmental Science and Forestry. Retrieved from ProQuest Dissertations and Theses.
(Publication No. 1534038).

Food and Agriculture Organization of the United Nations (FAO). 2011. FAOSTAT—Food Balance
Sheets. http://faostat.fao.org/.

Grewal, S. S., and P. S. Grewal. 2012. "Can Cities Become Self-Reliant in Food?" *Cities* 29(1): 1–11.
doi: dx.doi.org/10.1016/j.cities.2011.06.003.

Hall, C. A. S., R. Powers, and W. Schoenberg. 2008. "Peak Oil, EROI, Investments and the Economy in an Uncertain Future." In *Renewable Energy Systems: Environmental and Energetic Issues,*ed.
D. Pimentel, pp. 113–36. London: Elsevier.

Hall, C. A. S., S. B. Balogh, and D. J. R. Murphy. 2009. "What Is the Minimum EROI That a Sustainable Society Must Have?" *Energies* 2:25–47.

Hall, C. A. S., and J. W. Day Jr. 2009. "Revisiting the Limits to Growth after Peak Oil." *American
Scientist* 97:230–37.

Hall, C. A. S., and K. A. Klitgaard. 2011. *Energy and the Wealth of Nations: Understanding the Biophysical Economy*. New York: Springer.

Hall, M. 2011. "A Preliminary Assessment of Socio-ecological Metabolism for Three Neighborhoods within a Rust Belt Urban Ecosystem." *Ecological Modelling* 223(1): 20–31.doi: dx.doi
.org/10.1016/j.ecolmodel.2011.08.018.

Hamilton, J. 2009. "Causes and Consequences of the Oil Shock of 2007." In *Brookings Papers on Economic Activity*, ed. D. Romers and J. Wolfers, Spring, pp. 1–68. www.brookings.edu/economics/
bpea/bpea.aspx.

Heisler, G. M. 1986. "Effects of Individual Trees on the Solar Radiation Climate of Small Buildings."
Urban Ecology 9:337–59.

Heisler, G. M. 1991. "Computer Simulation for Optimizing Windbreak Placement to Save Energy
for Heating and Cooling Buildings." In *Trees and Sustainable Development: The Third International
Windbreaks and Agroforestry Symposium Proceedings, 1991 June 2–7*, pp. 100–104. Ridgetown,
Ontario: Ridgetown College.

Heisler, G. M., J. Walton, I. Yesilonis, D. Nowak, R. Pouyat, R. Grant, S. Grimmond, K. Hyde, and
G. Bacon. 2007. "Empirical Modeling and Mapping of Below-Canopy Air Temperatures in Bal-
timore, MD and Vicinity." In *Proceedings of the Seventh Urban Environment Symposium; 2007
September 10–13*. San Diego, CA: American Meteorological Society.

Li, R. 2012. "Analysis of Potential for Implementing Photovoltaic or Solar Water Heating Systems on
Residential Rooftops in Syracuse, NY." Master's Thesis, State University of New York College of
Environmental Science and Forestry. Retrieved from ProQuest Dissertations and Theses. (Publica-
tion No. 1534050).

McHale, M. R., E. G. McPherson, and I. C. Burke. 2007. "The Potential of Urban Tree Plantings to be
Cost Effective in Carbon Credit Markets." *Urban Forestry & Urban Greening* 6:49–60.

McPherson, E. G. 1993. "Evaluating the Cost Effectiveness of Shade Trees for Demand-Side Management." *Electricity Journal* 6(9): 57–65.

McPherson, E. G., D. J. Nowak, and R. A. Rowntree. 1994. "Chicago's Urban Forest Ecosystem: Results of the Chicago Urban Forest Climate Project (GTR GTR-NE-186)." Radnor, PA: USDA Forest Service, Northeastern Forest Experiment Station.

McPherson, E. G. and R. A. Rowntree. 1993. "Energy Conservation Potential of Urban Tree Planting." *Journal of Arboriculture* 19(6): 321–31.

McPherson, E. G., J. R. Simpson, P. J. Peper, S. E. Maco, and Q. Xiao. 2005. "Municipal Forest Costs and Benefits in Five Cities." *Journal of Forestry* 103(8): 411–16.

Montana State University (MSU) Extension. 2010. "Home Garden Soil Testing and Fertilizer Guidelines." MT200705AG. Revised May. http://msuextension.org/publications/yardandgarden/MT200705AG.pdf.

Murphy, D. J., M. H. P. Hall, C. A. S. Hall, G. Heisler, S. Stehman, and C. Anselmi-Molina. 2011. "The Relation between Land-Cover and the Urban Heat Island in Northeastern Puerto Rico." *International Journal of Climatology* 31(8): 1222–39.

Nowak, D. J., M. Kuroda, and D. E. Crane. 2004. "Tree Mortality Rates and Tree Population Projections in Baltimore, Maryland, USA." *Urban Forestry & Urban Greening* 2:139–47.

National Renewable Energy Laboratory (NREL). 2010. "Solar Radiation Data Manual for Flat-Plate and Concentrating Collectors." http://rredc.nrel.gov/solar/pubs/redbook/HTML/.

Onondaga County Department of Water Environment Protection (OCDWEP). Water Environment Protection. http://www.ongov.net/wep/we1901.html.

Simpson, J. R. 2002. "Improved Estimates of Tree-Shade Effects on Residential Energy Use." *Energy and Buildings* 34:1067–76.

Simpson, J. R., and E. G. McPherson. 1998. "Simulation of Tree Shade Impacts on Residential Energy Use for Space Conditioning in Sacramento." *Atmospheric Environment* 32(1): 69–74. doi: dx.doi.org/10.1016/S1352-2310(97)00181-7.

Solar Rating Certification Corporation (SRCC). 2011. http://www.solar-rating.org.

Solar Residential Power (SRP). 2011. http://www.srpnet.com/environment/earthwise/solar/default.aspx.

Sun, N., B. Hong, and M. H. Hall. 2013. "Assessment of the SWMM Model Uncertainties within the Generalized Likelihood Uncertainty Estimation (GLUE) Framework for a High Resolution Urban Sewershed." *Hydrological Processes*, doi: 10.1002/hyp.9869.

Sun, N. and M. H. Hall. 2013. "Coupling Human Preferences with Biophysical Processes: Modeling the Effect of Citizen Attitudes on Potential Urban Stormwater Runoff." *Urban Ecosystems*, doi: 10.1007/s11252-013-0304-5.

United Nations Economic Commission for Europe (UNECE). 2011. "UNECE, UN-HABITAT and Partners Hold Green Infrastructure Events in Run-up to Rio+20." http://www.unece.org/press/pr2011/11env_p04e.htm.

U.S. Census Bureau. 2012. American Fact Finder. http://factfinder2.census.gov/faces/nav/jsf/pages/index.xhtml.

U.S. Department of Agriculture (USDA) Forest Service. "New Software Puts Forest Ecology in Public Hands." March 10. http://www.fs.fed.us/news/2011/releases/03/i-tree.shtml.

U.S. Energy Information Agency (USEIA). 2010. The Public Policy Institute of New York State, Inc., Private Sector Insights on New York State Government, Economics, and Politics. http://ppinys.org/reports/jtf/2011/employ/average-retail-price-of-electricity2010–11.htm.

Green Jobs: Who Benefits?
Demographic Forecasting of Job Creation in U.S. Green Jobs Studies

KYLE GRACEY

MORE THAN TWENTY STUDIES HAVE ATTEMPTED TO ASSESS NET JOB CREATION through the growth in green jobs (Kammen, Kapadia, and Fripp, 2004; Center for Energy Economics, 2008). None have considered what the demographics of these jobholders might be. Using 2000–9 gender and race percentages from the Current Population Survey for detailed occupation and industry categories, a variety of periods of lagged linear regressions provide forecasts of the race, gender, and Latino and Hispanic ethnicity of these jobs through 2017. Many forecasts show poor statistical quality due to limited observations, especially with multiperiod lags. Despite this, most come close to the employment patterns in the Department of Labor's Employment Projections for 2018. Applying the forecasts to the categories of jobs considered in the existing green jobs studies, whites and males appear to occupy the majority of green jobs generated. This holds even if we assume an unrealistic, linear extrapolation of the percentage point growth in fractions of jobs held by women and minorities for the types of jobs most produced in these green jobs studies. However, if the green jobs studies are accurate, and even if the forecasts are biased by a dozen percentage points, overall women, blacks, Asians, and Hispanics and Latinos would still gain jobs in most studies considered, though blacks and Asians are relatively more susceptible to no gain in jobs if the percentage forecasts applied here are significantly far above the actual.

THE UNIVERSE OF GREEN JOBS STUDIES AND DEMOGRAPHICS OF GREEN JOBS

Since 1998, more than twenty (Kammen, Kapadia, and Fripp, 2004; Center for Energy Economics, 2008) studies have attempted to estimate the U.S. employment impact of green jobs (a term discussed in more detail below). Some modeled changes in the number and types of workers in a variety of primarily private sector industry categories and occupation types from new government investments or other policies, particularly the introduction of carbon prices. Some compare these job outputs to those from equivalent investments in traditional outputs, particularly equivalent amounts of electricity produced from coal, oil, or natural gas plants

171

compared to renewable energy (which typically excludes nuclear energy) electricity generation. Most attempt to forecast the impact of these investment or policy changes into the near future (see table 1). Others simply compare the current number and occupational categories of workers in facilities producing components necessary to generate "green" products (especially renewable energy) to those employed producing similar, traditional products (again, often coal-, oil-, or natural gas-fueled electricity).

Each study uses a different scope to define what jobs are "green." Some do not use the term at all, instead discussing "clean energy" jobs (those employed in firms producing renewable energy-based electricity). All studies include these renewable energy-based jobs. Some also include positions in mass transit, building and/or automobile energy efficiency improvements, and/or biofuels. The most expansive consider impacts on all types of jobs in the Census Bureau's Census Occupation Codes or all industries in the Census Industry Classification system (U.S. Census Bureau, 2009). In 2010, the U.S. Department of Labor announced its intent to begin defining and counting green jobs (Bureau of Labor Statistics, 2010b).

Some studies also consider additional characteristics that these green jobs will have or that the jobs will require, most commonly education level (ASES, 2008; White and Walsh, 2008) and wage or household income (Pollin et al., 2008; Pollin, Wicks-Lim, and Garrett-Peltier, 2009). *None, however, consider the gender or race of these employees*, while, for example, a recent projection of Recovery Act effects does briefly consider gender impacts (Romer and Bernstein, 2009). While gender disparities in jobs producing renewable energy in developing countries have been reviewed widely (see, for example, Skutsch, 2003 and Clancy, Oparaocha, and Roehr, 2004), evaluations and forecasts of green job creation in the United States lack these demographic considerations. Knowledge of which demographics of people will likely benefit most from green jobs may impact the desirability of policies designed to promote green jobs, provide information on which types of green jobs will impact which demographics most, and provide information that may aid in the adoption or termination of policies that impact these job demographics within the context of larger green jobs efforts.

MATERIALS AND METHODS

Defining the Scope of Green Jobs Studies

Taking into consideration the variable definition of green jobs discussed above, and rather than employing a particular definition to limit what supposedly "green jobs" studies were considered, I attempted to locate any study produced in 2000 or later that evaluated job impacts of policies or industries designed to reduce environmental impacts and that covered jobs in the entire United States, including all of the studies listed in Kammen, Kapadia, and Fripp (2004) and Center for Energy Economics (2008). From there, I narrowed the studies considered to those that calculated employment impacts for specific categories of jobs or specific industry classifications, since studies that only calculated total job creation in the United States would not provide sufficient detail to reliably calculate the race and gender of jobholders, given that these characteristics vary greatly depending on job category or industry (Bureau of Labor Statistics, 2009c; 2009b). Table 1 summarizes the studies

Table 1. GREEN JOBS STUDIES REVIEWED

Title (year of publication)	Year of impacts
Defining, Estimating, and Forecasting the Renewable Energy and Energy Efficiency Industries in the U.S. and Colorado (2008)	2030
Green Jobs Study (2008)	2013
Green Prosperity: How Clean-Energy Policies Can Fight Poverty and Raise Living Standards in the United States (2009)	Unspecified post-2009
Green Recovery: A Program to Create Good Jobs and Start Building a Low-Carbon Economy (2008)	2008–2010
Greener Pathways: Jobs and Workforce Development in the Clean Energy Economy (2008)	2008
Job Opportunities for the Green Economy: A State-by-State Picture of Occupations That Gain from Green Investments (2008)	2007
Redefining the Prospects for Sustainable Prosperity, Employment Expansion, and Environmental Quality in the US: An Assessment of the Economic Impact of the Initiatives Comprising the Apollo Project (2003)	Ten years after start of program (~2013)

considered after narrowing, including the year in which the job creation is expected to occur (either forecasted or current at the time of publication). The "Uncertainty and Error" section discusses the validity of these studies, including a review of some recent criticisms in the literature.

Demographic Data by Occupation and Industry

A comparable set of demographic data for these jobs is needed, ideally one that is based on the same Census Occupation and Industry Classification system. The Census Bureau's American Community Survey provides yearly information on detailed industry and occupation from 1996 onward (U.S. Census Bureau, 2009a). However, in 2006 the Census Bureau began including samples from individuals in group quarters,[1] and estimates comparing data from before and after this change are not recommended for any geographic scope where significant group quarters exist (U.S. Census Bureau, 2009a).

The Bureau of Labor Statistics Current Population Survey provides an alternative. Although from a smaller sample size than the American Community Survey (60,000 households monthly versus about 1.3 million people yearly) (Bureau of Labor Statistics, 2010a), it provides the same national, annual[2] demographic data for the same Census Industry and Occupation Classifications from 1995 forward. The classification systems were revised in 2003 to use the 2002 Census Occupation and Industry Classifications, and only corrections from 2000 onward have been produced (Ilg, 2010). This study uses published data on race, gender, and Hispanic or Latino identity from the Current Population Survey by detailed Census Occupation Classification and detailed Census Industry Classification (U.S. Census Bureau, 2009b) for 2003 through 2009, and unpublished versions of the same tables for 2000 through 2002 provided by Bureau of Labor Statistics economists (Ilg, 2010; Bowler, 2010).

These data provide a ten-year time series (ten observations) for each of 535 occupation and 317 industry categories for total number of workers and percentages of female, black, Asian, and Hispanic or Latino identity workers in each category and year. The exception is Asian percentages of jobholders by detailed occupation, for which data are only available from 2003 through 2009. Gender, race, and Hispanic or Latino identity are overlapping categories for individual workers, and data on, for example, race by gender are not available. Table 2 provides an example of the data set. Despite the examples in table 2, not all occupation or industries have ten years of data. Some years contain no data for unreported reasons, or if the number of workers nationally is below 50,000. Between seven and thirteen occupations and industries that report no data for these reasons in each demographic considered were dropped from consideration and are not a part of the industry and occupation totals above.

For the studies evaluating green jobs holders in previous years, applying that year of data to the categories of jobs considered shows which demographics of jobholders may be affected in each study. For considering projections of workers in future years, it is necessary to estimate the demographics for each job or occupation category in these years.

Pollin and Wicks-Lim (2008) consider what types of jobs would benefit most from increases in clean energy production and increased energy efficiency efforts in 2007 in table 3. For example, representative jobs most benefitting from increased solar power production include those that the Bureau of Labor Statistics codes as electrical engineer, electrician, industrial machinery mechanic, welder, metal fabricator, electrical equipment assembler, laborer, and construction manager. The table does not consider the number of workers who might be lost in other professions as a result of shifts in energy production or decreases or slower growth in energy production from increased energy efficiency. Looking at the 2007 demographics for the job categories in this table, Hispanics/Latinos are a minority in every category, never higher than 42.9 percent and usually much lower. Asians and blacks are even lower than this. Women make up a smaller percentage of most job categories compared to their share of overall jobs in the economy.

White and Walsh (2008) also only consider categories of jobholders currently in select renewable energy fields in table 4. Again, Hispanics and Latinos tend to have larger shares of the jobs considered compared to their overall fraction of the workforce, while the opposite is true for women. The table does not provide data on how many people work in the renewable energy industry.

Table 2. EXAMPLE OF CURRENT POPULATION SURVEY DEMOGRAPHIC DATA

	Percentage of Hispanic or Latino employees by occupation									
Year	*2000*	*2001*	*2002*	*2003*	*2004*	*2005*	*2006*	*2007*	*2008*	*2009*
Chief executives	3.1	2.3	2.8	3.3	3.7	3.8	4.6	5	4.8	4.6
General and operations managers	4.2	6.3	6.9	7.6	7.1	6.2	7.7	7.9	6.2	6

Pollin and coauthors (2008) estimate that 1.5 million more jobs would be created from $100 billion of spending on their "green recovery program" than on the same amount of spending on the oil industry or household consumption (see table 5). Unless all of

Table 3. JOB OPPORTUNITIES FOR THE GREEN ECONOMY: A STATE-BY-STATE PICTURE OF OCCUPATIONS THAT GAIN FROM GREEN INVESTMENTS

Green economy investment	Representa-tive job	2007			
		% female	% black	% Asian	% His./Lat.
Building retrofitting	Electrician	1.7	5.9	1.2	14.3
	Heating / air conditioning installer	0.9	6.3	2.2	13.2*
	Carpenter	1.9	5.6	1.8	26.9
	Roofer	0.9	4.9	0.1	42.9*
	Insulation worker	1.9	4.5*	0.6	
	Industrial truck driver	5.9	23	1.5	26.7*
	Construction manager	8.1	2.6	1.5	9.2
Mass transit	Civil engineer	11.5	2.9	8.8	6.1
	Rail track layer	—	—	—	19.5
	Electrician	1.7	5.9	1.2	14.3
	Welder	5.6	7.3	2.8	5.7
	Metal fabricator	28.9	12.4*	4.8	24.4*
	Engine Assembler	—	—	—	20
	Bus Driver	51.6	26.8	1.1	12.2*
	Dispatcher	55.1	11.6	1	12
Energy-efficient automobile	Computer software engineer	20.8	4.9	29.4	2.8
	Electrical engineer	8.6	6.9	13.5	4.1
	Engineering technician	22.4	8.3	5.9	11.2
	Welder	5.6	7.3	2.8	5.7
	Metal fabricator	28.9	12.4*	4.8	24.4*

Table 3. Job Opportunities for the Green Economy: A State-By-State Picture of Occupations That Gain from Green Investments *(continued)*

		2007			
Wind power	Engine assembler	—	—	—	20
	Environmental engineer	—	—	—	—
	Millwright	0.9	6.2	0.3	8.8
	Sheet metal worker	3.7	4.8	2.2	11.8*
	Machinist	5.2	5	5.2	12.1*
	Electrical equipment assembler	57.9	13.1	16.7	19.4*
	Industrial truck driver	5.9	23	1.5	26.7*
	Industrial production manager	16.7	4.7	3.7	9.8
	First-fine production supervisor	19.4	11.6	4.8	14.9*
Solar power	Electrical engineer	8.6	6.9	13.5	4.1
	Electrician	1.7	5.9	1.2	14.3
	Industrial machinery mechanic	3.2	8.3	2.6	11.3
	Welder	5.6	7.3	2.8	5.7
	Metal fabricator	28.9	12.4*	4.8	24.4*
	Electrical equipment assembler	57.9	13.1	16.7	19.4*
	Laborer	18.6	17.9	1.9	30
	Construction manager	8.1	2.6	1.5	9.2
Cellulosic biofuels	Chemical engineer	21.2	10.3	11.6	4.3
	Chemist	40.8	6.8	18.3	5.1
	Chemical equipment operator	15.4*	16.2*	4.4*	13.2*
	Chemical technician	32.4	7.4	6	14.5

		% female	% black	% Asian	% His/Lat
	2007				
	Industrial truck driver	5.9	23	1.5	26.7[*]
	Agricultural inspector	—	—	—	—
% of total workforce in 2007		46.4	11.0	4.7	14.0

[*]Data are from 2008 because data for 2007 were unavailable.
Source: Pollin and Wicks-Lim, 2008

Table 4. GREENER PATHWAYS: JOBS AND WORKFORCE DEVELOPMENT IN THE CLEAN ENERGY ECONOMY

		% female	% black	% Asian	% His/Lat
	2008				
Energy efficiency jobs at-a-glance	Construction laborer	3.1	7.7	1.9	44.1
	Sheet metal worker	4.8	6.2	1.2	11.8
	Insulation worker	1.9[*]	4.5[*]	0.6[*]	—
	Cement mason and concrete finisher	0.6[†]	7.4	0.1	57.7
	Heating, air conditioning, and refrigeration mechanic and installer	2	8.6	2.2	13.2
	Hazardous materials removal worker	—	—	—	—
	Carpenter	1.5	6	1.3	25.7
	Plumber, pipefitter, and steamfitter	1.4	6.4	0.6	19.5
	Electrician	1	5.9	2.7	16.2
	Boilermaker	—	—	—	—
Wind jobs at-a-glance	Laborers and freight, stock, and material movers	17.1	15.9	2.4	21.2

		2008			
		% female	% black	% Asian	% His/Lat
	Cutting, punching, and press machine setters, operators, and tenders	20.2	9.1	4	22
	Drilling, boring, and machine tool setters, operators, and tenders	—	—	—	22*
	Customer service representative	68.3	18.3	3.7	14.5
	Welders, cutters, solderers, and blazers	4.7	8.7	3.7	21
	Production, planning, and expediting clerks	58.2	8.9	3.7	7.3
	Machinist	6.9	7	4.2	12.1
	Maintenance and repair workers	3.5	10.2	2.4	13.7
Biofuels jobs at-a-glance	Laborers and freight, stock, and material movers	17.1	15.9	2.4	21.2
	Shipping, receiving, and traffic clerks	32.8	11.6	2.8	20.2
	Truck drivers; heavy and tractor-trailer	8.9	23.4	1.5	26.7
	Chemical equipment operators and tenders	15.4	16.2	4.4	13.2
	Chemical technician	35.2	18	6.9	7

		2008			
		% female	% black	% Asian	% His/Lat
	Electrical and electronic equipment repairers, commercial and industrial	—	—	—	—
	Sales representatives, wholesale and manufacturing, technical, etc.	27.3	3.9	3.8	8.6
% of total workforce in 2008		46.7 % female	11.0 % black	4.8 % Asian	14.0 % His./Lat.

*Data are from 2007 because data for 2008 were unavailable.
†Data are from 2009 because data for 2008 were unavailable.
Source: White and Walsh, 2008

those additional jobs go toward whites and males, which is unlikely given that these other demographics considered here make up at least some share of most of the job types and industries considered, all demographics of workers considered here will likely gain jobs in total, provided that the underlying studies are accurate (more sources of estimation uncertainty and error are discussed below), compared to the counterfactual cases in which energy efficiency and renewable energy investments, supportive policies, and expected sector growth do not occur.

Forecasting Demographics for Years after 2009

To compute their own forecasts of expected green jobs, all of the studies projecting future years of green jobs rely largely on input-output tables to estimate the sectoral impacts of investments or policy changes, specifically the impacts of changes in one sector on all other sectors. All of the studies use the Impact Analysis for Planning (IMPLAN) (Pollin and Wicks-Lim, 2008) input-output software. Without access to this software, or precise information on how each study's estimates were constructed (none are published in the peer-reviewed literature, though most include detailed but not comprehensive explanations of their models and assumptions), other strategies become necessary to attempt to forecast job demographics.

The limited number of observations for each demographic characteristic severely constrains the choice of forecasting models. Any multivariate regression that attempts to include other predictive variables in each time period would further reduce already limited

Table 5. GREEN RECOVERY: A PROGRAM TO CREATE GOOD JOBS AND START BUILDING A LOW-CARBON ECONOMY

Green economy investment	Representa-tive job	2009			
		% female	% black	% Asian	% His./Lat.
Smart grid	Computer software engineer	20.2	5.3	26.6	3.5
	Electrical engineer	9.4	5.1	17	5.1
	Electrical equipment assembler	59.4	11.6	13.2	28.8
	Machinist	5.4	5.1	5.7	15
	Construction laborer	2.7	7.4	1.9	44.2
	Operating engineer	1.5	5.5	0.8	13.7
	Electrical power line installer/repair	1.3	10	0.7	10.8
% of total workforce in 2009		47.3	10.7	4.7	14.0
		% female	% black	% Asian	% His/Lat

Source: Pollin et al., 2008

degrees of freedom. Following the method of Diebold and coauthors (2004), I consider autoregressive models of the form

$$y_t = a + \sum_{i=1}^{n} \beta_i y_{t-i} + u_t \tag{1}$$

which yields model errors of the form

$$u_t = \sum_{i=1}^{n} \left(\sum_{j=1}^{n-1} \beta_j^{n-j} \right) e_{t-i+1} \tag{2}$$

where $n \in [1..7]$, $t \in [2010..2017]$, and e_t has White Noise distribution $WN(0,\sigma^2)$.[3] Figure 1 shows an example of regressions with this model. Attempting to predict values beyond 2017 using this model would result in regressions with F-distributions with zero degrees of freedom. For models where more than one period of lag is considered, the maximum forecastable year is further reduced by one year for each additional lag period considered. Thus, eight successive

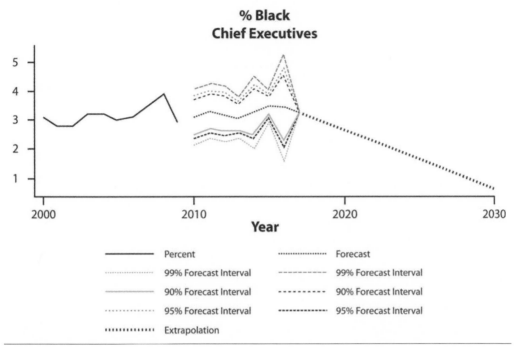

Figure 1. A Series of One-Period Lag Linear Regression Forecasts for the Percentage of Blacks Holding Occupations Coded as "Chief Executives"

years of one-period lags again yields a regression with an F-distribution with zero degrees of freedom and is not considered here.

All regressions were performed in Stata/SE 10.1 (StataCorp LP, 2009). Stata code for all regressions, forecasts, and postestimation tests discussed in this study are available from the author.

Despite the loss in observations and degrees of freedom from autoregressive processes of more than order one, the additional lag periods may provide better estimates of the forecasted years. Comparisons of the Akaike Information Criterion (AIC) across models of varying numbers of lagged regressors suggests which model provides the lowest forecast risk by assuming all models are approximations of the true process and values extra lags if they improve the forecast but penalizes additional lags or other regressors.[4] This is preferable in forecasting to the use instead of the Bayes or Schwarz Information Criterion, which assumes the existence of a true model (Armstrong, 2001). Table 6 presents a summary of AIC scores by autoregressive process. Figure 2 presents a histogram of which autoregressive process had the lowest/best AIC score for each demographic and occupation/industry.

Comparing the latest year of available forecasted values (2017) for each occupation code against the same occupations projected for 2018 in the Bureau of Labor Statistics Employment Projection table (which does not provide employment projections for detailed industry/occupation by gender/race/ethnicity but does provide detailed occupation projections for total workers in the economy) allows an additional check of the forecasting model's accuracy. The Employment Projection estimates are based on multivariable projections of factors that are believed to influence each occupation category's growth or decline (Bureau of Labor Statistics, 2009a). Table 7 compares the two projections.

Table 6. AIC SCORES BY DEMOGRAPHIC AND INDUSTRY/OCCUPATION DATABASE

Asian, Industry

Variable	Obs	Mean	Std. Dev.	Min	Max
AIC_1	1011	-4.043436	9.07499	-46.05707	21.33263
AIC_2	461	-5.321989	10.04734	-57.85435	18.61589
AIC_3	2	-14.5881	6.51269	-19.19327	-9.982933

Black, Industry

Variable	Obs	Mean	Std. Dev.	Min	Max
AIC_1	1661	1.987925	11.6139	-66.66119	37.32703
AIC_2	1064	.8188832	13.19493	-124.0927	33.55389
AIC_3	524	.5104573	12.65508	-74.28119	28.52877
AIC_4	170	-1.28286	13.76325	-39.16174	26.41997

Hispanic/Latino, Industry

Variable	Obs	Mean	Std. Dev.	Min	Max
AIC_1	1660	3.645581	11.41918	-47.72913	35.80178
AIC_2	1067	2.332412	12.36967	-54.10381	33.98428
AIC_3	529	1.607696	13.09098	-69.10397	29.12156
AIC_4	172	-2.042613	15.20435	-59.64277	27.4439

Female, Industry

Variable	Obs	Mean	Std. Dev.	Min	Max
AIC_1	1665	5.720758	13.10844	-83.47218	49.59357
AIC_2	1066	4.578044	13.29101	-56.9099	47.02958
AIC_3	529	3.661514	13.22128	-47.9027	43.93935
AIC_4	172	1.091639	14.08396	-37.84316	39.47191

Asian, Occupation

Variable	Obs	Mean	Std. Dev.	Min	Max
AIC_1	2251	-1.140123	11.23221	-97.11179	33.84206
AIC_2	1484	-1.520837	11.21848	-43.44164	32.73219
AIC_3	860	-3.006933	12.51348	-60.59088	30.50871
AIC_4	281	-6.953628	16.14255	-82.95504	26.6098

Black, Occupation

Variable	Obs	Mean	Std. Dev.	Min	Max
AIC_1	2335	4.389343	11.22309	-66.11866	41.97369
AIC_2	1539	3.699485	12.05429	-124.8761	39.82377
AIC_3	892	2.293809	13.41656	-70.51173	37.45194
AIC_4	294	-.4355545	16.76334	-89.03619	34.13867

Hispanic/Latino, Occupation					
Variable	*Obs*	*Mean*	*Std. Dev.*	*Min*	*Max*
AIC_1	2305	6.500856	11.99973	-84.02988	45.96317
AIC_2	1523	5.794316	12.05895	-60.19807	43.39228
AIC_3	829	3.53945	13.87875	-60.95013	41.05086
AIC_4	274	.9987584	16.42046	-74.73439	38.80769
Female, Occupation					
Variable	*Obs*	*Mean*	*Std. Dev.*	*Min*	*Max*
AIC_1	2328	6.829033	12.92031	-96.16654	60.57936
AIC_2	1542	6.332378	12.8418	-37.44624	56.87597
AIC_3	899	4.758618	14.15988	-69.96892	52.64983
AIC_4	294	1.225794	16.94505	-67.00991	46.71107

Note: AIC_x is the AIC value for *x* autoregression periods.

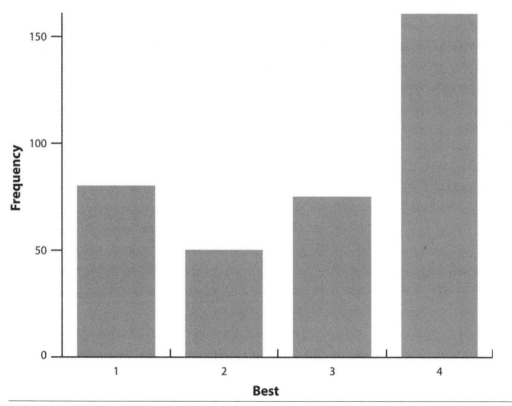

Figure 2. EXAMPLE OF BEST AIC SCORE HISTOGRAMS FOR YEAR 2010

Durbin's h-test is employed to check the assumption of serially uncorrelated errors (Armstrong, 2001). Results are summarized below. Regressions with Newey-West standard errors are also performed in addition to the original regressions with robust standard errors in case the error terms are serially correlated in addition to being heteroskedastic. Regressions with Newey-West standard errors in Stata do not compute root mean squared error, which is necessary for calculating confidence bands around the forecasts (see figure 1), so while the Newey-West regressions are used to examine the model, the robust standard error linear regressions are used for the out-of-sample forecasting (Hansen, 2010).

For the 2030 study (ASES, 2008), however, not only is this thirteen years outside of the predictive period, but the likelihood of cyclical impacts on demographic employment rates becomes more likely, especially if recessions occur in that period (Rives and Sosin, 2002; Clark and Summers, 1981). Calculating a simple linear extrapolation for 2017 through 2030, using both the observed and predicted data, while not likely a reliable predictor of actual demographic employment data, provides perhaps an extreme bound on the fraction of jobs held by each demographic. This still provides an interesting comparison of how much or little these demographics might occupy in the projected green jobs. Figure 1 includes an example of this extrapolation.

Table 7. COMPARISON OF 2018 EMPLOYMENT PROJECTIONS TO 2017 FORECASTS BY OCCUPATION CATEGORY

BLS projected (2018)	*Study forecasted (2017)*	*Difference*		
Accountants and auditors	1,570.0	Accountants and auditors	1733.636353	10%
Actors	63.7	Actors	32.666668	−49%
Actuaries	23.9	Actuaries	27.666666	16%
Advertising and promotions managers	43.9	Advertising and promotions managers	77.5	77%
Aerospace engineers	79.1	Aerospace engineers	132.166672	67%
Agents and business managers of artists, performers, and athletes	27.8	Agents and business managers of artists, performers, and athletes	43.333332	56%
Agricultural and food science technicians	23.8	Agricultural and food science technicians	48	102%
Agricultural and food scientists	35.9	Agricultural and food scientists	32.5	−9%

Note: The table presents a sample of the comparisons between 2018 projected data (left) and 2017 forecasted data (right) for total number of employees in the category. Overall, forecasted data exceeds projected data by about 11 percent across categories, but this averaged percentage is not weighted for the number of employees in each category. If the projected data are drawn from a better model (it is at least a more complex model) than the forecasted data from this study, it suggests that the forecasted data used here may, on average, overestimate the fractions of employment by the target demographics.

RESULTS

Demographics for Studies Using Past Years of Impact

For most categories, women and blacks occupy a smaller fraction of the jobs than they do for overall jobs in the economy. The opposite is true for Asians, and Hispanics and Latinos have as many job categories below the overall percentage in the economy as they do above. Again, though, that category is not weighted for the number of jobs held in each job category.

Figure 1 shows an example of the data produced from each linear regression forecast with robust standard error calculations, using one-period lags and forecast ranges using the root mean squared error, as well as the extrapolation calculation. Extrapolations were bottom- or top-coded at 0 percent or 100 percent, respectively. The *t*-statistics on many of the lagged regressors across the 100,000+ regressions calculated are low (approximately 20 percent of variables and constants with associated $p < .1$). However, *t*-statistics are less useful in forecasting since the percentages of the demographics in each job category may not change (that is, they may truly be zero) over some years, and yet this would still provide a forecast of future percentages if these values were true.

Still, with so few observations, the low *t*-statistics are troubling, especially given their even higher frequency in job categories with much fewer than ten observation years. Serially correlated errors would further affect the forecasted values. Testing for correlation and regressions to account for this is discussed later in this section. In 2017, the errors converge to the forecasted value because the seventh single-period lagged linear regression has so few observations that it returns a root mean squared error of zero. Expectedly, this occurs for all job categories with sufficient observations to forecast this far.

The AIC scores tend to show that the most lagged periods yield better model predictions, though not always. A single-period lagged regression also fares well across categories, with the advantage of allowing more prediction years. Figure 2 shows an example of the set of histograms for the same scores for models predicting year 2010, indicating for how many occupations or industries for that demographic the AIC score indicates that the particular number of lagged periods is the best model for predicting the 2010 fraction of employees. In general, though, none of the AIC scores are very high, and many are negative.

Durbin H-Test Summary

The mean Durbin alternative test for autocorrelation varied greatly among the regressions estimated (range of Prob > chi² ~[0.304. .0.986]), and with a mean ~0.531, suggesting that autocorrelation is likely present in most model specifications, and Newey-White standard error calculations would yield more accurate error bounds (though, again, not feasible for calculating the forecast intervals).

Linear Regression with Newey-White Errors

F-statistics are noticeably higher compared to the equivalent regression with robust standard error calculations. Overall, approximately ten percentage points more of the total number of regressions show variables and constants with $p < .1$, or at least improved t-statistics, compared to the robust standard error calculations. This also suggests serial correlation of errors.

We now consider the results of the forecasts when applied to studies that project green job creation for years after the year that the study was conducted.

GREEN PROSPERITY: HOW CLEAN-ENERGY POLICIES CAN FIGHT POVERTY AND RAISE LIVING STANDARDS IN THE UNITED STATES (POLLIN, WICKS-LIM, AND GARRETT-PELTIER, 2009)

This study considers the impact of $150 billion in U.S. federal stimulus money directed toward clean energy or fossil fuels, finding that, overall, clean energy spending generates more jobs, but the job creation is (unsurprisingly) distributed differently among industries between the two types of spending (see table 8). As the year is unspecified but meant to occur shortly after 2009, comparisons are made to the 2010 industry category predictions, using the lagged model prediction with the highest AIC score in each industry category (next four columns). Values below zero have been bottom-coded. Confidence intervals (90 percent) are in parentheses. Most confidence intervals are in the range of a few percentage points above or below the mean value, though a few categories showed very large confidence intervals (e.g., more than 15 percentage points above and below the mean for Hispanics/Latinos in the oil and gas extraction industry).

Some categories in the study were removed from the demographic comparison. These removals account for 44.41 percent of clean energy industry shares and 36.91 percent of fossil fuel industry shares. Calculations of demographic employment fractions were not made for these, since it is not clear from the study exactly which jobs from the original industry categories were included. Demographic percentages were weighted by the share of that industry for the clean energy spending and fossil fuel spending, with a summary of the weighted percentages calculated in the end.

Females, Asians, and blacks appear to occupy a larger share of the overall workforce if the stimulus were invested in fossil fuels instead of clean energy, while Hispanics/Latinos (and, implicitly, whites and men) gain more from investments in clean energy than from fossil fuels. However, given that about 40 percent of the industries are not calculated, the results for the full economy may vary significantly (for example, the "passenger and ground transportation" aggregate industry occupies almost an eight-percentage-point larger share in the clean energy investment scenario, and about eight more percentage points have been excluded from the clean energy industries than from the fossil fuel industries).

REDEFINING THE PROSPECTS FOR SUSTAINABLE PROSPERITY, EMPLOYMENT EXPANSION, AND ENVIRONMENTAL QUALITY IN THE US: AN ASSESSMENT OF THE ECONOMIC IMPACT OF THE INITIATIVES COMPRISING THE APOLLO PROJECT (2003)

This study, summarized in table 9 below, presents the detailed industry tables used in the preparation of the seminal Apollo Alliance green jobs study (Apollo Alliance, 2004). It

Table 8. INDUSTRY EMPLOYMENT SHARES BY ENERGY SECTOR

Industry	Industry share of clean-energy sector	Industry share of fossil fuels sector	2010 forecast (90% confidence interval)				Demographic % * industry share/100							
			Female	Black	Asian	His-panic/Latino	Female		Black		Asian		Hispanic/Latino	
							Clean	Fossil	Clean	Fossil	Clean	Fossil	Clean	Fossil
Farms	3.88%	1.10%												
Forestry, fishing, and related activities	1.03%	0.10%												
Mining														
Oil and gas extraction	0.28%	15.77%	23.6 (18.3–28.9)	6.0 (3.5–8.4)	3.3 (2.0–4.7)	13.0 (0.0–30.3)	0.066	3.7217	0.0168	0.9462	0.0092	0.5204	0.036	2.0501
Mining, except oil and gas	0.27%	1.55%	25.2 (20.4–30.1)	0 (0–1.1)	1.2 (0–4.1)	14.4 (9.9–18.9)	0.068	0.3906	0	0	0.0032	0.0186	0.039	0.2232
Support activities for mining	0.01%	0.25%	14.1 (12.5–15.7)	6.1 (4.6–7.7)	1.7 (0.4–3.1)	21.3 (18.2–24.4)	0.001	0.0353	0.0006	0.0153	0.0002	0.0043	0.002	0.05325
Utilities	0.26%	2.27%	19.7 (17.2–22.2)	10.1 (8.9–11.4)	2.0 (1.3–2.8)	9.7 (8.1–11.2)	0.051	0.4472	0.0263	0.2293	0.0052	0.0454	0.025	0.22019
Construction	25.69%	7.68%	9.8 (9.5–9.9)	5.5 (4.9–6.0)	1.6 (1.5–1.7)	22.6 (21.2–24.1)	2.518	0.7526	1.413	0.4224	0.411	0.1229	5.806	1.73568

Table 8. Industry Employment Shares By Energy Sector (continued)

Industry	Industry share of clean-energy sector	Industry share of fossil fuels sector	2010 forecast (90% confidence interval)				Demographic % * industry share/100							
			Female	Black	Asian	His-panic/Latino	Female		Black		Asian		Hispanic/Latino	
							Clean	Fossil	Clean	Fossil	Clean	Fossil	Clean	Fossil
Manufacturing: durable goods														
Wood products	0.81%	0.21%	17.5 (14.6–19.2)	9.5 (8.2–10.8)	1.5 (0.6–2.3)	14.1 (12.3–15.9)	0.142	0.0368	0.077	0.02	0.0122	0.0032	0.114	0.02961
Non-metallic mineral products	0.61%	0.23%	19.3 (17.5–21.1)	9.4 (6.3–12.5)	1.9 (1.4–2.5)	17.5 (15.4–19.7)	0.118	0.0444	0.0573	0.0216	0.0116	0.0044	0.107	0.04025
Primary metals	0.47%	0.38%												
Fabricated metal products	2.17%	1.65%												
Machinery	1.66%	0.63%												
Computer and electronic products	1.59%	0.18%	33.4 (31.9–34.9)	5.9 (4.7–7.1)	16.6 (15.7–17.6)	9.1 (7.5–10.7)	0.531	0.0601	0.0938	0.0106	0.2639	0.0299	0.145	0.01638

Electrical equipment, appliances, and components	0.85%	0.20%		31.6 (25.6–37.6)	11.9 (6.1–17.6)	6.1 (4.5–7.8)	9.8 (7.8–11.8)	0.269	0.0632	0.1012	0.0238	0.0519	0.0122	0.083	0.0196
Motor vehicles, bodies and trailers, and parts	0.28%	0.31%													
Other transportation equipment	0.04%	0.03%		41.5	—	—	51.1	0.017	0.0125	—	—	—	—	0.02	0.01533
Furniture and related products	0.23%	0.09%		26.3 (22.8–29.7)	6.3 (2.2–10.5)	3.4 (1.5–5.3)	18.8 (16.4–21.2)	0.06	0.0237	0.0145	0.0057	0.0078	0.0031	0.043	0.01692
Miscellaneous manufacturing	0.15%	0.19%		34.8 (16.7–53.0)	7.8 (6.2–9.4)	4.7 (0–10.1)	16.5 (13.8–19.3)	0.052	0.0661	0.0117	0.0148	0.0071	0.0089	0.025	0.03135
Manufacturing: nondurable goods															
Food and beverage and tobacco products	0.48%	0.50%													
Textile mills and textile product mills	0.09%	0.08%		51.0 (50.5–51.5)	6.6 (2.4–10.8)	4.7 (1.7–7.7)	12.2 (0–25.7)	0.046	0.0408	0.0059	0.0053	0.0042	0.0038	0.011	0.00976

Table 8. Industry Employment Shares By Energy Sector (*continued*)

Industry	Industry share of clean-energy sector	Industry share of fossil fuels sector	2010 forecast (90% confidence interval)				Demographic % * industry share/100							
			Female	Black	Asian	His-panic/Latino	Female		Black		Asian		Hispanic/Latino	
							Clean	Fossil	Clean	Fossil	Clean	Fossil	Clean	Fossil
Apparel and leather and allied products	0.07%	0.08%												
Paper products	0.18%	0.24%	40.8 (32.4–49.3)	14.6 (7.9–21.3)	3.7 (0–7.1)	48.7 (47.3–50.1)	0.073	0.0979	0.0263	0.035	0.0067	0.0089	0.088	0.11688
Print-ing and related support activities	0.20%	0.28%	33.5 (31.8–35.1)	8.2 (6.4–9.9)	4.4 (2.8–5.9)	19.9 (18.8–21.0)	0.067	0.0938	0.0164	0.2296	0.0088	0.0123	0.04	0.05572
Petroleum and coal products	0.14%	2.19%	20.7 (18.3–23.0)	17.1 (13.3–20.9)	3.8 (1.4–6.1)	12.4 (9.6–15.2)	0.029	0.4533	0.0239	0.3745	0.0053	0.0832	0.017	0.27156
Chemical products	0.37%	1.17%	34.3 (33.0–35.6)	11.4 (10.5–12.3)	6.5 (5.4–7.7)	10.1 (8.2–12.1)	0.127	0.4013	0.0422	0.1334	0.0241	0.0761	0.037	0.11817
Plastics and rubber products	0.81%	0.51%	28.6 (26.0–31.2)	10.5 (9.9–11.2)	3.1 (1.8–4.3)	14.7 (13.1–16.2)	0.232	0.1459	0.0851	0.0536	0.0251	0.0158	0.119	0.07497

			Retail trade											
Whole-sale trade	2.65%	3.55%	29.0 (28.2–29.8)	5.8 (4.5–7.1)	4.3 (4.2–4.4)	15.3 (14.6–16.0)	0.769	1.0295	0.1537	0.2059	0.114	0.1527	0.405	0.54315
Motor vehicle and parts dealers	0.79%	0.63%												
Food and beverage stores	1.05%	0.85%												
General merchandise stores	1.07%	0.87%												
Other retail	3.72%	3.00%												
			Transportation and warehousing											
Air trans-portation	0.14%	0.17%	40.5 (37.5–43.5)	13.0 (11.0–14.9)	6.8 (5.4–8.2)	8.5 (7.2–12.5)	0.057	0.0689	0.0182	0.0221	0.0095	0.0116	0.012	0.01445
Rail transpor-tation	0.42%	0.23%	6.6 (3.4–9.8)	12.1 (10.7–13.5)	1.5 (0.8–2.2)	8.6 (6.6–10.7)	0.028	0.0152	0.0508	0.0278	0.0063	0.0035	0.036	0.01978
Water transpor-tation	0.02%	0.04%	25.0 (15.3–34.7)	9.7 (6.5–12.9)	4.8 (1.1–8.5)	4.8 (0.1–9.6)	0.005	0.01	0.0019	0.0039	0.001	0.0019	1E03	0.00192
Truck transpor-tation	1.20%	1.40%	12.9 (11.2–14.6)	13.4 (12.0–14.8)	1.1 (0.7–1.5)	17.0 (16.1–17.8)	0.155	0.1806	0.1608	0.1876	0.0132	0.0154	0.204	0.238

Table 8. Industry Employment Shares By Energy Sector (continued)

Industry	Industry share of clean-energy sector	Industry share of fossil fuels sector	2010 forecast (90% confidence interval)				Demographic % * industry share/100							
			Female	Black	Asian	His-panic/Latino	Female		Black		Asian		Hispanic/Latino	
							Clean	Fossil	Clean	Fossil	Clean	Fossil	Clean	Fossil
Transit and ground passenger transportation	8.80%	0.25%												
Pipeline transportation	0.02%	0.96%	10.6	5	—	0	0.002	0.1018	0.001	0.048	—	—	0	0
Other transportation and support activities	0.62%	0.83%												
Warehousing and storage	0.33%	0.33%	28.9 (25.5–32.3)	22.7 (19.2–26.2)	3.1 (1.9–4.3)	24.9 (22.4–27.3)	0.095	0.095	0.0749	0.0749	0.0102	0.0102	0.082	0.082
						Information								
Publishing industries (includes software)	0.29%	0.37%												

Motion picture and sound recording industries	0.15%	0.18%												
Broadcasting and telecommunications	0.67%	0.86%												
Information and data processing services	0.12%	0.15%												
Federal reserve banks, credit intermediation, and related activities	1.32%	1.96%												
Insurance carriers and related activities	1.02%	1.15%	61.9 (60.0–63.7)	9.7 (8.6–10.7)	3.6 (3.1–4.1)	8.7 (8.1–9.4)	0.631	0.7119	0.0989	0.1116	0.0367	0.0414	0.089	0.10005

Finance and insurance

Table 8. Industry Employment Shares By Energy Sector (continued)

Industry	Industry share of clean-energy sector	Industry share of fossil fuels sector	2010 forecast (90% confidence interval)				Demographic % * industry share/100							
			Female	Black	Asian	His-panic/Latino	Female		Black		Asian		Hispanic/Latino	
							Clean	Fossil	Clean	Fossil	Clean	Fossil	Clean	Fossil
Funds, trusts, securities, commodity contracts, and other investments	1.87%	2.50%												
Real estate and rental and leasing, and other financial vehicles														
Real estate	2.70%	3.48%	49.1 (47.1–51.0)	8.3 (7.4–9.2)	3.8 (2.8–4.8)	12.1 (11.0–13.2)	1.326	1.7087	0.2241	0.2888	0.1026	0.1322	0.327	0.42108
Rental and leasing services and lessors of intangible assets	0.50%	1.02%	25.5 (23.3–27.7)	12.5 (11.1–13.9)	4.7 (3.2–6.2)	14.2 (13.7–14.6)	0.128	0.2601	0.0625	0.1275	0.0235	0.0479	0.071	0.14484
Professional, scientific, and technical services														
Legal services	0.90%	1.49%	56.5 (54.7–58.4)	7.2 (6.2–8.2)	2.7 (2.2–3.2)	7.9 (6.8–8.9)	0.509	0.8419	0.0648	0.1073	0.0243	0.0402	0.071	0.11771

Industry													
Computer systems design and related	0.11%	0.16%	25.9 (24.0–27.8)	6.3 (5.2–7.4)	17.3 (15.8–18.9)	4.9 (4.3–5.6)	0.028	0.0414	0.0069	0.0101	0.019	0.0277	0.005	0.00784
Miscellaneous professional, scientific, and technical services	6.00%	7.64%												
Management of companies and enterprises	1.04%	3.22%	73.2 (66.1–80.3)	8.5 (4.5–12.5)	4.9 (0.9–8.8)	7.4 (6.4–8.5)	0.761	2.357	0.119	0.2737	0.051	0.1578	0.077	0.23828
Administrative and waste management services														
Administrative and support services	4.82%	7.27%												
Waste management and remediation services	0.18%	0.22%	15.4 (13.8–16.9)	13.8 (12.1–15.6)	1.4 (0.1–2.7)	12.2 (9.4–15.0)	0.028	0.0339	0.0248	0.0304	0.0025	0.0031	0.022	0.02684
Educational services	0.75%	0.76%	74.9 (74.4–75.3)	11.0 (8.5–13.5)	3.7 (3.4–3.9)	9.1 (8.4–9.8)	0.562	0.5692	0.0825	0.0836	0.0278	0.0281	0.068	0.06916

Table 8. INDUSTRY EMPLOYMENT SHARES BY ENERGY SECTOR *(continued)*

Industry	Industry share of clean-energy sector	Industry share of fossil fuels sector	2010 forecast (90% confidence interval)				Demographic % * industry share/100							
			Female	Black	Asian	His-panic/Latino	Female		Black		Asian		Hispanic/Latino	
							Clean	Fossil	Clean	Fossil	Clean	Fossil	Clean	Fossil
Health care and social assistance														
Ambulatory health care services	1.85%	1.85%												
Hospitals	1.28%	1.28%	77.2 (75.8–78.7)	16.0 (15.0–16.9)	6.5 (6.2–6.7)	7.5 (6.3–8.8)	0.988	0.9882	0.2048	0.2048	0.0832	0.0832	0.96	0.096
Nursing and residential care facilities	0.94%	0.94%												
Social assistance	0.96%	0.96%	85.5 (84.8–86.2)	19.7 (18.4–21.1)	3.5 (2.8–4.3)	13.8 (12.5–15.1)	0.821	0.821	0.1891	0.1891	0.0336	0.0336	0.132	0.132
Arts, entertainment, and recreation														
Performing arts, spectator sports, museums, and related activities	0.58%	0.69%												

Accommodation and food services

							Women		Black		Asian		Hispanic/Latino	
							Clean	Fossil	Clean	Fossil	Clean	Fossil	Clean	Fossil
Amusements, gambling, and recreation industries	0.54%	0.59%												
Accommodation	0.51%	0.63%	57.3 (55.7–59.0)	14.7 (13.3–16.1)	7.7 (6.2–9.3)	24.4 (22.6–26.1)	0.292	0.361	0.075	0.0926	0.0393	0.0485	0.124	0.15372
Food services and drinking places	3.23%	3.80%	52.2 (51.6–52.8)	10.7 (10.2–11.2)	5.9 (5.6–6.2)	21.5 (20.1–23.0)	1.686	1.9836	0.3456	0.4066	0.1906	0.2242	0.694	0.817
Other services, except government	4.26%	4.83%	51.6 (51.1–52.1)	10.2 (9.5–10.8)	5.9 (5.5–6.3)	18.6 (17.9–19.4)	2.198	2.4923	0.4345	0.4927	0.2513	0.285	0.792	0.89838
Government														
Federal	0.09%	0.12%												
State and local	0.40%	0.61%												
Total	100%	99.71%					15.53	21.558	4.4059	5.5298	1.897	2.3213	10.93	9.22112

Table 9. THE TOTAL ONGOING ANNUAL ECONOMIC IMPACT OF APOLLO PROJECT INITIATIVES (AS OF YEAR 10): DETAILED SECTORAL RESULTS

Sector	Employment (permanent jobs)	2013 forecast % of labor force (90% confidence interval)				Employment (permanent jobs)			
		Female	Black	Asian	Lat./His.	Female	Black	Asian	Lat./His.
Agricultural products and services	94,351								
Forestry and fishery products	909								
Coal mining	0	5.2 (3.1–7.4)	0 (0–1.0)		1.7 (0.2–3.2)				
Crude petroleum and natural gas	1,205	27.5 (21.5–33.6)	6.6 (2.6–10.6)	2.2 (2.0–2.5)	9.2 (3.2–15.1)	331.38	79.53	26.51	110.86
Miscellaneous mining	0								
New construction	77,553	9.58 (9.4–9.8)	5.0 (4.6–5.4)	1.7 (1.6–1.7)	27.1 (24.8–29.4)	12,108.83	6,319.85	2,148.75	34,253.59
Maintenance and repair construction	48,844								
Food products and tobacco	7,546								
Textile mill products	5,989	60.3 (59.2–61.5)	3.1 (0–8.4)	7.1 (3.5–10.8)	21.8 (13.4–30.2)	3,611.37	185.66	425.22	1,305.60
Apparel	9,046								

Paper and allied products	7,294	38.6 (34.6–42.6)	0 (0–1.0)	1.9 (0–4.2)	22.7 (12.3–33.1)	2,815.48		138.59	1,655.74
Printing and publishing	11,180								
Chemicals and petroleum refining	6,523								
Rubber and leather products	10,350								
Lumber products and furniture	6,838								
Stone, clay, and glass products	8,320								
Primary metal	14,272	16.8 (15.3–18.3)	7.4 (6.2–8.5)	2.1 (2.0–2.3)	14.0 (12.5–15.6)	2,397.70	1,056.13	299.71	1,998.08
Fabricated metal products	23,388								
Machinery, except electrical	15,661								
Electric and electronic equipment	16,646								
Motor vehicles and equipment	13,394	27.7 (26.6–28.7)	13.1 (12.0–14.3)	7.2	9.4 (8.6–10.2)	3,710.14	1,754.61	964.37	1,259.04

Table 9. The Total Ongoing Annual Economic Impact of Apollo Project Initiatives (as of Year 10): Detailed Sectoral Results (*continued*)

Sector	Employment (permanent jobs)	% of labor force (90% confidence interval)				Employment (permanent jobs)			
		Female	Black	Asian	Lat./His.	Female	Black	Asian	Lat./His.
Transportation equipment, except motor vehicles	9,313	26.9 (25.2–28.6)	11.9 (10.0–13.9)	6.3 (6.3–6.3)	8.4 (6.9–9.9)	2,505.20	1,108.25	586.72	782.29
Instruments and related products	7,077								
Miscellaneous manufacturing	135	37.8 (35.9–39.6)	6.0 (5.5–6.5)	7.6 (5.9–9.2)	16.6 (11.9–21.3)	51.03	8.10	10.26	22.41
Transportation	45,267								
Communication	5,831	22.6	7.8	12.1	12.2	1,317.81	454.82	705.55	711.38
Electric, gas, water, sanitary services	1,209	28.9 (25.5–32.2)	8.3 (7.0–9.6)	3.5 (2.9–4.1)	7.1 (2.0–12.3)	349.40	100.35	42.32	85.84
Wholesale trade	150,896	29.3 (28.7–29.9)	7.4 (6.1–8.7)	4.2	15.6 (14.9–16.2)	44,212.53	11,166.30	6,337.63	23,539.78
Retail trade	319,123	48.9 (48.6–49.3)	9.7 (9.4–10.1)	7.9	12.5 (11.7–13.3)	156,051.15	30,954.93	25,210.72	39,890.38
Finance	23,572	52.1 (50.9–53.2)	8.7 (7.7–9.8)	4.8 (4.6–4.9)	10.1 (9.7–10.4)	12,281.01	2,050.76	1,131.46	2,380.77

					Women	Black	Asian	Lat/His
Insurance	16,644	61.9 (60.5–63.4)	10.7 (9.2–12.1)	3.7 (3.3–4.0)	9.4 (8.6–10.3)	10,302.64	1,780.91	615.83	1,564.54
Real estate	13,690	48.3 (45.6–51.0)	9.1 (8.4–9.9)	3.5 (2.2–3.8)	12.5 (11.5–13.5)	6,612.27	1,245.79	479.15	1,711.25
Hotels, lodging places, amusements	21,078								
Personal services	10,177	71.8 (70.1–73.4)	11.6 (11.1–12.0)	13.1 (13.1–13.2)	14.9 (13.7–16.2)	7,307.09	1,180.53	1,325.33	1,516.37
Business services	160,875	66.5 (66.1–66.9)	15.4 (13.9–16.8)	3.5 (1.6–5.3)	11.5 (11.4–11.6)	106,981.88	24,774.75	5,630.63	18,500.63
Eating and drinking places	57,185	52.2 (51.8–52.7)	10.7 (10.2–11.2)	6.3 (5.9–6.7)	23.1 (21.8–24.4)	29,850.57	6,118.80	3,602.66	13,209.74
Health services	71,690								
Miscellaneous services	90,423								
Households	8,923	92.1 (90.8–93.4)	6.4 (3.2–9.6)	1.4 (1.2–1.6)	42.4 (38.6–46.1)	8,218.08	571.07	124.92	3,783.35
Total	1,392,415					411,016	89,665	49,806	148,282
% of total jobs above						30%	6%	4%	11%
% of total workforce in 2013						45%	11%	4%	15%

Table 10. IMPACT OF GREEN CONSTRUCTION SPENDING BY NAICS INDUSTRIES

	2009–2013	% of labor force (90% confidence interval)				2013 *forecast* Number in labor force			
		Female	Asian	Black	Hispanic	Female	Asian	Black	Hispanic
Non-residential construction	7,497,566	9.6 (9.4–9.8)	3.4 (3.2–3.6)	5.0 (4.6–5.4)	27.1 (24.8–29.4)	764,064.86	270,606.31	397,950.45	2,156,891.44
Residential construction	461,443								
Electric power generation, transmission, and distribution	(41,745)	24.0 (19.1–28.9)	1.5 (1.4–1.6)	9.0 (7.2–10.7)	19.3 (16.1–22.6)	(10,018.80)	(626.18)	(3,757.05)	(8,056.79)
Water, sewage, and other systems	(10,401)								
Waste management remediation services	(4,398)	15.2 (12.9–17.6)	1.0 (0.2–1.8)	12.9 (11.2–14.6)	24.2 (23.3–25.2)	(668.50)	(43.98)	(567.34)	(1,064.32)
Total	7,902,466					753,377.57	269,936.15	393,626.06	2,147,770.34
% of total jobs created						10%	3%	5%	27%
% of total workforce in 2013						45%	11%	4%	15%

models approximately $300 billion worth of federal investments in a variety of renewable energy, energy efficiency, and greenhouse gas emission-reducing activities over ten years of economic impacts. It estimates that, by the end of the ten-year period, the initial investment more than pays for itself in government receipts, while generating 1.4 million jobs. One hundred and twenty-eight tables are presented for impacts in detailed industry sectors for each of the investment areas considered, as well as summary tables. Only the summary table from the study is evaluated here, although sufficient data exist to compare each table in the same manner.

Assuming 2013 as the end of the ten-year period, 2013 forecasted demographic percentages are compared to the projected number of total jobs from the study to estimate how many jobs would be generated for each demographic. The formatting for the forecasted percentages and the choice of forecast model for each industry category follow that in table 8.

Differences in industry aggregation led to approximately 33 percent of the projected jobs not being evaluated for their forecasted demographic division. Data from the "New Construction" and "Maintenance & Repair Construction" are combined and compared against the "Construction" column in the forecast data since these two categories cover the construction industry in the same way that the "Construction" category does.

The results indicate that, at least for the industry categories available for study, women will gain 30 percent of the new jobs estimated to be created, blacks 6 percent, Asians 4 percent, and Hispanics and Latinos 11 percent, though these fractions are smaller than the total fraction of jobs forecasted to be held by women, Asians, and Hispanics and Latinos in 2013.

GREEN JOBS STUDY (BOOZ ALLEN HAMILTON, 2009)

This study, with results shown in table 10, calculates the number of jobs created by the growth in the demand for Leadership in Energy and Environmental Design (LEED) buildings for the period 2000–2008, and forecasts the same employment and economic data for the period 2009–13. It predicts net job creation in five industry categories most related to green buildings at 7.9 million by 2013 from LEED building construction alone, though with a net loss of jobs in some industry categories. Employment impacts in each forecast year are not provided, so the estimate below instead applies the 2013 forecasted demographic percentages to the total 2009–13 job creation estimated. Thus, the actual (even assuming the forecasts are accurate) should vary a small amount due to differences in the demographic percentages across the years 2009–12 compared to 2013. The same formatting and data treatment methods as in the previous table apply here. Coverage is 99.87 percent of jobs affected since the Water, Sewage, and Other Systems category was removed due to differences in aggregation compared with the CPS industry categories.

Of the total jobs predicted to have been created, women occupy 10 percent, blacks 5 percent, Asians 3 percent, and Hispanics and Latinos 27 percent. Latinos and Hispanics appear to gain more jobs in LEED-related occupations compared to their overall projected share of jobs in 2013, as do blacks (though by a much slimmer margin). Women, especially, and Asians are forecasted to occupy a smaller fraction of the LEED-related jobs than in the U.S. economy overall.

DEFINING, ESTIMATING, AND FORECASTING THE RENEWABLE ENERGY AND ENERGY EFFICIENCY INDUSTRIES IN THE UNITED STATES AND IN COLORADO (ASES, 2008)

The study, with results summarized in table 11, estimates the change in select jobs for three scenarios above the baseline assumption of renewable energy industry growth. The table contains the job creation assumptions for the "advanced case" of both aggressive technological improvements and government policies and spending. The extrapolated values for 2030 are used to calculate the number of employees in each demographic holding these estimated jobs. Again, the extrapolated values can at best be thought of as extreme values of where the demographics could develop, not reliable forecasts. The same formatting and other data treatment approaches from previous tables are repeated. Employment numbers for each job category are estimated from a bar graph and may be +/– 1,000.

Interestingly, even in this extreme example, the demographics considered still occupy minority shares, overall, of the jobs estimated to have been created, at least for the categories of jobs shown (but only barely for Hispanics and Latinos). Women hold 30 percent of the jobs, blacks 21 percent, Asians, 18 percent, and Latinos and Hispanics 49 percent.

DISCUSSION

Green Jobs: Who Benefits?

The forecasts and evaluations from this study can be viewed in two ways. First, women, Asians, blacks, and those of Hispanic or Latino ethnicity are forecasted to hold a minority of the green jobs that these studies indicate have been or will be produced, with whites and males occupying the majority. In that sense, these demographics may be expected to benefit the least from green job growth or programs that promote green jobs.

Second, however, even if women, Asian, black, and Hispanic and Latino workers will constitute minorities of green jobs holders, that does not mean they will not benefit at all from a growth in green jobs. All occupy minority shares of the total workforce today, so it is not surprising that they would occupy minority shares in the near future, especially for those demographics that are far below 50 percent. Even if the forecasted fractions in future years are biased by a dozen percentage points, in some cases, these demographics still show net increases in jobs. For some studies, though, the margin for error is much smaller.

All of the green jobs studies that calculate a net change in jobs in the U.S. estimate that total jobs available will grow with a shift toward more green jobs. This is largely based on calculations that green industries, particularly renewable energy electricity generation (and energy efficiency savings that divert the need for some increased energy production) are more labor-intensive than their nonrenewable alternatives.

Many studies also do not provide information on job categories created through induced or indirect[5] jobs that are generated as a result of the creation of the direct jobs. These jobs, everything from accountants to housekeepers, may be smaller in number than the direct jobs created, but may more favorably employ the demographics of workers left out of the

Table 11. U.S. Jobs Created By Renewable Energy in 2030 Compared to 2007 (Total Jobs Created—Selected Occupations)

		2030 extrapolated %				total jobs			
		Women	Black	Asian	Hispanic/Latino	Women	Black	Asian	Hispanic/Latino
Accountant	95,000	91.3	0.0	12.1	100.0	86,735	—	11,495	95,000
Chemist	22,000	0.0	100.0	0.0	76.6	—	22,000	—	16,852
Computer systems analyst	38,000	6.9	0.0	40.8	51.2	2,622	—	15,504	19,456
Construction manager	28,000	0.0	0.0	0.0	28.8	—	—	—	8,064
cost estimator	28,000	46.5	2.4	13.4	0.0	13,020	672	3,752	—
Electrician	90,000	6.8	41.2	54.5	18.9	6,120	37,080	49,050	17,010
Environmental scientist	21,000	31.5	0.0	1.4	0.0	6,615	—	294	—
Iron and steel worker	10,000	100.0	51.9	0.0	0.0	10,000	5,190	—	—
IT manager	19,000	0.0	0.0	7.5	100.0	—	—	1,425	19,000
Mechanical engineer	38,000	10.0	0.0	9.0	0.0	3,800	—	3,420	—
Management analyst	41,000	39.3	69.7	9.1	97.2	16,113	28,577	3,731	39,852
Power line worker	23,000	0.0	8.7	16.3	38.8	—	2,001	3,749	8,924
Sheet metal worker	21,000	47.0	29.9	0.0	0.0	9,870	6,279	—	—
Welder	41,000	0.0	15.9	1.0	64.7	—	6,519	410	26,527
Total	515,000					154,895	108,318	92,830	250,685
% of total						30%	21%	18%	49%

majority of direct green jobs. Most studies considered here model aggregate indirect and induced jobs.

Uncertainty and Error

Several sources of error likely reduce the estimation accuracy of the forecasted demographics. First, the Current Population Survey exhibits sampling and nonsampling errors that bias the previous year percentages (Bureau of Labor Statistics, 2006). The forecast model adds omitted variable bias since it does not assume to be the exact, true model, and many factors may affect labor force participation by these demographics in particular industries and occupations (Reskin, McBrier, and Kmec, 1999), none of which are considered here. The trends that have driven changes in demographic participation in 2000–2009, and that thus implicitly drive the forecasted years, may vary in coming years (for example, a possible slowdown in the growth of Hispanic and Latino fractional occupation), biasing the forecasts. The limited number of observations disrupts the model fit to the data. If the errors are serially correlated, the use of linear regressions with robust rather than Newey-White error calculations may further misrepresent the errors. Attempts to account for and introduce random, compounding errors for each year of forecasting produced an unknown computation error in Stata, so the forecast confidence intervals in years after 2009 are likely too narrow.

It is not certain that the same demographics of workers who occupy these occupation and industry categories overall will occupy them in green jobs with the same frequency. Perhaps female chemical engineers will choose more biofuel jobs, while male chemical engineers will seek out petroleum companies. We do not know.

These forecasts treat each change in the demographics of employment as independent. In reality, changes in the employment rates in some categories of jobs will likely affect the rate at which other jobs are filled by certain demographics.

Even if we did understand the patterns of green job employment, we would have to assume that the studies themselves are accurate in their overall job estimates. A few studies have criticized the methodologies of some of the green jobs research considered here (Center for Energy Economics, 2008; Morriss et al., 2009), though criticism of the job creation estimates of fossil fuel investments also exist (Ochs Center for Metropolitan Studies, 2011). These criticisms, like most of the studies considered, have also not been published in peer-reviewed journals, though some or all of their criticisms may be valid nonetheless.

FURTHER RESEARCH

At the minimum, future green jobs studies could include demographic data in their calculations, whether they are reports about current green jobs or estimates of future green jobs scenarios. A more sophisticated modeling of demographic changes from these green jobs policies would allow for more reliable demographic forecasts, particularly if the demographics could be incorporated into the existing input-output modeling that the studies (or future studies) use to derive their data. Future estimates might also want to incorporate additional demographics, such as worker age, or race and ethnicity by gender, to further subdivide the types of workers who might be expected to hold green jobs.

Understanding if certain demographics show noticeably varying rates of green job adoption versus nongreen job adoption in the otherwise same occupation or industry category also seems important. Research might also consider what policies, such as targeted job training or recruitment programs, could shift the demographics of green jobs workers, and whether such shifts would be desirable. Do different demographics of workers show higher or lower average performance in green jobs, especially compared to equivalent nongreen jobs, and if so, why? All of these questions and more remain unanswered, even as interest in green jobs continues.

NOTES

I am indebted to Drs. Dan Black and Sabina Shaikh at the University of Chicago for their thoughtful review, to Fay Booker at the University of Chicago for Stata troubleshooting, and to my session participants at the U.S. Society for Ecological Economics conference for helpful ideas in extending this work in the future. An April 2011 analysis and October 2011 update, "Green Jobs for Youth: An Analysis of Youth in the Green Economy," with Michael Davidson, begins to explore the age composition of U.S. green jobs.

1. "A [Group Quarter] facility is a place where people live or stay that is normally owned or managed by an entity or organization providing housing and/or services for the residents" (U.S. Census Bureau, 2009a).

2. Although demographic data are also available on a monthly basis over the same time period, they are not available at the level of detailed Census Occupation or Industry Classification. Using monthly data would provide more observations but would also require longer out-of-sample forecasts.

3. This assumption, though common for time series, is unverifiable since Stata does not permit Bartlett's or Portmanteau white noise tests for multiple panel IDs, such as in these demographic data sets.

4. Stata's AIC command assumes that the number of observations used for estimation (T) and the number of observations (N) in total are always equal, which is not true for forecasts. Instead, the AIC is calculated directly by using the stored regression values AIC = ln(_result(4)/_result(1))*10+(1+_result(3))*2, where _result(4) returns the residual sum of squares, _result(1) returns T, _result(3) returns the autoregression period, and 10 is replaced by the appropriate N (StataCorp LP, 2009).

5. Indirect jobs are those that support the direct green jobs but do not necessarily perform functions directly related to the provision or construction of the "green" product or service. This includes support staff such as accountants, secretaries, and lawyers. Induced jobs are those created by the other jobholders spending the money they earn at their job. These jobs could include things like housekeepers or store owners (Pollin, Wicks-Lim, and Garrett-Peltier, 2009).

REFERENCES

Apollo Alliance. 2004. *New Energy for America: The Apollo Jobs Report. Good Jobs & Energy Independence.* 2004. Institute for America's Future, Center on Wisconsin Strategy, and Perryman Group. http://apolloalliance.org/downloads/resources_ApolloReport_022404_122748.pdf.

Armstrong, J. S. 2001. *Principles of Forecasting: A Handbook for Researchers and Practitioners.* Norwell, MA: Kluwer Academic Publishers.

ASES (American Solar Energy Society). 2008. *Defining, Estimating, and Forecasting the Renewable Energy and Energy Efficiency Industries in the U.S. and Colorado.* American Solar Energy Society and Management Information Services, Inc. http://ases.org/images/stories/ASES/pdfs/CO_Jobs _Final_Report_December2008.pdf.

Booz Allen Hamilton. 2009. *Green Jobs Study.* Washington, DC: U.S. Green Building Council. http://www.usgbc.org/ShowFile.aspx?DocumentID=6435.

Bowler, Mary. 2010. RE: [cps] 2000–2002 CPS table 18. E-mail message to author, April 5.

Bureau of Labor Statistics. 2006. *Employment and Earnings.* Washington, DC: U.S. Department of Labor. http://www.bls.gov/cps/eetech_methods.pdf.

Bureau of Labor Statistics. 2009a. *Employment by Occupation, 2008 and Projected 2018.* Washington, DC: U.S. Department of Labor, Division. ftp://ftp.bls.gov/pub/special.requests/ep/ind-occ.matrix/ occupation.xls.

Bureau of Labor Statistics. 2009b. *Highlights of Women's Earnings in 2008.* Washington, DC: U.S. Department of Labor. http://www.bls.gov/cps/cpswom2008.pdf.

Bureau of Labor Statistics. 2009c. *Labor Force Characteristics by Race and Ethnicity, 2008.* Washington, DC: U.S. Department of Labor. http://www.bls.gov/cps/race_ethnicity_2008.htm.

Bureau of Labor Statistics. 2010a. *Current Population Survey, Household Data Annual Averages, Employed Persons by Detailed Industry, Sex, Race, and Hispanic or Latino Ethnicity.* 2000–2009. Washington, DC: U.S. Department of Labor. http://www.bls.gov/cps/tables.htm.

Bureau of Labor Statistics. 2010b. "Green Jobs." Washington, DC: U.S. Department of Labor. http://www.bls.gov/green/.

Bureau of Labor Statistics. 2010c. *Labor Force Statistics from the Current Population Survey Overview.* Washington, DC: U.S. Department of Labor. http://www.bls.gov/cps/cps_over.htm.

Center for Energy Economics. 2008. *Green Jobs: A Review of Recent Studies.* Austin: Center for Energy Economics, Bureau of Economic Geology, University of Texas at Austin. http://www.beg.utexas .edu/energyecon/documents/CEE_Green_Jobs_Review.pdf.

Clancy, J., S. Oparaocha, and U. Roehr. 2004. "Gender Equity and Renewable Energies." Internationale Konferenz für Erneuerbare Energien, Bonn. http://www.genanet.de/fileadmin/downloads/ gm_rn04_en/TBP12-gender.pdf.

Clark, Kim B., and Lawrence H. Summers. 1981. "Demographic Differences in Cyclical Employment Variation." *Journal of Human Resources* 16(1): 61–79.

Diebold, F. X., R. J. Barro, J. E. Marthinsen, R. Carbaugh, B. V. Yarbrough, R. M. Yarbrough, P. Mourdoukoutas, B. Kaufman, J. L. Hotchkiss, and T. Hyclak. 2004. *Elements of Forecasting.* Cincinnati: South-Western.

Hansen, Bruce. 2010. *Distribution of Least Squares.* Madison, WI: University of Wisconsin-Madison. http://www.ssc.wisc.edu/~bhansen/390/390Lecture16.pdf.

Ilg, Randy E. 2010. RE: [cps] multi-year CPS table 11? E-mail to author, February 16.

Kammen, D. M., K. Kapadia, and M. Fripp. 2004. "Putting Renewables to Work: How Many Jobs Can the Clean ENERGY Industry Generate?" RAEL Report, Renewable and Appropriate Energy Laboratory, University of California, Berkeley.

Morriss, Andrew P., William T. Bogart, Andrew Dorchak, and Robert E. Meiners. 2009. "Green Jobs Myths." University of Illinois Law & Economics Research Paper No. LE09-001.

Ochs Center for Metropolitan Studies. 2011. *A Fraction of the Jobs: A Case Study of the Job Creation Impacts of Completed Coal-Fired Power Plants between 2005 and 2009.* Chattanooga, TN: Ochs Center for Metropolitan Studies. http://www.ochscenter.org/documents/fractionofthejobs.pdf.

Perryman Group. 2003. *Redefining the Prospects for Sustainable Prosperity, Employment Expansion, and Environmental Quality in the US: An Assessment of the Economic Impact of the Initiatives Comprising the Apollo Project.* Waco, TX: Perryman Group.

Pollin, Robert, and Jeannette Wicks-Lim. 2008. *Job Opportunities for the Green Economy: A State-by-State Picture of Occupations That Gain from Green Investments.* Amherst,: Political Economy Research Institute, University of Massachusetts, Amherst.

Pollin, Robert, H. Garrett-Peltier, J. Heintz, and H. Scharber. 2008. *Green Recovery: A Program to Create Good Jobs and Start Building a Low-Carbon Economy.* Washington DC: Center for American Progress.

Pollin, Robert, J. Wicks-Lim, and H. Garrett-Peltier. 2009. "Green Prosperity: How Clean-Energy Policies Can Fight Poverty and Raise Living Standards in the United States." Amherst: Political Economy Research Institute, University of Massachusetts, Amherst.

Reskin, B. F., D. B. McBrier, and J. A. Kmec. 1999. "The Determinants and Consequences of Workplace Sex and Race Composition." *Annual Review of Sociology* 25(1): 335–61.

Rives, J. M., and K. Sosin. 2002. "Occupations and the Cyclical Behavior of Gender Unemployment Rates." *Journal of Socio-Economics* 31(3): 287–99.

Romer, Christina, and Jared Bernstein. 2009. "The Job Impact of the American Recovery and Reinvestment Plan." January 8, 2009. http://otrans.3cdn.net/45593e8ecbd339d074_l3m6bt1te.pdf.

Skutsch, M. 2003. "Tooling Up for Gender in Energy." Unpublished.

StataCorp LP. 2009. *Stata S/E 10.1.* College Station, TX: StataCorp LP.

U.S. Census Bureau. 2008. "A Compass for Understanding and Using American Community Survey Data: What General Data Users Need to know." Washington, DC: U.S. Census Bureau, Housing and Household Economic Statistics Division.

U.S. Census Bureau. 2009a. "A Compass for Understanding and Using American Community Survey Data: What PUMS Data Users Need to Know. " Washington, DC: U.S. Census Bureau, Housing and Household Economic Statistics Division.

U.S. Census Bureau. 2009b. "Industry and Occupation." Washington, DC: U.S. Department of Labor. http://www.census.gov/hhes/www/ioindex/view.html.

White, S., and J. Walsh. 2008. "Greener Pathways: Jobs and Workforce Development in the Clean Energy Economy." Madison: Center on Wisconsin Strategy.

Great Lakes, Great Debates

Facilitating Public Engagement
on Offshore Wind Energy Using
the Delphi Inquiry Approach

ERIK NORDMAN, JON VANDERMOLEN,
BETTY GAJEWSKI, AND AARON FERGUSON

INTRODUCTION

LAND-BASED WIND ENERGY IS A MATURE, ESTABLISHED ELECTRICITY-GENERATING technology. The U.S. Energy Information Administration reported that in 2009, wind turbines generated 10,886 megawatt-hours (MWh) of electricity, enough to power 6.7 million homes (Energy Information Administration, 2011a, 2011b). Offshore locations, including the Great Lakes, offer exceptional wind resources with the potential to produce 50 gigawatts (GW) of electricity-generating capacity (U.S. Department of Energy, 2008). One wind development firm has already proposed an offshore wind farm off Michigan's Lake Michigan coast (Scandia Wind Offshore, 2010). However, there is considerable debate over whether offshore wind energy development is appropriate and acceptable in coastal West Michigan. Tourism is a multi-billion-dollar industry in Michigan with beach and waterfront activities among the most popular with shoreline visitors (Costa, 2010). The West Michigan area in particular boasts miles of sandy beaches, quaint towns, and recreation opportunities ranging from charter fishing to kite surfing. With such popular tourism and recreational resources possibly at stake, the West Michigan Wind Assessment used a facilitated group discussion called a Delphi Inquiry to understand the conditions, if any, under which offshore wind energy development in Lake Michigan could be acceptable to residents of West Michigan. This chapter summarizes the resulting thoughts and concerns expressed by the stakeholder participants in this Delphi Inquiry.

THE DELPHI INQUIRY

The Delphi Inquiry (also known as a Delphi Method or Delphi Process) is "a qualitative method used to combine expert knowledge and opinion to arrive at an informed group consensus on a complex problem" (Donohoe and Needham, 2009, p. 416). The Delphi Inquiry is not a randomly sampled survey of public opinion. Instead it is a facilitated iterative discussion among participants with relevant knowledge of the subject in question. The Delphi Inquiry method has been used in many different fields, including management of the Grand Traverse Bay watershed (Ludlow, 1975) and wind turbine noise ordinances in Michigan (Alberts, 2007).

Over the years Delphi Inquiries have used many approaches, but the foundation of this structured communication technique for complex problems usually involves the following:

- An opportunity for participants to contribute their views on the topic
- A request for feedback from participants on these contributions
- The compilation of feedback and then an assessment of the group judgment
- An opportunity for participants to revise their views based on this compilation
- The possibility of consensus within an anonymous format (Linstone and Turoff, 1975)

The complex problem for the West Michigan Wind Assessment's Delphi Inquiry was *Under what conditions, if any, would West Michigan communities find offshore wind energy development in Lake Michigan acceptable?*

This "big picture" problem was reduced into a series of smaller questions addressing the following:

- The benefits of offshore wind energy development in Lake Michigan
- Ways in which communities in shoreline counties could capture those benefits
- The challenges of offshore wind energy development in Lake Michigan
- Ways to mitigate those challenges
- Specific topics about which residents would like more information

Public meetings held during 2010 on offshore wind energy development in Michigan have indicated that coastal residents hold a wide range of views on offshore wind energy development (Klepinger and Public Sector Consultants, 2010). For example, some West Michigan residents espouse a preservationist perspective in which they believe it is inappropriate to build wind farms in Lake Michigan no matter what benefits might come to their coastal communities. The project team made sure that all questions were open to such perspectives.

Participants

The study area comprised five lakeshore counties: Allegan, Ottawa, Muskegon, Oceana, and Mason (figure 1). Mason County was not part of the original West Michigan Wind Assessment study plan. It was included in the Delphi Inquiry because the Aegir Offshore Wind Energy Project was originally proposed for an area offshore from Mason and Oceana counties (near Ludington, Michigan). The Aegir project has since been revised to include locations offshore from Muskegon and Ottawa counties (near Holland and Muskegon, Michigan).

Figure 1. Five West Michigan Counties Included in Delphi Inquiry

During the summer of 2010, the project team created a list of possible Delphi Inquiry participants based on the following considerations:

- Participation from within all five counties in the study area
- Geographic diversity within these five counties including both shoreline and inland communities
- Diversity of professional expertise
- A minimum of forty invited participants from each county to contribute to the Delphi Inquiry

The invited participants possessed a diversity of professional expertise, including marina managers, ministers, fishing charter captains, engineers, business development authorities, township supervisors, county board members, tribal governments, college professors, shoreline property owner associations, local utilities, and many others. This participant diversity was not random but was purposefully selected so that a broad range of perspectives would be represented in the Delphi Inquiry. The number of invited participants ranged from forty-one in Ottawa County to twenty-six in Oceana County. Since the goal of forty invited participants per county was difficult to reach in rural Oceana and Mason counties, these counties were merged into one group. Actual participation totaled thirty-five and ranged from six people in Allegan County to twelve people in Muskegon County representing a broad mix of professional backgrounds (figure 2).

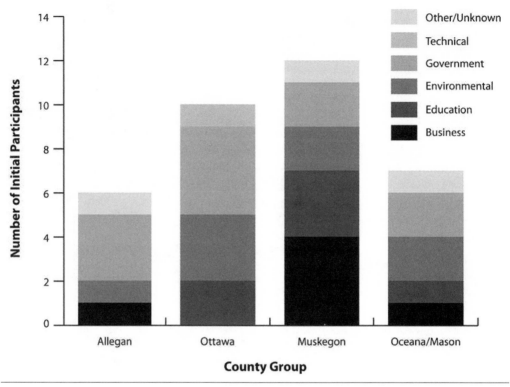

Figure 2. PARTICIPATION IN THE DELPHI INQUIRY

Providing background information on the problem to the participants is standard practice in a Delphi Inquiry (Donohoe and Needham, 2009). The project team sent all participants two prepublication draft issue briefs, one on the economic and social dimensions of offshore wind energy and the other on environmental and technical dimensions. These issue briefs synthesized the state of the science on offshore wind energy development. Final versions of these and other issue briefs are or will be made publicly available through the West Michigan Wind Assessment website.

Facilitating the Discussion through the Delphi Inquiry

The Delphi Inquiry for this project consisted of three rounds of questions (figure 3). The questionnaire was administered through a web-based tool (Zoomerang). Participants logged into the online survey under a self-generated code name to ensure anonymity. Each county group participated in its own separate Delphi Inquiry with its own developing set of concerns.

In Round 1, participants were asked to respond to five open-ended questions:

1. What are the key benefits to local communities, if any, of offshore wind energy development in Lake Michigan?
2. How can West Michigan communities best capture these benefits?

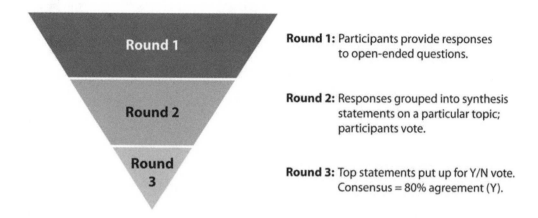

Round 1: Participants provide responses to open-ended questions.

Round 2: Responses grouped into synthesis statements on a particular topic; participants vote.

Round 3: Top statements put up for Y/N vote. Consensus = 80% agreement (Y).

Figure 3. THE DELPHI INQUIRY PROCESS USED IN THIS PROJECT

3. What are the key challenges facing offshore wind energy development in Lake Michigan?
4. What are some ways of mitigating these challenges, if any?
5. What topics do communities need more information about in order to make informed decisions on offshore wind energy development in Lake Michigan?

The questionnaire instructions clearly stated that a response such as "Offshore wind energy development is unacceptable under any conditions" is an appropriate response to any of the questions above. This instruction was included to address specific concerns that the Delphi Inquiry was open to all points of view regarding offshore wind energy development in Lake Michigan. This is illustrated in the example question below:

> Based on your understanding of offshore wind energy development, what would you identify to West Michigan communities as the most important benefits of wind energy development in Lake Michigan? Please list up to three benefits, in no particular order. An acceptable answer is "There are no benefits from offshore wind energy development in Lake Michigan for West Michigan communities."

In Round 2, participants reviewed the statements of all group members and selected three statements that, in their view, were most important. The statements were organized based on the five categories (benefits, challenges, etc.) presented in Round 1. Statements that were selected by 50 percent or more of the participants advanced to Round 3. For example, a statement regarding the benefits of offshore wind energy was

> Offshore wind energy is a cleaner alternative to fossil fuels and nuclear energy.

In Round 3, the Delphi participants were simply asked to indicate whether they agreed with the statements that were advanced from Round 2. As in the previous rounds, the statements were organized by category (benefits, challenges, etc.). Each of the five categories also included an alternative statement indicating that offshore wind energy development in Lake Michigan was unacceptable. The alternative statement was included whether or not such a statement was identified and advanced from previous rounds. For example in the benefits category, one of the benefit statements was

> Offshore wind energy development in Lake Michigan would be more acceptable to West Michigan communities if it reduces pollution and reduces dependence on fossils fuels and nuclear energy.

The alternative statement for the benefit category was

> There are no benefits to local communities from offshore wind energy development in Lake Michigan.

Round 3 begins the process of obtaining consensus for the advanced statements. The goal of a Delphi Inquiry was to arrive at an informed group consensus on a complex challenge. There is no standard definition of "consensus" in the literature or how to define consensus in the Delphi method. For this project, consensus was defined as 80 percent agreement on a statement by Delphi participants in Round 3. That is, if a statement was affirmed by at least 80 percent of the participants in Round 3, it was concluded that consensus was reached for that statement.

RESULTS

The participants in each of the county groups were able to reach consensus on at least one statement in Round 3 (table 1). For example, Allegan County arrived at consensus on twelve statements, while the Oceana/Mason counties group reached consensus on only one. Most of the consensus statements were related to the categories of "challenges" and "information gaps" of offshore wind energy development (figure 4). Only one consensus statement, from the Allegan County group, included consensus on the environmental benefits of offshore wind energy development. In terms of the topics most of the consensus statements were related to visibility concerns and economics (figure 5).

Benefits of Offshore Wind Energy Development in Lake Michigan

Only the Allegan County group arrived at consensus on a statement related to the benefits of offshore wind energy development in Lake Michigan. This group identified the primary benefit as reducing pollution and dependence on fossil fuels and nuclear energy.

Table 1. NUMBER OF CONSENSUS STATEMENTS ARRIVED AT BY EACH COUNTY GROUP

Statement type	*County*			
	Allegan	Ottawa	Muskegon	Oceana/Mason
Round 3 statements	21	15	16	9
Final consensus	12	5	8	1

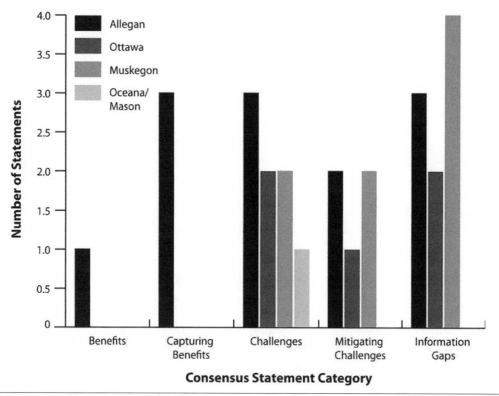

Figure 4. MOST CONSENSUS STATEMENTS RELATED TO CHALLENGES AND INFORMATION GAPS

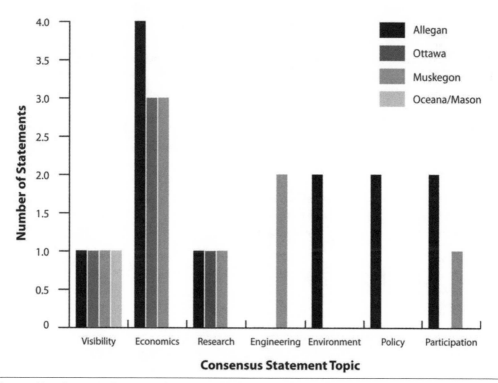

Figure 5. MOST CONSENSUS STATEMENTS WERE ASSOCIATED WITH ECONOMICS AND WIND FARM VISIBILITY

Capturing the Benefits

The Allegan County group was also the only group reaching consensus on statements related to ways that local communities could capture the benefits of offshore wind energy development in Lake Michigan. These methods were identified by the Allegan County group as the following:

- Providing more complete details on offshore wind energy development that anticipate the information needs of local residents
- Establishing state and local energy policies, including wind energy, and coordinating local planning efforts
- Soliciting and arranging for input from all sides of the issue and encouraging an open, flexible approach to offshore wind energy development

Key Challenges Facing Offshore Wind Energy Development

Every county group, including the Oceana/Mason group, reached consensus on at least one statement related to the challenges of offshore wind energy development in Lake Michigan. All groups reached consensus on a statement similar to the one below (the county group(s) that reached consensus on the statements are listed in parentheses):

> Before offshore wind energy development in Lake Michigan could be considered acceptable, proposed projects must recognize concerns about aesthetics and reduce possible related impacts on coastal businesses and property values. (Allegan, Ottawa, Muskegon, Oceana/Mason)

Other "challenge" consensus statements related to economics and engineering included responses to this statement: Before offshore wind energy development in Lake Michigan could be considered acceptable:

- The economic and financial costs of offshore wind energy must be analyzed, including utility costs, construction and maintenance costs, and outsourcing concerns. (Ottawa, Muskegon, Allegan)
- Project developers must demonstrate that local communities will be net beneficiaries (i.e., the benefits are greater than the costs) from offshore wind energy development. (Allegan)
- Certain engineering and design challenges must be overcome, including the technical/economic feasibility, safe placement, transmission, and ice on and around the turbines. (Muskegon)

Mitigating the Challenges

All of the county groups, except Oceana/Mason, arrived at consensus on approaches to mitigating the challenges of offshore wind energy development in Lake Michigan. The mitigation approaches ranged from additional research and development to policy and public participation. Below are the responses to the statement: A way to mitigate the challenges of offshore wind energy development in Lake Michigan and make it more acceptable is to

- Conduct more research, including lessons learned from communities where full-scale offshore wind farms or pilot projects have been built (Ottawa, Muskegon)
- Encourage more assertive leadership on renewable energy issues, especially from state government and local utilities (Allegan)
- Encourage public participation by hosting town hall meetings on offshore wind energy development (Muskegon)
- Provide more diverse opportunities for targeted education and outreach efforts (Allegan)

Information Gaps

The county groups arrived at consensus on more statements related to information gaps than any other aspect of offshore wind energy development. Questions about economic impacts dominated the responses to the statement: Offshore wind energy development in Lake Michigan might be considered more acceptable if communities had more information about

- Turbine visibility and potential effects on shoreline property values and tourism (Muskegon)
- The full costs and benefits of offshore wind energy development compared to onshore development and fossil fuels (Muskegon, Allegan)
- The transparent evaluation of risks and opportunities of offshore wind energy development, especially with respect to job creation. (Ottawa, Allegan)
- The economic impacts on utility rate-payers, including subsidies for offshore development (Muskegon)
- The technical feasibility of such projects, including year-round operation and production potential (Muskegon)
- The comprehensive environmental impacts, including effects on wildlife, fishing, recreational boating, and shipping (Allegan)

Evaluation

The final round of the Delphi Inquiry included questions about the Delphi process itself. Of the twenty-eight participants who answered the wrap-up questions, six (21 percent) reported being more knowledgeable about offshore wind energy development as a result of the Delphi Inquiry. None of the respondents from the Oceana/Mason group reported that their level of knowledge of offshore wind energy had changed. Six (21 percent) of the respondents found offshore wind energy development in Lake Michigan more acceptable after going through the Delphi Inquiry process, while two (8 percent) found it less acceptable now (table 2). A large majority (93 percent) of participants agreed that the project team acted openly and transparently in administering the Delphi Inquiry.

Table 2. Changes in Acceptance of Offshore Wind Energy Resulting from the Delphi Inquiry

Change in acceptance	*Oceana/Mason*	*Muskegon*	*Ottawa*	*Allegan*
I find offshore wind energy in Lake Michigan *more acceptable* now.	3 (43%)	1 (14%)	0 (0%)	2 (33%)
My opinion of offshore wind energy development in Lake Michigan *has not changed.*	4 (57%)	5 (71%)	8 (100%)	3 (50%)
I find offshore wind energy development in Lake Michigan *less acceptable* now.	0 (0%)	1 (14%)	0 (0%)	1 (17%)

DISCUSSION

As expected, each county group clearly had a range of opinions about offshore wind energy development in Lake Michigan, yet all the groups were able to reach consensus on at least one statement. No group arrived at consensus on one of the alternative statements that offshore wind energy development in Lake Michigan is unacceptable under any circumstances. This suggests that most group members may be open to the idea of offshore wind energy development in Lake Michigan as long as certain conditions are met.

The one topic that every group agreed on, as demonstrated by the highest percentage in agreement overall, was concern about the visual impact of an offshore wind farm. In some groups this concern was expressed as a challenge and other groups identified it as an information gap, but the sentiment was consistent.

Economics was another common theme among the consensus statements. These statements were found mostly among the "challenge" and "information gap" categories. These spanned topics such as how offshore development will impact electricity rates, affect employment, and shoreline property values.

Allegan County was the only group to reach consensus about the benefits of offshore wind energy development and ways in which local communities can capture those benefits. The only benefit on which consensus was reached in any group was about the potential to reduce pollution and fossil fuel consumption. Participants from counties outside of Allegan were unable to agree that offshore wind energy development offers any benefits to local communities. This suggests that if future offshore wind projects in Lake Michigan are to be acceptable to local communities, the projects must provide some benefits to the communities and those benefits need to be clearly articulated.

The Delphi Inquiry proved to be an appropriate technique for stimulating discussion and improving the level of knowledge among participants. Outside of the Oceana/Mason group, nearly 30 percent of the participants reported feeling more knowledgeable about offshore wind energy. One participant in the Allegan group felt less knowledgeable, which may be indicative of the complexity of the issue. The Oceana/Mason group, where the Aegir Offshore project was originally proposed, expressed the least level of consensus and no change in the level of knowledge compared to the start of the Delphi Inquiry. The Delphi Inquiry did not change the opinions of most participants on offshore wind energy in Lake Michigan, but among those that did change, most moved toward a more favorable opinion. The vast majority of participants agreed that the project team administered the Delphi Inquiry in a transparent and open manner, which suggests that this is an appropriate tool for engaging the public in a discussion of a complex and controversial issue.

The West Michigan Wind Assessment project team has written a series of issue briefs summarizing the state of the science about wind energy development from environmental, social, and economic perspectives. The team used the Delphi Inquiry results to tailor its outreach efforts to address the most pressing concerns and information gaps as suggested by the participants.

It is important not to draw too broad a conclusion from this Delphi Inquiry. The participants were selected based on their professional expertise in business, government, and engineering, or for their location-based knowledge as residents of coastal communities. The participants were not a random sample of the population, so the conclusions cannot be applied to the population as a whole. This is not a flaw in the process but rather the nature of the Delphi Inquiry technique. The Delphi Inquiry results do suggest, however, that informed professionals with wide-ranging views can reach agreement on certain aspects of a controversial topic like offshore wind energy development. The Delphi Inquiry results can help inform future research projects, public opinion polls, and policy decisions.

CONCLUSIONS

The individual consensus statements from the four county groups can be aggregated to answer the "big picture" question that introduced this chapter. According to the results of this Delphi Inquiry, offshore wind energy development in Lake Michigan could be acceptable to the participants if:

- It reduces pollution and dependence on fossil fuels
- The visual impact is minimal
- Property values and tourism are not significantly harmed
- Coastal communities benefit from the projects
- The public has ample opportunity to participate in the siting process
- Projects do not lead to substantial utility rate increases
- Projects do not harm wildlife, recreation, and fishing activities
- Technical challenges are overcome, such as ice buildup and transmission

The Delphi Inquiry participants generated consensus statements on a variety of relevant topics. The Delphi Inquiry process proved to be a useful method for facilitating a group discussion on what has become an emotionally charged issue in West Michigan. The groups were most in agreement on the challenges and information gaps related to offshore wind energy development in Lake Michigan. Economic concerns dominated the discussion in these areas. There was little agreement on the benefits of offshore wind energy development. The results of the process can assist local decision-makers in understanding the issues to be considered in siting wind energy developments as well as provide a road map for future investigations on the public acceptance of offshore wind farms in the Great Lakes and beyond.

NOTE

The West Michigan Wind Assessment team thanks the Delphi Inquiry participants for their honest assessments and willingness to share their perspectives on a controversial issue. Without the participants, this project would not have been possible. We also thank the staff at Michigan Sea Grant and the project stakeholder steering committee for their comments and suggestions. This project was sponsored by Michigan Sea Grant College Program, R/CCD-11, under NA100AR4170071 from National Sea Grant, NOAA, U.S. Department of Commerce, and funds from the State of Michigan. A version of this chapter was released as West Michigan Wind Assessment Issue Brief No. 4, "Citizen Views on Offshore Wind: Benefits, Challenges, and Information Gaps."

REFERENCES

Alberts, D. J. 2007. "Stakeholders or Subject Matter Experts: Who Should Be Consulted?" *Energy Policy* 35(4): 2336–46.

Costa, B. 2010. "2009 Visitor Profile—Michigan." Prepared for the Michigan Economic Development Corporation by D.K. Shifflet & Associates, Ltd. http://web4.canr.msu.edu/mgm2/econ/MIindex.htm.

Donohoe, H., and R. Needham. 2009. "Moving Best Practice Forward: Delphi Characteristics, Advantages, Potential Problems, and Solutions." *International Journal of Tourism Research* 11:415–37.

Energy Information Administration. 2011a. "Electric Power Monthly Table 1.1.A Net Generation—Other Renewables: Total—All Sectors." http://www.eia.gov/cneaf/electricity/epm/epm_sum.html.

Energy Information Administration. 2011b. "Electricity Sales, Revenue, and Price Table 5A Residential Average Monthly Bill by Census Division, and State." http://www.eia.gov/cneaf/electricity/esr/esr_sum.html.

Klepinger, M., and Public Sector Consultants. 2010. "Report of the Michigan Great Lakes Wind Council." http://www.michiganglowcouncil.org/GLOWreportOct2010_with%20appendices.pdf.

Linstone, H., and M. Turoff. 1975. Introduction to *In The Delphi Method: Techniques and Applications*, ed. H. Linstone and M. Turoff. Reading, MA: Addison-Wesley.

Ludlow, J. 1975. "Delphi Inquiries and Knowledge Utilization." *In The Delphi Method: Techniques and Applications*, ed. H. Linstone and M. Turoff. Reading, MA: Addison-Wesley.

Scandia Wind Offshore. 2010. The Aegir Project. http://www.scandiawind.com/Aegirproject.html.

U.S. Department of Energy National Renewable Energy Laboratory. 2008. "20% Wind Energy by 2030: Increasing Wind Energy's Contribution to the US Electricity Supply." DOE/GO-102008-2567. http://www.nrel.gov/docs/fy08osti/41869.pdf.

Endogenous Environmental Discounting and Climate-Economy Modeling

PHILIP SIRIANNI

THE DEBATE OVER HOW TO DISCOUNT PUBLIC (ENVIRONMENTAL) VERSUS PRIVATE (capital) investments in dynamic climate-economy models is well documented: Conventional private discounting does not explain the divide between the near-term costs of reducing emissions and the associated far-term reductions in climate damages. We propose an endogenization of discount rates that hinges on the following assumption of human behavior: We tend to react quickly to imminent dangers but slowly, or not at all, to far-distant ones. Specifically, the current period's environmental discount rate is modeled so that it is directly related to the difference between contemporaneous temperature and a "catastrophic" temperature bound: As global atmospheric temperature rises toward the bound, the environmental discount rate declines, and sustainability of the environment becomes a greater concern. Using a dual-rate discounting approach so as to maintain conventional discount rates for private investment, we implement the solution in a popular integrated assessment model (Nordhaus and Yang, 1996). The results are compared with those of other popular solution concepts, and it is demonstrated that in most cases an endogenous discounting approach is consistent with more stringent emissions reduction strategies. However, the discounting assumptions made here are not enough to justify the level of emissions reductions recommended by the *SternReview* (Stern, 2007), particularly in the nearer term.

INTRODUCTION

Debates over discounting future utilities in economic growth models with microeconomic foundations date back to the inception of modern long-term growth models themselves. High discount rates characterize agents' relative impatience, and a greater emphasis is placed on nearer-term costs and benefits. The addition of environmental components to growth models complicates the discounting concerns to an even greater extent. Ethical considerations regarding the welfare of future generations and how to deal with private versus public projects play crucial roles in the choice of "the appropriate" discount rate. Not surprisingly, in long-term climate-economy models, the higher the discount rate, the smaller is the reduction in near-term emissions, and the lower is the weight placed on future climate damages in cost-benefit analyses (i.e., the smaller is the investment in the public project).

In economic growth models (without environmental components), Ramsey (1928) among others advocates a nondiscounted utilitarian approach in which the benevolent social planner maximizes the sum of utilities across time. However, as Koopmans (1960) demonstrates, such an approach—though perhaps desirable from ethical perspectives—leads to excessively high savings rates when compared with historical outcomes. Fisher (1930) suggests that discount rates should be chosen according to social norms, quality of life, and in general a concern for other members of society. Although a common modeling practice is to assign a nonzero, and often constant, discount rate in economic growth frameworks, the literature on nonzero, nonconstant discount rates is extensive. Henderson and Bateman (1995) and Laibson (1997) treat discount rates as time-varying parameters that are assumed to have a hyperbolic shape. Theoretical justifications for nonconstant, endogenous discount rates are often rooted in habit formation with respect to consumption and wealth accumulation (see, for example, Obstfeld, 1990; Becker and Mulligan, 1997; and Schumacher, 2006).

In growth models with environmental components, the use of nonzero, constant discount rates raises additional concerns. A comprehensive review of discounting and the environment is found in Portney and Weyant (1999). Theoretical details on discounting and climate change are examined rigorously in many studies (see, for earlier examples, Nordhaus, 1997, and Lind and Schuler, 1998). A crucial insight is that more stringent greenhouse gas mitigation policies such as those called for in the *SternReview* (Stern, 2007) or the Kyoto Protocol are difficult to justify with conventional discount rates that are in line those used to discount private projects, especially for the developed countries that bear the larger mitigation burdens. Furthermore, the discount rates selected must be consistent with other parameters in the model as well as historical observations regarding savings and investment rates. (See, for example, the Nordhaus, 2007 critique of the *SternReview*, 2007.) Some researchers use empirical observations on human behavior and psychology (Harvey, 1994; Heal, 1998) or uncertainty (Weitzman, 1999; Gollier, 2002) to justify time-varying (declining) discount rates.

An important question remains: Why should the discount rate applied to the accumulation of private capital also apply to projects related to the reduction of carbon emissions? Furthermore, how should these (different) discount rates be determined? As a partial answer to the latter question, Cropper, Aydede, and Portney (1992) aim to empirically identify public discount rates for environmental projects and conclude that these discount rates are significantly lower than their private project counterparts. Exploring this notion in a theoretical framework, Borissov and Shakhnov (2011) add dual-rate discounting to Stokey's (1998) model and show that the growth rate of emissions depends on the ratio of discount rates for private and environmental capital. In an effort to reconcile the empirical observations of dual rates with the known discounting issues associated with long-term climate-economy modeling, Yang (2003) develops a dual-rate discounting framework in the context of an integrated assessment model. The discount rate for environmental investment is low, while the discount rate for investment in private capital is set such that historical observations of savings rates are consistent with the economic module used in the study.

We should point out that dual-rate discounting is not advocated by all economists. For instance, it is argued by Tol (2003) that dual-rate discounting is unnecessary because the same results can be generated by making the assumption of a changing risk aversion parameter, a key determinant of income elasticity of consumption in many economic growth models. However, it is unclear as to what would cause risk aversion to be altered over time. Brunnermeier and Nagel (2008) find no evidence that wealth shocks affect risk aversion.

Given the empirical evidence for dual rates, we proceed within that framework. However, it is only recently that endogenous discounting in environmental models has been explored. Tsur and Zemel (2009) examine discount rates that are endogenous to environmental policy. Ayong Le Kama and Schubert (2007) use an economic growth model to assess, from theoretical perspectives, the impacts of a discount rate that is altered when the stock of "environment" changes. Their model is parsimonious, as there is no capital accumulation, and consumption is derived directly and exclusively from environmental amenities. Thus, there is one discount rate that applies, and it is assumed to be positively related to environmental quality. They identify convergence paths of environmental quality, which occur generically for any parametric specification of endogenized discount rates.

Based on the literatures discussed above, questions and issues surrounding the discounting debate can be summarized as follows. First, there is the empirical evidence from contingent valuation literatures that discount rates for environmental projects are significantly lower than discount rates for investments in private capital, the latter of which are estimated based on historical rates of saving. Second, when near-sighted agents develop mounting concerns over long-term sustainability, a nonconstant discount rate that varies with environmental or other factors is justifiable. The present project aims to link these two lines of research. To address the first issue, we apply the dual-rate discounting approach from Yang (2003), in which the discount rate for private investment differs from the discount rate for environmental investment. To address the second issue, we extend the analysis by incorporating endogenously determined discount rates into a dynamic climate-economy modeling framework. The discount rate varies positively with environmental quality à la Ayong Le Kama and Schubert (2007). Specifically, we assume that as global atmospheric temperature rises toward the six-degree Celsius "catastrophic" level suggested by the IPCC (2007) report, the discount rate for public investment declines proportionately. We implement the solution in a modified version of the popular integrated assessment model (IAM) of Nordhaus and Yang (1996) to see what levels of emissions reductions are justifiable given these assumptions about discounting.

The literature on discounting (exogenous or hyperbolic) in integrated assessment models of many types is abundant.[1] Although theoretical issues involving endogenous discount rates in environment-economy models are coming to the forefront of environmental economics, endogenous discounting has not yet been implemented in an IAM. However, it is only with an IAM that the effects of endogenous discounting on regional carbon control rates, optimal carbon taxes, and other macroeconomic variables can be empirically estimated through model simulations.

The next section discusses the generic frameworks for using dual-rate discounting and endogenous environmental discounting in particular. The third section provides the algorithmic procedure used to solve the RICE-B (Yang and Sirianni, 2010) model with uniform and dual-rate discounting (exogenous and endogenous). The fourth section presents simulation results in comparison with some other popular solution concepts employed in the literature. The first section concludes and discusses possibilities for future research.

MODELING DUAL-RATE DISCOUNTING WITH
ENDOGENOUS ENVIRONMENTAL DISCOUNT RATES

In Ramsey-type economic growth models, what is often referred to as "the discount rate" (r) to be used in the cost-benefit analyses of projects can actually be decomposed into two components: r = ρ + θg. Here, ρ is the rate at which future utilities are discounted. It is often referred to as the "pure rate of time preference" and is a reflection of agents' impatience regardless of the rate at which they will grow richer (or poorer) in the future. The second term in the above expression, θg, is a growth-related rate. Specifically, θ is the elasticity of marginal utility with respect to consumption,[2] and g is the growth rate of agents' incomes. Thus, for a given value of ρ, a higher g increases "the discount rate"; for a given growth rate of income, increasing impatience causes r to increase as well. This chapter is primarily concerned with changes in the pure rate of time preference (for a given g). For that reason, a change in the discount rate is hereby assumed to come about from a change in the policymakers' inferred pure rate of time preference.

Consider the following four (distinct) objective functions:

$$Max\ V = \int_0^\infty e^{-\rho t} U_i(X_i(t),\ Y(t))dt \tag{1}$$

$$Max\ V = \int_0^\infty e^{-\rho(Y(t))t} U_i(X_i(t),\ Y(t))dt \tag{2}$$

$$Max\ V = \int_0^\infty U_i(X_i(t,\rho_x),\ Y(t,\rho_y))dt \tag{3}$$

$$Max\ V = \int_0^\infty U_i(X_i(t,\rho_x),\ Y(t,\rho_y(Y(t))))dt \tag{4}$$

In equation (1), a constant pure rate of time preference applies to both X_i (the private good) and Y (the public good, i.e., environmental quality). This is the "conventional" approach to discounting. In equation (2), the same pure rate of time preference applies to both goods; however, the rate depends on the level of the public good. This characterization resembles the discounting assumption made in Ayong Le Kama and Schubert (2007). The assumption that $\rho'(Y(t) > 0$ indicates that the pure rate of time preference declines as environmental quality declines. Equations (3) and (4) represent exogenous dual-rate discounting and endogenous dual-rate discounting, respectively.

Yang (2003) suggests the dual-rate discounting approach of equation (3) to deal with the inherent difficulties of conventional discounting in long-term modeling that are outlined in the previous section. Specifically, private investments in Yang (2003) are subject to a conventional pure rate of time preference of 3 percent per year, while public investments in carbon control are subject to a 0.2 percent per year rate. As long as X_i and Y are not substitutable, the results are time-consistent.[3] To connect the discount rate with environmental quality, it is here that we extend this literature by further incorporating a characterization of human behavior that hinges on the following assumption: We react more quickly to near-term dangers than we do to far-distant dangers. Thus, when the temperature rises due to increased carbon emissions and the buildup of carbon concentration in the atmosphere (which, in an integrated assessment framework, would be related to Y(t) in the above objective functions), the pure rate of time preference declines, and agents become more concerned with long-term sustainability of the environment. Specifically, the pure rate of time preference can be characterized as follows:

$$\rho_t(temp_t) = f(temp_t - \overline{temp}) = a(temp_t - \overline{temp})^b \tag{5}$$

$$f'(temp_t - \overline{temp}) > 0 \tag{6}$$

For the main analysis, we use a linear formulation for equation (5) ($b = 1$). The parameter a is calibrated so that the initial value of the endogenous rate of pure time preference is (a) equal to the rate that matches historical observations of savings rates, and (b) consistent with other parameters of the model. The upper bound on temperature (i.e., the "catastrophic" level) is assumed to be six degrees Celsius, as advised by the IPCC (2007), and the initial temperature in the first period ($t = 0$) of the model is 0.71 degrees Celsius above the preindustrial level (the initial condition of the RICE-B model). This implies that the value of $a = -0.00567$ in the linear formulation so that $\rho_0 = 0.03$. As temperature changes over time, the pure rate of time preference adjusts accordingly. To examine the sensitivity of the results, we then use a quadratic formulation ($b = 2$). Because the discount rate under the quadratic formulation would decline more rapidly in temperature, we would expect to see higher carbon control rates shifted to the nearer term when compared with the linear formulation. Using the same convention for calibration, $a = 0.00107$ in the quadratic formulation. Of course, many functional forms for equation (5) are possible, and they would depend on the modeler's subjective criteria. The following section discusses the integrated assessment model in which these endogenous pure rates of time preference are implemented.

SCENARIO DESIGN AND SOLUTION ALGORITHM

The RICE model has many versions. Modeling details are documented extensively in Nordhaus and Yang (1996), Nordhaus and Boyer (2000), and Yang (2008). The interested reader is hereby referred to these sources. To summarize, the RICE model adapted for this study has six regions: USA (United States), OHI (Other High Income countries), EU (European Union countries), CHN (China), EEC (Eastern European countries and the Former Soviet Union), and ROW (the Rest of the World). This model is a modification of RICE named RICE-B (RICE with the Bern-CC model), which is introduced in Yang and Sirianni (2010) to study the impacts of a climate policy in which each region's mitigation burden is based on its share in aggregate carbon concentration. The base year of the model is 2000; the time horizon is 250 years in five-year time steps. RICE-B is coded in GAMS language.

The RICE model treats climate change as a stock externality phenomenon. Regional carbon emissions (flow variables) contribute to global carbon concentration (a stock variable). Changes in carbon concentration affect temperature, and the damages due to temperature increases affect regional welfare. The optimal control problem has two choice variables: investment in private capital and investment in public (environmental) capital. The private capital component evolves according to the standard Ramsey-type capital accumulation equations. The public capital component is characterized by a carbon control rate that falls between zero and 1: "Business-as-usual" (or a no-control baseline) implies that the carbon control rate is zero.

The simulations of the next section are based on the following scenarios:

- *Benchmark—Scenario 1 (conventional discounting)*: A constant pure rate of time preference of 3 percent per year applies to both private and public investments.
- *Scenario 2 (near-zero discounting)*: A constant pure rate of time preference of 0.2 percent per year applies to both private and public investments.
- *Scenario 3 (dual-rate exogenous discounting)*: Pure rates of time preference of 3 percent and 0.2 percent per year apply to private and public investments, respectively.
- *Scenario 4 (uniform endogenous discounting)*: A pure rate of time preference that follows equation (5) applies to both private and public investments.
- *Scenario 5 (dual-rate endogenous discounting)*: A constant pure rate of time preference of 3 percent per year applies to private investments; a pure rate of time preference that follows equation (5) applies to public investments.

Efficient solutions for which the climate externality is fully internalized are obtained for each of the above scenarios using the "color-preserving" or "quasi-equitable" social welfare weights from Yang and Sirianni (2010).[4]

A final note on the algorithmic procedure used for solving Scenarios 3 and 5 is warranted. The algorithm is a modification of the *tatonnement* procedure documented in Yang (2003):

1. Set the pure rate of time preference to 3 percent per year. Solve for the optimal paths of private investment, given arbitrary paths for regional carbon control rates (say, zero for all regions and all time periods).
2. Set private investment to the paths that are determined in step 1. Set the discount rate to 0.2 percent per year (Scenario 3), or allow the discount rate to evolve according to equation (5) (Scenario 5). Solve for the optimal paths of carbon control rates.
3. Set control rates to the paths determined in step 2. Set the discount rate to 3 percent per year. Solve for the optimal paths of private investment.
4. Repeat steps 2 and 3 until the paths of control rates and private investment are rendered invariant to subsequent iterations.

ANALYSIS OF SIMULATION RESULTS

Due to the large number of both economic and climate variables in the RICE-B model, we do not present simulation results for all of these variables. Instead, we focus on the time paths of public and private investment so that the results are more easily compared with those in Yang (2003). Specifically, we present results for emissions, (private) investment, and carbon control rates (public investment), for each of the scenarios described above. To summarize, the endogenized environmental discount rate in Scenario 5 falls from 3 percent to 0.1 percent over the time horizon of the model using the linear formulation, and 3 percent to 0.01 percent using the quadratic formulation. Figure 1 shows twenty-first-century projections of the environmental discount rate for both formulations. The simulation results we present in this section suggest that the endogenous dual-rate discounting in Scenario 5 justifies higher carbon control rates than both exogenous dual-rate discounting (Scenario 3) and conventional uniform discounting (Scenario 1). This is true under both formulations of equation (5), the second (quadratic) of which we analyze in the second subsection. As expected, the assumption of quadratic discounting requires more stringent emissions reductions.

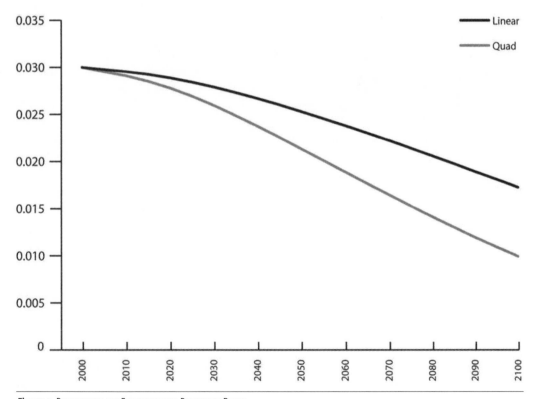

Figure 1. PROJECTION OF ENDOGENOUS DISCOUNT RATES

Linear Endogenous Discounting

Figures 2–4 display the efficient regional profiles for investment, carbon control rates, and emissions, respectively, under each of the five scenarios for USA and CHN, two key players in climate change negotiations. It is clear that the private investment profiles for both dual-rate scenarios (Scenarios 3 and 5) are very close to those under conventional discounting. However, regional carbon control rates in Scenario 5 are higher and emissions are lower (figures 3 and 4), particularly in the longer term, due to the endogenous (and declining) discount rate used for environmental investments. For USA, twenty-first-century optimal control rates are in the range of 10–12 percent under conventional discounting, and 11–18 percent under the endogenous dual-rate assumption of Scenario 5. For CHN, they are in the range of 6–12 percent under conventional discounting, but rise to 17 percent by the end of the century under Scenario 5.

Using the metric employed by Yang (2003), tables 1–3 report the relative deviations of key variables from the benchmark case in Scenario 1 (conventional uniform discounting). In table 1, it is not surprising that the assumption of near-zero uniform discounting requires a large and increasing amount of private investment by each region: by the end of the twenty-first century, an efficient outcome requires that private investment is nearly 50 percent higher than with conventional discounting, and that the average regional carbon tax (or "social cost" of carbon) exceeds $600 per ton by the middle of the century. The results in tables 2 and 3 indicate that the corresponding carbon control rates are more than twice as high for each region throughout the time horizon, and emissions are significantly lower. For instance, USA's emissions in 2015 are 87.1 percent of those under conventional discounting.

The uniform endogenous rate of Scenario 4 shows a similar and expected pattern. However, since this rate is assumed to be higher initially and then decline as sustainability of the environment becomes a greater concern, private investment is not as high as under the assumption of near-zero discounting initially, but it increases rapidly over the time horizon; that is, in comparison with uniform near-zero discounting, the rate at which investment deviates from the benchmark case is higher. Similarly, it can be seen that by the end of the century, carbon control rates increase to more than three times that of conventional discounting for all regions, and emissions are in the range of 65 percent (for ROW) to 85 percent (for EEC). Because both private and environmental investments are discounted at the same rate (which is endogenous to temperature in this scenario), it is obvious that this particular scheme relies on an extreme and unrealistic assumption about discounting, especially with respect to private investment. Nevertheless, the results are provided for comparison.

Although perhaps desirable from ethical perspectives, the rates used in Scenarios 2 and 4 suffer from a known empirical problem as discussed in the introduction: private investment profiles are too high when compared with historical outcomes. To reconcile this, we now turn to the results of the dual-rate discounting approaches of Scenarios 3 and 5. Because the dual-rate approach allows conventional discount rates (of 3 percent) to be applied to private investment, the profile of this variable over the time horizon matches very closely with the conventional discounting case of Scenario 1. In fact, as seen in table 1, private investment in the dual-rate cases of Scenarios 3 and 5 is always in the range of 97 percent to 100.4 percent of the level of private investment in Scenario 1. However, the public investment in carbon control deviates from the benchmark, as shown in table 2. In the dual-rate exogenous case of Scenario 3, the environmental discount rate remains at 0.2 percent for the entire time horizon. For the dual-rate endogenous case, the environmental discount rate declines as temperature

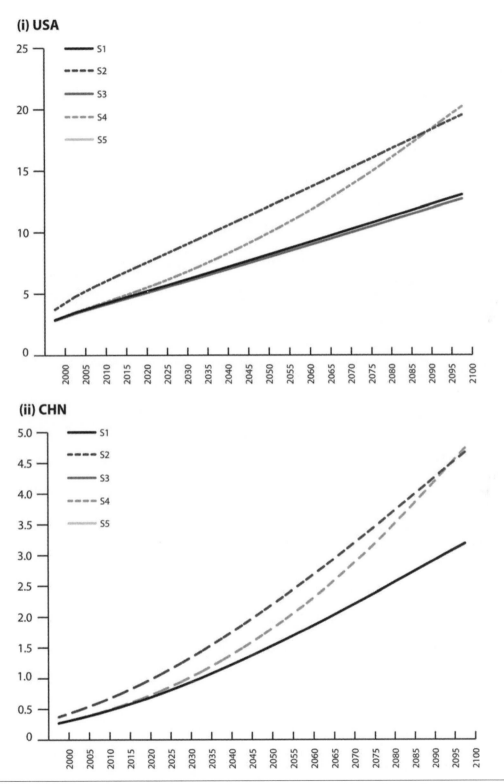

(i) USA

(ii) CHN

Figure 2. Linear Endogenous Discounting: Investment across Scenarios for Selected Regions (trillions of 2000US$)

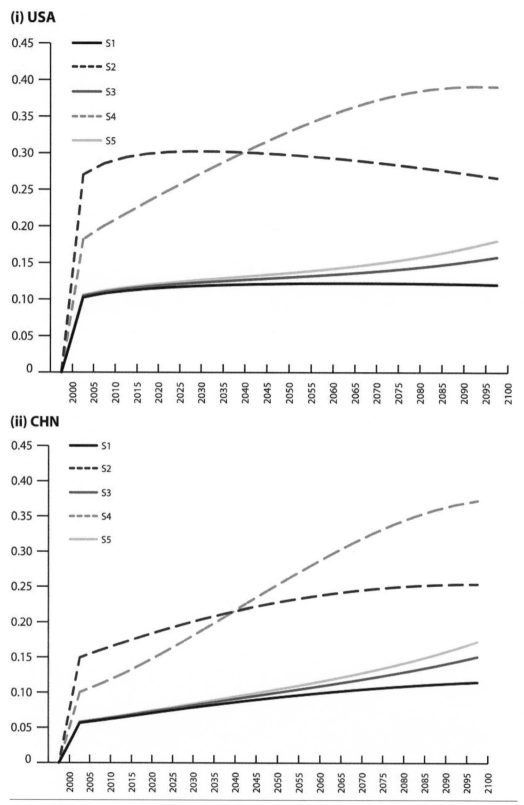

(i) USA

(ii) CHN

Figure 3. LINEAR ENDOGENOUS DISCOUNTING: CARBON CONTROL RATES ACROSS SCENARIOS FOR SELECTED REGIONS

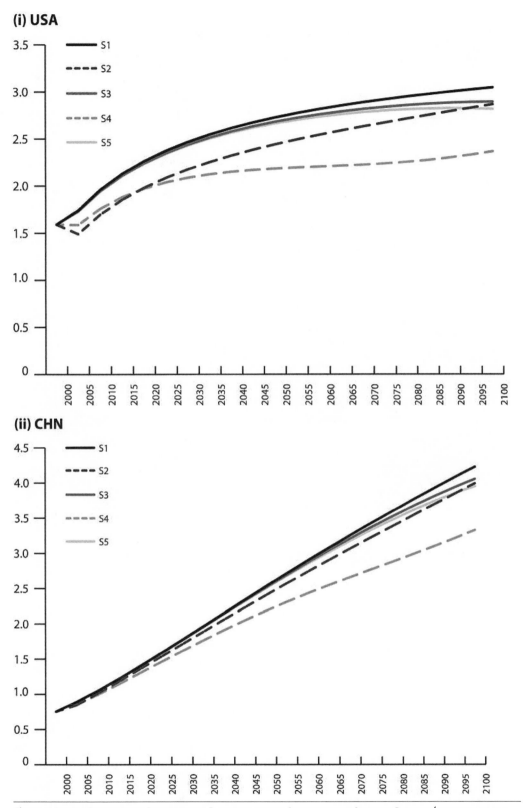

Figure 4. Linear Endogenous Discounting: Emissions across Scenarios for Selected Regions (gigatons of carbon equivalent)

Table 1. Investment: Relative Changes from Conventional Uniform Discounting (Scenario 1)

	2015	2020	2025	2050	2100
USA					
U, 0.2%	1.435	1.447	1.455	1.474	1.497
D, Exo	0.978	0.977	0.976	0.975	0.974
U, Endo	1.032	1.048	1.068	1.197	1.550
D, Endo	0.978	0.977	0.976	0.975	0.974
OHI					
U, 0.2%	1.454	1.458	1.461	1.472	1.489
D, Exo	0.987	0.986	0.986	0.981	0.970
U, Endo	1.039	1.056	1.075	1.204	1.546
D, Endo	0.987	0.986	0.986	0.981	0.970
EU					
U, 0.2%	1.451	1.458	1.462	1.474	1.492
D, Exo	0.991	0.991	0.990	0.988	0.981
U, Endo	1.038	1.055	1.075	1.205	1.551
D, Endo	0.991	0.991	0.990	0.988	0.981
CHN					
U, 0.2%	1.410	1.416	1.420	1.437	1.464
D, Exo	1.000	1.000	1.000	1.000	0.998
U, Endo	1.029	1.043	1.060	1.171	1.486
D, Endo	1.000	1.000	1.000	1.000	0.998
EEC					
U, 0.2%	1.434	1.438	1.441	1.453	1.477
D, Exo	0.992	0.991	0.990	0.987	0.983
U, Endo	1.032	1.047	1.065	1.183	1.511
D, Endo	0.992	0.991	0.990	0.987	0.983
ROW					
U, 0.2%	1.403	1.411	1.417	1.433	1.463
D, Exo	1.003	1.003	1.003	1.004	1.003
U, Endo	1.025	1.039	1.056	1.167	1.486
D, Endo	1.003	1.003	1.003	1.004	1.003

rises. As a result, for USA, control rates are 1.024 times larger in 2015 and 1.312 times larger by 2100 in the dual-rate exogenous case when compared with the benchmark. In the dual-rate endogenous discounting scheme, control rates are 1.5 times larger by 2100. Other regions display a similar pattern, and the requisite reduction in emissions from the benchmark case (table 3) is not as large as in the uniform discounting cases of Scenarios 2 and 4.

We now give a view of the results from a different perspective. Tables 4–6 present the relative changes from the endogenous dual-rate discounting of Scenario 5. Because this is the new proposal, it is useful to examine the differences between this scenario, specifically,

Table 2. CARBON CONTROL RATES: RELATIVE CHANGES FROM CONVENTIONAL UNIFORM DISCOUNTING (SCENARIO 1)

	2015	*2020*	*2025*	*2050*	*2100*
USA					
U, 0.2%	2.630	2.611	2.587	2.457	2.211
D, Exo	1.024	1.027	1.031	1.066	1.312
U, Endo	1.945	2.040	2.139	2.659	3.250
D, Endo	1.041	1.047	1.054	1.111	1.498
OHI					
U, 0.2%	2.650	2.628	2.601	2.462	2.211
D, Exo	1.024	1.027	1.032	1.067	1.312
U, Endo	1.946	2.042	2.142	2.663	3.253
D, Endo	1.041	1.047	1.054	1.112	1.499
EU					
U, 0.2%	2.648	2.626	2.600	2.462	2.211
D, Exo	1.024	1.027	1.032	1.067	1.313
U, Endo	1.946	2.042	2.142	2.663	3.254
D, Endo	1.041	1.047	1.054	1.112	1.499
CHN					
U, 0.2%	2.640	2.618	2.591	2.455	2.208
D, Exo	1.024	1.028	1.032	1.067	1.313
U, Endo	1.947	2.042	2.141	2.661	3.242
D, Endo	1.041	1.047	1.054	1.113	1.500
EEC					
U, 0.2%	2.649	2.626	2.598	2.459	2.210
D, Exo	1.024	1.028	1.032	1.067	1.313
U, Endo	1.947	2.042	2.142	2.662	3.249
D, Endo	1.041	1.047	1.054	1.112	1.499
ROW					
U, 0.2%	2.638	2.615	2.588	2.453	2.205
D, Exo	1.024	1.028	1.032	1.067	1.314
U, Endo	1.946	2.041	2.140	2.656	3.228
D, Endo	1.041	1.047	1.054	1.113	1.500

relative to the other scenarios. If one examines table 4, a result that stands out immediately is the similarity of Scenario 5 with the dual-rate exogenous case of Scenario 3. The investment profiles are identical for all regions and all time periods. It is also not surprising that, for all regions, investment matches closely with that under the conventional discounting of Scenario 1, although there is a slight deviation in the longer term. These scenarios will, by construction, yield similar results in this capacity. The table shows that Scenarios 2 and 4, on the other hand, yield significantly higher investment profiles when compared with Scenario 5. The uniform, near-zero discounting assumption requires investment that is approximately

Table 3. EMISSIONS: RELATIVE CHANGES FROM CONVENTIONAL UNIFORM DISCOUNTING (SCENARIO 1)

	2015	2020	2025	2050	2100
USA					
U, 0.2%	0.871	0.875	0.879	0.895	0.941
D, Exo	0.991	0.990	0.989	0.983	0.950
U, Endo	0.884	0.871	0.859	0.801	0.777
D, Endo	0.989	0.988	0.986	0.977	0.925
OHI					
U, 0.2%	0.946	0.950	0.952	0.946	0.937
D, Exo	0.995	0.994	0.993	0.988	0.949
U, Endo	0.924	0.916	0.907	0.855	0.772
D, Endo	0.994	0.992	0.991	0.983	0.923
EU					
U, 0.2%	0.939	0.943	0.945	0.942	0.943
D, Exo	0.996	0.995	0.994	0.989	0.953
U, Endo	0.921	0.912	0.902	0.851	0.783
D, Endo	0.994	0.993	0.992	0.984	0.928
CHN					
U, 0.2%	0.971	0.971	0.969	0.950	0.944
D, Exo	0.998	0.998	0.998	0.993	0.959
U, Endo	0.940	0.931	0.921	0.863	0.787
D, Endo	0.997	0.997	0.996	0.989	0.935
EEC					
U, 0.2%	0.973	0.976	0.976	0.971	0.979
D, Exo	0.996	0.996	0.995	0.991	0.962
U, Endo	0.938	0.931	0.923	0.882	0.850
D, Endo	0.995	0.994	0.994	0.987	0.943
ROW					
U, 0.2%	0.918	0.912	0.904	0.872	0.867
D, Exo	0.998	0.998	0.997	0.991	0.943
U, Endo	0.918	0.902	0.885	0.784	0.650
D, Endo	0.997	0.996	0.995	0.985	0.909

40–50 percent higher, while the relative deviation of private investment under the uniform endogenous assumption is initially 2–6 percent higher across regions but rises over the time horizon to become 50–60 percent higher.

It is with the optimal carbon control rates that we see significant departures of Scenarios 1 and 3 from Scenario 5's projections, particularly in the longer term. Because the discount rate declines as temperature rises over time, the carbon control rates are higher in the long term under Scenario 5 when compared with Scenarios 1 and 3. Table 5 shows that control rates under conventional discounting assumptions are just 66.7 percent of those under the

Table 4. INVESTMENT: RELATIVE CHANGES FROM ENDOGENOUS DUAL-RATE DISCOUNTING (SCENARIO 5)

	2015	*2020*	*2025*	*2050*	*2100*
USA					
U, 3%	1.023	1.024	1.024	1.026	1.027
U, 0.2%	1.468	1.481	1.490	1.512	1.537
D, Exo	1.000	1.000	1.000	1.000	1.000
U, Endo	1.055	1.073	1.094	1.229	1.592
OHI					
U, 3%	1.013	1.014	1.015	1.019	1.031
U, 0.2%	1.473	1.478	1.482	1.500	1.536
D, Exo	1.000	1.000	1.000	1.000	1.000
U, Endo	1.052	1.070	1.091	1.227	1.595
EU					
U, 3%	1.009	1.009	1.010	1.013	1.019
U, 0.2%	1.463	1.471	1.476	1.493	1.521
D, Exo	1.000	1.000	1.000	1.000	1.000
U, Endo	1.047	1.065	1.086	1.220	1.580
CHN					
U, 3%	1.000	1.000	1.000	1.000	1.002
U, 0.2%	1.410	1.415	1.420	1.436	1.467
D, Exo	1.000	1.000	1.000	1.000	1.000
U, Endo	1.028	1.042	1.059	1.170	1.488
EEC					
U, 3%	1.008	1.009	1.010	1.013	1.018
U, 0.2%	1.446	1.451	1.455	1.472	1.503
D, Exo	1.000	1.000	1.000	1.000	1.000
U, Endo	1.040	1.056	1.075	1.198	1.538
ROW					
U, 3%	0.997	0.997	0.997	0.996	0.997
U, 0.2%	1.399	1.407	1.412	1.428	1.459
D, Exo	1.000	1.000	1.000	1.000	1.000
U, Endo	1.023	1.036	1.052	1.162	1.482

dual-rate endogenous discounting scenario, and 87.5 percent of those under the dual-rate exogenous assumptions.[5]

It is clear that carbon control rates are higher under dual-rate endogenous discounting when compared with dual-rate exogenous discounting. However, the cross-regional average control rate for developed countries is around 10 percent over the period from 2010 to 2030. Although this average rate is higher than that under both conventional and dual-rate exogenous discounting, it still falls short of the *Stern Review*'s (Stern, 2007) prescription of 30 percent control rates now, rising to 70 percent for developed countries by midcentury. More

Table 5. Carbon Control Rates: Relative Changes from Endogenous Dual-Rate Discounting (Scenario 5)

	2015	2020	2025	2050	2100
USA					
U, 3%	0.961	0.955	0.949	0.900	0.667
U, 0.2%	2.527	2.494	2.455	2.211	1.476
D, Exo	0.984	0.981	0.979	0.959	0.876
U, Endo	1.868	1.949	2.030	2.392	2.169
OHI					
U, 3%	0.961	0.955	0.949	0.899	0.667
U, 0.2%	2.546	2.510	2.468	2.213	1.475
D, Exo	0.984	0.981	0.979	0.959	0.875
U, Endo	1.870	1.950	2.032	2.395	2.171
EU					
U, 3%	0.961	0.955	0.949	0.899	0.667
U, 0.2%	2.544	2.508	2.466	2.213	1.475
D, Exo	0.984	0.981	0.979	0.959	0.875
U, Endo	1.870	1.950	2.032	2.394	2.170
CHN					
U, 3%	0.961	0.955	0.948	0.899	0.667
U, 0.2%	2.536	2.500	2.458	2.207	1.472
D, Exo	0.984	0.981	0.979	0.959	0.876
U, Endo	1.870	1.950	2.031	2.391	2.161
EEC					
U, 3%	0.961	0.955	0.949	0.899	0.667
U, 0.2%	2.545	2.508	2.465	2.211	1.474
D, Exo	0.984	0.981	0.979	0.959	0.876
U, Endo	1.870	1.950	2.032	2.393	2.167
ROW					
U, 3%	0.961	0.955	0.948	0.899	0.667
U, 0.2%	2.534	2.497	2.455	2.204	1.470
D, Exo	0.984	0.981	0.979	0.959	0.876
U, Endo	1.870	1.949	2.030	2.387	2.152

stringent emissions reductions are justifiable with endogenous dual-rate discounting; however, such draconian reductions in emissions are only justifiable with extreme assumptions about discounting. Comparing the relative changes of carbon control rates in Scenario 5 with those of Scenarios 2 and 4, the carbon control rates in the latter scenarios are significantly higher over the entire time horizon.

Last, table 6 shows the relative changes in emissions across regions and time when compared with Scenario 5. Emissions under the dual-rate exogenous case of Scenario 3 are quite

Table 6. Emissions: Relative Changes from Endogenous Dual-Rate Discounting (Scenario 5)

	2015	*2020*	*2025*	*2050*	*2100*
USA					
U, 3%	1.011	1.012	1.014	1.023	1.082
U, 0.2%	0.881	0.886	0.891	0.916	1.018
D, Exo	1.002	1.003	1.003	1.006	1.027
U, Endo	0.894	0.882	0.870	0.820	0.841
OHI					
U, 3%	1.007	1.008	1.009	1.017	1.083
U, 0.2%	0.952	0.958	0.960	0.962	1.015
D, Exo	1.001	1.002	1.002	1.005	1.028
U, Endo	0.930	0.923	0.915	0.870	0.836
EU					
U, 3%	1.006	1.007	1.008	1.016	1.077
U, 0.2%	0.945	0.949	0.952	0.957	1.016
D, Exo	1.002	1.002	1.002	1.005	1.027
U, Endo	0.926	0.918	0.909	0.865	0.844
CHN					
U, 3%	1.003	1.003	1.004	1.011	1.069
U, 0.2%	0.974	0.974	0.972	0.961	1.010
D, Exo	1.001	1.001	1.002	1.005	1.026
U, Endo	0.942	0.934	0.924	0.873	0.842
EEC					
U, 3%	1.005	1.006	1.007	1.014	1.061
U, 0.2%	0.978	0.982	0.983	0.984	1.039
D, Exo	1.001	1.001	1.002	1.004	1.021
U, Endo	0.943	0.936	0.929	0.894	0.901
ROW					
U, 3%	1.003	1.004	1.005	1.016	1.101
U, 0.2%	0.921	0.915	0.909	0.885	0.954
D, Exo	1.002	1.002	1.002	1.007	1.038
U, Endo	0.921	0.906	0.889	0.797	0.715

close to those under the dual-rate endogenous case. In fact, out to 2050, the difference is less than 1 percent, with emissions under Scenario 3 being slightly higher. A larger difference can be seen when comparing Scenario 5 with Scenario 1. By the end of the century, emissions are approximately 6 percent (EEC) to 10 percent (ROW) higher using the conventional discounting assumption of Scenario 1. As predicted, given the previous discussion of control rates, it is only when compared with the more extreme assumptions of Scenarios 2 and 4 that emissions are higher under Scenario 5.

Sensitivity of Results: Quadratic Endogenous Discounting

Because we present a nonconventional formulation of discount rates, we now present some evidence regarding the sensitivity of the results displayed in the previous subsection. However, we focus our efforts more narrowly here. Specifically, we compare the results of model runs under Scenario 5 using linear endogenous discounting with those under quadratic endogenous discounting. Recall from figure 1 that the quadratic discount rates decline more rapidly when compared with the linear formulation.

Tables 7 and 8 show deviations (under Scenario 5) of the quadratic formulation from the linear formulation of discount rates for control rates and emissions. For all regions, it is clear that control rates are significantly higher under quadratic endogenous discounting, and the gap between quadratic and linear formulations increases in the longer term. Given this result, the deviations of emissions display a predictable pattern.

Figures 5 and 6 display carbon control rates and emissions projections, respectively, for USA. The results are quite sensitive to the functional form used in equation (5): the "policy ramp" is much more pronounced using the quadratic formulation. If we examine figure 5, control rates using this functional form range from 20 percent initially to nearly 80 percent by the end of the century for USA. The *Stern Review* (2007) recommends cuts of 30 percent immediately, increasing to 70 percent by midcentury. The discounting assumption made here produces results that are closer to Stern's recommendations when compared to the linear formulation, but the control rates are still lower. Under these assumptions, USA reduces 30 percent by 2040 and does not get to 70 percent until nearing the end of the century.

Table 7. CARBON CONTROL RATES: RELATIVE DEVIATION FROM LINEAR FORMULATION

	2015	*2020*	*2025*	*2050*	*2100*
USA	1.840	1.929	2.028	2.666	4.375
OHI	1.840	1.930	2.029	2.670	4.402
EU	1.840	1.930	2.029	2.670	4.408
CHN	1.840	1.930	2.029	2.666	4.290
EEC	1.840	1.930	2.029	2.668	4.364
ROW	1.840	1.929	2.028	2.660	4.175

Table 8. EMISSIONS: RELATIVE DEVIATION FROM LINEAR FORMULATION

	2015	*2020*	*2025*	*2050*	*2100*
USA	0.889	0.873	0.856	0.740	0.258
OHI	0.925	0.914	0.901	0.798	0.241
EU	0.922	0.910	0.896	0.793	0.264
CHN	0.941	0.930	0.916	0.813	0.317
EEC	0.940	0.930	0.918	0.832	0.437
ROW	0.922	0.904	0.884	0.729	0.031

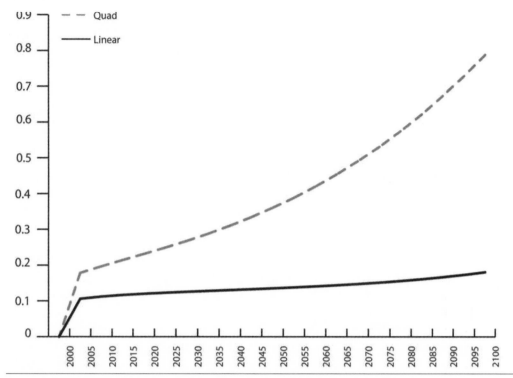

Figure 5. CARBON CONTROL RATE FOR USA: LINEAR VERSUS QUADRATIC ENDOGENOUS DISCOUNTING

In figure 6, emissions for USA increase until 2035 and then begin to decline. The Kyoto Protocol required that industrialized countries reduce emissions to 1990 levels. For USA, these levels are the equivalent of approximately 1.3 gigatons of carbon equivalent (although the United States did not ratify the treaty and is not required to reduce its emissions of greenhouse gases). As evidenced by figure 6, such levels are not achieved until 2085.

As a final note, we point out that the private investment profile (not shown) is, by construction, identical using both formulations.

CONCLUSION

It is reasonable to assume that different discount rates should be applied to different projects. This chapter endogenizes the "environmental" discount rate used in dynamic climate-economy modeling and separates it from conventional rates used to discount private investments. Specifically, contemporaneous environmental discount rates are assumed to be a function of the difference between contemporaneous temperature and a "catastrophic" upper bound on temperature of six degrees Celsius, as advised by the most recent IPCC report. The simulation results presented above demonstrate that endogenous discount rates of this type lead to more stringent emissions reductions across all regions when compared with conventional discounting methods. However, draconian reductions in emissions such as those prescribed by the *Stern Review* (2007) are not justifiable with the endogenous discounting approaches used in this study.

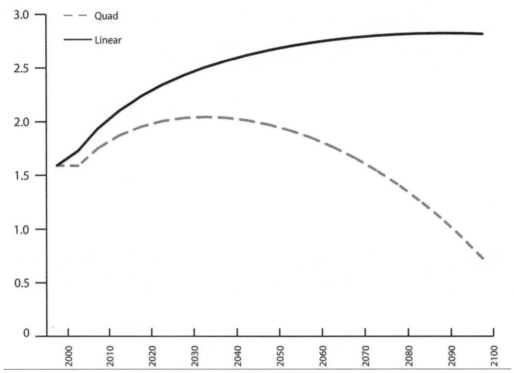

Figure 6. EMISSIONS FOR USA: LINEAR VERSUS QUADRATIC ENDOGENOUS DISCOUNTING (GIGATONS OF CARBON EQUIVALENT)

A vital question remains to be answered: Is there a better characterization of discount rates, and if so, how do we identify them? One possibility is to continue using survey results to identify not only the values of the discount rates applied to environmental projects, but also the factors that influence the determination of these values. If we accept the assertion that environmental discount rates vary with temperature, then it seems plausible that discount rates may vary with, say, carbon concentration; that is, discount rates are altered as a "catastrophic parts per million" value is approached.

Future research in this area will examine alternative specifications of an endogenous discount rate and deduce general mathematical properties of endogenous environmental discounting including, but not limited to, time consistency. In addition, an endogenization of both public and private discount rates will likely lead to different investment profiles, as will heterogeneous/country-specific discount rates. One thing is clear: Policymakers must pay close attention to the parametric assumptions that are made in dynamic climate-economy models, especially with regard to the choice of discount rates.

NOTES

1. See Tol (1999); Hope, Anderson, and Wenman (1993); Hasselmann et al. (1997) just to name a few.
2. Log utility implies that θ equals 1.

3. If equality of discounted marginal utility over time does not hold, then the result is time-inconsistent.
4. These weights are chosen optimally through numeric searching procedures so that the (heterogeneous) control rates are based on each region's historical, current, and projected future contributions to carbon concentration.
5. The relative changes of carbon control rates for these two scenarios are the same across regions.

REFERENCES

Ayong Le Kama, A., and K. Schubert. 2007. "A Note on the Consequences of an Endogenous Discounting Depending on the Environmental Quality." *Macroeconomic Dynamics* 11(2): 272–89.

Becker, G. S., and C. B. Mulligan. 1997. "The Endogenous Determination of Time Preference." *Quarterly Journal of Economics* 112(3): 729–58.

Borissov, K., and K. Shakhnov. 2011. "Sustainable Growth in a Model with Dual-Rate Discounting." *Economic Modelling* 28:2071–74.

Brunnermeier, M. K., and S. Nagel. 2008. "Do Wealth Fluctuations Generate Time-Varying Risk Aversion? Micro-evidence on Individuals' Asset Allocation." *American Economic Review* 98(3): 713–36.

Cropper, M., S. Aydede, S., and P. R. Portney. 1992. "Rates of Time Preference for Saving Lives." *American Economic Review* 82(2): 469–72.

Fisher, I. 1930. *The Theory of Interest*. New York: Macmillan Company.

Gollier, C. 2002. "Discounting an Uncertain Future." *Journal of Public Economics* 85(2): 149–66.

Harvey, C. M. 1994. "The Reasonableness of Non-constant Discounting." *Journal of Public Economics* 53(1): 31–51.

Hasselmann, K., S. Hasselmann, R. Giering, V. Ocana, and H. V. Storch. 1997. "Sensitivity Study of Optimal CO_2 Emission Paths Using a Simplified Structural Integrated Assessment Model (SIAM)." *Climatic Change* 37(2): 345–86.

Heal, G. 1998. *Valuing the Future: Economic Theory and Sustainability*. New York: Columbia University Press.

Henderson, N., and I. Bateman. 1995. "Empirical and Public Choice Evidence for Hyperbolic Social Discount Rates and the Implications for Intergenerational Discounting." *Environmental and Resource Economics* 5(4): 413–23.

Hope, C. W., J. Anderson, and P. Wenman. 1993. "Policy Analysis of the Greenhouse Effect—an Application of the PAGE Model." *Energy Policy* 15:328–38.

IPCC (Intergovernmental Panel on Climate Change.) 2007. *Fourth Assessment Report* (AR4). http://www.ipcc.ch/.

Koopmans, T. C. 1960. "Stationary Ordinal Utility and Impatience." *Econometrica* 28(2): 287–309.

Laibson, D. 1997. "Golden Eggs and Hyperbolic Discounting." *Quarterly Journal of Economics* 112(2): 443–77.

Lind, R. C., and R. E. Schuler. 1998. "Equity and Discounting in Climate-Change Decisions." In *Economics and Policy Issues in Climate Change*, ed. W. D. Nordhaus. Washington, DC: Resources for the Future.

Nordhaus, W. D. 1997. "Discounting in Economics and Climate Change: An Editorial Comment." *Climatic Change* 37(2): 315–28.

Nordhaus, W. D. 2007. A review of the *Stern Review on the Economics of Climate Change*. *Journal of Economic Literature* 45(3): 686–702.

Nordhaus, W. D., and J. Boyer. 2000. *Warming the World: Economic Models of Global Warming.* Cambridge: MIT Press.

Nordhaus, W. D., and Z. Yang. 1996. "A Regional Dynamic General-Equilibrium Model of Alternative Climate-Change Strategies." *American Economic Review* 86(4): 741–65.

Obstfeld, M. 1990. "Intertemporal Dependence, Impatience, and Dynamics." *Journal of Monetary Economics* 26(1): 45–75.

Portney, P., and J. Weyant, eds. 1999. *Discounting and Intergenerational Equity.* Washington, DC: Resources for the Future.

Ramsey, F. P. 1928. "A Mathematical Theory of Saving." *Economic Journal* 38(152): 543–59.

Schumacher, I. 2006. "On Optimality, Endogenous Discounting and Wealth Accumulation." CORE Discussion Paper No. 2006/103.

Stern, N. 2007. *The Economics of Climate Change: The "Stern Review."* New York: Cambridge University Press.

Stokey, N. L., 1998. "Are there limits to growth?" *International Economic Review* 39: 1–31.

Tol, R. S. J. 1999. "Time Discounting and Optimal Emission Reduction—an Application of FUND. *Climatic Change* 41:351–62.

Tsur, Y., and A. Zemel. 2009. "Endogenous Discounting and Climate Policy." *Environmental and Resource Economics* 44(4): 507–20.

Weitzman, M. L. 1999. "Just keep discounting, but . . ." In *Discounting and Intergenerational Equity*, ed. P. R. Portney and J. P. Weyant. Washington, DC: Resources for the Future.

Yang, Z. 2003. "Dual-Rate Discounting in Dynamic Economic-Environmental Modeling." *Economic Modelling* 20(5): 941–57.

Yang, Z. 2008. *Stategic Bargaining and Cooperation in GHG Mitigations: An Integrated Assessment Modeling Approach.* Cambridge: MIT Press.

Yang, Z., and P. Sirianni. 2010. "Balancing Contemporary Fairness and Historical Justice: A Quasi-Equitable Proposal for GHG Mitigations." *Energy Economics* 33(5): 1121–30.

A Genuine Metric for Assessing Business Sustainability

MATTHEW P. H. TAYLOR, DARRELL BROWN,
DAVID E. ERVIN, JIM THAYER, AND BRETT CASSIDY

SUSTAINABILITY MEASUREMENT BY FIRMS HAS STEADILY INCREASED OVER THE LAST decade, driven by an expansion of issues addressed in sustainability reports and a broadening of the relevant stakeholders. As a voluntary process, this process is conducted using a diverse collection of metrics and methodologies, stemming from the unique needs and requirements of individual firms and their operating environments. The resulting heterogeneity in sustainability reporting makes verification, interpretation, and use of the reported information to assess progress difficult if not impossible. A necessary next step in the field of enterprise-level sustainability is the development of a standard methodology for measuring and assessing a firm's total effects on sustainability. Genuine Metrics adapts the five-capital framework of Genuine Savings, a macroeconomic sustainability metric used by the World Bank, to develop a comprehensive measure of an individual organization's progress towards sustainability.

INTRODUCTION

As sustainability has become an increasingly prevalent focus of society, diverse stakeholder groups, including consumers, businesses, academia, civil society organizations, and government, have made increasing efforts to shift economic activity toward a sustainable path. Sustainability has been identified as an "emerging megatrend" in the business community, reflecting changes in the reality of growing resource scarcity and social concerns, both of which alter the nature of the competitive environment (Lubin and Esty, 2010, p. 44). Organizations are increasingly planning, adopting goals, implementing initiatives, and transforming processes in the name of sustainability. Indeed, in the past decade the active management of sustainability issues has spread from mission-oriented pioneers to many traditionally unconcerned industries (Makower, 2011, p. 5). The evaluation of these efforts, however, lacks a standard, rigorous, and comprehensive framework, exacerbating uncertainty regarding the efficacy of these efforts.

Evaluating an organization's relationship to sustainability involves two key processes: (1) gathering and reporting information regarding the organization's activities and their impacts on sustainability, and (2) analyzing and interpreting that information to gauge the progress those impacts have on achieving sustainability itself. The Global Reporting Initiative (GRI) has emerged as the most widely used sustainability reporting framework for organizations, providing a holistic, standardized, and flexible foundation (Bernhart, 2009, pp. 26–28; Makower, 2011, p. 15). Currently, no complementary standardized framework for interpreting these reports in terms of progress on sustainability exists; furthermore, there is no methodology for evaluating sustainability that is commonly accepted and utilized by organizations.

Although many sustainability metrics and measurement systems have been proposed, they incompletely capture the full range of sustainability issues, fail to provide a clear signal regarding overall impact on sustainability, or lack sound theoretical grounding. The ideal sustainability metric has a strong scientific foundation while providing a holistic and comprehensive measurement of sustainability. Furthermore, the heterogeneity of existing metrics and measurement approaches render reported sustainability information confusing, incomparable, and difficult to utilize (Ranganathan, 1998, p. 3). We propose a framework for interpreting organization level sustainability performance, coined "Genuine Metrics," that meets the necessary requirements and provides a standardized means of sustainability assessment. With its roots in the economic theory of genuine savings, a macroeconomic sustainability indicator used by the World Bank (Hamilton et al., 1997, p. 1; Pearce and Atkinson, 1993, pp. 104–5), Genuine Metrics (GM) provides a comprehensive framework for assessing and interpreting an organization's diverse impacts on sustainability in a common numeraire, dollars, laying the foundation for improvement in our capability to assess sustainability.

DEFINING THE CONCEPT OF SUSTAINABILITY

Organizations have struggled to define the concept as sustainability has expanded and moved from academic discussions into common business vernacular. Competing definitions of sustainability abound, varying across disciplines and between contexts. These range from broad holistic approaches adopting a societal perspective to more narrow definitions focusing on how an organization's sustainability performance impacts its competitiveness. The lack of common understanding is problematic, generating uncertainty and confusion about what is meant by the term. Further, this diversity has resulted in the propagation of a variety of sustainability measurement and assessment approaches. Measuring and assessing sustainability performance in a manner that produces consistent and actionable information requires harmonization in how we define the concept. This analysis adopts the Brundtland definition of sustainability, "meeting the needs of the present generation without compromising the ability of future generations to meet their needs" (WCED, 1987, p. 41), as a starting point because of its commonality and its consistent use within the literature, providing some cohesiveness for future work and relevance to the existing literature.

Two salient aspects of the Brundtland definition have implications meriting discussion. First, sustainability deals with intergenerational equity, taking into consideration the opportunities, threats, and level of welfare bequeathed to posterity. Second, it maintains a broad definition of "needs," commonly discussed in terms of three broad categories: economic, social, and environmental. Economic needs include the human-made commodities, tools, equipment, and knowledge that contribute to our prosperity. Similarly, social needs include the relationships, networks, laws, and other institutions of our society, all making important contributions to our well-being. Environmental needs include a broad range of natural commodities and ecosystem services. Actual needs and their satisfaction often blur these conceptual boundaries, depending on each other and exhibiting significant complementarities.

Adopting a systems perspective is useful in understanding the nature of sustainability. To continually meet human needs requires economic sustainability, itself being dependent upon sustaining the overarching society that provides the context for economic activity. However, if this process destroys our natural environment to the point that society ceases to function, our economic activity is inherently unsustainable, hence the importance of a holistic perspective when considering sustainability. Analyzing the trade-offs and complementarities between the environment, society, and economic activity is central to understanding how our actions impact our long-term sustainability.

Similarly, sustainability is inherently a global macroeconomic concept. The translation of sustainability into microeconomic terms requires careful interpretation because the effects caused by the smaller scale must be interpreted in terms of macroeconomic sustainability, requiring a broader social perspective. An individual agent can only be as sustainable as the economy, society, and natural environment in which it operates. Thus, the notion that an organization is "sustainable" is empty if we know nothing about the sustainability of the natural, social, and economic environments within which it operates. Assessment of an organization's impact does not tell us if the organization is sustainable itself, but rather whether or not the organization is contributing positively or negatively to the sustainability of the larger society. While this distinction may appear to be purely semantic, it is important to recognize when constructing a means to assess and interpret the sustainability of an organization.

Adopting a systems perspective creates the problem of defining the boundaries of an organization, its activities, and its impacts on its operating environment—the scope of assessment matters and will be discussed in more detail below.

STATE OF ORGANIZATIONAL SUSTAINABILITY EFFORTS: MANAGING, REPORTING, AND INTERPRETING IMPACTS

Being an unregulated and voluntary process, the approaches to managing, reporting, and interpreting organizational sustainability performance span a wide range. The existing diversity is not surprising given the independent development of the purposes, methods, and uses of such activities. Underlying this heterogeneity is a consistent trend of an increasing prevalence of active management, reporting, and interpretation of sustainability issues.

Managing Sustainability Impacts

Growing attention to sustainability issues has led to increasingly active internal management of related issues on the part of organizations, evidenced by the burgeoning prevalence of corporate endeavors to explicitly define and address how sustainability relates to the mission of those organizations and to create and identify positions and individuals within the firm responsible for managing sustainability (Deloitte, 2010, p. 8). As sustainability issues become more relevant to business, we can expect increasing attention given to the management of sustainability concerns within, if not across, industries, leading to an increased need for the evaluation of the effectiveness of sustainability initiatives by internal and external stakeholders (Lubin and Esty, 2010, pp. 48–49).

Key challenges in moving the organizational management of sustainability forward are translating the aims and outcomes of narrowly focused sustainability initiatives into broadly defined objectives of sustainability, and then reconciling them with competing organizational goals (Adams and Frost, 2008, pp. 299–300; Deloitte, 2010, pp. 3–7). Similarly, firms struggle to consistently apply existing metrics across geographic, cultural, and functional areas (Adams and Frost, 2008, p. 294). For example, contributions to charities that address community social needs provide nonfinancial social benefits that management may find difficult to communicate quantitatively. This indicates the distinct usefulness of a standardized framework for assessing sustainability impacts. From the external stakeholder perspective, information regarding sustainability impacts needs to be conveyed in an accessible and understandable manner satisfying the full range of their diverse interests.

Reporting Sustainability Impacts

Such a framework has emerged within the *reporting* aspect of sustainability evaluation; the Global Reporting Initiative[1] (GRI) is the most widely used organizational reporting framework, providing a crucial step toward a widely accepted and relatively standardized process (Bernhart, 2009, p. 27; Makower, 2011, p. 15). The GRI and other voluntary nonfinancial reporting initiatives originated from environmental reporting efforts in the 1980s, broadening over time to include social and nonmandatory financial issues. Such sustainability reporting among Fortune Global 250 companies rose from 35 percent in 1998 to 64 percent in 2004 (Kolk, 2008, pp. 3–6). In 2011 such reporting was conducted by 95 percent of the Fortune Global 250 (KPMG, 2011, p. 6). This trend has exhibited similar resilience within the broader business community by maintaining a modest yet steady increase throughout the recent downturn in the business cycle (Makower, 2011, p. 15).

Motivation for sustainability reporting arises both internally, driven by changing organizational cultures, management values, and green marketing opportunities, and externally, from market, regulatory, and stakeholder pressures (Ervin, 2011a). Sustainability reporting's purpose is to provide information on the environmental and social impacts of corporate operations to an increasingly large and diverse audience of external stakeholders, including an indication of what measures and initiatives are in place to promote future improvement. As pressure from stakeholders—including governments, consumers, shareholders, and the community at large—for reliable information concerning sustainability issues continues to increase, effective organizations will adapt and require continued advances in their sustainability reporting capabilities (Kolk, 2008, p. 3; Lubin and Esty, 2010, p. 49).

Without standards or prescribed guidelines for reporting, however, sustainability reporting is varied and largely unaudited, resulting in minimal comparability and low credibility. Previous research found bias toward reporting positive outcomes, framing these outcomes in descriptive terms that cannot be used in benchmarking, comparisons, or goal setting (Hubbard, 2009, p. 181). A rigorous reporting framework, such as the GRI, supports sustainable outcomes by working to ensure that stakeholders, both internal and external, are well informed with complete relevant information, both positive and negative. Most current sustainability reporting is process oriented, providing information on what initiatives are in place. While processes are important, their outcomes determine the sustainability of a society and provide the basis on which the processes must be evaluated. Reporting the impacts of processes will help successful sustainability initiatives to be recognized as such, increasing the efficiency and effectiveness with which society is guided to its sustainable path.

Interpreting Sustainability Impacts

Effective sustainability reporting integrates the environmental, economic, and social aspects of performance to holistically assess the trade-offs facing decision makers (Adams and Frost, 2008, p. 290). Sustainability metrics are essential to help companies understand and assess the impacts of sustainability initiatives, to communicate those results, and to provide investors with evidence of returns generated by these activities, from both a financial and a sustainability perspective (Lubin and Esty, 2010, p. 49).

Logically and accurately connecting sustainability actions and sustainability outcomes is of the utmost importance for organizations (Deloitte, 2010, p. 3). Organizational activities' impacts on competitiveness, profitability, and solvency must be understood, and so must their impacts on all dimensions of society's sustainability. Assessment of environmental, economic, and social impacts of an organization must be integrated in a manner that translates and speaks directly to the essence of sustainability. To do this, the science behind measuring sustainability must continue its progression (Makower, 2011, p. 15).

SUSTAINABILITY METRICS: STATE OF THE ART

A useful organization-level sustainability metric must capture the complexity of sustainability in a simple metric that is meaningful and understandable. In addition, a metric must be flexible enough to meet individual organizations' unique requirements while remaining standardized and comparable (Ness et al., 2007, p. 506). Existing sustainability metrics typically take one of three approaches: (1) the dashboard approach, such as the GRI or the balanced scorecard, presenting a set of individual indicators addressing a spectrum of sustainability issues; (2) the composite index approach, such as the Human Development Index (HDI) or Environmental Sustainability Index (ESI), where a set of indicators are normalized, weighted, and aggregated into a single numerical value that reflects some degree of sustainability; and (3) the physical measure approach, such as the ecological footprint, typically involving metrics derived from the natural sciences to measure the impact and feasibility of economic activity. In addition, at the macroeconomic scale there are measures of "green" national accounts and the calculation of net, or "genuine," savings (Hamilton, 1994, pp. 155–68; Stiglitz, Sen, and Fitoussi, 2009, pp. 234–49).

Despite their usefulness and popularity, each of the first three approaches is problematic when attempting to holistically assess an organization's impact on sustainability. Dashboards of indicators preserve the richness and complexity inherent in sustainability issues, yet the individual indicators often lack harmonization or a means of aggregation; their heterogeneity makes their interpretation difficult, notably when different indicators provide conflicting results. Stakeholders are left with little understanding regarding how each of the individual impacts relate in terms of furthering sustainability. Dashboards make interorganizational comparisons difficult, if not impossible, especially when the indicators comprising each dashboard differ (Ranganathan, 1998, p. 7), as is the case in the GRI reporting framework.

Composite indices reduce the complexity of interpreting multiple indicators yet are plagued by problems of their own. The procedures for constructing the indices are typically made explicit, yet the underlying assumptions, values, and the relation between the index and sustainability are not (Stiglitz, Sen, and Fitoussi, 2009, p. 239). In many cases their construction is highly arbitrary, and while useful for benchmarking, their interpretation in regards to their overall impact on sustainability remains difficult; without an origin, above which is sustainable and below which is not, the link between an index and progress toward sustainability is lacking.

Physical metrics, such as those used to monitor environmental outcomes, are commonly used as sustainability performance indicators. A major drawback to these metrics is they are rarely directly comparable to each other or to other indicators of economic and social performance. Furthermore, they seldom allow for changing technology or the increased efficiency with which resources can be used (Stiglitz, Sen, and Fitoussi, 2009, p. 245).

Organizations often rely upon anecdotal evidence and qualitative descriptions of their sustainability policies and processes to convey their organization's performance and its relation to sustainability. While informative, such discussions fail to perform a rigorous and meaningful sustainability assessment. Similarly, a focus on individual products may be misleading regarding the overall organization if the products studied are not representative of the organization's entire suite of products, if the assessment fails to consider impacts from overhead and administrative activities, or both. Anecdotal or product-based reporting may result in little connection between the information presented and true sustainability. As such, the organization is the appropriate unit of analysis when considering sustainability at the microeconomic scale. What, then, would be the characteristics of an ideal organizational sustainability metric? While by no means exhaustive, table 1 highlights seven important qualities of a meaningful metric for an organization's contribution to a sustainable economy.

Perhaps the most important criterion, and the least frequently met, is that the metric be grounded in rigorous scientific theory. Being *theoretically sound* implies that, in addition to requiring metrics to be measured, normalized, weighted, and aggregated in a scientifically sound manner, there is a clear, observable, and direct relationship between what is being measured and sustainability theory itself (Bohringer and Jochem, 2007, p. 2). Proposals for sustainability metrics frequently do not include such a discussion. Second, a sustainability indicator, whether macro or microeconomic, must be *comprehensive*, assessing and integrating the relevant environmental, economic, and social issues of sustainability (Bernhart, 2009, p. 26; Bohringer and Jochem, 2007, p. 2; Ranganathan, 1998, p. 2). Simultaneous assessment of the multidimensional trade-offs when economic activities impact social and environmental issues is complex and difficult (Hockerts, 1999, p. 25); however, such an assessment makes explicit the actual trade-offs being made. A successful sustainability metric incorporates all aspects of such trade-offs while minimizing the complexity of its presentation and interpretation.

A meaningful sustainability metric is *actionable*, effectively informing decision making (Hockerts, 1999, p. 36; Veleva and Ellenbecker, 2000, p. 106), and useful, providing a clear

Table 1. KEY SUSTAINABILITY METRIC CHARACTERISTICS

Theoretically sound	The metric is grounded in theory that is consistent with prevailing science and provides a direct link to the definition of sustainability.
Comprehensive	The metric addresses and integrates economic, environmental, and social issues.
Transparent	The methodological, mechanical, and normative processes and assumptions are made explicit.
Feasible	The metric can be implemented in practice.
Pliant	The metric can be used to assess a broad range of organization types across a broad range of industries.
Comparable	Applications of the metric are done consistently, resulting in different organizations' assessments being comparable.
Actionable	The metric provides concerned stakeholders with clear and useful information regarding sustainability.

indication of how an organization's operations impact sustainability. A metric for enterprise sustainability, through its theoretical linkages to sustainability theory, provides a clear answer to whether the organization is or is not contributing to a sustainable society. Thus, an origin—above which is considered progress toward sustainability and below which is not—is an important characteristic for any metric that aims to indicate sustainability. *Transparency*, in both the mathematical procedures and the underlying and supporting normative assumptions, is an important characteristic because understanding mechanical construction is crucial for its credibility in decision making (Bernhart, 2009, p. 26; Bohringer and Jochem, 2007, p. 3; Veleva and Ellenbecker, 2000, p. 106).

More practical criteria are the *feasibility* of the metric's implementation and the *pliancy* of its application. Feasibility implies that the necessary data are, or can be, available with acceptable precision and are reliable, verifiable, and consistent (Bohringer and Jochem, 2007, p. 2; Veleva and Ellenbecker, 2000, p. 105). Similarly, the need to compare sustainability impacts of different firms across different industries requires pliancy, meaning the indicator can be applied in a standardized and consistent manner that yields comparable results (Ranganathan, 1998, p. 2; Veleva and Ellenbecker, 2000, p. 105). Equally important are the ability to track an organization's performance and progress over time (Bernhart, 2009, p. 26; Ranganathan, 1998, p. 2) and the ability to implement the metric given existing business practices (Hockerts, 1999, p. 36).

If, as indicated by trends in corporate behavior, sustainability is an emerging "megatrend," it will continue to play an important role in defining the business landscape; understanding what that means and how to assess it is important for all stakeholders concerned with the issue. Further, if sustainability is an imperative social objective, accurately evaluating the impacts that consumer and business actions have on achieving that objective is paramount, informing effective decision making (Ness et al., 2007, p. 499). This need is intensified because sustainability is outside of, and sometimes at odds with, the more well-established socioeconomic goals of efficiency, growth, and equity.

Economics is the study of allocating scarce resources to satisfy the satisfaction of our competing needs. As such, economic theory provides us with a natural starting point for constructing the means for rigorously assessing sustainability. What follows is an introduction to the economic theory of sustainability; drawing directly from this we propose a framework for interpreting an organization's contribution to sustainability. This framework lays the foundation for moving forward in the development and improvement of our capability to assess the impacts of our actions in terms of sustainability.

SUSTAINABILITY AND ECONOMIC THEORY

The Brundtland Report's definition of sustainability translates well into economic theory. Within economics, sustainability is widely interpreted as a condition requiring intergenerational equity, defined as a requirement for nondeclining per capita opportunities for well-being, or utility, over time (Pezzey and Toman, 2005, pp. 124–25). Nondeclining per capita utility across generations implies a sustainable state in which the current generation's actions are not compromising the well-being of posterity. Uncertainty regarding the preferences of future generations, regarding technology, and regarding their actual realization of potential well-being implies that at best we can preserve their *opportunities* to achieve a level of personal welfare equivalent to what is currently enjoyed. This sustainability condition is consistent with the Brundtland definition and can be assessed using economic theory.

An economy's ability to provide well-being to individuals, that is, providing flows of goods and services, is dependent upon wealth, that is, the stock of productive assets or the capital stock, in the economy (Stiglitz, Sen, and Fitoussi, 2009, p. 17). Changes in the total capital stock directly impact the ability of an economy to produce flows of economically desirable goods in the future, providing a direct link to the notion of sustainability. The maintenance of our capital stocks is required to maintain levels of well-being through time (Goodwin, 2003, pp. 2–3).

Economists normally employ a four-capital-stock framework, including human-made physical capital (referred to as physical capital hereafter), human capital, social capital, and natural capital, to recognize the breadth of goods and services that contribute to well-being and the variety of resources required to produce those benefits. The wealth of an economy at time t can be expressed as the summed value of its capital stocks:

$$Total\ Wealth = TK_t = K_{m,t} + K_{h,t} + K_{s,t} + K_{n,t} \tag{1}$$

Physical capital, K_m, is the social value of man-made buildings, equipment, and infrastructure in an economy. Physical capital is derived from natural capital that has been significantly altered and augmented by humankind to improve its productivity and usefulness. Human capital, K_h, is the social value of individuals' skills, abilities, and knowledge within an economy, taking into account both innate abilities and nurtured skills, knowledge, and physical health. Social capital, K_s, represents the full value of social networks, institutions and relationships conducive to well-being, while K_n is natural capital. Natural capital incorporates a broad range of ecosystem assets, such as minerals, timber, and fresh water, and ecosystem services, such as recreational and cultural opportunities, pollution assimilation, and biodiversity (Goodwin, 2003, pp. 3–7). Theoretically, the value of each asset should be equal to the discounted net private and public benefits produced over the asset's lifetime (Stiglitz, Sen, and Fitoussi, 2009, pp. 241–44).

Working toward a sustainability condition, we move to per capita wealth, given by

$$Wealth\ Per\ Capita = w = \frac{TK_t}{P_t} = \frac{K_{m,t} + K_{h,t} + K_{s,t} + K_{n,t}}{P_t} \qquad (2)$$

where P_t is population at time t. The maintenance of society's per capita wealth, that is, productive assets, over time then provides us with a condition for a sustainable economy that is consistent with our definition:

$$\frac{TK_{t+1}}{P_{t+1}} \geq \frac{TK_t}{P_t} \qquad (3)$$

This condition implies that the change in wealth per capita over time, $\dot{w}$, provides us with an indication of potential sustainability. When $\dot{w} < 0$, we observe a decline in wealth per capita over time, indicating declining per capita opportunities for the realization of well-being and implying unsustainable economic activity during that time. When $\dot{w} \geq 0$, wealth per capita is nondeclining, implying constant or increasing opportunities for per capita well-being and a potentially sustainable path for society.

The presentation of (2) and (3) highlights a contentious element within the economics of sustainability—the substitutability of capital stocks. Relating the changes in capital stocks additively implies unending substitutability between capital stocks; decreases in natural or social capital can be compensated for with investments in physical or human capital, and so forth. For some, this assumption is dangerously misleading because the relationship between some capital stocks is potentially complementary in nature. This may be especially true where certain forms of capital are critical to the functioning and productivity of the complementary capital stocks. Having sufficient natural water sources to run a production process is a salient example. Furthermore, for these "critical capital stocks" a threshold may likely exist; degradation of these stocks beyond the thresholds potentially leads to costly irreversibilities, rendering these assets largely unsubstitutable in those ranges (Pearce and Barbier, 2000, pp. 23–24; Toman, 1994, pp. 405–9).

This argument represents an ecological economics perspective, necessitating the additional use of an appropriate suite of physical indicators to ensure that critical levels are maintained (Stiglitz, Sen, and Fitoussi, 2009, p. 17). While typically framed in terms of natural capital, these critical capital stocks, K_i^{C*}, could theoretically be found within any of the human, social, or natural capital stocks. These critical capital stocks will have a threshold, K_i^{C*} above which the level of capital must be maintained to ensure sustainability (Ervin, 2011b). Thus, an additional constraint yields a stricter sustainability condition, given by

$$\frac{TK_{t+1}}{P_{t+1}} \geq \frac{TK_t}{P_t} \ , \quad K_i^C \geq K_i^{C*} \ , \quad \forall i = 1,...,N \qquad (4)$$

Sustainability condition (4) represents the notion of *strong sustainability* (where natural and physical capital are assumed to be complementary), whereas the weaker condition, (3), connotes *weak sustainability* (where natural and physical capital are assumed to be substitutable). Assuming their existence, the identification of critical capital stocks and their respective thresholds is an essential component to fully grasping the economics of sustainability. The current understanding of these critical stocks is largely incomplete, making strong sustainability a relatively intractable concept. However, humankind's historical ability to circumvent some natural resource constraints through technological innovation and investments in human capital has led to a split consensus on the nature of capital stock substitutability. Economists such as Robert Solow (1993, pp. 167–68) reject the legitimacy of strong sustainability, whereas others, notably Herman Daly (1996, pp. 54–55), advocate its importance. Still others argue that neither polar position is generally accurate because the degree of substitutability or complementarity of capital stocks depends on the particular situation being analyzed (Castle, Berrens, and Polasky, 1996, pp. 482–85).

Regardless of one's perspective on capital stock substitution, it is clear that weak sustainability is a precondition for strong sustainability, making it a logical starting point for assessing progress toward sustainability. If an economy does not meet the more tractable weak sustainability condition, it will certainly not meet that of strong sustainability. Conversely, if it meets the weak sustainability condition, an economy could potentially meet the more stringent constraint of strong sustainability. Future research involving strong sustainability should draw from ecology, sociology, and economics to further define and understand the roles of these critical assets and their substitutability, complementarity, and potential irreversibility.

World Bank researchers have used this sustainability framework as the basis for a macroeconomic sustainability metric (Hamilton, 1994, pp. 165–66; Hamilton and Atkinson, 1996, pp. 676–78; Hamilton et al., 1997, pp. 3–13; Pearce and Atkinson, 1993, pp. 104–5). Originally proposed as a savings rule to indicate weak sustainability, the metric begins with investment from national income accounts. After adjusting this measure of investment for depreciation of physical and natural capital stocks, the rule purports that an economy is on an unsustainable path if the adjusted level of investment is negative. Following the notation of Pearce and Barbier (2000, pp. 92–94), this measure, deemed Genuine Savings and denoted by S_g, is given by

$$S_g = I - dK_m - dK_n \tag{5}$$

where dK_m is the depreciation of an economy's aggregate physical capital stock's useful life and dK_n is given by

$$dK_n = dK_{rc} + dK_{nrc} + dK_{es} = r_{rc} \cdot (h - g) + r_{nrc} \cdot (e - d) + wtp_{es} \cdot (q - a) \tag{6}$$

where bold letters denote column vectors of assets. The valuation of natural capital requires explicit distinction between ecosystem services (dK_{es}) and natural commodities, both renewable (dK_{rc}) and nonrenewable (dK_{nrc}). The total change in value of the stock of a given renewable commodity is given by the difference between the quantity harvested (h) and the quantity regenerated (g) over a period of time, valued at the per unit rent (r_{rc}). Similarly, the value of a change in a nonrenewable resource stock, for example, mineral deposits, is given by the change in existing quantity, total units extracted (e) less new discoveries (d), valued at the per unit rent (r_{nrc}). Change in the value of the stock of ecosystem services is determined by the change in the environment's capacity to provide these services—the difference between damages (q) to that capacity and the assimilation (a) of those damages—valued by per unit willingness-to-pay (wtp_{es}) estimates for the avoidance of the degradation of those services.[2] Ecosystem services are largely nonmarket goods, requiring the use of nonmarket valuation techniques.

Further expansions of the Genuine Savings framework include investments in human capital and advances in technology (Hamilton et al., 1997, pp. 10–13). The resulting metric approximates net investment in total capital over time, providing a clear indication of potential sustainability. Again using the notation of Pearce and Barbier (2000, pp. 92–97), Genuine Savings is given by

$$S_g = I - dK_m + dK_h - dK_n + PV(T) \tag{7}$$

where dK_h is the sum of national expenditures on higher education and $PV(T)$ is the present value of technological advance.

Genuine Savings largely meets our criteria for beginning to develop a meaningful sustainability metric. Crucially, the derivation is *grounded in peer-reviewed economic theory*. From an economics perspective Genuine Savings is the theoretically correct macroeconomic indicator of weak sustainability, stemming from a clear and consistent framework (Stiglitz, Sen, and Fitoussi, 2009, p. 244). Genuine Savings is *comprehensive* in its inclusion of economic, social, and environmental aspects of sustainability. While the actual calculation presented in (7) falls short of the theoretically complete measure put forth in (3) (a shortcoming stemming primarily from the omission of social capital considerations and practical data limitations), the Genuine Savings framework provides the starting basis for a comprehensive and holistic assessment, leaving room for progress to be made toward a more complete measure including strong sustainability elements.

The practical considerations—*transparency* and *consistency*—are clearly met. The data required for calculating Genuine Savings are widely available macroeconomic data. Furthermore, although the valuation of nonmarket goods and services is sometimes criticized in the literature, the monetization and aggregation procedures used by Genuine Savings come directly from accepted economic practices and are fully disclosed in a calculation manual published by the World Bank (Bolt, Matete, and Clemens, 2002). Consistency requires the ability to apply the metric across a wide variety of countries in a standardized manner. To meet this, Genuine Savings is frequently normalized by gross national income (GNI), allowing comparison between diversely sized and developed economies.

Perhaps most importantly, Genuine Savings provides a clear and useful signal to stakeholders regarding a nation's performance in making progress toward sustainability; where $S_g < 0$, we have a clear indication that the economy is operating unsustainably because there has been a net depletion in wealth (Ness et al., 2007, p. 502). Thus, the economics literature provides a rigorous interpretation of weak sustainability, defined in a manner that can be empirically tested. While this has been recognized and applied to macroeconomic behavior, an enterprise level equivalent has not been proposed until now; we proceed with the construction of GM.

GENUINE METRICS: A THEORETICAL FRAMEWORK FOR ASSESSING BUSINESS SUSTAINABILITY

Adapting the weak sustainability condition in (3) to an enterprise level sustainability indicator follows the same theoretical procedure as the construction of Genuine Savings. Appropriate adaptations are made to reflect the smaller-scaled unit of analysis. The following provides a theoretical framework for a rigorous assessment of an organization's net contribution to a nation's sustainable development.

An organization's actions should be interpreted as contributing positively or negatively toward an economy's sustainability and can be evaluated by assessing the resulting net capital stock changes, or their net impact on societal wealth. Interpreting an individual organization's impact in per capita terms is not feasible because in assessing society's sustainability organizations' net contributions will ultimately be interpreted in the aggregate using the national change in population. Similarly, concerns over capital stock substitution and threshold levels of critical capital stocks become relatively moot. Assessment of strong sustainability and existing levels of critical capital stocks are important in the aggregate, but an individual agent's contribution will not necessarily coincide with the character of aggregate change. Thus, the validity of strong sustainability concerns at larger scales does not fundamentally change the interpretation of a firm's impacts on sustainability in a meaningful way.

Because the aggregate impacts are what ultimately inform us about a society's sustainability, the summed assessments of each agent's contribution should theoretically equal the impact assessed at the macroeconomic level. This highlights the importance of not double-counting impacts on the microeconomic level and raises the issue of clearly defining boundaries for determining which agents are responsible for each impact. We propose that only an organization's direct impacts are counted when assessing their impact on sustainability. Direct impacts include the waste streams and investments occurring from an organization's processes and resource inputs directly used in the production of final goods and services. Indirect effects, such as upstream emissions that result from the production of an input, are not included; such impacts are owned by the upstream supplier, just as emissions from a product's use down the supply chain are owned by the end user.

This specification requires differentiating an individual organization from its supply chain and is potentially problematic because an organization's policies can have important consequences on the behavior of upstream suppliers. Similarly, an organization's production practices often have important consequences for the end of a product's life cycle (Linton, Klassen, and Jayaraman, 2007, p. 1079). Isolating an organization's activities from these outcomes may appear unwarranted; however, establishing causation between one firm's policy and another's actions and the degree of influence would be necessary to make such a case. In essence, we assume the supplier and the end user make decisions regarding how materials and products are produced, transported, and disposed of.

Furthermore, in the microeconomic context, financial assets, an essential fifth form of capital, must be considered in addition to physical, natural, human, and social capital (Dyllick and Hockerts, 2002, p. 133). Financial capital serves as a store of value and is essential to the management of an organization's wealth and activities. The inclusion of financial capital is based upon the assumption that such assets could be used to invest in other capital stocks at any given point in time, increasing the real wealth of society. Although not typically considered in the Genuine Savings literature, including a nation's financial capital when calculating its total wealth has been suggested, where net financial capital would equal net foreign financial assets or net debt (Hamilton, 1994, p. 158). The inclusion of financial capital at the microeconomic level is consistent with Genuine Savings theory, and this measure of stored wealth must be included when considering the net impact of an organization's activities. Therefore, we move from the four capital framework outlined above toward a five-capital framework that takes explicit account of changes in stocks of financial capital (Goodwin, 2003, p. 3). If an organization has legal ownership of a financial asset that is a store of productive value, it should be included in that organization's holdings of total capital stock.

Properly accounting for an organization's spending on research and development (R&D) raises further questions regarding what should be counted as an expense and what should be treated as an investment in technology. Despite relatively common definitions, the guidelines for treating R&D spending provided by the United States Generally Accepted Accounting Principles (GAAP) and the International Financial Reporting Standards (IFRS) differ. Whereas GAAP conservatively requires all R&D spending to be treated as expenses, the IFRS is more lenient than GAAP, allowing for the capitalization of R&D spending if the following criteria are met (Gornik-Tomaszewski and Millan, 2005, pp. 42–44):

1. Feasibility of intangible asset's completion for use
2. Intention on completing the asset for use
3. Ability for the asset to be used
4. Demonstration of how the asset will be used productively
5. Availability of resources for the asset to be completed and used
6. Ability to measure expenses attributable to development of the asset

We follow the IFRS guidelines, contending that spending on R&D that meet these criteria should be counted as investments in the existing stock of knowledge and technology. Improvements in the productivity of existing wealth will have an important impact on the ability of a given capital stock to provide goods and services and are an important element in moving from a paradigm of economic growth to one of sustainable development. Spending that advances technology and grows the stock of human capital should be counted as an investment.

Adapting (3) to account for financial capital and allowing for positive or negative net investment in each capital stock over a given period results in our base equation for GM, given by

$$GM = \dot{K}_m + \dot{K}_h + \dot{K}_s + \dot{K}_n + \dot{K}_f + PV_{R\&D} \tag{8}$$

where $PV_{R\&D}$ is the present value of expected net returns from research and development, and $\dot{K}_m$, $\dot{K}_h$, and $\dot{K}_s$, annual changes in man-made, human, and social capital stocks, are given by

$$\dot{K}_m = \sum_{i=1}^{N_m} \left(i_{m,i} - d_{m,i} \right) + \dot{INV} \tag{9}$$

$$\dot{K}_h = \sum_{i=1}^{N_h} \left(i_{h,i} - d_{h,i} \right) \tag{10}$$

$$\dot{K}_s = \sum_{i=1}^{N_s} \left(i_{s,i} - d_{s,i} \right) \tag{11}$$

From (9) we see that the change in physical capital over time is given by investment (i_m) in a vector of plants, property, and equipment, over the period less the period's depreciation of the useful life (d_m) of the vector of existing physical capital, plus net changes in inventories (INV). Capital stocks for which functional markets exist are valued using observed market prices; while using market prices to value changes in physical capital is potentially problematic (Sen, 1999, pp. 80–81; Stiglitz, Sen, and Fitoussi, 2009, p. 244), we start by assuming that market prices conceptually reflect the social net present value of the capital asset. Significant departures from that assumption can be treated by adjusting prices due to noncompetitive factors at the empirical stage.

The quantification and valuation of investments and decrements to human ($\dot{K}_h$) and social (K_s) capital are less straightforward; although theoretically they require the same approach, observable market prices rarely exist, making nonmarket valuation necessary. Investments in human capital (i_h) include investments in the health, education, and training of the workforce, whereas decrements to the workforce's productivity (d_h) include impacts such as health issues, layoffs, or harmful working conditions. Investments in social capital (i_s) include activities such as the support, financially or otherwise, for community-building programs, charitable organizations, and social institutions, whereas predatory corporate behavior and corporate criminal activity, for example, fraud and corruption, degrade community networks and trust (d_s).

Similar to (6) above, the term $\dot{K}_n$ is given by

$$\dot{K}_n = \dot{K}_{rc} + \dot{K}_{nrc} + \dot{K}_{es} = \sum_{i=1}^{N_{rc}} r_{rc,i} \cdot (h_i - g_i) + \sum_{i=1}^{N_{nrc}} r_{nrc,i} \cdot (e_i - d_i) + \sum_{i=1}^{N_{es}} wtp_{es,i} \cdot (q_i - a_i) \quad (12)$$

where h, e, and q are the same as before, and i_{rc}, i_{nrc}, and i_{es} are investments in renewable natural capital stocks, nonrenewable natural capital stocks, and the capacity to provision ecosystem services, respectively. Whereas calculation of the rents paid to marketable renewable and nonrenewable capital stocks can usually be calculated using market prices and extraction costs, estimates of nonmarket renewable and nonrenewable resources and the willingness to pay for ecosystem service must rely upon nonmarket valuation methods.

Theoretically, the identification of change in financial capital is concerned with changes in the value stored in financial assets owned by the firm. Recognizing this as a stock concept, the balance sheet provides the necessary information needed to measure the change in value stored in financial assets owned by an organization over time. Ownership is a key element, and financial liabilities must be accounted for, providing us with a measurement of net financial assets. Thus, a firm's financial capital at a given point of time is given by

Financial Capital = Cash + Cash Equivalents + Long-Term Financial Assets +
Accounts Receivable − Accounts Payable − Other Outstanding Debt \quad (13)

where Long-Term Financial Assets are distinguished based upon their treatment by accountants, largely differing from cash and cash equivalents based upon their degree of liquidity and the intent of the firm.

The interpretation of GM is analogous to that of Genuine Savings. When GM < 0, the organization's activities have had a negative net effect on societal wealth over the given period of time, indicating a detrimental impact on the potential sustainability of the nation. When

GM ≥ 0, the organization has had either a positive or zero net effect on societal wealth over the given time period. Just as Genuine Savings is normalized by GDP for comparison purposes, comparing the net impact of an organization with another requires the normalization of GM to account for varying sizes of operations, perhaps by sales or another appropriate metric of scale. Prenormalized values are important to consider, providing insight into the magnitude of an organization's impacts, while normalizing allows for comparison and is important to consider when benchmarking (Pearce and Atkinson, 1993, p. 105). The following case study provides an illustrative application of GM, followed by a discussion of the concept's merits, complications, and future needs.

GENUINE METRICS CASE STUDY: SUSTAINABLE HARVEST

Genuine Metrics is ultimately intended to be an easy-to-use, open source, spreadsheet-based tool providing the necessary conversion, monetization, and aggregation of user-provided inputs. We present a case study representing the first alpha test of the concept using an elementary first-generation calculator. We test the overall methodology of GM, flesh out the theoretical details, demonstrate an actual application of GM, and identify aspects of the process and methodology that require future research—both in the development of the GM calculator and the direction of future case studies.

Sustainable Harvest is a coffee importer based in Portland, Oregon. The firm adopted a business model it refers to as "relationship coffee." Sustainable Harvest's operations invest heavily in educating coffee farmers and building long-term relationships between growers and buyers. The firm staffs local offices in Mexico, Tanzania, and Peru with employees trained to interact and assist the growers. In addition, the firm actively manages and monitors its environmental impacts, publishing information on its activities through an annual sustainability report and third-party certification programs.

Our study focused on Sustainable Harvest's operations throughout the 2009 fiscal year. The firm's key sustainability initiatives during the period involved contributing 1–2 percent of sales revenue to charitable foundations, investing heavily in educating the farmers in their new information technology systems, holding the firm's annual workshop bringing together farmers, Sustainable Harvest employees, and buyers from around the world, and initiating a tree-planting project in which thousands of trees were planted on and around the farms of Tanzanian coffee growers. These activities represent investments in social capital, human capital, and natural capital, respectively.

Figure 1 shows the estimated net change in each of the five individual capital stocks from Sustainable Harvest's operations, shown as a percentage of income. Aggregating the net change in financial, physical, natural, human, and social capital stocks resulted in Sustainable Harvest having a net investment in capital equivalent to approximately 2.36 percent of that year's income, indicating a net contribution to societal wealth and sustainability over the course of 2009.

Implementation of the GM framework highlights the importance of including financial assets and inventories when considering a firm's net contribution to societal wealth. While the firm did experience depreciation on equipment during the course of the year, the relatively large decrement shown in figure 1 is primarily driven by fluctuations in inventories. These inventory fluctuations are closely related with accounts payable and accounts receivable, resulting in a

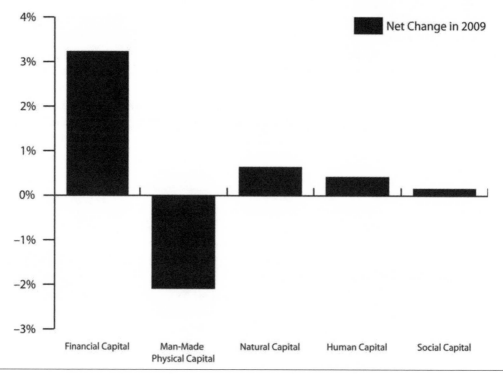

Figure 1. Net Change of Individual Capital Stocks for the Fiscal Year of 2009, as Percentage of Income

notable portion of the fluctuation in financial assets; if these financial assets were not considered, the picture of Sustainable Harvest's net impact on total capital stocks would be misleading.

This case study illustrates the potential effectiveness of meaningful sustainability initiatives. Despite Sustainable Harvest's resource consumption and carbon emissions generated through shipping, travel, and power use, it had a net positive impact on natural capital over the course of the year. The tree-planting project represented a significant investment in carbon sequestration capacity, more than offsetting the firm's negative impacts on natural capital during 2009.

The case study revealed two shortcomings in the current methodology: (1) feasibility of data collection, and (2) state of the valuation procedures. While much of the necessary data was collected, the process was far from exhaustive. Much of the physical data necessary, such as the material input used in office supplies and the organization's resulting solid waste streams, were not available and not feasible to collect. Existing data may be insufficient for conducting detailed analyses such as GM, yet organizations have limited resources for more extensive data collection. Establishing a feasible long-term data collection protocol is essential to future studies.

The current state of the GM calculator requires improvement in the sophistication and breadth of its valuation procedures. Within economics there is a significant body of literature regarding the nonmarket valuation of natural resources and ecosystem services. While this case study includes the value of carbon emissions and sequestration, there are a host of other eco-system services that have not been, yet should be, included in a GM assessment. Similarly, labor economics offers much information regarding investments in human capital, their impact on productivity, and methods of valuing those impacts. In its current state, GM only considers expenditure on employee education under investments in human capital, valued at cost.

However, it is probable that a one-dollar investment results in a more than one-dollar increase in the value of human capital. As such, the cost of the investment is used as a lower-bound estimate of the associated increase in human capital. It is likely that this is an underestimate, and it is clear that different types of educational expenditure of the same size will likely result in heterogeneous impacts on human capital. GM will be expanded to be more inclusive of an organization's impacts on human capital, and the valuation methods will be updated.

The most problematic valuation, and the one requiring the most future work, regards that of social capital. Unlike human and nonmarket natural capital, there is little literature to draw from, and most is conceptual rather than practical. The current understanding of these capital stocks limits our ability to confidently estimate the true value of such investments. As with human capital, we valued investments in social capital at cost, taking the value as a lower bound.

To demonstrate the potential to use GM to analyze alternative strategies we provide three alternative GM estimates in figure 2 using different valuations and assuming different investment scenarios. Scenario 1 holds Sustainable Harvest's activities constant while valuing investments in human capital at two to one ($1 spent on training yields $2 of human capital) and valuing investments in social capital at three to one ($1 spent on social capital investments yields $3 of social capital). The assumption of a positive return on human and social capital investments improves Sustainable Harvest's net contribution to societal wealth. Scenarios 2 and 3 maintain these valuation assumptions yet assume that Sustainable Harvest did not engage in all of its sustainability initiatives during the period. Scenario 2 assumes that charitable donations were not made, whereas Scenario 3 assumes further that the tree-planting project, the grower education, and the charitable donations were not made either. Stripping away Sustainable Harvest's sustainability initiatives clearly reduces the firm's contribution to societal wealth. For a firm with a marginally positive contribution to societal wealth, it is clear that GM helps communicate how sustainability initiatives impact sustainability itself and how they compare to each other.

DISCUSSION OF GENUINE METRICS

The framework outlined by Genuine Savings and adopted by Genuine Metrics provides a theoretically consistent methodology for evaluating sustainability. GM represents a decidedly utilitarian approach to assessing change in the potential well-being of future generations. Alternative approaches to assessing well-being have merits and should be further explored; however, GM provides a theoretically sound framework for assessing the trade-offs made by organizational activities in regards to sustainability. Genuine Metrics, as with Genuine Savings, is a starting point for assessing potential sustainability and should be interpreted as such.

Similarly, the quantification and monetization procedures effectively reduce complex and diverse information into dollar values, allowing for their aggregation and comparison. Critics of this approach argue it is oversimplified and reductionist, and they are correct that some information is indeed lost when monetizing these impacts (Bell and Morse, 2008, pp. 92–97; Goodwin, 2003, pp. 2–3). However, real-world trade-offs are made between vastly different goods and services; natural resources and social capital are frequently traded for each other and other commodities in market and political processes, implicitly if not explicitly. Recognizing and addressing this truth improves our understanding of these decisions and how they affect

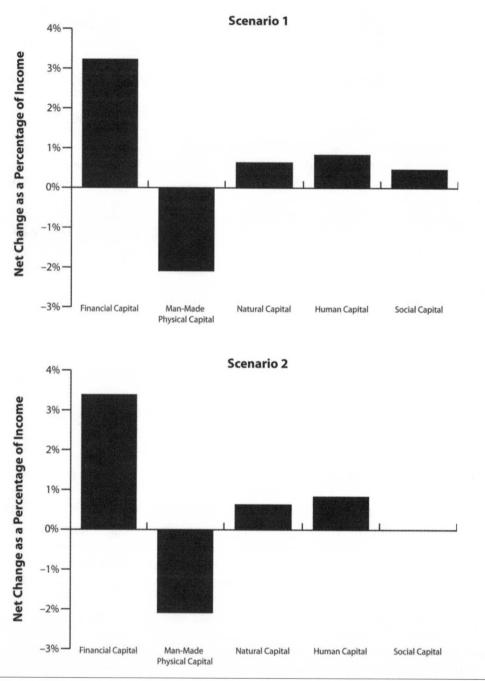

Figure 2. HYPOTHETICAL GM ESTIMATE SCENARIOS 1, 2, AND 3

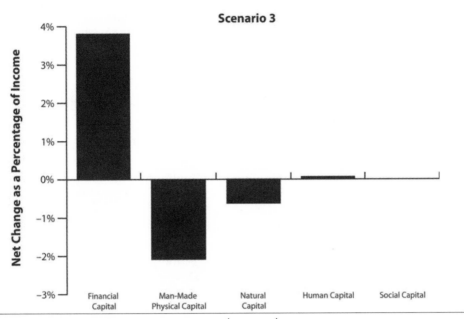

Figure 2. HYPOTHETICAL GM ESTIMATE SCENARIOS 1, 2, AND 3 (CONTINUED)

sustainability. The quantification and monetization process forces analysts to consider the relationships between these resources and the trade-offs that are being made, revealing which relationships are least understood and require more extensive research. Evaluating a complex system such as sustainability, a critical societal objective, requires some level of reduction.

While contentious in some circles, using monetary terms as the basis for analysis provides a convenient means of measurement due to its broad acceptance as the primary way to express and understand value. Being the dominant form of exchange and communication in the business world also favors its adoption in sustainability measurement and reporting. When important qualitative information is lost in the monetization process, it should be identified and included in any final evaluation, especially when considering strong sustainability. Given economists' limited understanding of nonmarket valuation, a strong case exists for including a detailed qualitative analysis with any assessment such as GM. Economics has developed a wide array of valuation techniques; however, the applications are far from exhaustive and the methodologies are not without contention. The literature has recognized the difficulty of fully implementing measurement systems such as Genuine Savings because of deficiencies in non-market valuation (Stiglitz, Sen, and Fitoussi, 2009, p. 17). This shortcoming is important to recognize, yet it is not a sufficient reason to abandon further development of the framework. The difficulties with implementing the concept should instead stimulate further research to develop and improve the existing body of knowledge to increase the framework's feasibility.

An important next step for the GM project is updating and expanding the valuation procedures so that they are using the most accurate, current, and defensible estimates as possible. Continually updating the GM calculator to reflect future improvements in methodologies and estimates should be a regular part of the GM program. Impacts that cannot be reliably quantified or monetized serve as an excellent indication that those impacts, and their relation to sustainability, warrant further research on their theoretical connection and practical

Table 2. COMPARISON OF TOTAL NET CHANGE IN CAPITAL AS PERCENTAGE OF INCOME

Scenario	Estimated Net Change in 2009
1	3.10%
2	2.78%
3	1.66%

evaluation. In light of these issues, the use of GM to interpret an organization's sustainability should be done with supplemental qualitative analysis that addresses limitations of the methodology and changes in processes. An example may include a description of any significant equity effects due to changes in capital stocks, that is, who wins and loses.

Despite these limitations, GM provides a meaningful contribution to the evaluation of organizational sustainability, moving the practice toward a more rigorous, scientifically defensible process based upon peer-reviewed economic theory. The GM approach fundamentally shifts the way an organization's actions are interpreted away from a cost-benefit flow paradigm toward one of investments, stocks, and wealth, the essential elements of sustainable development. The method isolates the change in society's wealth that results from an agent's activities over a period of time, calculating whether a net positive or negative change has occurred. Such a calculation will likely be most beneficial when done year after year, providing a time series that indicates whether or not an organization is on a trajectory toward having a positive contribution to sustainability. This would allow organizations to assess the effectiveness of sustainability initiatives and policy changes.

Perhaps the most useful feature of GM is the ability to aid in benchmarking and decision making. Internally, the management of sustainability requires a framework for comparing the returns, in terms of sustainability, from various initiatives. An organization facing a suite of potential initiatives will benefit from a framework that aids in maximizing the impact of its efforts in terms of sustainability, generating the greatest net contribution to societal wealth. A tool that helps decision makers grasp the expected outcome of their actions in terms of sustainability makes it an increasingly actionable and defensible objective. GM scales well and can be used internally to assess individual projects, branches, departments, or the entire organization. Similarly, organizations can use past performance to benchmark initiatives and assess future outcomes.

The decision making of external stakeholders would similarly benefit from organizations' use of GM. Besides providing interested parties with a comprehensive, easily interpreted view of an organization's contribution to sustainability, normalizing GM to control for the scale of economic activity would allow comparisons across organizations and industries. Investors and managers alike would be better informed regarding the success of firms' sustainability initiatives as well as potential risks. Regulators and managers could potentially identify best practices within and across industries, making GM assessments useful benchmarking tools.

In addition to further improving the valuation procedures, increased testing through more case studies is an important next step for developing GM. As with the Sustainable Harvest study, it is expected that future applications will continue to reveal aspects of the concept and the calculator that require development and greater sophistication. Developing a body of case studies will allow researchers to begin benchmarking and highlighting best practices. Utilizing existing data collected as part of other reporting and evaluation initiatives, such as the GRI, is an important component to increasing the effectiveness and efficiency of GM applications. Also, qualitative comparisons of GM outcomes with GRI assessments could identify strengths and weaknesses in each approach.

CONCLUSION

The increasing importance of sustainability issues in the management, reporting, and evaluation of corporations has been accompanied by the development of a broad range of enterprise-level sustainability indicators and measurement approaches. However, these metrics fall short of satisfying one or more of the accepted characteristics necessary for a sustainability indicator to be useful and meaningful. Furthermore, the diversity of definitions and perspectives of sustainability has exacerbated the disconnect between these indicators and sustainability itself, leaving the existing metrics largely incapable of providing any indication of progress on sustainability. Making sense of the proliferation of sustainability initiatives requires some standardization on the definition and interpretation of sustainability and how it relates to individual organizations.

The GM framework developed here provides a methodology for assessing an organization's activities' contribution to a sustainable economy that provides a clear, useful, and easily interpretable indication of those impacts. The methodology is grounded in the economic theory of sustainability and Genuine Savings, providing a direct link between what is meant by sustainability and what is measured, and ensuring that the actions of the present generation do not compromise the ability of posterity to achieve its own well-being. GM has the potential to provide a comprehensive assessment of sustainability, one that provides clear and useful information concerning an organization's impacts on sustainability to both internal and external stakeholders.

Although the framework is useful as a conceptual construct, the practical implementation of GM requires future research in the development of a readily available calculator with extensive databases for estimating credible biogeophysical and monetary effects. Without this easy-to-use calculator and reliable data, GM will likely see limited application. Of key importance, whether working within this framework or not, is gaining a greater understanding of the impacts that firm's activities have upon social capital and their relation to sustainability in general. Limitations in the art of nonmarket valuation pose a significant hurdle for fully employing GM; further research and determination will continue to improve the understanding of our actions and sustainable outcomes.

NOTES

1. See www.globalreporting.org/Home.
2. Many ecosystem services come directly from renewable and nonrenewable natural resources. Thus their respective valuation may overlap. When assessing the value of change in natural capital, much care must be taken to not double-count the values provided by natural resources and ecosystem services.

REFERENCES

Adams, C. A., and G. R. Frost. 2008. "Integrating Sustainability Reporting into Management Practices." *Accounting Forum* 32(4): 288–302.

Bell, Simon, and Stephen Morse. 2008. *Sustainability Indicators: Measuring the Immeasurable?* London: Earthscan Publications.

Bernhart, M. 2009. "The Rules of the Game: Global Standards Can Help Organizations Communicate Their Sustainability Efforts Clearly and Credibly." *Communication World* 26(5): 24–28.

Bohringer, Christoph, and Patrick E. P. Jochem. 2007. "Measuring the Immeasurable: A Survey of Sustainability Indices." *Ecological Economics* 63(1): 1–8.

Bolt, Katharine, Mampite Matete, and Michael Clemens. 2002. "Manual for Calculating Adjusted Net Savings." http://www.worldbank.org.

Castle, E., R. Berrens, and S. Polasky. 1996. "Economics of Sustainability." *Natural Resources Journal* 36:715–30.

Daly, Herman E. 1996. *Beyond Growth: The Economics of Sustainable Development.* Boston: Beacon Press.

Deloitte LLC. 2010. "Sustainability in Business Today: A Cross-Industry View." http://www.deloitte.com.

Dyllick, Thomas, and Kai Hockerts. 2002. "Beyond the Business Case for Corporate Sustainability." *Business Strategy & the Environment* 11(2): 130–41.

Ervin, D. 2011a. "The Economics of Sustainable Business: Theory and Evidence." In *Designing Sustainable Products, Services and Manufacturing Systems*, ed. Amaresh Chakrabarti, Sudarsan Rachuri, Prabir Sarkar, and Srinivas Kota. Singapore: Resource Publishing Services. 1–22.

Ervin, D. 2011b. "Notes on the Economics of Weak and Strong Sustainability." Working paper, Department of Economics, Portland State University.

Goodwin, Neva R. 2003. "Five Kinds of Capital: Useful Concepts for Sustainable Development." Global Development and Environment Institute, Working Paper No. 03–07. Medford, MA: Tufts University.

Gornik-Tomaszewski, Sylwia, and Miguel A. Millan. 2005. "Accounting for Research and Development Costs: A Comparison of U.S. and International Standards." *Review of Business* 26(2): 42–47.

Hamilton, Kirk. 1994. "Green Adjustments to GDP." *Resources Policy* 20(3): 155–68.

Hamilton, Kirk, and Giles Atkinson. 1996. "Air Pollution and Green Accounts." *Energy Policy* 24(7): 675–84.

Hamilton, Kirk, Giles Atkinson, and David W. Pearce. 1997. "Genuine Savings as an Indicator of Sustainability." www.cserge.ac.uk.

Hockerts, K. 1999. "The SustainAbility Radar: A Tool for the Innovation of Sustainable Products and Services." *Greener Management International* 25:29–49.

Hubbard, G. 2009. "Measuring Organizational Performance: Beyond the Triple Bottom Line." *Business Strategy and the Environment* 18(3): 177–91.

Kolk, A. 2008. "Sustainability, Accountability and Corporate Governance: Exploring Multinationals' Reporting Practices." *Business Strategy and the Environment* 17(1): 1–15.

KPMG. 2011. "KPMG International Survey of Corporate Responsibility Reporting 2011." http://www.kpmg.com.

Linton, J. D., R. Klassen, and V. Jayaraman. 2007. "Sustainable Supply Chains: An Introduction." *Journal of Operations Management* 25(6): 1075–82.

Lubin, D. A., and D. C. Esty. 2010. "The Sustainability Imperative." *Harvard Business Review* 88(5): 42–73.

Makower, Joel. 2011. "State of Green Business 2011." GreenBiz Group Inc. http://www.greenbiz.com.

Ness, B., E. Urbel-Piirsalu, S. Anderberg, and L. Olsson. 2007. "Categorising Tools for Sustainability Assessment." *Ecological Economics* 60(3): 498–508.

Pearce, David W., and Giles D. Atkinson. 1993. "Capital Theory and the Measurement of Sustainable Development: An Indicator of 'Weak' Sustainability." *Ecological Economics* 8:103–8.

Pearce, David W., and Edward Barbier. 2000. *Blueprint for a Sustainable Economy*. London: Earthscan.

Pezzey, John C. V., and Michael A. Toman. 2005. "Sustainability and Its Economic Interpretations." In *Scarcity and Growth Revisited: Natural Resources and the Environment in the New Millennium*, ed. Ralph David Simpson, Michael A. Toman, and Robert U. Ayres, pp. 121–41. Washington, DC: Resources for the Future.

Ranganathan, Janet. 1998. "Sustainability Rulers: Measuring Corporate Environmental and Social Performance." WRI Sustainable Enterprise Initiative. http://www.wri.org/wri/.

Sen, Amartya. 1999. *Development as Freedom*. New York: Knopf.

Solow, Robert. 1993. "An Almost Practical Step toward Sustainability." *Resources Policy* 19(3): 162–72.

Stiglitz, Joseph E., Amartya Sen, and Jean-Paul Fitoussi. 2009. *Report by the Commission on the Measurement of Economic Performance and Social Progress*. Paris: Commission on the Measurement of Economic Performance and Social Progress.

Toman, Michael A. 1994. "Economics and 'Sustainability': Balancing Trade-Offs and Imperatives." *Land Economics* 70(4): 399–413.

Veleva, V., and M. Ellenbecker. 2000. "A Proposal for Measuring Business Sustainability: Addressing Shortcomings in Existing Frameworks." *Greener Management International* 31:101–20.

World Commission on Environment and Development (WCED). 1987. *Our Common Future*. Oxford: Oxford University Press.

The Case for "Improvement" in Corporate Sustainability Indicators

RICHARD GROGAN

BUILDING A GREEN ECONOMY IS, AT LEAST IN PART, PREDICATED ON OPEN AND HONest dialogue with stakeholders about organizations' progress with respect to sustainability. In the private sector, this progress is currently communicated through corporate sustainability reports, which supplement existing government-mandated reports. These reports were the subject of this research study, which content-analyzed 330 corporate sustainability reports from all multiple-reporting (reporting more than once) U.S. corporations during the first ten years (1999–2009) of the Global Reporting Initiative (GRI), now the world's largest sustainability reporting framework. The data reveal some improvement among core sustainability indicators, yet the current philosophy underlying the world's largest reporting frameworks will at some point prevent significant further improvement. Recent statements from the GRI and other reporting frameworks have validated that actual sustainability improvement is not a consideration. Statements at both the GRI's biennial meeting in 2010, and from the Association for the Advancement of Sustainability in Higher Education's (AASHE) Sustainability Tracking, Assessment and Rating System (STARS) program, a university reporting framework, indicate that these organizations wish to avoid judgments about an individual organization's "sustainability." Thus, at present, "improvement" does not indicate an organization is getting *more sustainable*, but rather that it is getting *better at reporting*. I argue that simply reporting for reporting sake gets us no closer to a sustainability transition, and thus we ought to move toward evaluating whether companies are actually improving with respect to sustainability. This could be accomplished through the development of a "Gross Sustainability" (GS) measure using reporting data.

BACKGROUND

Building a green economy requires measures and indicators that allow both the architects of and stakeholders within that economy to know whether what they are building is actually "green," or, given the events of the past five years, whether anything is really being "built" at all. Scholars, NGOs, and associations have all been working to develop and promote a series of indicator "frameworks" over the past two decades to address this question. Nowhere is this effort more public and more prevalent than in the corporate sector, where these measures take the form of corporate sustainability reporting, which is also commonly known as "Corporate Social Responsibility" (CSR), "Environmental, Social and Governance" (ESG), and increasingly, "Sustainability Reporting" (all nonfinancial reports will be referred to in this chapter as "sustainability reports"); reporting is often one component of companies' larger "corporate citizenship," or "corporate social responsibility" (CSR) efforts. These reporting frameworks in corporations are rooted in a long history of financial reporting, which is and has been provided in a standardized format within the guidelines of the U.S. Securities and Exchange Commission (SEC), or one of several country- or region-specific regulatory agencies.

While companies (or occasionally other types of organizations, such as nonprofits or government agencies) are not required to report non-financial indicators, there is evidence that the SEC in the United States is heading in that direction; recent actions include requiring disclosures concerning business risks from climate change (Lehmann, 2009), and consideration of standardized sustainability indicators for future reporting schemes (SEC, 2009). Among those that already report nonfinancial indicators, the most widely accepted framework is the Global Reporting Initiative (GRI).

Sustainability reporting must be considered in the context of sustainable development, a concept that implies that corporations can hold both growth and sustainability as complementary values. This idea is theoretically challenging, in that corporations are bound to seek profits for their shareholders by their articles of incorporation, and thus must continue to grow. Yet at least some theoretical concepts of sustainability (such as "strong sustainability," e.g., Lawn, 2006; Brekke, 1997, which severely restricts substitutability of natural capital and makes unrestrained growth difficult) would seem to be at odds with a paradigm encouraging growth, certainly unrestrained growth. Still, organizations are operationalizing elements of sustainability by increasingly introducing quantifiable sustainability practices and disclosing them publicly in sustainability reports.

Sustainability reporting, or at least thinking beyond the financial "bottom line" of a company, can be traced to the concept of externalities, introduced by Pigou (1920) and, later, Coase (1960). Social responsibility at the corporate level can be traced to the 1960s (Salzmann, Ionescu-Somers, and Steger, 2005). As early as the 1940s however, there are accounts of a broader commitment to *stake*holders, implying an audience beyond *share*holders (Norman and MacDonald, 2004). In the 1980s, the concept of stakeholder involvement in corporate strategic decisions appeared through the work of scholars such as Edward Freeman, whose 1984 work *Strategic Management: A Stakeholder Approach*, is commonly cited as early evidence of what would eventually be called "social" sustainability in corporations.

To make these theoretical concepts explicit, alternative (compared to strictly financial) reporting began to emerge in the form of environmental indicators. These were eventually combined with social indicators to create "sustainability reports." The process of sustainability reporting generally follows a set of guidelines or a framework of indicators within which a company measures and reports its sustainability-related activities.

The basis of the indicators included in the earliest sustainability reports was in financial accounting, in what was termed "triple bottom line accounting" or "sustainable accounting." Sustainable accounting is credited to Elkington (1999), who developed the concept during the 1990s. Combining his version with the work of other scholars, the concept of sustainable accounting has evolved from its first iteration, which employed traditional methods of accounting to make damage to the environment from business activities financially explicit, to later work, which defines two additional "bottom lines," social and environmental, beyond the financial bottom line (Lamberton, 2005).

Multiple reporting frameworks have emerged since this earlier work to provide the growing interest in measuring corporate sustainability with a format for systematically measuring and reporting it. Perrini and Tencati (2006) found that over one hundred such frameworks and reporting schemes existed at one time or another for this purpose. The frameworks that still exist today exhibit a range of comprehensiveness, from the triple-bottom-line-rich GRI, to the London Benchmarking Group's tool that helps companies evaluate contributions from a single philanthropic project, such as a day of volunteerism to remove trash from a local river, or a company-wide fund-raising drive to benefit a charitable organization (LBG, 2008). Additionally, some companies create and use their own proprietary frameworks.

One framework has emerged as the clear frontrunner: the GRI. In the absence of a formal standard for sustainability reporting, the GRI has become the de facto standard; a recent KPMG study found that nearly 80 percent of companies reporting on sustainability use the GRI (KPMG International, 2008), and in early SEC deliberations on potential sustainability reporting standards, the SEC formally recognized that the GRI is rapidly becoming the standard worldwide (SEC, 2009). Harnessing this momentum, GRI director Ernst Ligteringen unveiled a charge at the GRI's 2010 conference in Amsterdam to all of the world's companies—corporations and SMEs—to report using the GRI by 2015 or explain publicly why they choose not to (GRI, 2010).

The GRI was piloted by 20 organizations in 1999, and by 2010, 1,866 international organizations participated in reporting using the GRI's G3 guidelines (GRI, 2011). The G3 guidelines represent the third iteration of guidelines, with each revision reflecting changes driven by a stakeholder input process (GRI, 2009; KPMG International, 2008); the latest version, G4, is currently under development. The GRI specifies indicators ranging from quantitative, such as the amount of energy or materials used in a specific industrial process, to qualitative, such as the narrative details of employee training programs (GRI, 2008).

CURRENT CHALLENGES IN REPORTING RESEARCH

A review of research on corporate sustainability reporting over the past decade reveals several challenges, among them a continued inability to produce a strong "business case" for sustainability (e.g., Brammer and Millington, 2008; Callan and Thomas, 2009; Godfrey, Merrill, and Hansen, 2009), issues with the comparability of reports (e.g., Cerin, 2002; Slater and Gilbert, 2004), and finally, the subject of this chapter, the question of whether companies are making measurable progress on sustainability issues. This issue can be explained through two different lenses: the first is an established line of questioning evident from the literature regarding the purpose of reporting, and the second builds upon this line of questions to pose a broader, more philosophical question about reporting: Is reporting getting us any closer to sustainability?

First, there are concerns that sustainability reports are merely marketing tactics; the popular term "greenwashing" is one manifestation of this controversy. Though many reporting companies have a dedicated sustainability or social responsibility department or office, some companies house these operations within marketing, public relations, or public affairs offices, thus contributing to the marketing-driven perception. The "greenwashing" accusation implies that corporate sustainability efforts are window dressing, and thus their sustainability efforts address issues at the margin without approaching core issues.

A review by Kolk (2004) revealed that while categories of sustainability indicators proliferated in the 1990s, there has been little evidence to support an increase in the "sustainable" activities included in those reports. In part because of this, several scholars support the view that sustainability reporting is little more than a marketing and public relations vehicle (e.g., Cerin, 2002; Dunphy, Griffiths, and Benn, 2002; Marshall and Brown, 2003; O'Donovan, 2002; Perrini and Tencati, 2006).

The second lens examines the concept of "improvement" in sustainability performance as a way of measuring progress toward sustainability; however, defining improvement can be problematic. The GRI, for example, views improvement in a literal sense; that is, improvement equals *getting better at reporting*. Getting better at reporting includes addressing a suite of problems that scholars and stakeholders have identified with reports (some of which were mentioned earlier); to address limited comparability among firms, for example, the GRI has introduced sector-specific supplemental reports. These reports ostensibly allow stakeholders to compare, for example, electric utilities or auto companies with other companies in their sector, instead of with a global sample of all reporting companies from every industry. The GRI has also welcomed the trend of increased auditing ("assurance") to ensure the validity of companies' sustainability disclosures.

The drive to get better at reporting is also manifested in awards—distributed on an annual basis—to companies that have the "best" reports, which according to one large award-granting body, the Corporate Register, are measured along "five essential elements": "content, communication, credibility, commitment, and comparability" (Corporate Register, 2011). The GRI and other reporting frameworks such as AASHE STARS make it clear that their frameworks are not intended for use as a ranking system of the sustainability of a particular organization, but as a way of rating a company's report. AASHE says as much about its STARS system: "STARS is a rating system, NOT a ranking system" (AASHE, n.d.). The GRI, while espousing comparability as a foundation of its reporting framework, is "committed to the Framework's continuous improvement" and states the organization's core goal as the "mainstreaming of disclosure" (GRI, 2007), without explicit mention of an end goal for these disclosures.

Thus, the award and ranking processes that do exist are conceived as ranking the *best reports*, not the most sustainable companies (or, in AASHE's case, universities). This is perhaps a small detail, yet the conflation of *who is a great sustainable reporter* with *who is a great sustainability leader or champion* has an important implication for the purpose of sustainability reporting: Is the purpose of reporting to get better at reporting ("reporting for reporting's sake"), or is it to push for a more sustainable world? And further, what should be the purpose of reporting? By implication, and assuming that supporters of the aforementioned frameworks want a more sustainable world, the concept underlying the frameworks appears to be, using the words of U.S. Supreme Court Justice Louis Brandeis, that "sunlight is the best disinfectant;" that is, by making sustainability information transparent, companies will get better at sustainability as well.

What is missing from the present conception of reporting—as a general rating system not a ranking system—is goal setting, and more importantly, accountability. Both of these issues are left to individual organizations that may or may not wish to create actionable targets or goals for themselves. In part, this is intuitive, since the ultimate accountability for any public corporation is its shareholders, as defined in its articles of incorporation.

The problem with defining improvement as *getting better at reporting* instead of some measure of *acting in a more sustainable way* is that on a global scale we risk ignoring the sum total of the calculations within these reports, and the debate about what corporate sustainability ought to mean, to instead serve the pedantic concerns of the reports themselves. Fear of this evolution is not without precedent; for example, in education, the increased importance of standardized tests during the past decade has resulted in accusations of "teaching to the test" instead of concentrating on "education" more broadly. In this way these tests become a proxy for education and foreclose conversation on the broader—and likely much more contested— term "education" (e.g., Hudley and Wells, 2011; Nichols and Berliner, 2007; Thomas, 2005).

In designing the justification for this chapter, it is difficult to transfer the concept of improvement in reporting to improvement in sustainability when, it has been argued, sustainability is itself a contested concept (Thompson, 2010). However, given that GRI reports (the subject of this study) are built around a triple-bottom-line conception of sustainability (i.e., environmental, social, and economic "bottom lines") (Elkington, 1999), the indicators therein offer clues as to how companies are defining sustainability and, further, how they are trending—toward acting more or less sustainably. Further, terming the reports "corporate sustainability reports" indicates that, at least semantically, they may serve as proxies for a *corporate sustainability*, even though we as a society likely disagree on whether they represent *sustainability*.

In terms of improvement, I suggest that we are missing a real opportunity to use these reports to understand whether reporting is getting us anywhere in the global calculus that is our progression toward a sustainability transition (or not). This study examines the question of whether reporting is getting us any closer to sustainability by determining whether companies improved or declined in their sustainability performance across a subset of GRI indicators. The GRI's environmental sustainability indicators were chosen as the data set for this study because examining quantitative indicators makes improvement more objective than qualitative aspects of sustainability. For example, within the GRI framework, environmental indicator EN16 asks companies to report greenhouse gas (GHG) emissions. It is assumed for the purpose of this study that a higher GHG number from the previous year is *less sustainable* than a lower GHG number. Thus, a lower GHG number from the previous year is an improvement for sustainability. By contrast, improvement in the company's report—measured by an award or some other third-party certification—serves no purpose in determining our progress toward sustainability; it only reinforces the complaint lodged above that reports are marketing exercises and self-serving. Still, given the contested nature of any fixed interpretation of sustainability, the author's improvement judgments for each of the indicators included in the analysis are provided in appendix 1 in the spirit of transparency.

GROSS SUSTAINABILITY (GS)

Most of the data in sustainability reports in the sample appeared in its raw, or "gross" form, instead of in a "normalized" way, where "normalized" represents reporting in the context of another (typically financial) indicator. To extend the GHG emissions (EN16) example begun above further, Company X might report its gross emissions as one million tons of CO_2 emitted in year Y. A normalized version of that indicator would suggest that, for example, if Company X earned $1 million in revenue, its emissions were one ton of CO_2 per $1 in revenue. This normalized figure can be thought of as a measure of a company's sustainability efficiency; that is, if Company X's revenue increases at a higher rate than its CO_2 emissions, the ratio of one ton of CO_2 per $1 in revenue will tip in the favor of sustainability.

Though efficiency gains are to be lauded, this study focused on the data in their "gross" form (and, as described in the "Method" section, the few cases where data were presented as normalized, it was converted to gross). The author created indicators of "Gross Sustainability" (GS) for each variable to measure whether companies in the sample improved or declined in terms of their sustainability performance. The justification for this approach is that efficiency gains may expand a company's financial bottom line, but increases in gross emissions output slow a global sustainability transition. Stated differently, even if companies are improving their efficiency, gross increases are not helpful in the global drive to reduce overall emissions.

RESEARCH QUESTIONS

The study uses two primary research questions to investigate the research challenge highlighted above.

> RQ-1: Of companies that have produced multiple sustainability reports, what are the most commonly reported indicators among them?
>> RQ-1a: By how much have these commonly reported indicators improved/declined?

RQ-1 is included because previous literature (e.g., Cerin, 2002; Slater and Gilbert, 2004) indicated comparability problems, and thus the potential fractured nature of specific indicators suggested that an analysis based on the most commonly reported indicators could yield more valid conclusions about improvement.

METHOD

This study utilizes quantitative content analysis (e.g., Riffe, Lacy, and Fico, 2005), though there is considerable space for in-depth qualitative analyses of this data set in future research. Quantitative indicators are the focus of this study because it is exploratory, and given reported inconsistencies in the literature (e.g., Slater and Gilbert, 2004), it was unclear to what extent qualitative indicators could be categorized for analysis of improvement over time.

This section first describes the data collection and identification processes, which resulted in the creation of a database that the author believes to be unique in the field of corporate sustainability indicators research. This is followed by a discussion of the coding process and the challenges encountered in collecting these data.

Data Identification and Collection

Multiple sources were used to collect these data. Collectively, the data populate a new database that consists of the names of companies that have produced sustainability reports, the years they have reported (within the years 1999–2009), and the associated environmentally focused quantitative indicators contained within the reports.

Though products such as KLD STATS detail some of the same indicators as are outlined in sustainability reports, these products do not detail which companies have produced multiple reports over multiple years. Meetings with colleagues and librarians at Michigan State University, and additional research and networking internationally, revealed no comprehensive databases of sustainability reports organized by company and by year. There is one known global source of this information, though it is unknown whether it is categorized as outlined above, given that the organization holds this information as proprietary (Corporate Register employee, personal communication, March 2, 2010).

Given these challenges, the author created a new database of global organizations that have reported over the decade 1999–2009. This time frame was chosen because 1999 was the first year companies reported using the GRI, which is a relevant milestone for the field. Also, 2009 was the last year for which there was a significant volume of reports available at the time the study was conducted (winter/spring 2010).

The GRI's website includes a chart of company reports per year (it is not cumulative; if Company X reports in 2000 and in 2001, the chart does not indicate that); and this became the foundation of the new database. The new database shows that 1,811 organizations, headquartered across sixty-eight countries, reported at least once between 1999 and 2009. Of the 1,811 companies, 853 reported more than once, and of those, 78 were U.S.-headquartered companies. These U.S.-headquartered companies are the focus of this study for two reasons: first, the author is most familiar with U.S.-based organizations, having studied them extensively and worked in three such organizations; second, U.S. companies are relatively "new" to sustainability reporting when compared with peer organizations in Europe, and thus U.S. companies provide an interesting case study and point of comparison for future studies.

Report Collection

Reports were collected and analyzed in both hardcopy and electronic format, depending on availability. Many reports are available from specially designated sections of company websites; these are commonly called "sustainability" or "corporate responsibility" pages. Additionally, reports can sometimes be found within the "investors" section of company web pages alongside a company's 10-K filings, annual reports, and other financial documents. There are also online clearinghouses of sustainability reports. The clearinghouses used for this study were Corporate Register (Corporate Register, 2012), and Social Funds (Social Funds, 2012).

Finding the earliest reports in the sampling frame presented the greatest challenge. Using contact information located in sustainability reports, emails were sent to corporate sustainability directors and via generic "contact us" pages and were followed up with phone calls. When they could be located, these early reports were mailed in hardcopy.

After collection, a final check was performed to ensure that the reports were in fact GRI-compliant or had used GRI guidelines in their preparation. It became apparent early on that some reports in the GRI's list were not, in fact, GRI-compliant, thus necessitating this final check. If reports were on the list but were not GRI-compliant, they were not included in the final sample.

Sample

As mentioned above, the sampling frame is 1999–2009, during which time there were seventy-eight U.S. headquartered organizations that reported multiple times. Three of these organizations were not included in the final sample because only one sustainability report was available, and thus, improvement could not be assessed.

The final sample of seventy-five companies produced a total of 330 reports, which were collected for analysis. The reports ranged in length from 14 pages (Strategic Sustainability Consulting, 2009), to 332 pages (Newmont Mining, 2007). The companies in the sample span twenty-four industry sectors and range in annual revenue from $142,000 to $477 billion, though the majority of companies are large entities, as average revenue is just over $42 billion. The smallest company has just three employees, while the largest company employs 465,000; the average number of employees for a U.S.-headquartered company in this sample is 91,356.

Report Coding

Each of the 330 reports was coded for core environmental (EN) indicators specified by the GRI's G3 guidelines. Only core indicators were analyzed because, according to the GRI, every company should be able to report on core indicators, and thus these offer the best chance of comparability. The GRI separates indicators into "core" and "additional" categories. In theory, every company should be able to produce a report using the core indicators, with the opportunity for companies to achieve a higher "Adherence Level" (the highest adherence level is A+; directionality is commensurate with a standard primary school grading scale) by also measuring and including additional indicators.

The G3 guidelines are the third release of guidelines by the GRI, making analysis of previous versions potentially problematic; however, the GRI provides a conversion document via its website to allow users to interpret indicators released under previous versions in the language of the G3 guidelines. This study utilized this document to ensure the consistent coding of indicators across guideline updates.

To collect the data, a coding sheet was developed (appendix 2) that includes all of the core G3 environmental indicators. The sheets were left blank on the reverse side to allow room to record variation in reporting within each indicator (see data challenges section below). Due to the amount of variation, the code sheet was complemented by a spreadsheet into which each new variant was entered; additionally, as new variants were discovered, a retroactive analysis was conducted to ensure that this variant had not been missed in previously analyzed reports.

The reports were analyzed between January 2010 and April 2010. Due to the time frame, some 2009 reports were not yet available. For these reports, individual companies were contacted (per the sampling methods above) and asked to provide the reports when available, even if they were in a preproduction phase. If these reports did not arrive by April 2010, they were excluded from the sample. Analysis was limited to eight reports per day to avoid coding fatigue, which can result in missed data points or diminished thoroughness (Riffe, Lacy, and Fico, 2005). At the end of each coding day, data were entered into a master spreadsheet.

Data Challenges and Corrections

There were four primary data challenges that influenced the coding and analysis, each of which is detailed below. First, companies interpret and report each of the core indicators liberally; there are seventeen quantitative, core environmental indicators in the G3 guidelines, yet companies in this sample reported these indicators in 181 different variations (for example, listing a wide range of air or water pollutants; see appendix 1 for a complete list of all of the variations).

Second, these indicators were not designed as survey items, nor were they created for later analysis using quantitative data techniques; the absence of intentional research design resulted in multiple additional challenges, among them the "double-barreled" configuration of some individual indicators. An example is indicator EN20: "NOx, SO_2 and other significant air emissions by type and weight" (GRI, 2008). NOx and SO_2 comprise two data points (as do "type and weight"), while "other significant air emissions" resulted in twenty-three additional variants of emissions, including VOCs and methane.

A third challenge was conversion of normalized data to GS, where the required information for the calculation either did not exist or was unavailable. Where possible, the units of normalization, such as sales volume or other financial data, were accessed in annual reports and from company websites. If the calculation was not clearly replicable after these steps,[1] the indicator was excluded from the data.

A final notable challenge resulted from units of measurement. The GRI has specific unit-of-measurement guidelines for reporting data per category; energy usage, for example, is reported in gigajoules, water usage is reported in cubic meters, and most emissions are reported in metric tons. However, many companies report data consistent with their own internal data collection systems, resulting in vast inconsistency across companies. For this study, all of the data were converted from proprietary units to the GRI-specified unit of analysis for each indicator prior to analysis.

ANALYSIS AND MEASURES

After completing the data entry from the code sheets, the data were transferred to the Statistical Package for Social Sciences (SPSS) for processing. First, descriptive statistics were calculated to determine commonly reported indicators (RQ-1). Next, change variables were computed for each year and for the entire span of years captured for each company, to determine improvement or decline in specific indicators (RQ-1a). Improvement (or decline) was calculated through a dummy variable, in which a 1 or a zero was assigned to improvement or decline, respectively, from year to year; if a company reduced its absolute carbon dioxide (CO_2) emissions, for example, from 2000–2001, they would receive a 1. Alternatively, if their emissions increased over that time period, they received a zero.[2]

RESULTS

Descriptive results are provided in this section, beginning with commonly reported indicators (RQ-1) over the sampling frame (1999–2009). Next, improvement and decline for each of the commonly reported indicators are presented both across the entire sample and by percentage of companies (RQ-1a).

RQ-1: Of companies that have produced multiple sustainability reports, what are the most commonly reported indicators among them?

The seventeen core environmental sustainability indicators are shown in table 1 below, with higher percentages indicating more commonly reported indicators. These results represent the entire sample of multireport organizations (seventy-five U.S.-headquartered companies). Note that the 181 variations of core environmental indicators were recombined to the original seventeen for presentation in this table.

Table 1. COMMONLY REPORTED GRI CORE ENVIRONMENTAL INDICATORS 1999–2009: U.S. (HQ) COMPANIES (G3 TERMINOLOGY & ORDER)

Indicator	*Percentage reporting*
Aspect: Materials	
EN1: Materials used by weight or volume	22.20%
EN2: Percentage of materials used that are recycled input materials	10.00%
Aspect: Energy	
EN3: Direct energy consumption by primary energy source	78.70%
EN4: Indirect energy consumption by primary source	11.90%
Aspect: Water	
EN8: Total water withdrawal by source	69.00%
Aspect: Biodiversity	
EN11: Location and size of land owned, leased, managed in, or adjacent to protected areas of high biodiversity value outside protected areas	32.20%
EN12: Description of significant impacts of activities, products, and services on biodiversity in protected areas and areas of high biodiversity value outside protected areas	38.60%
Aspect: Emissions, effluents, and waste	

Indicator	*Percentage reporting*
EN16: Total direct and indirect greenhouse gas emissions by weight	89.40%
EN17: Other relevant indirect greenhouse gas emissions by weight	11.60%
EN19: Emissions of ozone-depleting substances by weight	13.40%
EN20: NOx, SO_2 and other significant air emissions by type and weight	55.60%
EN21: Total water discharge by quality and destination	20.40%
EN22: Total weight of waste by type and disposal method	68.40%
EN23: Total number and volume of significant spills	23.70%
Aspect: Products and services	
EN26: Initiatives to mitigate environmental impacts of products and services, and extent of mitigation	66.30%
EN27: Percentage of products sold and their packaging materials that are reclaimed by category	24.00%
Aspect: Compliance	
EN28: Monetary value of significant fines and total number of nonmonetary sanctions for noncompliance with environmental laws and regulations	37.10%
$n = 330$	

From the table, it is clear that the most commonly reported indicators (more than 50 percent reporting across the ten-year time horizon) are EN3 (direct energy consumption by primary energy source) (78.70 percent), EN8 (total water withdrawal by source) (69.00 percent), EN16 (total direct and indirect greenhouse gas emissions by weight) (89.40 percent), EN20 (NOx, SO_2, and other significant air emissions by type and weight) (55.60 percent), and EN22 (total weight of waste by type and disposal method) (68.40 percent).

Though EN26 (initiatives to mitigate environmental impacts of products and services, and extent of mitigation) was also reported over 50 percent of the time, analysis showed that this indicator was primarily reported as qualitative (it is intended as a quantitative indicator by the GRI), and thus it was not included in the coding other than to indicate presence / absence.

RQ-1a: By how much have these common measures improved/declined?

Improvement or decline in the GS measure is presented in two ways: first, based on the raw data across all of the companies in the sample, represented in table 2. Second, the percentage of companies that improved their sustainability performance for each of the commonly reported core indicators is shown in table 3; this second table corrects for reporting multiple iterations of one indicator by one company. Since indicators EN20 (NOx, SO$_2$, and other significant air emissions by type and weight) and EN22 (total weight of waste by type and disposal method) are written as "double-barreled," the most commonly reported variations of these indicators are included in table 2 and table 3.

DISCUSSION

Commonly Reported Indicators

RQ-1 revealed the commonly reported core GRI environmental indicators from 1999 to 2009. It is not surprising that the most commonly reported indicators are also the "low-hanging" fruit of environmental measurement: EN3 (direct energy consumption by primary energy source), EN8 (total water withdrawal by source), EN16 (total direct and indirect greenhouse gas emissions by weight), EN20 (NOx, SO$_2$, and other significant air emissions by type and weight), and EN22 (total weight of waste by type and disposal method). With the exception of EN16, companies likely already have systems in place to capture these data because of utility billing (e.g., electricity, water, and waste disposal) or because they must operate within specific emission tolerances (in the case of EN20).

Improvement

Results from RQ-1a indicate that between 2006 and 2009, there is an improvement trend among commonly reported indicators EN3, EN8, EN16, and EN20 (NOx). While this trend can be partially explained by additional data points in those years resulting from an increase in the number of reports, it is an important benchmark by which future reports can be tracked, assuming that the number of reports and the number of indicators reported continues to increase (as has been the trend for GRI reporters since 1999).

Limitations

The primary limitation to this study was the design of the data within sustainability reports. The data in sustainability reports were not intended for this type of analysis, and as a result, the author encountered numerous challenges, many of which are detailed in the "Data Challenges and Corrections" section above.

Second, the findings indicated a trend of improvement noticeable in 2006–9; however, the global economy underwent a tumultuous period during these years, which might have impacted some of the indicators. For example, CO$_2$ emissions might have been lower for a manufacturer in 2008 due to lower production rates or sales numbers, rather than any particular sustainability initiative.

Table 2. Percentage of Improvements by Year: Commonly Reported Indicators

Indicator	1999–2000		2000–2001		2001–2002		2002–2003		2003–2004		2004–2005		2005–2006		2006–2007		2007–2008		2008–2009	
	n	%	n	%	n	%	n	%	n	%	n	%	n	%	n	%	n	%	n	%
EN3: Direct energy consumption by primary energy source	2	0.0	8	37.5	9	33.3	19	68.4	33	54.5	39	58.9	61	42.6	87	44.8	98	54.1	35	60.0
EN8: Total water withdrawal by source	2	50.0	3	0.0	4	75.0	13	76.9	15	86.7	25	60.0	30	63.3	35	45.7	50	60.0	19	68.4
EN16: Total direct and indirect greenhouse gas emissions	2	50.0	5	20.0	6	33.3	18	66.7	25	48.0	31	48.4	46	52.2	61	47.5	67	68.6	28	78.6
EN20: NOx	0	0.0	1	0.0	3	0.0	5	80.0	8	75.0	11	81.8	17	70.6	15	73.3	19	78.9	5	80.0
EN20: SO2	0	0.0	3	33.3	3	33.3	4	75.0	7	57.1	9	66.7	15	73.3	14	78.6	18	61.1	5	80.0
EN20: VOC	0	0.0	1	0.0	1	0.0	7	71.4	9	33.3	11	63.6	16	56.3	16	81.3	13	92.3	5	60.0
EN22: Hazardous waste (amount)	3	33.3	7	14.3	11	54.5	33	63.6	46	54.3	52	51.9	73	54.7	82	56.1	104	51.9	46	60.1

TABLE 3. PERCENTAGE OF COMPANIES IMPROVING BY YEAR AND COMMONLY REPORTED INDICATORS

Indicator	1999–2000		2000–2001		2001–2002		2002–2003		2003–2004		2004–2005		2005–2006		2006–2007		2007–2008		2008–2009	
	N	%	N	%	n	%	n	%	n	%	n	%	n	%	n	%	n	%	n	%
EN3: Direct energy consumption by primary energy source	1	0.0	2	50.0	2	50.0	7	85.7	8	37.5	9	66.7	14	35.7	19	57.9	24	62.5	11	72.7
EN8: Total water withdrawal by source	2	50.0	3	0.0	4	75.0	11	72.7	13	84.6	19	52.6	24	54.2	29	37.9	38	57.9	16	62.5
EN16: Total direct and indirect greenhouse gas emissions	2	50.0	5	20.0	6	33.3	15	66.7	22	54.5	25	48.0	32	56.3	43	48.8	50	64.0	21	81.0
EN20: NOx	N/A	N/A	1	0.0	3	0.0	5	80.0	8	75.0	11	81.8	17	70.6	15	73.3	19	78.9	5	80.0
EN20: SO2	N/A	N/A	3	33.3	3	33.3	4	75.0	7	57.1	9	66.7	15	73.3	14	78.6	18	61.1	5	80.0
EN20: VOC	N/A	N/A	1	0.0	1	0.0	7	71.4	9	33.3	11	63.6	16	56.3	16	81.3	13	92.3	5	60.0
EN22: Hazardous waste (amount)	N/A	N/A	1	0.0	2	0.0	6	66.7	9	77.8	12	50.0	14	50.0	15	66.7	18	38.9	9	66.7

CONCLUSION

An essential question underlying this chapter is whether what is being measured in sustainability reports is "sustainability" at all. We as a society cannot agree on what sustainability is (sustainability as *contested concept*), the argument goes, so how are we to measure it? Further, sustainability is constantly evolving, so how do we measure a moving target? Some companies have addressed this issue semantically by calling their reports CSR reports or ESG reports and leaving the term "sustainability" out of the title (e.g., Anheuser-Busch, 2002; Chevron, 2007). Others have framed reports as a company's "progress" on sustainability, or its "journey" toward sustainability (e.g., Freeport-McMoRan, 2008; Newmont Mining, 2007), a nod to sustainability as a path and not an end in and of itself. Still, the GRI calls itself "a network-based organization that has pioneered the development of the world's most widely used *sustainability reporting* framework" (emphasis added) (GRI, 2007), and so the implication is that the reports are measuring a form of sustainability.

Given that, highlighting the potential conflation of *who is a great sustainable reporter* with *who is a great sustainability leader or champion* is important for understanding two questions that should be considered as reporting continues to evolve: (1) Is the purpose of reporting to get better at reporting ("reporting for reporting's sake") or to push for a more sustainable world? and (2) What *should* be the purpose of reporting?

Before these questions can be answered, we need a consistent measure of progress toward sustainability, and a measure like GS is a good start. The results suggest that improvement (as specified by GRI indicators) is occurring along four core indicators under the *reporting for reporting's sake* model; how much, and whether companies are improving fast enough is up for debate. Some will argue that efficiency improvements are good enough, and that overall sustainability progress (GS) cannot come at the cost of economic progress. It will be up to future researchers to continue to refine the GS measure and perhaps create a normalized or efficiency measure for sustainability reporting ("NS" or "ES" perhaps) to compare with GS. Regardless, without a final goal for business sustainability, or a serious accountability mechanism, *reporting for reporting's sake*, while useful so far according to the results of this study, is limited in its potential to impact a global sustainability transition.

The results and discussion thus far have not addressed the second question highlighted above: *What should be the purpose of reporting*; it is to this question that I now turn. If the purpose of reporting is to get better at reporting, then corporate sustainability is nothing more than another commodification of sustainability—turning sustainability reporting into a cottage industry complete with consultants, legal experts, and data analysts. If, however, the purpose of reporting is something greater—working toward a better world perhaps, or examining the boundaries of corporate influence in the realm of sustainability—and reporting is just a first step along that journey, then that is a very different (and more productive) conversation.

Regardless, it is essential to gather more data and evidence to determine whether reporting is the driver of companies' GS improvements, and further, whether improvement is occurring among indicators that are more difficult to measure, such as in the social sphere of sustainability. This raises an interesting issue regarding accountability and goals; two features I argue are essential to future sustainability reporting efforts. The logic that improvement automatically follows reporting only works to a particular threshold—likely some point where financial concerns begin to outweigh the other two bottom lines (environmental, social). At this point, a new dilemma emerges: how far to do we push companies past lower returns, and into territory where they become less financially sustainable in service to their environmental and social obligations; that is, toward a true balance of the three bottom lines, approximating an integrated and holistic sustainability. It is at this point that we may begin to know the limits of corporate sustainability, and it will likely require something beyond voluntary sustainability disclosure to make progress in this scenario.

Future Research

This research yields three primary opportunities for future research. First, as a direct result of this chapter, the sample, U.S.-based companies, should be expanded to include other global reporters who have reported multiple times. Though the data challenges, particularly inconsistencies in measurement, are sure to grow more complex, the extra data points from an additional 500 or 1,000 reports would strengthen the results outlined above, or may serve to highlight important regional differences. Primarily, additional data could possibly illustrate broader trends.

Next, future endeavors could expand the work from environmental sustainability measures to include GRI measures of social sustainability and long-term financial sustainability. Though the judgments used for coding may be more theoretically complex, the potential to show trends beyond the "low-hanging fruit" of commonly reported environmental issues could provide for a rich dialogue.

Finally, future studies could create efficiency or normalization corporate sustainability measures (perhaps ES or NS) to compare with GS to begin to understand just what level of efficiency companies are able to achieve, and whether those efficiencies have a meaningful impact on GS. At some point, gross emissions must be reduced in order to avoid catastrophic climate and social shifts.

Appendix 1. List of Variables, Units, and Judgments

Variable Name	Variable Description	Units	Judgments
EN1	Materials used by weight or volume	Metric tons	1 (improvement) = Decrease
EN1a	Natural gas used *as a material* (not as fuel source)	Cubic meters	1 = Decrease
EN1b	Plastic resins	Metric tons	1 = Decrease
EN1c	Corrugated	Metric tons	1 = Decrease
EN1d	Sodium chloride	Metric tons	1 = Decrease
EN1e	Dextrose	Metric tons	1 = Decrease
EN1f	Tobacco	Metric tons	1 = Decrease
EN1g	Wrapping and packaging materials	Metric tons	1 = Decrease
EN1h	Cigarette paper	Metric tons	1 = Decrease
EN1i	Coal as a material	Metric tons	1 = Decrease
EN1j	Oil as a material	Cubic meters	1 = Decrease

Variable Name	Variable Description	Units	Judgments
EN1k	Paper	Metric tons	1 = Decrease
EN1l	Wood	Metric tons	1 = Decrease
EN1m	Nonferrous metals (e.g., aluminum, copper)	Metric tons	1 = Decrease
EN1n	Plastics	Metric tons	1 = Decrease
EN1o	Glass	Metric tons	1 = Decrease
EN1p	Ferrous metals	Metric tons	1 = Decrease
EN1q	Adhesives, coatings, solvents, paints	Metric tons	1 = Decrease
EN1r	Resins (liquid/volume)	Cubic meters	1 = Decrease
EN1s	Wood (reported as volume)	Cubic meters	1 = Decrease
EN2	Percentage of materials used that are recycled	Percent	1 = Increase
EN2a	Paper	Percent	1 = Increase
EN2b	Manila and nontraditional paper	Percent	1 = Increase
EN2c	Packaging	Percent	1 = Increase
EN2d	Cups	Percent	1 = Increase
EN2e	Polyester	Percent	1 = Increase
EN3	Direct energy consumption	Gigajoules	1 = Decrease
EN3a	Energy consumption from oil (energy units)	Gigajoules	1 = Decrease
EN3b	Energy consumption from natural gas (energy units)	Gigajoules	1 = Decrease
EN3c	Energy consumption from coal	Gigajoules	1 = Decrease
EN3d	Energy consumption from hydro	Gigajoules	1 = Increase
EN3e	Energy consumption from grid	Gigajoules	1 = Decrease
EN3f	Energy consumption from fuel (Fairmount—Fuel #400) (Energy units)	Gigajoules	1 = Decrease
EN3g	Energy consumption "electricity"	Gigajoules	1 = Decrease
EN3h	Jet fuel (energy units)	Gigajoules	1 = Decrease
EN3i	Biogas	Gigajoules	1 = Increase

Variable Name	Variable Description	Units	Judgments
EN3j	Propane (energy units)	Gigajoules	1 = Decrease
EN3k	Wood (scrap)	Gigajoules	1 = Increase
EN3l	Diesel oil	Gigajoules	1 = Decrease
EN3m	LPG (liquefied petroleum gas)	Gigajoules	1 = Decrease
EN3n	District heating (steam & chilled)	Gigajoules	1 = Decrease
EN3o	Energy consumption from "green"/renewable electricity	Gigajoules	1 = Increase
EN3p	"Other" energy consumption (reported as "other")	Gigajoules	1 = Decrease
EN3q	Biodiesel (volume)	Cubic meters	1 = Increase
EN3r	Gasoline	Gigajoules	1 = Decrease
EN3t	Nuclear	Gigajoules	1 = Decrease
EN3u	"Total" energy	Gigajoules	1 = Decrease
EN3v	Biofuels	Gigajoules	1 = Increase
EN3w	Ethanol	Gigajoules	1 = Increase
EN3x	Hydrogen	Gigajoules	1 = Increase
EN3y	Energy from "Fuel"	Gigajoules	1 = Decrease
EN3a1	Energy consumption from oil (volume)	Cubic meters	1 = Decrease
EN3b1	Energy consumption from natural gas (volume)	Cubic meters	1 = Decrease
EN3f1	Energy consumption from fuel (Fairmount—Fuel #400) (Volume)	Cubic meters	1 = Decrease
EN3h1	Jet fuel (volume)	Cubic meters	1 = Decrease
EN3j1	Propane (volume)	Cubic meters	1 = Decrease
EN3j2	Propane (weight of material)	Metric tons	1 = Decrease
EN3k1	Wood (scrap) (weight of material)	Metric tons	1 = increase
EN3l1	Diesel oil (volume)	Cubic meters	1 = Decrease
EN3r1	Gasoline (volume)	Cubic meters	1 = Decrease
EN4	Indirect energy consumption	Gigajoules	1 = Decrease
EN8	Withdrawal (as original indicator notes)	Cubic meters	1 = Decrease
EN8a	Water "consumed"	Cubic meters	1 = Decrease

Variable Name	Variable Description	Units	Judgments
EN8b	Water taken from stressed areas	Cubic meters	1 = Decrease
EN8c	Surface water	Cubic meters	1 = Decrease
EN8d	Well water / groundwater	Cubic meters	1 = Decrease
EN8e	Municipal water	Cubic meters	1 = Decrease
EN8f	Ocean water	Cubic meters	1 = Decrease
EN8g	Withdrawal (as original indicator notes—measured in weight)	Metric tons	1 = Decrease
EN11	Location & size of land (original indicator)	1 or 0	1 = Increase
EN11a	Total acreage	Square kilometers	1 = Increase
EN12	1 = Yes, 0 = No	1 or 0	1 = Increase
EN12a	Undisturbed	Square kilometers	1 = Increase
EN12b	Disturbed by company	Square kilometers	1 = Decrease
EN12c	Permanently restored / restored	Square kilometers	1 = Increase
EN12d	Set aside / protected	Square kilometers	1 = Increase
EN16	Direct carbon emissions by weight	Metric tons CO2 equivalent (e)	1 = Decrease
EN16a1	Travel	Metric tons CO2e	1 = Decrease
EN16a2	Purchased electricity	Metric tons CO2e	1 = Decrease
EN16a3	Auto / Fleet	Metric tons CO2e	1 = Decrease
EN16a4	Air travel	Metric tons CO2e	1 = Decrease
EN16a5	Freight	Metric tons CO2e	1 = Decrease
EN16a6	Purchased heating oil	Metric tons CO2e	1 = Decrease
EN16a7	Commuting	Metric tons CO2e	1 = Decrease
EN16b	Perfluorocarbon (PFC) emissions (direct)	Metric tons	1 = Decrease
EN17	Indirect (scope 3) emissions	Metric tons CO2e	1 = Decrease
EN19	Emissions of ozone-depleting substances by weight	Metric tons / CFC-11e	1 = Decrease
EN20	NOX	Metric tons	1 = Decrease
EN20a	SOX	Metric tons	1 = Decrease
EN20b	VOC (included as emissions, not greenhouse gas (GHG) or ozone-depleting)	Metric tons	1 = Decrease
EN20c	Particulates	Metric tons	1 = Decrease

Variable Name	Variable Description	Units	Judgments
EN20d	Mercury	Metric tons	1 = Decrease
EN20e	Carbon monoxide (CO)	Metric tons	1 = Decrease
EN20f	Superfund Amendments and Reauthorization Act (SARA) Air (formerly Comprehensive Environmental Response, Compensation, and Liability Act (CERCLA)[a]	Metric tons	1 = Decrease
EN20g	"Total"—generic	Metric tons	1 = Decrease
EN20h	Ammonia	Metric tons	1 = Decrease
EN20i	Hydrochloric acid	Metric tons	1 = Decrease
EN20j	N-methyl pyrrolidone	Metric tons	1 = Decrease
EN20k	Ethylene glycol	Metric tons	1 = Decrease
EN20l	Xylene	Metric tons	1 = Decrease
EN20m	Other	Metric tons	1 = Decrease
EN20n	HAP (hazardous air pollutants)	Metric tons	1 = Decrease
EN20o	Arsenic	Metric tons	1 = Decrease
EN20p	Lead	Metric tons	1 = Decrease
EN20q	Selenium	Metric tons	1 = Decrease
EN20r	Formaldehyde	Metric tons	1 = Decrease
EN20s	Hydrogen fluoride	Metric tons	1 = Decrease
EN20t	Phenol	Metric tons	1 = Decrease
EN20u	Styrene	Metric tons	1 = Decrease
EN20v	Sulfur hexafluoride (SF6)	Metric tons	1 = Decrease
EN20w	Methane	Metric tons	1 = Decrease
EN20x	Nitrogen	Metric tons	1 = Decrease
EN21	Water discharge—impaired (volume)	Cubic meters	1 = Decrease
EN21a	Water discharge—nonimpaired	Cubic meters	1 = Decrease
EN21b	SARA Water	Metric tons	1 = Decrease
EN21c	Biochemical oxygen demand	Metric tons	1 = Decrease
EN21d	Chemical oxygen demand	Metric tons	1 = Decrease

Variable Name	Variable Description	Units	Judgments
EN21e	Total suspended solids	Metric tons	1 = Decrease
EN21f	Water discharge (total)	Cubic meters	1 = Decrease
EN21g	Nitrates	Metric tons	1 = Decrease
EN21h	Phosphorous	Metric tons	1 = Decrease
EN21i	Hydrocarbons	Metric tons	1 = Decrease
EN21j	To surface water	Cubic meters	1 = Decrease
EN21k	To groundwater	Cubic meters	1 = Decrease
EN21L	Total dissolved solids	Cubic meters	1 = Decrease
EN21m	Coliform	Cubic meters	1 = Decrease
EN21n	Metals	Metric tons	1 = Decrease
EN21o	Water discharge—measured in weight (21)	Metric tons	1 = Decrease
EN21p	Biochemical oxygen demand (BOD)—measured in volume (21c)	Cubic meters	1 = Decrease
EN21q	Total suspended solids—measured in volume (21e)	Cubic meters	1 = Decrease
EN21r	Water discharge (total)—in weight (21f)	Metric tons	1 = Decrease
EN22	Total waste	Metric tons	1 = Decrease
EN22a	Waste-to-energy	Metric tons	1 = Increase
EN22b	Recycle/recovery/reuse	Metric tons	1 = Increase
EN22c	Treatment (when given together, divided in half)	Metric tons	1 = Decrease
EN22d	Incineration	Metric tons	1 = Decrease
EN22e	Landfilled	Metric tons	1 = Decrease
EN22f	Hazardous waste	Metric tons	1 = Decrease
EN22g	Nonhazardous waste	Metric tons	1 = Decrease
EN22h	Hazardous waste disposed	Metric tons	1 = Decrease
EN22i	Hazardous waste recycled	Metric tons	1 = Increase
EN22j	Paper recycled	Metric tons	1 = Increase
EN22k	Metal recycled	Metric tons	1 = Increase
EN22l	Oil recycled	Cubic meters	1 = Increase
EN22m	Total chemical waste	Metric tons	1 = Decrease
EN22n	Chemical waste treated	Metric tons	1 = Decrease

Variable Name	Variable Description	Units	Judgments
EN22o	Chemical waste incinerated	Metric tons	1 = Decrease
EN22p	Chemical waste landfilled	Metric tons	1 = Decrease
EN22q	Chemical waste recycled	Metric tons	1 = Increase
EN22r	Total solid waste	Metric tons	1 = Decrease
EN22s	Solid waste incinerated	Metric tons	1 = Decrease
EN22t	Solid waste landfilled	Metric tons	1 = Decrease
EN22u	Solid waste recycled	Metric tons	1 = Increase
EN22v	Hazardous waste-to-energy	Metric tons	1 = Increase
EN22w	Hazardous waste incinerated	Metric tons	1 = Decrease
EN22x	Aqueous treatment	Metric tons	1 = Decrease
EN22y	Hazardous aqueous treatment	Metric tons	1 = Decrease
EN22z	Computer/e-waste recycling	Metric tons	1 = Increase
EN22aa	Nuclear waste	Cubic meters	1 = Decrease
EN22bb	Hazardous waste treated	Metric tons	1 = Decrease
EN22cc	Hazardous waste stored on site	Metric tons	1 = Decrease
EN22dd	Ash produced	Metric tons	1 = Decrease
EN22ee	Ash landfilled	Metric tons	1 = Decrease
EN22ff	Composted	Metric tons	1 = Increase
EN22gg	Ash reused	Metric tons	1 = Increase
EN22aa1	Nuclear waste—weight	Metric tons	1 = Decrease
EN23	Number of spills	Number	1 = Decrease
EN23a	Number of spills—petroleum	Number	1 = Decrease
EN23b	Volume of spills—petroleum	Cubic meters	1 = Decrease
EN23c	Volume of spills (total, not differentiated)	Cubic meters	1 = Decrease
EN23d	Maritime oil spills (number)	Number	1 = Decrease
EN23e	Number of chemical spills	Number	1 = Decrease
EN23f	Volume of chemical spills	Cubic meters	1 = Decrease

Variable Name	Variable Description	Units	Judgments
EN23g	Number of "other" spills	Number	1 = Decrease
EN23h	Volume of "other" spills	Cubic meters	1 = Decrease
EN26	1 = Yes, 0 = No	1 or 0	1 = Increase
EN27	1 = Yes, 0 = No	1 or 0	1 = Increase
EN27a	Batteries	Percent	1 = Increase
EN27b	Misc %	Percent	1 = Increase
EN28	Monetary value of significant fines	US Dollars	1 = Decrease
EN28a	Number of nonmonetary sanctions for noncompliance with environmental laws and regulations	Number	1 = Decrease

ᵃ http://www.epa.gov/superfund/policy/sara.htm.

Appendix 2. Coding Sheet

CODE SHEET: G3 GUIDELINES, "CORE" INDICATORS

Environment Performance Indicators

Aspect: Materials

EN1—Materials used by weight or volume
EN2—Percentage of materials used that are recycled input materials

Aspect: Energy

EN3: Direct energy consumption by primary energy source
EN4: Indirect energy consumption by primary source

Aspect: Water

EN8: Total water withdrawal by source

Aspect: Biodiversity

EN11: Location and size of land owned, leased, managed in, or adjacent to protected areas of high biodiversity value outside protected areas
EN12: Description of significant impacts of activities, products, and services on biodiversity in protected areas and areas of high biodiversity value outside protected areas

Aspect: Emissions, Effluents, and Waste

EN16: Total direct and indirect greenhouse gas emissions by weight
EN17: Other relevant indirect greenhouse gas emissions by weight
EN19: Emissions of ozone-depleting substances by weight
EN20: NOx, SO$_2$ and other significant air emissions by type and weight
EN21: Total water discharge by quality and destination
EN22: Total weight of waste by type and disposal method
EN23: Total number and volume of significant spills

Aspect: Products and Services

EN26: Initiatives to mitigate environmental impacts of products and services, and extent of impact mitigation
EN27: Percentage of products sold and their packaging materials that are reclaimed by category

Aspect: Compliance

EN28: Monetary value of significant fines and total number of nonmonetary sanctions for non-compliance with environmental laws and regulations

NOTES

1. If the indicator was normalized based on "total net sales," for example, and that exact number was not available in the financial data (and called the same thing), the indicator was excluded from the database. This standard was created to enhance replicability.
2. Please see appendix 1 for a list of improvement/decline judgments for each of the 181 variations.

REFERENCES

Anheuser-Busch. 2002. *Environmental, Health & Safety Report.* http://www.corporateregister.com/.
Association for the Advancement of Sustainability in Higher Education (AASHE). N.d. *The STARS Program: AASHE's Sustainability Tracking, Assessment & Rating System.* www.aashe.org/files/documents/STARS/stars_overview.ppt.
Brammer, S., and A. Millington. 2008. "Does It Pay to be Different? An Analysis of the Relationship between Corporate Social and Financial Performance." *Strategic Management Journal* 29:1325–43.
Brekke, K. A. 1997. *Economic Growth and the Environment: On the Measurement of Income and Welfare.* Brookfield, VT: Edward Elgar.
Callan, S. J., and J. M. Thomas. 2009. "Corporate Financial Performance and Corporate Social Performance: An Update and Reinvestigation." *Corporate Social Responsibility and Environmental Management* 16(2): 61–78.

Cerin, P. 2002. "Communication in Corporate Environmental Reports." *Corporate Social Responsibility and Environmental Management* 9:46–66.

Chevron. 2007. *2007 Corporate Responsibility Report.* http://www.chevron.com/news/publications/#b3.

Coase, R. H. 1960. "The Problem of Social Cost." *Journal of Law and Economics* 3:1–44.

Corporate Register. 2011. *Categories & Awards Help.* http://www.corporateregister.com/crra/help/crrahelp.html.

Corporate Register. 2012. *About Corporate Register.com.* http://www.corporateregister.com/about.html.

Dunphy, D., A. Griffiths, and S. Benn. 2002. *Organizational Change for Corporate Sustainability.* London: Routledge.

Elkington, J. 1999. *Cannibals with Forks: Triple Bottom Line of 21st Century Business.* Gabriola Island, BC: New Society Publishers.

Freeman, R. E. 1984. *Strategic Management: A Stakeholder Approach.* Boston: Pitman Publishing.

Freeport-McMoRan Copper & Gold. 2008. *Working Toward Sustainable Development Report.* http://www.fcx.com/envir/sus_reports.htm.

Godfrey, P. C., C. B. Merrill, and J. M. Hansen. 2009. "The Relationship between Corporate Social Responsibility and Shareholder Value: An Empirical Test of the Risk Management Hypothesis." *Strategic Management Journal* 30:425–45.

GRI. 2007. *What Is GRI?* http://www.globalreporting.org/AboutGRI/WhatIsGRI/.

GRI. 2008. *Sustainability Reporting Guidelines.* Version 3.0. .

GRI. 2009. *History.* http://www.globalreporting.org/AboutGRI/WhatIsGRI/History/OurHistory.htm.

GRI. 2010. GRI announces its 2015 and 2020 goals and launches G3.1 public comment at first day of Amsterdam Conference. Press release, May 26, 2010. http://www.amsterdamgriconference.org/index.php?id=39&item=33.

GRI. 2011. GRI Reports List. http://www.globalreporting.org/ReportServices/GRIReportsList/reportslist.htm.

Hudley, C., and B. Wells. 2011. "The Case for Translational Research in Education." Commissioned essay for the American Educational Research Association. http://www.aera.net/uploadedFiles/Meetings_and_Events/2012_Annual_Meeting/CynthiaHudley_AERA%20essay%20June%201_11.pdf.

Kolk, A. 2004. "A Decade of Sustainability Reporting: Developments and Significance." *International Journal of Environment and Sustainable Development* 3(1): 51–64.

KPMG International. 2008. *KPMG International Survey of Corporate Responsibility Reporting 2008.*October. http://www.kpmg.com/Global/en/IssuesAndInsights/ArticlesPublications/Pages/Sustainability-corporate-responsibility-reporting-2008.aspx.

Lamberton, G. 2005. "Sustainability Accounting: A Brief History and Conceptual Framework." *Accounting Forum* 29:7–25.

Lawn, P. A. 2006. "Sustainable Development: Concept and Indicators." In *Sustainable Development Indicators in Ecological Economics,*ed. Philip Lawn, pp. 13–51. Northampton, MA: Edward Elgar.

Lehmann, E. 2009. "SEC Turnaround Sparks Sudden Look at Climate Disclosure." *New York Times,* July 13.

London Benchmarking Group (LBG). 2008. *Improving the Measurement and Management of Community Involvement.* http://www.lbg-online.net/lbg.

Marshall, R. S., and D. Brown. 2003. "Corporate Environmental Reporting: What's in a Metric?" *Business Strategy and the Environment* 12:87–106.

Newmont Mining. 2007. *Beyond the Mine: The Journey towards Sustainability*. http://www.newmont.com/sustainability.

Nichols, S., and D. Berliner. 2007. *Collateral Damage: How High-Stakes Testing Corrupts America's Schools*. Cambridge: Harvard University Press.

Norman, W., and C. MacDonald. 2004. "Getting to the Bottom of 'Triple Bottom Line.'" *Business Ethics Quarterly* 14(2): 243–62.

O'Donovan, G. 2002. "Environmental Disclosures in the Annual Report: Extending the Applicability and Predictive Power of Legitimacy Theory." *Accounting, Auditing & Accountability Journal* 15(3): 344–71.

Perrini, F., and A. Tencati. 2006. "Sustainability and Stakeholder Management: The Need for New Corporate Performance Evaluation and Reporting Systems." *Business Strategy and the Environment* 15:296–308.

Pigou, A. C. 1920. *The Economics of Welfare*. London: Macmillan.

Riffe, D., S. Lacy, and F. G. Fico. 2005. *Analyzing Media Messages: Using Quantitative Content Analysis in Research*. Mahwah, NJ: Lawrence Erlbaum Associates.

Salzmann, O., A. Ionescu-Somers, and U. Steger. 2005. "The Business Case for Corporate Sustainability: Literature Review and Research Options." *European Management Journal* 23(1): 27–36.

Slater, A., and S. Gilbert. 2004. "The Evolution of Business Reporting: Make Room for Sustainability Disclosure." *Environmental Quality Management*, Autumn, 41–48.

Social Funds. 2012. *Sustainability Report Center*. http://www.socialfunds.com/report/.

Strategic Sustainability Consulting. 2009. *Sustainable Growth. 2009 Sustainability Report*. http://www.sustainabilityconsulting.com/sustainability-report/.

Thomas, R. M. 2005. *High-Stakes Testing: Coping with Collateral Damage*. Mahwah, NJ: Erlbaum.

Thompson, P. B. 2010. *The Agrarian Vision: Sustainability and Environmental Ethics*. Lexington: University Press of Kentucky.

U.S. Securities and Exchange Commission (SEC). 2009. Investor Advisory Committee, Briefing Paper No. 1, July 27. www.sec.gov/spotlight/invadvcomm/iacmeeting072709-briefingpaper.pdf.

Evolutions in Methods and Technology for Research in Pro-environmental Behavior

DOUGLAS L. BESSETTE AND ROBERT B. RICHARDSON

MOTIVATING PRO-ENVIRONMENTAL BEHAVIOR IS FUNDAMENTAL TO THE TRANSITION to a green economy and demands an understanding of the determinants of human behavior generally. Most examinations of the factors that influence behavior rely upon stated-preference surveys, and survey research has long been associated with several types of error or bias, including reactivity, satisficing, recall error, and social desirability bias. Similarly, revealed-preference methods also have shortcomings that limit their usefulness in understanding the determinants of behavior. The experience sampling method has been used to collect information about the context and content of the daily life of individuals, and the method has potential to contribute to the analysis and understanding of the determinants of pro-environmental behaviors. We examined the evolution in research on pro-environmental behavior and explored the potential of the experience sampling method to be deployed using mobile-phone technology to analyze the determinants of behavior. The objective was to develop and test a robust, rapidly deployable, and near real-time instrument for examining individuals' attitudes, values, well-being, and private-sphere pro-environmental behaviors. By combining questions about daily experiences with multimedia and direct behavioral monitoring, we concluded that the use of smart phones in experience sampling can be effective in the analysis of behavior and its determinants.

ECOLOGICAL ECONOMICS AND PRO-ENVIRONMENTAL BEHAVIOR RESEARCH

Transitioning to a green economy will require behavioral changes at multiple levels and scales. It will require individuals, communities, firms, and institutions to investigate their private- and public-sphere behaviors at a personal, corporate, and geopolitical level. Pro-environmental behaviors (PEB), or actions that aim to reduce the use of materials and energy from the environment and minimize effects to the structure of and dynamics of ecosystems (Stern, 2000), must increase as a share of all behaviors if achieving sustainability is a true objective. How to achieve such an increase remains unclear, however, primarily because altering behavior is so difficult. Even incentives for prosocial behavior financially often fail to achieve their objectives (e.g., Charness and Gneezy, 2009; Gneezy and Rustichini, 2000). Nevertheless, it is the responsibility of ecological economists, if for lack of a better contestant, to advance an understanding of the determinants of PEBs and incorporate those findings into the literature related to business, regulatory and even household, or private-sphere, affairs. Understanding the motivations to engage in PEBs will be critical in the development of policies or incentives necessary to promote PEBs, such as reuse, recycling, using public transit, installing energy-efficient appliances, and conserving energy.

Motivating PEBs demands an understanding of the determinants of human behaviors. For over a century, behavioral scientists, social psychologists, behavioral economists, and sociologists have developed a number of theories to explain the factors, conditions, and processes that shape human behavior. Fishbein and Ajzen (1980) have studied the influences of attitudes and intentions. Schwartz (1973) argues behavior is influenced by prosocial personal norms. Kasser (2010) emphasizes the role of individual values. Guagnano, Stern, and Dietz (1995) have investigated the power of a combination of values, beliefs, and norms, and more recently, Stern (2000) has suggested that the determinants of behavior may include socioeconomic constraints that are wholly external to the individual. Neoclassical economic theory assumes that individual decisions are based on a specific definition of rational self-interest, while Simon (1952) argues that individuals "satisfice," or more simply do the best they can under the circumstances. Until recently, much of this behavioral research has existed outside the realm of or only contributed diminutively to socio-environmental study. As a result, a multitude of perspectives from various disciplines have shaped policies that aim to influence behavior, resulting in an array of financial and nonfinancial incentives, rewards, regulations, and penalties.

Yet almost all of these perspectives rely on a single method to investigate behavioral determinants: the single-administration paper, telephone, or computer survey. Despite the large number and wide variety of theories, the manner of investigating behavioral determinants through individual and household surveys has been particularly consistent over the years. The use of surveys in the analysis of behavior involves the collection of data about particular determinants that are hypothesized to influence behavior, such as stated beliefs, intentions, values, or knowledge, and that determinant is then tested as a predictor of a particular behavior or group of behaviors using statistical analysis. Variation in the specifics of each determinant obviously makes for unique approaches within single theoretical frameworks. In the end, competing theories are compared and judged by the significance of determinants' respective ability to predict and explain behaviors. Determinants that are poor predictors are rejected and determinants that consistently predict significant associations with certain behaviors receive the lion's share of attention and research.

Regrettably the line between winners and losers, or the good predictors and bad predictors, is difficult to discern. And this lack of clarity often promotes adjustments that are mostly theoretical. For example, if general attitudes fail to predict behavior, then perhaps specific attitudes predict behaviors more accurately. If attitudes and intentions fail to predict behavior, then perhaps how individuals perceive their own behavioral control needs to be considered (Ajzen, 1991). If prosocial norms fail to predict behavior, perhaps values and beliefs need to be considered in the model. Perhaps most radically, if determinants wholly internal to the individual show little consistency in predicting behavior, perhaps it is an individual's external context and the socioeconomic constraints he or she faces that are most important.

These theoretical adjustments then may often come as the result of two considerations. Either the determinants selected are not the actual—or only—determinants of behavior, or the determinants selected, or their proxies, have been incorrectly measured or described. Both of these considerations typically encourage the researcher to tweak or reject only the theory and then try again in similar experiments. A more systemic source of error, wholly unspecific to a particular theoretical framework, may be the result of stated-preference methods such as surveys themselves and in certain cases may magnify or ameliorate specific behavioral determinants.

Before discussing the errors themselves, it is first necessary to acknowledge that the current critique of sample surveys is only possible, and warranted, because of recent developments both in methods and technology. Survey research has long been associated with several types of error or bias, including reactivity, satisficing, recall error, and socially desirability bias (Bailey, 2007; Suchman, 1962). Significant effort has been expended in mitigating each type of bias, some to a point of irrelevance. Yet none can be entirely eliminated, and as a result, reliance on a single method may limit the potential of behavioral science to understand motivations for behavioral change. This is of particular importance as regards social-psychological investigations in which the reliance on one method allows for no way to distinguish trait variance from method variance (Campbell and Fiske, 1959).

Economists would argue that revealed-preference models and methods avoid many of the shortcomings that are associated with stated-preference approaches (Carson et al., 1996). Yet these models and methods are usually confined to the study of consumption and market behaviors, and thus they are limited with respect to investigating other private-sphere behaviors, including many PEBs. Similar to stated-preference approaches, such revealed-preference methods also have shortcomings that limit their usefulness in understanding the determinants of behavior.

We examine the evolution in research on pro-environmental behavior and explore the potential of the experience sampling method to be deployed using mobile-phone technology to analyze the determinants of behavior.

METHODS AND TECHNOLOGY: EVOLUTIONS IN PRO-ENVIRONMENTAL BEHAVIOR RESEARCH

Advances in research methods and their applications are related in part to the limitations of specific theories as well as to evolutions in technology. Within the behavioral sciences, the application of methods and technologies in research is shaped by the concepts, theories, and language of academic disciplines. Social psychologists who adopt rational choice theories tend to focus on the internal processes of the individual and, given their orientation, frequently apply single-administration surveys that examine attitudes and values in their research. Economists and sociologists often focus on the external context, or the structural, institutional, and socioeconomic constraints each individual faces, and revealed-preference models or market analysis are more common in their research methods. The recent rise in application of interdisciplinary models and research has led to an integration of methods. Behavioral economists and neuroeconomists who study brain imagery during decision making integrate research approaches from both psychology and economics (Shogren and Taylor, 2008; Weber et al., 2007). Rational-choice theorists offer reinterpretations of earlier models that take into account both internal and external constraints (Ajzen, 1991).

This recent dedication to examining both individuals' context and constraints in socioenvironmental research is for the most part an attempt to close the value-action gap, or the empirical reality that attitudes and beliefs fail to predict behavior (Blake, 1999). Such attempts more than ever require the melding of methods and methodologies. No longer can researchers simply examine market behaviors or survey data regarding beliefs or values about climate change or geo-engineering (e.g., Mercer et al., 2011). In order to successfully close the value-action gap, new methods and new technologies must be integrated. The experience sampling method (ESM), the subject of this chapter, has been used primarily for specific time-of-day-sensitive investigations and has required substantial financial, human, and capital resources. However, ESM can now be applied rather effortlessly in a variety of research contexts because of advances in mobile-phone technology. Incorporating ESM and smart phones allows for real-time analysis of individual behaviors and flexible investigations into the determinants of those behaviors and also reduces many of the biases and problems with validity commonly associated with other methods of social research.

ESM developed out of a "large body of research demonstrating the inability of people to provide accurate retrospective information on their daily behavior and experience" (Csikszentmihalyi and Larson, 1987, p. 526). Its primary focus was to collect "information about both the context and content of the daily life of individuals . . . to capture daily life as it is directly perceived from one moment to the next, affording an opportunity to examine fluctuations in the stream of consciousness and the links between the external context and the contents of the mind" (Hektner, Schmidt, and Csikszentmihalyi, 2007, p. 6). While ESM's more general purpose is to study subjective experience by capturing respondents in various life situations and recording their psychological reactions (Csikszentmihalyi and Larson, 1987), it provides a unique approach for examining the determinants of human behavior.

ESM has been used to identify regularities in the stream of consciousness and then relate these regularities to characteristics of the person (e.g., age, aptitude, physiological arousal, well-being), of the situation (e.g., challenges of a job, being a university student), or of the interaction between the person and the situation (e.g., the dynamics of one's personal relationships). ESM can also be used to triangulate behaviors and their determinants. Hektner, Schmidt, and Csikszentmihalyi (2007, p. 125) argue that ESM research centers on "the contexts of daily life, the experiential content of life, and the links between context and content"; we argue that it is this very focus on context and content that makes ESM a potentially -valuable research method for examining PEBs.

Scientists engaging in laboratory studies that ask individuals to describe feelings and behavior often receive responses that are not typical of experience encountered in real-life situations. In quality-of-life studies, complex phenomena that are often temporally or spatially contingent are often only presented as global assessments. When data are gathered in retrospect and outside the context of the life situation, distortions and rationalizations may become significant. Studies of time budgeting often present unclear links between behavior and psychological states (Csikszentmihalyi and Larson, 1987).

In attempting to address these shortcomings, Scollon, Kim-Prieto, and Diener (2003) argue that in a couple of decades of development, five particular strengths of ESM have emerged. First, ESM allows researchers to better understand the contingencies of behavior. Second, ESM removes the respondent from the lab and places her back into real-life situations. Third,

ESM allows for the investigation of "within-person processes" (Scollon, Kim-Prieto, and Diener, p. 8). Fourth, ESM avoids memory and recall bias and the use of heuristics. Finally, ESM alleviates the need for multiple methods to study psychological phenomena. While this fifth and final characteristic of ESM might be true for some, we believe ESM should still be used in tandem with more common methods of investigation.

Perhaps surprisingly, beepers were the technology that allowed for the initial ESM investigations. Beepers allowed researchers to alert respondents and elicit self-report data at randomized points in time (Csikszentmihalyi and Larson, 1987). Respondents would receive a signal and then enter their answer to the proposed question in a journal or research booklet. As opposed to the diary method, which was in wide use before the initial ESM studies and provided "dry and generalized" results "without much discrimination" and "according to predictable scripts," ESM typically generated rich and unique data (Hektner, Schmidt, and Csikszentmihalyi, 2007, p. 34). Beepers were eventually replaced by mobile telephones, but only as signaling devices, and personal digital assistants (or PDAs such as Palm Pilots) often only as recording devices. ESM thus has for most of its history required substantial resources, including time, money, and human capital. As opposed to survey-based approaches, ESM studies require researchers to engage, sometimes continuously, with their respondents for days and weeks, if not months or years. This engagement is often in the form of signaling, which as stated above relies on an electronic instrument that emits stimulus signals according to a random schedule. Due to this high level of resources and commitment, it has been argued that ESM studies are not appropriate for all types of investigation. ESM is designed to capture individuals' representation of experience as it occurs, within the context of daily life, and thus is best suited to measure dimensions of experiences that are contingent on context, such as time, place, space, and activity (Hektner, Schmidt, and Csikszentmihalyi, 2007). Global and retrospective questions have not generally been considered useful or cost-effective.

Investigations of PEBs would certainly benefit from the snapshot-style approach that is commonly used in ESM studies. For example signaling a person on "garbage day" and asking her to report the quantity or type of refuse or recyclable materials she has produced would, because of recall error, generate more accurate data than asking her a week or month later to summarize her behavior. However, identifying the individual's values, beliefs, intentions, or attitudes often requires asking more global or retrospective questions. For example, asking an individual about his specific value orientation, such as his beliefs concerning the social redistribution of income, does not necessarily warrant questions designed for a specific time of day or week or context. This is not to say that there are not benefits from asking such a question in specific contexts. Certainly one can imagine two situations where the individual might answer that same question differently, and both situations might elicit different responses than those produced by his participation in a focus group or laboratory experiment. Yet what is lost in such a discussion is that new technologies, such as smart phones, are capable of reducing the cost of ESM studies to a point that makes such concerns unnecessary. ESM can be used to elicit and capture both snapshot and global phenomena.

Kahneman and Krueger (2006) and Kahneman and coauthors (2004) attempted to supplant ESM with an alternate version entitled the Day Reconstruction Method, or DRM. DRM relies on a combination of experience sampling and time diaries and was "designed specifically to facilitate accurate emotional recall" (Kahneman and Krueger, 2006, p. 10). Some have argued that DRM is preferred because it is less expensive to execute, it may be easier than ESM, and it provides similarly valid and accurate data. Hektner, Schmidt, and

Csikszentmihalyi (2007, p. 277), however, argue that DRM is subject to the same biases that more standard diary-reliant methods are, and that DRM very well "might provide information that distorts reality." Recent advances in smart phone technology have made DRM somewhat obsolete, as these phones dramatically reduce the cost of deploying ESM studies (e.g., Killingsworth and Gilbert, 2010).

Previous ESM studies required researchers to provide significant amounts of instruction to respondents regarding the signaling device and the ESM form, or the booklet in which the respondents were to record their answers. While respondents surely still require an introduction to the study, its intentions, and instructions on how to respond to signals, using mobile phones as both signaling and recording devices reduces the amount of instruction required by a considerable degree—presuming the respondent is already knowledgeable about using certain features of her phone. There are other advantages to reducing the necessary introduction and instruction, namely, reducing the impact of the study on the respondents' day-to-day activities, such as reducing reactance effects.

To this point, there have only been a few forays into using broadband mobile phones and ESM to study social-psychological phenomena, only one of which relied exclusively on ESM and the Apple iPhone. Killingsworth and Gilbert (2010) used ESM and the iPhone to study mind-wandering and its deleterious effects on individuals' happiness. Karapanos and coauthors (2009) used DRM to examine individuals' user-experiences with iPhones, but did not use iPhones as the survey instrument. Hicks and coauthors (2010) developed a Droid-powered personal data collection system called AndWellness. As of 2012, this system had yet to be deployed.

Most of the literature regarding the use of mobile phones in social-psychological research does not reside in social-psychological or methodological journals but instead resides in computer science, information systems, and consumer research journals. As a result the focus remains on the development of the mobile technology and the purported advantages such technology will afford social scientists. Little empirical evidence or supposition, however, exists regarding the second-order advantages, or the advantages to social-psychological and behavioral research that come about exclusively because of these technical advantages. Not only are costs reduced and sampling made easier, but the very phenomena being investigated are being investigated more clearly and accurately.

One of these advantages to incorporating broadband mobile technology into ESM studies is real-time data collection and analysis. Since ESM is necessarily longitudinal in format, instantaneous data collection and analysis allows for the creation of a flexible research instrument. Researchers cannot only monitor participants as if they were typing their answers into a computer in a laboratory, but they can also alter the composition of the survey instrument so as to personalize it to each respondent or time period. While computer programming allows for such real-time composition, because survey-based approaches typically endure for only a few minutes, adjustments generally cannot take into account contextual variables like time or social or cultural events, especially those that are unpredictable. Using mobile phones as both the signaling and recording device allows for such incorporation.

Using mobile technology to implement ESM studies increases the number and variety of arenas appropriate for experiential research. Such devices also allow for ESM and ESM-style approaches to move beyond personal experience and psychological and phenomenological investigation. ESM and mobile phones allow for investigations of both stated and revealed preferences and may provide greater detail and accuracy by accounting for the ecological context of both. Integrating both approaches to a research design is a way to avoid many of the shortcomings of either type of method. Adamowicz, Louviere, and Williams (1994) used revealed-preference methods in a study of visitation at recreation sites to observe respondents' market behavior, and then a stated-preference model to explain the choice of one alternative over the other as a function of the attributes of sites. Brownstone, Bunch, and Train (2000) examined both survey responses and revealed behavior in two waves, with the survey data preceding the market observations by fifteen months. Both waves of data were gathered via survey, either telephone or mail.

Certainly these joint-model studies provide data that offer advantages over studies that use singular approaches. Yet in doing joint-model studies, researchers face higher costs and higher resource requirements. Many of these types of studies are longitudinal or require the use of multiple samples. The validity concerns regarding the use of multiple samples are known and require considerable effort on the part of the researcher to mitigate. ESM when combined with broadband mobile technologies offers a low-cost alternative or at least can supplement many joint-model studies. No longer do all researchers need to rely on conducting separate investigations—admittedly many researchers still do and would not benefit from ESM-style studies. However, for many, ESM surveys allow for simultaneous investigations, both surveying to acquire stated preferences and monitoring market behavior to acquire revealed preferences.

Brown and Kasser (2005) have called for additional research into value orientations as determinants of pro-environmental attitudes and PEBs, particularly in ways that account for recall error and biases associated with socially desirability responding (SDR). The application of ESM and broadband mobile technology may be able to contribute to this call by reducing SDR through directly monitoring individual behaviors, as opposed to relying solely on self-reporting.

We tested this application of ESM and mobile technology, the Apple iPhone in particular, in a study of sophomore-level students at Michigan State University (MSU) during four one-week periods in January and February 2011. The study had three primary objectives. The first objective was to develop and test a robust, rapidly deployable, and near real-time instrument for measuring individuals' attitudes, values, well-being, and private-sphere PEBs. The second objective was to use the instrument in the examination and interpretation of the relationship between attitudes, values, well-being, and PEBs. The third objective was to attempt to reduce the errors and biases often found in previous socio-environmental studies, studies that identified either through explicit means or implicitly through their content their intended pro-environmental goal, vis-à-vis measures of pro-environmental attitudes and behaviors.

The burdens of ESM described above were lessened by the use of the respondent's own mobile phone as both the signaling and recording device. As opposed to carrying a journal, PDA, or beeper, the respondent needed only carry a mobile phone, a device she or he likely carries regularly. The study used short message service (SMS) messaging almost exclusively and psychometric Likert-scale questions as the primary mode of question and response. This allowed the participant to quickly engage and disengage with the instrument and the survey. This was an improvement upon other studies that have focused on the development of web-based applications that require respondents to log in or engage physically and cognitively with the survey instrument for greater periods of time (Hicks et al., 2010; Killingsworth and Gilbert, 2010; Uy et al., 2010). This integrated approach also encourages more accurate self-reporting of activities and behavior, phenomena that researchers consider to be time-sensitive measures, as well as more in-depth queries that use interactive multimedia like videos, web pages, audio broadcasts, news articles, and photographs, including media generated by the research subject.

VALUES AND SUBJECTIVE WELL-BEING AS DETERMINANTS OF PEBS

Schwartz (1992, 1994) identifies ten types of basic priorities people have across the world, including *self-enhancement* values (i.e., power and achievement) and *self-transcendent* values (i.e., benevolence and universalism). Other scholars associate several *extrinsic* or *materialistic* goals with Schwartz's (1994) self-enhancement values, including financial success, image, and status (Grouzet et al., 2005; Kasser and Ryan, 1996; Ryan et al., 1999; Schmuck, Kasser, and Ryan, 2000). They associate other types of *intrinsic* goals with Schwartz's (1994) self-transcendent values, including self-acceptance, affiliation, and community feeling.

Past research shows that self-enhancing and extrinsic values have been associated with attitudes and values that are inconsistent with environmental stewardship (Saunders and Munro, 2000; Good, 2007; Schwartz, 1992; Schultz et al., 2005) and behavior that is ecologically detrimental (Richins and Dawson, 1992; Brown and Kasser, 2005: Gatersleben et al., 2008; Kasser, 2005, 2011). On the other hand, self-transcendent and intrinsic values and goals have been associated with attitudes and values that *are* consistent with environmental stewardship (Schultz et al., 2005; Gatersleben et al., 2008; Kasser, 2005) and behavior that *is* ecologically sensitive or pro-environmental (Sheldon and McGregor, 2000; Brown and Kasser, 2005; Kasser, 2011). In addition, Ahuvia and Wong (2002), Banerjee and Dittmar (2008), and Kasser and coauthors (1995) argue that the two primary causes of high materialistic or extrinsic values are (1) social modeling, such as exposure to people or messages suggesting that "money, power, possessions, achievement, image and status are important aims to strive for in life" (Kasser, 2010, p. 92), and (2) insecurity, such as economic hardship, poor interpersonal relationships, hunger, personal self-doubt, or social exclusion. Thus, individuals exposed to a high degree of materialistic social modeling or insecurity are more likely to hold materialistic or extrinsic values than are those who are exposed to a lesser degree of the same. As such, those individuals are not likely to exhibit PEBs.

Regarding subjective well-being, research has shown (Kasser and Ryan, 1993, 1996; Sheldon and Kasser, 1998; Sheldon et al., 2004) that intrinsically oriented individuals report greater well-being than those who focus on extrinsic values. Brown and Kasser (2005) report positive correlations between subjective well-being and PEBs, ultimately concluding that "happy people live in more ecologically responsible ways because such individuals hold intrinsically oriented values" (p. 360). All of this research suggests one fairly straightforward supposition: individuals who hold intrinsically oriented values are more likely to lead happier lives and perform more PEBs than those individuals who hold extrinsically oriented values.

This study included questions that asked each participant about her values, subjective well-being, and pro-environmental behavior. In order to examine both values and well-being, questions were asked about the participant's level of satisfaction, both for the day and in general, and about the specific contributions to that level of satisfaction. For example, participants were asked about the effect that their personal relationships, personal finances, or health had on their level of satisfaction. Asking each individual about these effects was intended to examine whether or not each effect or value contributed to overall satisfaction. If, as Rokeach (1968) suggests, values are the psychological representations of what people believe is important in life, then those individuals who report no effect for a particular question can be thought not to hold or be pursuant of that particular value. As opposed to asking an individual "how much he or she values a particular [goal or value]," asking "what effect does [this value] have on your level of satisfaction" releases the individual from having to self-identify his or her motivations and instead should provide responses that more closely represent his or her real attachment to values.

Regarding PEB, the current study focused on the individual choices regarding diet, transportation, and housing, as these are typically identified as the most environmentally consequential human activities (Brown and Leon, 1999). Brown and Kasser (2005, p. 358) identify that "meat eaters who drive many miles per week and live in large houses have larger ecological footprints than do vegetarians who use public transportation and live in small homes." The study also focused on respondents' recycling behavior, as many previous studies have used recycling as their primary pro-environmental variable (e.g., Guagnano, Stern, and Dietz, 1995; Hopper, 1991; De Young, 1988–89; Corral-Verdugo, 1997). The study also inquired about the participants' technology choices, such as the age and type of their computers, televisions, gaming systems, and automobiles. These questions were intended to examine the frequency with which participants exchanged and upgraded technology.

The study also measured how often the individuals dined outside their homes and identified the foods and beverages individuals kept in their refrigerators through photographs. Photographs were also used to characterize participants' recycling behaviors. The study also asked about the individuals' transportation choices on multiple days throughout the week. These self-reports and photographs were thought to be more accurate than would be those reports gained through reflective single-administration surveys that suffer from recall error and biases, such as telescoping, part-whole effects, and satisficing. The use of ESM allowed for this type of longitudinal behavioral monitoring.

Participants were also asked to watch short videos on their devices and respond to three questions immediately afterward. Each video used a unique approach to inform its viewers about renewable energy, sustainability, and climate change. Videos were chosen based in part on their attempts to appeal to either a self-transcendent or self-enhancement value-orientation. Upon conclusion of each video, the participants were asked to measure the video's scientific content and expertise and were then asked about the accuracy of statements made during the video. The intent of these questions was to determine the effectiveness of each message, to examine the participants' reactions to each, and to gauge the level of trust the narrators were able to achieve. It was thought that individuals who showed self-transcendent value-orientations would react differently than those having self-enhancement value-orientations.

Individuals were then classified based on responses as either having a self-transcendent value-orientation or a materialistic value-orientation. Individuals were also classified as either engaging or not engaging in particular pro-environmental behaviors. Finally, respondents were asked Likert-scale questions about their subjective well-being.

Although survey-based research studies typically report only one response rate (i.e., the proportion of recruits for the study sample who agree to participate in the study), ESM trifurcates the response rate to include a volunteer rate, a signal-response rate, and an attrition rate. The proportion of recruits who agree to participate in an ESM-based research study is known as the volunteer rate. The signal-response rate then describes the proportion of signals for which responses are completed, and the attrition rate describes the proportion of participants who do not complete subsequent waves of data collection. Attrition rates only apply to those studies that are longitudinal (i.e., those that contain more than one data collection period per population).

For this study, 7,862 students were contacted by e-mail with a message explaining that researchers at MSU were looking for individuals to participate in an iPhone study. The primary tasks associated with participation were described in the e-mail as answering questions sent to them as text messages, taking photographs of various aspects of their behavior, and watching brief video clips. They were instructed that approximately five questions a day would be sent to them no earlier than 8:00 A.M. and no later than 9:00 P.M. for a period of seven days. Completion of a short paper survey at the conclusion of the survey was also required. Students were asked to respond to the e-mail if they were interested in learning more about participating in the study.

In total, 114 students were recruited and sent a letter of consent via e-mail, which contained more detailed instructions, the specific dates and times that their examination period would begin and end, and notice that each would receive a $20 cash payment as an incentive for participating. They were instructed that their receiving the incentive was not dependent upon their answering every question. Of the 114 students, $n = 71$ (62.3 percent) students agreed to participate. This study's volunteer rate was 0.89 percent, which was not unexpected based on the narrow technological requirements of the study and would likely have been much higher if the researchers were able to recruit all students with any type of broadband mobile phones with camera features, which are currently more common. Regardless of the low volunteer rate, samples of this size are not uncommon for ESM studies (e.g., Feldman Barrett, 2004) and studies with as few as five or ten participants can still provide rich data that can be used reliably in statistical analyses (Hektner, Schmidt, and Csikszentmihalyi, 2007).

Respondents received between 37 and 41 questions during the one-week periods, or an average of 5.57 questions per day, depending on which examination period they participated. In total 2,777 questions were sent to the participants, and 2,725 were answered, amounting to a signal-response rate of 98.1 percent. Only 52 questions were not answered, and of these, 23 (44.2 percent) were video responses and 9 (17.3 percent) were photograph responses, and those questions required the greatest effort on the part of the participants. Study sample and response rates are summarized in table 1.

This signal-response rate of 98.1 percent is much higher than those rates reported from previous ESM studies, providing immediate support for preliminary assumptions about the benefits of ESM studies using mobile-phone technology. Typical signal-response rates range from 70 to 80 percent (e.g., Csikszentmihalyi and Larson, 1987; Hormuth, 1986; Larson et al., 2002; Zuzanek, 1999; Mannell, Zuzanek, and Aronson, 2005) and rates among university

Table 1. STUDY SAMPLE AND RESPONSE RATES

Initial contacts	*Recruits*	*Volunteers*	*Volunteer rate*
2,762	114	71	62.3%
Questions	*Questions asked*	*Responses*	*Signal-response rate*
Text response	1,925	1,905	99.0%
Video response	639	616	96.4%
Photograph response	213	204	95.8%
Total	2,777	2,725	98.1%

students can range from 50 to 75 percent depending on both hardware and whether or not follow-up signals are used (Zuzanek, 1999; Feldman Barrett, 2004). Follow-up signals were used in this study.

None of the studies mentioned above used mobile phones as either signaling devices or as reporting devices. In addition, this study was the only one to ask respondents to take photographs or to watch and react to videos. While the latter is not likely to be incorporated quickly into more typical ESM studies, the former could be a valuable addition, helping researchers to gain insight into the ecological context of participants' responses or even their psychological states, possibly through providing photographs that represent one's mood. While the photograph response questions had the lowest signal-response rate (95.8 percent), it was still a much higher rate than those seen in previous studies.

In order to examine participants' self-reported well-being and PEB, participants were asked two types of questions regarding their subjective well-being (SWB). The first type of question asked them to report their general level of satisfaction with their lives. This question was asked twice, once on the first day of the research period and once on the last day. The other SWB questions asked respondents about their levels of satisfaction on particular days—these were randomly asked throughout the week and at different times of day. The participants' responses to these questions were then combined to form three variables: total SWB (TOTAL SWB), general SWB (GEN SWB), and snapshot SWB (SNAP SWB). TOTAL SWB was a weighted average of all level of satisfaction questions; GEN SWB was a weighted average of only the general level of satisfaction questions (asked at the beginning and end of each research period), and SNAP SWB was a weighted average of only the random daily level of satisfaction questions.

A respondent's pro-environmental behavior (PEB) was measured using two methods. The first asked the respondent to report on certain behaviors that he or she had performed during the day. These ranged from manner of primary transport (e.g., walking, bus, automobile, biking) to the length of time the individual spent using the computer, talking on the phone, or watching television, or the number of meals the individual ate at a restaurant or at home. The second method of inquiry required the individual to photograph his or her behavior. The respondent was asked to photograph her recycling and the inside of her refrigerator, as well as the type of television set and video-game system she owned. At no point was a participant asked if or why he did or did not engage in a particular behavior.

Chi-square tests were performed on each of the SWB variables and on the participants' recycling behavior (REC = 1 if participant recycles; 0 if not) and transportation behavior (TRANS = 1 if participant walks, bikes, or uses public transit; 0 if participant drives an automobile), as well as a weighted average of the two (PEB = 2 if participant recycles and does not drive; 1 if participant recycles and drives or does not recycle and walks, bikes, or uses public transit; 0 if participant does neither). Other behaviors either did not demonstrate sufficient variance or demonstrated variance that was dependent upon the specific day, date, or time the signal was received; for example, time spent online was much higher on weekdays than on weekend days, across all examination periods. As a result these behaviors were left out of the analysis. The results of analysis are shown below in table 2.

The results in table 2 show that there is no significantly positive or negative relationship between the respondents' self-reported SWB and their PEBs. There are many possible reasons no association was found, such as problems related to extrapolation, SDR, and recall error. Regardless of whether respondents are aware of the researchers' intentions, it is possible that individuals overreport PEB. Regarding recall errors, this study's investigation of PEBs took only a snapshot

Table 2. RESULTS OF ANALYSIS OF SUBJECTIVE WELL-BEING AND PRO-ENVIRONMENTAL BEHAVIOR

Variable 1	*Variable 2*	*df*	*N*	^{2} *critical value*	^{2} *statistic*	*Asymp. signif.*	*Pearson's R (correl.)*
TOTAL SWB	REC	23	56	35.2	23.2	0.45	–0.119
TOTAL SWB	TRANS	46	70	62.8	35.8	0.86	0.077
TOTAL SWB	PEB	92	70	115.4	81.3	0.78	–0.048
GEN SWB	PEB	36	70	51.0	47.4	0.10	–0.072
SNAP SWB	PEB	60	70	79.1	49.1	0.84	0.002

of the respondents' behavior. And thus it is difficult to generalize, even within the sample. Were the signals sent on different days or the examination period to take place in a different month, it is possible that the participants' reported PEBs would be different. Yet these contextual variables or external coordinates of experience are certainly important to recognize and raise questions regarding individuals' own reports of their generalized behavior. The fact that snapshots are so variable raises questions about the veracity of individuals' retrospective and generalized reports.

These variables are subject to a great deal of underlying constraints and effects, particularly in a sample of university sophomores, some living in campus residence halls or with parents. Such constraints may limit individual choice regarding recycling, transportation, and other PEBs. These concerns certainly need to be considered and may imply only that a much weaker relationship than hypothesized exists within this sample regarding SWB and PEB. Alternatively, it may be that resources, situations, and constraints external to the individual dominate variables like SWB elsewhere as well, making such correlations between SWB and PEB superfluous.

Nevertheless, this study demonstrated that broadband mobile devices are not only capable of being used in ESM studies, but in fact, may be preferable to the PDAs, written research journals, and beeper technology used in previous studies. The high signal-response rate (98.1 percent) suggests that the burden of ESM studies is reduced significantly with the incorporation of mobile-phone technology. When combined with multimedia and direct behavioral monitoring, as well as the considerable reduction in financial and human resources necessary to enact such research, mobile device-driven ESM studies are an attractive alternative to single-administration surveys, focus groups, interviews, and many laboratory experimental designs used to examine human behavior. Furthermore the study confirmed that when used with smart phones, ESM has the capacity to integrate both stated- and revealed-preferences approaches to analyzing behavior and its determinants.

IMPLICATIONS FOR SOCIO-ENVIRONMENTAL RESEARCH

The study's methodological and instrumental application has two possible consequences for future research. The first concerns ESM and the second concerns ESM's setting in socio-environmental research as a whole. Regarding the former, mobile phones make ESM studies simpler to implement, less expensive than alternative approaches, and likely more accurate in eliciting valid data. Replacing PDAs, beepers, and research journals with mobile phones likely reduces the participants' burden and certainly reduces the researchers' burdens. Such reductions should allow for greater flexibility, larger sample sizes, and more accurate data, as respondents no longer need carry additional materials during the research period. Yet the mobile phone device can potentially accomplish much more than what previous instruments afforded. The audio, photographic, and video capabilities of broadband mobile phones increase the type of questions and interactions available to the researcher. Furthermore, instead of relying on self-reported attitudes, emotions, times, locations, and behaviors, respondents can now provide researchers with real, objective evidence of the same.

The study not only used the respondents' own technology and thus reduced technology costs, but it also did not require training or extensive instruction to the respondents regarding that technology. Whereas other studies have advised developing web-based applications to assist in the design, deployment, and analysis stages of mobile-phone-driven ESM research (e.g., Hicks et al., 2010; Killingsworth and Gilbert, 2010; Uy, Foo, and Aguinis, 2010), this research suggests that such efforts may backfire. Not only can initial costs be significant, but the cognitive requirement of the respondents may also be increased, requiring greater physical or cognitive engagement with the device. Such an increase would erode one of the significant advantages afforded by mobile-phone instrumentation, that is, the reduced burden such technology affords the respondent.

The second consequence, for socio-environmental research specifically may also be profound. ESM has been shown previously to be effective in reducing recall errors and biases and if used appropriately, it can likely eliminate SDR, satisficing, and part-whole effects. Brown and Kasser (2005) argued that their research regarding values and pro-environmental attitudes especially needed to be replicated in a manner that focused on mitigating SDR and recall error. ESM, when used with mobile phone technology, can also reduce researchers' reliance on self-reporting, a key source of inaccuracy in socio-environmental surveys according to Corral-Verdugo (1997). This is possible because the technology allows the researcher to directly monitor the respondents' behavior through the use of the device's camera. The study used the camera to verify individuals' recycling behavior, their television and videogame behaviors, and their food purchases. Such phenomena, which are important to socio-environmental investigations, may be inaccurately self-reported or even degraded through SDR or satisficing. Using the phone's photographic capabilities provided this study with a possible way around such biases and errors.

ESM's two greatest advantages may be its focus on ecological validity and intrapersonal variation. Lab-based experiments, computer-aided and telephone surveys, focus groups, and interviews all extract the respondent from his or her natural environment. Yet ESM and broadband mobile phones allow for direct access, which is of particular relevance in socio-environmental research, as most is typically aimed in at least some way at measuring individuals' relationship with their environment. The study allowed researchers to investigate that relationship while the respondent experienced, both physically and cognitively, the environment in question. The exact benefits of such measurement were outside the purview of the study but certainly warrant future investigation.

Furthermore, as socio-environmental researchers become more and more interested in comparing individuals' values, well-being, and pro-environmental attitudes, ESM's focus on intrapersonal variation is key. While the sample population may be fairly homogenous in terms of age and university class, as was the case in the study, other factors certainly play a role in their behavior, well-being, and value orientations. Vehicle ownership, gender, employment status, and housing status are variables that can be controlled. Individuals' families, their family's income, their distance to school and work, their class schedule, their clothes (personal appearance was one of the values examined), and their extracurricular activities all likely play a role yet are much more difficult to control. ESM studies allow for much greater control regarding these often-intrapersonal variables or else can incorporate them as independent variables.

Whether or not to focus on the individual or on communities with regards to PEBs will likely remain a case-by-case decision. Yet being able to effectively investigate both the motivations to engage in PEBs and the constraints that hold individuals back from acting pro-environmentally requires being able to increase and decrease the level of detail regarding investigation and analysis at will. ESM, when deployed with smart phones, allows for a level of detail that has been until now unavailable to socio-environmental researchers. Using ESM is less expensive and easier than ever before, and while we do not suggest that single-administration surveys be abandoned, they may effectively be supplemented with alternative methods like ESM.

Achieving sustainability will not be easy; however, in order to do so, learning how to both measure and encourage PEBs will be critical. Ecological economists need to be quick to adopt new methods and use new technologies in order to both lead those efforts and help achieve society's objectives.

REFERENCES

Adamowicz, W., J. Louviere, and M. Williams. 1994. "Combining Revealed and Stated Preferences Methods for Valuing Environmental Amenities." *Journal of Environmental Economics and Management* 26:271–92.

Ahuvia, A., and N. Y. Wong. 2002. "Personality and Values Based Materialism: Their Relationship and Origins." *Journal of Consumer Psychology* 12:389–402.

Ajzen, I. 1991. "The Theory of Planned Behavior." *Organizational Behavior and Human Decision Processes* 50:179–211.

Ajzen, I., and M. Fishbein. 1980. *Understanding Attitudes and Predicting Social Behavior*. Englewood Cliffs, NJ: Prentice Hall.

Bailey, Kenneth D. 2007. *Methods of Social Research*. 4th edition. New York: Free Press.

Banerjee, R., and H. Dittmar. 2008. "Individual Differences in Children's Materialism: The Role of Peer Relationships." *Personality and Social Psychology Bulletin* 34:17–31.

Blake, J. 1999. "Overcoming the 'Value-Action Gap' in Environmental Policy: Tensions between National Policy and Local Experience." *Local Environment* 4(3): 257–78.

Brown, K. W., and T. Kasser. 2005. "Are Psychological and Ecological Well-Being Compatible? The Role of Values, Mindfulness, and Lifestyle." *Social Indicators Research* 74:349–68.

Brown, M., and W. Leon. 1999. *The Consumer's Guide to Effective Environmental Choices*. New York: Three Rivers.

Brownstone, D., D. S. Bunch, and K. Train. 2000. "Joint Mixed Logit Models of Stated and Revealed Preferences for Alternative-Fuel Vehicles." *Transportation Research Part B* 34:315–38.

Campbell, D. T. and D. Fiske. 1959. "Convergent and Discriminant Validation by the Multitrait-multimethod Matrix." *Psychological Bulletin* 56(2): 81–105.

Carson, Richard T., Nicholas E. Flores, Kerry M. Martin, and Jennifer L. Wright. 1996. "Contingent Valuation and Revealed Preference Methodologies: Comparing the Estimates for Quasi-Public Goods." *Land Economics* 72(1): 80–99.

Charness, G., and U. Gneezy. 2009. "Incentives to Exercise." *Econometrica* 77(3): 909–31.

Corral-Verdugo, V. 1997. "Dual 'Realities' of Conservation Behavior: Self-report vs. Observations of Re-use and Recycling Behavior." *Journal of Environmental Psychology* 17:135–45.

Csikszentmihalyi, M., and R. W. Larson. 1987. "Validity and Reliability of the Experience Sampling Method." *Journal of Nervous and Mental Disease* 175(9): 526–36.

De Young, R. 1988–89. "Exploring the Difference between Recyclers and Non-recyclers: The Role of Information." *Journal of Environmental Systems* 18:341–51.

Feldman Barrett, L. 2004. "Feelings or Words? Understanding the Content in Self-Report Ratings of Emotional Experience." *Journal of Personality and Social Psychology* 87(2): 266–81.

Fishbein, M., and I. Ajzen. 1975. *Belief, Attitude, Intention, and Behavior: An Introduction to Theory and Research*. Reading, MA: Addison-Wesley.

Gatersleben, B., J. Meadows, W. Abrahamse, and T. Jackson. 2008. "Materialistic and Environmental Values of Young People." Unpublished. University of Surrey.

Gneezy, U., and A. Rustichini. 2000. "A Fine Is a Price." *Journal of Legal Studies* 29 (January): 1–17.

Good, J. 2007. "Shop 'Til We Drop? Television, Materialism and Attitudes about the Natural Environment." *Mass Communication and Society* 10:365–83.

Grouzet, F. M. E., T. Kasser, A. Ahuvia, J. M. Fenandez-Dols, Y. Kim, and S. Lau. 2005. "The Structure of Goal Contents across 15 Cultures." *Journal of Personality and Social Psychology* 89:800–816.

Guagnano, G. A., P. A. Stern, and T. Dietz. 1995. "Influences on Attitude-Behavior Relationships: A Natural Experiment with Curbside Recycling." *Environment and Behavior* 27(5): 699–718.

Hektner, J. M., J. A. Schmidt, and M. Csikszentmihalyi. 2007. *Experience Sampling Method: Measuring the Quality of Everyday Life*. Thousand Oaks, CA: Sage.

Hicks, J., N. Ramanathan, D. Kim, M. Monibi, J. Selsky, M. Hansen, and D. Estrin. 2010. "AndWellness: An Open Mobile System for Activity and Experience Sampling." *Wireless Health,* October 5–7, 1–10.

Hopper, J. R. 1991. "Recycling as Altruistic Behavior: Normative and Behavioral Strategies to Expand Participation in a Community Recycling Program." *Environment and Behavior* 23(2): 195–220.

Hormuth, S. E. 1986. "The Sampling of Experiences In Situ." *Journal of Personality* 54:262–93.

Kahneman, D., and A. B. Krueger. 2006. "Developments in the Measurement of Subjective Well-Being." *Journal of Economic Perspectives* 20(1): 3–24.

Kahneman, D., A. B. Krueger, D. A. Schkade, N. Schwarz, and A. A. Stone. 2004. "A Survey Method for Characterizing Daily Life Experience: The Day Reconstruction Method (DRM)." *Science* 306(5702): 1776–80.

Karapanos, E., J. Zimmerman, J. Forlizzi, and J.-B. Martens. 2009. "User Experience over Time: An Initial Framework." Paper presented at the 2009 conference of the Special Interest Group on Computer-Human Interaction, April 4–9, Boston.

Kasser, T. 2005. "Frugality, Generosity, and Materialism in Children and Adolescents." In *What Do Children Need to Flourish? Conceptualizing and Measuring Indicators of Positive Development*, ed. K. A. Moore and L. H. Lippman, pp. 357–73. New York: Springer Science.

Kasser, T. 2010. "Ecological Challenges, Materialistic Values, and Social Change." In *Positive Psychology as Social Change*, ed. R. Biswas-Diener, pp. 89–108. New York: Springer.

Kasser, T. 2011. "Cultural Values and the Well-Being of Future Generations: A Cross-National Study." *Journal of Cross-Cultural Psychology* 42(2): 206–15.

Kasser, T., and R. M. Ryan. 1993. "A Dark Side of the American Dream: Correlates of Financial Success as a Central Life Aspiration." *Journal of Personality and Social Psychology* 65:410–22.

Kasser, T., and R. M. Ryan. 1996. "Further Examining the American Dream: Differential Correlates of Intrinsic and Extrinsic Goals." *Personality and Social Psychology Bulletin* 22:280–87.

Kasser, T., R. M. Ryan, M. Zax, and A. J. Sameroff. 1995. "The Relations of Maternal and Social Environments to Late Adolescents' Materialistic and Prosocial Values." *Developmental Psychology* 31:907–14.

Killingsworth, M. A., and D. T. Gilbert. 2010. "A Wandering Mind Is an Unhappy Mind." *Science* 330:932.

Larson, R. W., G. Moneta, M. H. Richards, and S. Wilson. 2002. "Continuity, Stability, and Change in Daily Emotional Experience across Adolescence." *Child Development* 73:1151–65.

Mannell, R. C., J. Zuzanek, and R. Aronson. 2005. "Internet/Computer Use and Adolescent Leisure Behavior, Flow Experiences and Psychological Well-Being: The Displacement Hypothesis." Paper presented at the Eleventh Canadian Congress on Leisure Research, May 17–20, Nanaimo, British Columbia.

Mercer, A. M., D. W. Keith, et al. 2011. "Public Understanding of Solar Radiation Management." *Environmental Research Letters* 6(4): 1–9.

Richins, M. L., and S. Dawson. 1992. "A Consumers Values Orientation for Materialism and Its Measurement: Scale Development and Validation. *Journal of Consumer Research* 19:303–16.

Rokeach, M. 1968. *Beliefs, Attitudes, and Values.* San Francisco: Jossey-Bass.

Ryan, R. M., V. I. Chirkov, T. D. Little, K. M. Sheldon, E. Timoshina, and E. L. Deci. 1999. "The American Dream in Russia: Extrinsic Aspirations and Well-Being in Two Cultures." *Personality and Social Psychology Bulletin* 25:1509–24.

Saunders, S., and D. Munro. 2000. "The Construction and Validation of a Consumer Orientation Questionnaire (SCOI) Designed to Measure Fromm's (1955) 'Marketing Character' in Australia." *Social Behavior and Personality* 28:219–40.

Schmuck, P., T. Kasser, and R. M. Ryan. 2000. "Intrinsic and Extrinsic Goals: Their Structure and Relationship to Well-Being in German and U.S. College Students." *Social Indicators Research* 50:225–41.

Schultz, P. W., V. V. Gouveia, L. D. Cameron, G. Tankha, P. Schmuck, and M. Franek. 2005. "Values and Their Relationship to Environmental Concern and Conservation Behavior." *Journal of Cross-Cultural Psychology* 36:457–75.

Schwartz, S. H. 1973. "Normative Explanations of Helping Behavior: A Critique, Proposal and Empirical Test." *Journal of Experimental Social Psychology* 9:349–64.

Schwartz, S. H. 1992. "Universals in the Content and Structure of Values: Theoretical Advances and Empirical Tests in 20 Countries." In *Advances in Experimental Social Psychology*, vol. 25, ed. M. P. Zanna, pp. 1–65. Orlando, FL: Academic.

Schwartz, S. H. 1994. "Are There Universal Aspects in the Structure and Contents of Human Values?" *Journal of Social Issues* 50(4): 19–45.

Scollon, C. N., C. Kim-Prieto, and E. Diener. 2003. "Experience Sampling: Promises and Pitfalls, Strengths and Weaknesses." *Journal of Happiness Studies* 4:5–34.

Sheldon, K. M., and T. Kasser. 1998. "Pursuing Personal Goals: Skills Enable Progress but Not All Progress Is Beneficial. *Personality and Social Psychology Bulletin* 24:1319–31.

Sheldon, K. M., and H. McGregor. 2000. "Extrinsic Value Orientation and the Tragedy of the Commons." *Journal of Personality* 68:383–411.

Sheldon, K. M., R. M. Ryan, E. L. Deci, and T. Kasser. 2004. "The Independent Effects of Goal Contents and Motives on Well-Being: It's Both What You Pursue and Why You Pursue It." *Personality and Social Psychology Bulletin* 30(4): 475–86.

Shogren, J. F., and L. O. Taylor. 2008. "On Behavioral-Environmental Economics." *Review of Environmental Economics and Policy* 2(1): 26–44.

Simon, H. 1952. "Comments on the Theory of Organizations." *American Political Science Review* 46:1130–39.

Stern, Paul C. 2000. "Toward a Coherent Theory of Environmentally Significant Behavior." *Journal of Social Issues* 56(3): 407–24.

Suchman, Edward A. 1962. "An Analysis of 'Bias' in Survey Research." *Public Opinion Quarterly* 26(1): 102–11.

Uy, M. A., M.-D. Foo, and H. Aguinis. 2010. "Using Experience Sampling Methodology to Advance Entrepeneurship Theory and Research." *Organizational Research Methods* 13(1): 31–54.

Weber, B., A. Holt, C. Neuhaus, P. Trautner, C. Elger, and T. Teichert. 2007. "Neural Evidence for Reference-Dependence in Real-Market Transactions." *NeuroImage* 35:441–47.

Zuzanek, J. 1999. "Experience Sampling Method: Current and Potential Research Applications." Paper presented at the Workshop on Time-Use Measurement and Research, May 27–28, Washington, DC.

Contributors

Stephen Balogh is a PhD candidate in the Graduate Program in Environmental Science at the State University of New York College of Environmental Science and Forestry. He holds an MS degree in environmental science from SUNY-ESF. Prior to coming to ESF, he was a licensed physical therapist and environmental writer. He studies energy systems and urban ecology. His dissertation examines the food and fuel flows in Syracuse, NY from a systems perspective.

Douglas L. Bessette is currently pursuing a PhD in geography at the University of Calgary. His research involves structuring complex decision-making processes so as to achieve higher quality decisions, particularly in the development of regional and national energy strategies. He holds a BA from the University of Michigan and an MS from Michigan State University.

Darrell Brown is the Les Fahey/KPMG Accounting Fellow and a Fellow in the Institute for Sustainable Solutions at Portland State University. With an undergraduate degree in forestry and a PhD in accounting, he teaches and researches at the intersection of business sustainability and measurement. He teaches metrics for understanding, reporting, and evaluating social and environmental impacts of organizations and the odd managerial accounting or accounting information systems class. His current research interests include measurement issues related to organizational impacts on social and natural systems and valuation of ecosystem services. He is also interested in how organizational reporting practices influence sustainability-oriented behaviors, both internally and externally to the organization.

Brett Cassidy holds an MBA in sustainable business from Portland State University. He is an outdoor industry professional and enjoys backpacking with his wife, climbing mountains, and racing bikes in the mud.

David Dempsey has spent thirty years in environmental policymaking and is the author of an environmental history of Michigan, Ruin and Recovery. He has also authored or coauthored six other environmental and history books. A native of Michigan, he now lives in Minnesota. He holds a Master's degree in natural resources policy and law from Michigan State University.

David E. Ervin is a Professor of Environmental Management, Professor of Economics, and Fellow in the Institute for Sustainable Solutions at Portland State University. He teaches the economics of business environmental management and sustainability, among other topics. His research program includes voluntary business sustainability initiatives, ecosystem service management and urban regions, and the environmental impacts of genetically engineered crops.

Joshua Farley is Associate Professor in Community Development and Applied Economics and Fellow at the Gund Institute for Ecological Economics at University of Vermont. He is coauthor with Herman Daly of *Ecological Economics: Principles and Applications* (2nd ed., 2010).

Aaron Ferguson attained a BS in natural resources management with a minor in economics from Grand Valley State University. Currently he is working toward an MS in public administration from Grand Valley State University. His career objectives are to work in a consulting role around sustainable planning, triple bottom line analysis, and climate resilience research.

Catherine Foley holds a Master's of Science in environmental science from the State University of New York College of Environmental Science and Forestry and a Master's of Public Administration from the Maxwell School, Syracuse University. Her work focuses on analysis of citizen opinions and community participation.

Betty Gajewski holds a BS in environmental sciences and an MS in communications from Grand Valley State University and pursued postgraduate studies in environmental planning at Michigan State University. Currently a Research Assistant with the Annis Water Resources Institute at GVSU, she has worked on a broad range of environmental issues, such as developing watershed information and education strategies, crafting community policies and plans, and addressing the environmental obligations of businesses.

Kyle Gracey is a Director for SustainUs and Student Pugwash USA, President of the Board of Directors of the Truman Scholars Association, Chair of the Treaties Task Force for the Society for Conservation Biology, and on the board for Engineers for a Sustainable World and Green21. He holds an MS in geophysical science and public policy from the University of Chicago. His research has been presented by the International Trade Union Confederation, United Nations, U.S. Green Building Council, and BlueGreen Alliance, among others.

Richard Grogan is the Regional Director of the New Hampshire Small Business Development Center, in Keene, NH, and an adjunct professor at Antioch University New England. He works closely with small businesses daily, while continuing to write and teach about sustainability in a variety of forums.

Myrna Hall is a Research Associate in the Department of Environmental Studies, State University of New York College of Environmental Science and Forestry, and director of the University's Center for Urban Environment. Her work focuses on spatial modeling of ecosystems that links human decisions, preferences, and behaviors and economic indicators, with ecosystem services and sociological impacts. In particular she has done extensive modeling of land use change in the northeastern United States, Central and South America, and Puerto Rico.

Jonathan M. Harris is Director of the Theory and Education Program at the Tufts University Global Development and Environment Institute. He is coeditor of *Twenty-First Century Macroeconomics: Responding to the Climate Challenge* (2009) and author of *Environmental and Natural Resource Economics: A Contemporary Approach* (2006).

William M. Hayes, a retired educator and former land commissioner, continues to develop the theory and practice of sustainable development with ecosystem science, ecological economics, and integrated resource management. He is also coauthor of the Ego'n'Empathy Hypothesis proposed as the centerpiece for ecological economic theory.

David Korten is Cochair of the New Economy Working Group, President of the Living Economies Forum, and Chair of the Board of Directors of *YES!* magazine. He is author of *Agenda for a New Economy: From Phantom Wealth to Real Wealth* and the international bestselling *When Corporations Rule the World*. He holds MBA and PhD degrees from the Stanford Graduate School of Business and is a former faculty member of the Harvard Business School.

Ruiqi Li holds an MS in environmental science at the State University of New York College of Environmental Science and Forestry. Her research interests include renewable energy, urban sustainability, and GIS spatial analysis.

Ed Lorenz is Reid-Knox Professor of History and Political Science at Alma College in Michigan and Director of the Public Affairs Institute at Alma. He has served since 1998 on the Executive Committee of the Pine River Superfund Task Force, an U.S. Environmental Protection Agency community advisory group. He is the author of *Civic Empowerment in an Age of Corporate Greed*, published by Michigan State University Press in 2012.

Bobbi S. Low is Professor of Resource Ecology and Conservation in the School of Natural Resources at the University of Michigan and a Faculty Associate of the Institute of Social Research and of the Center for the Study of Complex Systems. Her current research specialties include the relevance of life history theory and behavioral ecology to conservation, and the evolution of sex differences.

Gary D. Lynne is Professor, Department of Agricultural Economics and School of Natural Resources, University of Nebraska–Lincoln. He focuses both teaching and research attention on the behavioral economic dimension of natural resource, ecosystem, and environmental problems. His research has especially been concentrated on understanding conservation and sustainability choices by the farming population.

Erik Nordman is an Associate Professor of Natural Resource Management at Grand Valley State University in Allendale, Michigan, specializing in natural resource policy and economics. He was awarded a Fulbright Scholar grant to teach and conduct wind energy research at Kenyatta University in Nairobi, Kenya, for the 2012–13 academic year.

Skyler Perkins attended the University of Vermont, where he majored in global studies and focused on ecological economics and Spanish. He has sought ways to communicate on global sustainability issues through film media that chronicles hiking, skiing and engagement with diverse communities. He also currently writes for Izilwane.org.

Robert B. Richardson is Assistant Professor of Sustainable Development in the Department of Community Sustainability at Michigan State University. His research interests relate to the role of ecosystem services in supporting the well-being of households and communities.

Kristen A. Sheeran is Vice President of Knowledge Systems at Ecotrust and Director of Economics for Equity and the Environment Network.

Philip Sirianni holds a PhD in economics from Binghamton University and teaches in the Division of Economics and Business at the State University of New York College at Oneonta. In his current research projects, Professor Sirianni uses econometric methods and dynamic climate-economy modeling to examine the efficacy of policies for reducing greenhouse gas emissions from economic and environmental perspectives.

Ning Sun holds a PhD in environmental science at the State University of New York College of Environmental Science and Forestry, in Syracuse, NY. Her PhD research involved urban storm water modeling, green infrastructure simulations, and storm water management. She now works in the Hydrology Group at the University of Washington as a research associate. Her current research focuses on simulation of extreme climate events and their effects on urban water quality.

Matthew P. H. Taylor is a PhD student in economics at the University of California, Riverside. The work presented in this volume was part of the research he conducted for David Ervin and Darrell Brown while earning his MS in economics from Portland State University.

Jim Thayer is the founding Principal at Resilience Consulting. His work focuses on sustainability, resilience, and energy conservation. At the Cadmus Group, he led an effort with special emphasis on measuring the effectiveness of carbon management initiatives and sustainability programs. His prior experience includes over twelve years launching and leading a series of advanced technology companies into more than sixty international markets. He holds a BA from Reed College, an MBA in international finance from the American Graduate School for International Management, and teaches international marketing at Portland State University and sustainability at Marylhurst University.

Jon VanderMolen is a Technical Call-in at Grand Valley State University's Annis Water Resources Institute. He holds a BS in natural resources management from Grand Valley State University and has worked on numerous coastal management projects ranging from renewable energy assessments to invasive species monitoring.

Matthew A. Weber is a Postdoctoral Research Economist at the U.S. Environmental Protection Agency. His research interests are efficient and equitable management of natural resources, particularly water. His research methods span qualitative and quantitative approaches. He enjoys immersion-learning of rivers whenever possible.